Dialogues in the Dark

HARVARD-YENCHING INSTITUTE MONOGRAPH SERIES 146

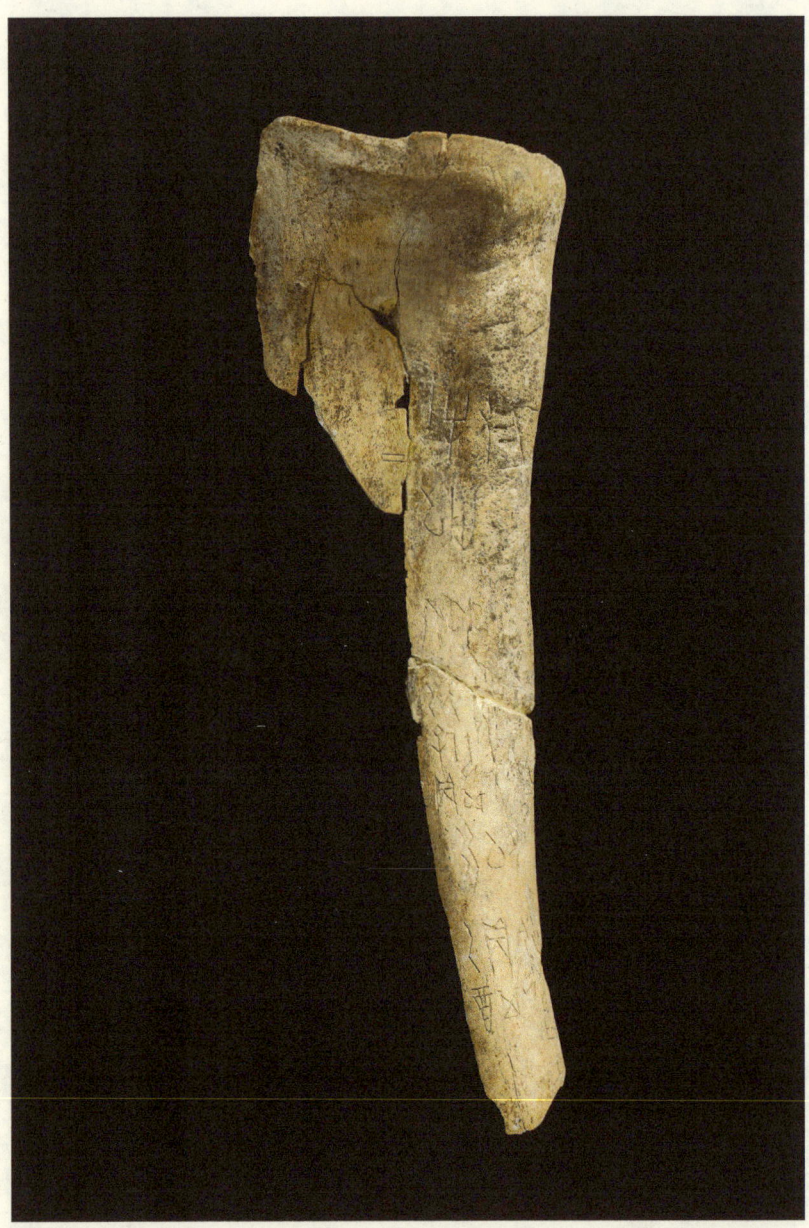

Frontispiece: Oracle bone, China. Inscribed bone, Shang dynasty, circa 1400–1050 BCE, 7 × 19.6 cm. Courtesy of ROM (Royal Ontario Museum), Toronto, Canada. ©ROM. 960.237.477; 960.237.541.

Dialogues in the Dark

*Interpreting "Heavenly Questions"
across Two Millennia*

Nicholas Morrow Williams

Published by the Harvard University Asia Center
Distributed by Harvard University Press
Cambridge (Massachusetts) and London, 2025

© 2025 by the President and Fellows of Harvard College
All rights reserved. No part of this publication may be reproduced, translated, stored in a retrieval system, or transmitted in any form or by any means, electronic, mechanical, photocopying, recording or otherwise, without prior written permission from the publisher.

Published by the Harvard University Asia Center, Cambridge, MA 02138

The Harvard University Asia Center publishes a monograph series and, in coordination with the Fairbank Center for Chinese Studies, the Korea Institute, the Reischauer Institute of Japanese Studies, and other faculties and institutes, administers research projects designed to further scholarly understanding of China, Japan, Korea, Vietnam, and other Asian countries. The Center also sponsors projects addressing multidisciplinary and regional issues in Asia.

The Harvard University Asia Center gratefully acknowledges the generous support of the Harvard-Yenching Institute, whose funding contributed to the publication of this book.

The Harvard-Yenching Institute, founded in 1928, is an independent foundation dedicated to the advancement of higher education in the humanities and social sciences in Asia. Headquartered on the campus of Harvard University, the Institute provides fellowships for advanced research, training, and graduate studies at Harvard by competitively selected faculty and graduate students from Asia. The Institute also supports a range of academic activities at its fifty partner universities and research institutes across Asia. At Harvard, the Institute promotes East Asian studies through annual contributions to the Harvard-Yenching Library and publication of the *Harvard Journal of Asiatic Studies* and the Harvard-Yenching Institute Monograph Series.

Library of Congress Cataloging-in-Publication Data

Names: Williams, Nicholas Morrow, author. | Qu, Yuan, approximately 343 B.C.-approximately 277 B.C. Tian wen. | Qu, Yuan, approximately 343 B.C.-approximately 277 B.C. Tian wen. English (Williams)
Title: Dialogues in the dark : interpreting "Heavenly Questions" across two millennia / Nicholas Morrow Williams.
Other titles: Harvard-Yenching Institute monograph series ; 146.
Description: Cambridge : Harvard University Asia Center, 2025. | Series: Harvard-Yenching Institute monograph series ; 146 | Includes bibliographical references and index. | English; Chinese with English translation.
Identifiers: LCCN 2024055572 (print) | LCCN 2024055573 (ebook) | ISBN 9780674299993 (hardcover) | ISBN 9780674301733 (epub)
Subjects: LCSH: Qu, Yuan, approximately 343 B.C.-approximately 277 B.C. Tian wen. | Qu, Yuan, approximately 343 B.C.-approximately 277 B.C.—Criticism and interpretation. | Liu, Zongyuan, 773–819—Criticism and interpretation. | Wang, Yi, active 89–158—Criticism and interpretation. | Chinese poetry—History and criticism.
Classification: LCC PL2661.T53 W55 2025 (print) | LCC PL2661.T53 (ebook) | DDC 895.11/1—dc23/eng/20250422
LC record available at https://lccn.loc.gov/2024055572
LC ebook record available at https://lccn.loc.gov/2024055573

Index by Arc Indexing, Inc.

Printed by Books International, 22883 Quicksilver Drive, Dulles, VA 20166, USA (www.booksintl.com). The manufacturer's authorized representative in the EU for product safety is LOGOS EUROPE, 9 rue Nicolas Poussin, 17000, La Rochelle, France (e-mail: Contact@logoseurope.eu).

*for my mother, who taught me to read
not just by sight, but also by intuition*

Contents

List of Illustrations and Tables	ix
Acknowledgments	xi
Prologue: No History without Hermeneutics	1
1 The Poem's Earliest Interpretations	21
Appendix: Text One: "Heavenly Questions" as Read by Han Scholars	75
2 Liu Zongyuan's Critique and Affirmation of "Heavenly Questions"	126
Appendix: Text Two: "Heavenly Questions" as Read by Liu Zongyuan	175
3 Towards the Modern Interpretation	216
Appendix: Text Three: "Heavenly Questions" as We Can Read It Today	264
Epilogue: No Literature without Lacunae	311
Bibliography	319
Index	339

Illustrations and Tables

Frontispiece

Shang oracle bone, courtesy of Royal Ontario Museum   ii

Figures

1 Bees and vipers, illustration from *Chuci tuzhu* by Xiao Yuncong   143

2 Rushou, illustration from *Chuci tuzhu* by Xiao Yuncong   153

3 *Wang Guowei*, drawing by Kong Kai Ming   256

Tables

1 Prosodic irregularity in the *Shijing*   63

2 Prosodic irregularity in the "Heavenly Questions"   63

3 Analysis of rhymes in two quatrains of "Heavenly Questions"   65

Acknowledgments

In keeping with this book's theme (the dialogic nature of interpretation), it is fitting that the book has developed organically out of my exchanges with colleagues and students. It all started in 2014, when Ron Egan invited me to give a talk at Stanford University, and I used the opportunity to begin diving into the works of Liu Zongyuan, little knowing where it would lead. My studies of "Heavenly Questions" ("Tianwen" 天問) proceeded in 2015 with the help of the reading group at Hong Kong Baptist University, organized by that redoubtable scholar of the *Chuci* 楚辭 and much more, Timothy W. K. Chan. The congenial group of colleagues, including our friend Mei Ah Tan, encouraged me to plunge into the "Heavenly Questions," though at the time I still found the text utterly baffling.

A few years later, I was submerged in a translation of the entire *Elegies of Chu* anthology and so was already grappling with "Heavenly Questions" again by necessity, when a series of new opportunities intervened. In 2019, a stimulating collaboration, led by Martin Dinter, between the University of Hong Kong and King's College London, was the first occasion for me to present some tentative thoughts on the crux of quatrain 56. That same spring I had the opportunity to give lectures at both Beijing Normal University–Hong Kong Baptist University United International College, Zhuhai and National Tsing Hua University, Hsinchu, where I developed my ideas on the crux and its significance for the poem as a whole. I remain enormously grateful to my hosts at these two lectures, Chen Zhi 陳致 in Zhuhai and Hsu Ming-chuan 許銘全 in Taiwan.

The year 2019 culminated in Wolfgang Behr's generous invitation for me to conduct a mini-seminar devoted solely to the poem at the University of Zurich. The reactions of Professor Behr and the splendid students who attended the three-day seminar in that snowy December gave me some new confidence that this direction was worth pursuing further.

At that point, fate took a hand. When Luke Bender kindly invited me to present a talk on it at Yale University in March 2020, I was still not committed enough to the "Heavenly Questions" project and was instead intending to talk on an entirely new and different topic. The interruption of the pandemic postponed the presentation at Yale, like many others. By the time Luke arranged for a makeup talk by Zoom the following March, I had had enough time mulling over the "Heavenly Questions" to present an entire lecture just on the poem. A week later, another remote event, the "Worst Chinese Poetry" conference in Hong Kong, organized by Tom Mazanec, Li Xiaorong, and Xu Hangping, gave me the chance to pull together some thoughts about Wang Yi, and some of these have made it into the second chapter of this book. Finally, during a three-week quarantine in a hotel room with a partial view of Victoria Harbor (very, very partial—largely obscured by a concrete wall), I enjoyed enough tranquility to read through the remainder of Gadamer's *Truth and Method*, which helped me to see that the "Heavenly Questions," apart from its intrinsic interest, could also be a model of other things.

By this time, as the result of some combination of timely prodding by colleagues and fortuitous circumstances, I was able to formulate the main contents of this book and complete its writing after moving to Arizona in the summer of 2021, with the additional inspiration of another Zoom workshop with Fudan University, organized by Miao Xiaojing and Guo Xi'an. In May 2022, I also presented some of the ideas in chapter 3 at the "Reading Tang Literature across Disciplines" workshop, organized by myself, at the Eide Center in Sarasota, Florida, and I am grateful to all the participants in those events. Finally, Zhu Xi gave valuable suggestions on rhyming, and Edward L. Shaughnessy provided several important corrections to the manuscript.

But the above narrative leaves out another indispensable factor in the production of this book, namely, my students, especially at the University of Hong Kong, who patiently accompanied me in my obsession with the "Heavenly Questions" through several weeks of class in spring 2019. It was really my teaching experiences there and at other Hong Kong universities, and getting to know outstanding undergraduate students like Li Jiaxuan, Li Linhe, Fu Xinci, Au-yeung Wai Ching, and Luo Andi, as well as my three brilliant Ph.D. students Fung Ka Yi, Yu Yuming, and Travis Chan, that changed my whole outlook on classical Chinese and helped me to appreciate it as a living form of expression.

I would also like to thank my curious and often questioning students here at Arizona State University, on whom I have also inflicted a few verses of "Heavenly Questions," as well as my inspiring colleagues, and especially the hardworking staff at the university library: Liu Qian, who unfortunately left us in 2024, was able to acquire most of the books that I needed; and the Interlibrary Loan office, which was able to borrow the other ones.

I am ever grateful to my family for distracting me from, and giving greater purpose to, my work; this time especially to Hunter Kiyoshi, born as I was finishing up the first draft of this book. And finally, this book is dedicated to my mother, now suffering from the ravages of Alzheimer's, who throughout her long careers as teacher, librarian, and mother was also a fine poet and hermeneutician.

PROLOGUE

No History without Hermeneutics

> In truth history does not belong to us, but rather we to history. Long before we come to understand ourselves consciously in retrospect, we understand ourselves reflexively within the family, society, and country in which we live. The focus of subjectivity is a distorting mirror. The self-contemplation of the individual is merely a flicker in the closed circuit of historical life.
>
> — Hans-Georg Gadamer, *Truth and Method*[1]

Readers of Chinese literature, fatigued by the unremitting flood of commentary to their cherished sources, are often tempted to throw up their hands in exhaustion and call for a return to the text itself. Their historically-minded colleagues then remind them that the true meaning of the original text has been obscured by cultural and linguistic change, and that a hundred commentaries and references are needed simply to reconstruct the surface meaning of the text. While both reactions are justified, neither is fully reasonable. It is indeed always essential to return to the earliest sources and not to trust in the biased interpretations of later readers, but the text is also already embedded in a historical context with which it is in dialogue, and its interpretation relies on myriad assumptions and implications which are not explicit. Moreover, even within its own context the meaning of an individual message is not indisputable: "the focus of subjectivity is a distorting mirror." Rather than identifying a true

---

1. Translation from Gadamer, *Wahrheit und Methode*, 261: "In Wahrheit gehört die Geschichte nicht uns, sondern wir gehören ihr. Lange bevor wir uns in der Rückbesinnung selber verstehen, verstehen wir uns auf selbstverständliche Weise in Familie, Gesellschaft und Staat, in denen wir leben. Der Fokus der Subjektivität ist ein Zerrspiegel. Die Selbstbesinnung des Individuums ist nur ein Flackern im geschlossenen Stromkreis des geschichtlichen Lebens." Cf. published translation in *Truth and Method*, 288–89.

kernel of meaning, our goal can only be to understand within a tradition of interpretation, both past and present.

One of the Chinese texts that best exemplifies the embeddedness of the text both in history and hermeneutic tradition is the long poem "Heavenly Questions" ("Tianwen" 天問), attributed to Qu Yuan 屈原 (fl. ca. 300 BCE). This poem, an extended inquiry into the background assumptions of early Chinese thought, opens with questions about well-known events from the past, such as the formation of the cosmos or the founding of the Zhou dynasty. But precisely because the background to these questions must have been well-known when the poem was created, much of this background is omitted from the text itself. Thus, any interpretation of the text by later readers, even as early as the Han dynasty, had to be at the same time an exploration of Shang mythology, of Zhou history, of Chu politics, and many other topics. Beyond all of these historical topics, moreover, the history of the poem's interpretation itself presents one strand in Chinese intellectual history, which needs to be understood as well.

"Heavenly Questions" is a poem of ninety-five rhymed quatrains, in a loose tetrasyllabic meter similar to that predominant in the earliest anthology of Chinese poetry, the *Shijing* 詩經 (Book of odes). The poem is included in a Han anthology, the *Chuci zhangju* 楚辭章句 (Elegies of Chu, with chapter-and-verse commentary), compiled by Wang Yi 王逸 (ca. 89–ca. 158). While many of the poems in this anthology deal with the experiences of the banished courtier Qu Yuan or similar figures, "Heavenly Questions" is unique in asking questions about objective reality, about the cosmos and history. It touches on the creation of the world, the division of Heaven and Earth, and the configuration of astronomical bodies. It then turns to prehistoric legends, particularly the quelling of the great flood by Gun 鯀 and Yu 禹. The poem then deals with various geographical information, considering the extremities of the cardinal directions, and rumors about various strange creatures; this passage has much in common with the mytho-geographical miscellany *The Classic of Mountains and Seas* (*Shanhaijing* 山海經). Starting about one-third through the total length of the poem, it becomes more focused on historical personages, and loosely follows the traditional chronology of the Xia, Shang, and Zhou dynasties, asking questions about prominent individuals and events. A point of special interest is the Zhou conquest of the Shang, occupying quatrains 65–75. The poem then considers miscellaneous examples of good and bad leadership, and concludes with cryptic questions that are sometimes taken as referring to Qu Yuan's own circumstances.²

We today can appreciate the coherence of the poem and its distinctive theme, inquiring whether Heaven aids the worthy and punishes the wicked. But this is only because of the exegetical labors of many scholars over the past two thousand years. By the end of the twentieth century, there were detailed commentaries identifying the historical events to which each quatrain refers, and lucid scholarship summing up the content and themes of the poem. In 1982, You Guoen's 游國恩 (1899–1978) remarkable summation of traditional scholarship on the poem, *Tianwen zuanyi* 天問纂義 (Compiled interpretations of the "Heavenly Questions"), was published posthumously. In this work, You quotes key examples of traditional scholarship for each quatrain, then sifts through them and adds his own opinion of the correct interpretation at the end. Though difficulties remain, and in many cases the reader may still quibble with You's choices, the book makes clear that most lines in the poem are intelligible and form a coherent poem. A more concise and accessible treatment was Lin Geng's 林庚 (1910–2006) "Tianwen lunjian" 天問論箋 (Discussion and commentary to "Heavenly Questions"), remarkable for its unwavering attempt to read into the poem a distinctive message about historical destiny.³ Kominami Ichirō's 小南一郎 essay on the poem also attempts to analyze its overall structure and clarify the narrative sequence of the poem in a convincing way.⁴ Finally, Huang Linggeng's 黃靈庚 commentary to the poem within his complete collated edition of the *Chuci zhangju*, which was published in 2007, also built on this scholarly tradition while resolving certain cruxes in ways as consistent as possible with the original commentary.⁵

The conclusive result of this effort is that it is possible to read the "Heavenly Questions" today with some confidence about what the questions themselves mean, and the historical contexts in which they are set. Thus, this volume presents an annotated translation of the poem as we

---

2. At a couple of places, the numbering of the quatrain relies on some arbitrary decisions and could vary slightly. My numbering is based on the edited text as I read it in "Text Three" below, which for convenience I apply to the discussion throughout this book.

3. Lin Geng, "Tianwen lunjian," originally published in 1983.

4. Kominami Ichirō, "Tenmon hen no seiri."

5. Huang Linggeng, ed., *Chuci zhangju shuzheng*.

can understand it today, with the benefit of past scholarship ("Text Three" below). But one thing that an overview of the scholarly tradition on the poem reveals—in particular, what one garners from You Guoen's masterful compilation—is that the way an informed reader can approach the poem today is often quite distinct from how it appeared to a reader of the Han or Tang dynasties. That difficulty will be illustrated at length below, in the first two translations of the poem, one in the context of Han scholarship ("Text One: 'Heavenly Questions' as Read by Han Scholars"), and the second from the perspective of an erudite poet-scholar of the Tang ("Text Two: 'Heavenly Questions' as Read by Liu Zongyuan"). For most of its history, the poem was so challenging to read that it seemed to many readers not to be a coherent poem at all, but rather a messy, baffling congeries of puzzling questions.

Our understanding of "Heavenly Questions," then, is not simply a restoration of an original understanding, but is rather a historical project that has continued for many lifetimes. It is not a matter simply of discovering or rediscovering historical artifacts (though this played a key role), but also a question of interrogating the text and other early texts. Our understandings of the poem have resulted from the ongoing investigations and discussions of readers and scholars over centuries, who have tried to read the original questions, answer them, and pose their own questions about ancient Chinese history. We cannot understand what the very words of the poem say without participating ourselves in this age-old hermeneutical project, in which the true meaning of the questions is itself the answer we seek to find.

A Crux and Its Resolution

To illustrate the limits of the kind of interpretive process going on here, we might begin with one extraordinary crux, in comparison with which the rest of the poem is actually relatively straightforward. Consider the following eight Chinese characters (which form the first couplet within a rhyming quatrain, although they have not always been recognized as such):[6]

---

6. In general, I aim to follow the text of "Heavenly Questions" in Huang Linggeng's authoritative *Chuci zhangju shuzheng*, 2:995–1260 (*juan* 3). This couplet may be found on p. 1150.

該秉季德
厥父是臧

The meaning of these lines is not at all obvious, though they do succeed a passage on the origin myth of the Shang dynasty, so we might surmise they have something to do with Shang mythology. The character *fu* 父 for "father" stands out as being self-explanatory, but it is unclear whose father is being referred to.

The first two characters here, *gai bing* 該秉, already pose a problem, since they are both normally read as verbs with related meanings, and the conjunction of the two seems awkward. Wang Yi's commentary thus offers these remarks, first glossing the two verbs and then proposing a paraphrase for them:

> *Gai* 該 means to "encompass." *Bing* 秉 means to "maintain." The "father" refers to [Shang ancestor] Xie 契. *Ji* 季 means *mo* 末 "tip, latter, remnant, legacy." *Zang* 臧 means "excellent." These lines say that [Shang dynastic founder] Tang 湯 embraced and maintained the virtue inherited from his ancestors, and cultivated the excellent endeavors of his forefathers, so that Heaven aided him to become the ruler of the people.
> 該, 苞也。秉, 持也。父, 謂契也。季, 末也。臧, 善也。言湯能包持先人之末德, 脩其祖父之善業, 故天祐之以為民主也。

In light of the commentary provided by Wang Yi, we might translate these two lines of the original poem as follows:

> Encompassing and maintaining the virtue of his legacy,　該秉季德
> [Tang 湯] showed the same excellence as his father.[7]　厥父是臧

The gloss on the word *gai* 該 as "encompass" is awkward, but not impossible, given that the primary meaning of *gai* is something like "possess." This identification of *gai* as a verb, syntactically, then naturally leads to the tagging of the second word in the line as another coordinate verb. Wang Yi identifies the subject of both these verbs based on the preceding passage, which has referred to Tang, also known as Cheng Tang 成湯, the founding ruler of the

---

7. This is the translation provided in "Text One: 'Heavenly Questions' as Read by Han Scholars," following chapter 1.

Shang dynasty, who is said to have overthrown the Xia dynasty and established the Shang as supreme. On the other hand, the syntax that results from reading both *gai* and the succeeding character *bing* as parallel verbs is unusual for pre-Qin texts, which rarely employ two coordinate verbs when a single one would suffice. Moreover, it is surprising that the text should refer to Tang's father, who is not a prominent figure in the transmitted historical records.[8] The commentary's explanation that *fu* 父 means "ancestor," not "father," is admissible, but again not strongly compelling.

In light of the various weaknesses of this explanation, we may already regard it with some suspicion, but readers familiar with the Han-era commentary to the *Elegies of Chu* in Wang Yi's *Chuci zhangju* will be even less convinced, since that commentary has long been criticized, both in premodern and modern times, for its misreadings. The passage quoted above does not seem to have done a good job even of parsing the original text, nor has it offered a particularly compelling interpretation of its meaning. On the other hand, despite all these limitations of the commentary, there is no alternative way to parse the text here that is obvious even to a modern reader. This passage is a crux of ancient Chinese literature, and without any alternative commentary surviving from the Han, we might have little choice but to accept this ancient interpretation, as many readers did before the twentieth century.

At the turn of that century, however, a dramatic discovery offered a new source of evidence for this problem. In 1899, Wang Yirong 王懿榮 (1845–1900), who was chancellor of the Directorate of Education under the Qing, noticed that the so-called "dragon bones" he had purchased seemed to be inscribed with ancient writing. Though Wang committed suicide during the Boxer Rebellion and its occupation of Beijing, he shared his discovery with his friend Liu E 劉鶚 (1857–1909), who published the very first transcriptions and rubbings of the oracle bones in 1903.[9] These inscriptions carved onto cow scapulae and turtle plastrons are authentic divination records from the Shang dynasty, dating back before 1000

---

8. According to *Shiji*, Tang's father's name was Zhukui 主癸; see *Shiji*, 3.92.

9. For an overview of this episode, see Wilkinson, *Chinese History*, 758–59; for a scholarly introduction to these sources, see Keightley, *Sources of Shang History*. Peter Hessler's *Oracle Bones* treats some important episodes in their discovery in context of contemporary Chinese society.

BCE. They had lain buried under the ground at various sites, primarily the Shang capital of Anyang 安陽, for some three millennia. Thus, they had not been accessible, so far as we know, to scholars of the Han dynasty, so Wang Yi's commentary had to speculate about Tang and his ancestors with little concrete information about the Shang ancestors.

The oracle bones offered a transformative new body of evidence about remote antiquity, including the protagonists mentioned in these lines. Towards the end of 1914, the philologist Luo Zhenyu 羅振玉 (1866–1940) published *Yinxu shuqi kaoshi* 殷虛書契考釋 (Examination of the documents of the Yin sites), in which he identified the personal name of Wang Hai 王亥 among the texts. This name occurs very frequently in the inscriptions. One example is a relatively long text containing the following line (see frontispiece):

> Divined on the *yisi* day, the great exorcism, offering the sacrifice ascending towards high ancestor Wang Hai. [10]
> 乙巳貞：大禦其陟于高祖王亥。

This confirmed that Wang Hai was one of the principal Shang ancestors, worshipped in the second millennium BCE. Though there were references to him in various transmitted texts, mostly compiled around the Han dynasty, this was material confirmation that he was known far, far earlier.

Luo Zhenyu was a friend and collaborator of Wang Guowei 王國維 (1877–1927), the transformative scholar of Chinese history, classics, and literature. Wang immediately recognized this name as equivalent to the Shang ancestor mentioned in various early texts such as *The Classic of Mountains and Seas* and *Bamboo Annals* (*Zhushu jinian* 竹書紀年), a chronicle of early dynasties that was lost and only rediscovered in the third century CE.[11] It is telling that both of these sources with close connections to "Heavenly Questions," but somewhat peripheral to the classical canon, turned out to preserve authentic information about the Shang dynasty, which had been neglected or obscured in the primary histories compiled

---

10. *Jiaguwen heji*, no. 32916. The verb *zhi* 陟 here has the specific meaning of ascending to join the ancestors; see Shirakawa Shizuka, *Jitō: fukyūban*, 609.

11. Wang Guowei, "Yin buci zhong suo jian xiangong xianwang kao." On their friendship, see Zhang Lianke, *Wang Guowei yu Luo Zhenyu*.

by Han scholars. The gradual inclusion of less prestigious but still authentic historical sources is a major theme in the history of scholarship on the "Heavenly Questions."

Wang argued that "Wang Hai" was equivalent with a number of figures with the Wang surname who were mentioned in other early texts, typically a Shang ancestor identified as the son of Wang Ming 冥:[12] Wang He 核 in *Shiben* 世本, Wang Zhen 振 in *Shiji* 史記, and Wang Gai 垓 in *Hanshu* 漢書;[13] but also identified, for instance, as Wang Bing 冰, who first harnessed oxen, in *Lüshi chunqiu* 呂氏春秋 (Annals of Lü Buwei), which relates closely to other lore on Wang Hai.[14] Moreover, Wang Guowei showed that this was the same personage being referred to in quatrain 56 of "Heavenly Questions," whom the earliest commentators had not even recognized as a proper name. Wang also consulted about the matter with the Japanese scholar Naitō Torajirō 内藤虎次郎 (1866–1934), styled Naitō Konan 内藤湖南, who in July 1916 had published a study of the topic in *Geibun zasshi* 藝文雜誌, pointing out the mention of Wang Hai in *Bamboo Annals*.[15] Wang Guowei further identified another figure named Wang Heng 恆 in the oracle bone inscriptions as well. Wang Hai and Heng were both sons of Wang Ming 冥 (or Ji 季), also mentioned elsewhere in the oracle bone inscriptions.[16] In 1923, Wang finally presented his own polished insights in his compilation of scholarly studies, *Guantang jilin* 觀堂集林.

In his finished study, Wang directly quotes *The Classic of Mountains and Seas* on Wang Hai:

---

12. Wang identifies all of these as mistranscriptions based on graphic similarity. Wang Guowei, "Yin buci zhong suo jian xiangong xianwang kao," 416.

13. See *Shiben*, 5; *Shiji*, 3.120; *Hanshu*, 20.882.

14. See Xu Weiyu, ed., *Lüshi chunqiu jishi*, 17.450.

15. Specifically, the Modern-Text version. Naitō also understands Wang Hai as an inventor, perhaps the first to domesticate oxen. On the friendship of Naitō and Luo Zhenyu, beginning in 1899, see Fogel, *Politics and Sinology*, 101. The importance of the *Bamboo Annals* will become clear in the third chapter below. This study was based on Wang Guowei's views, and Naitō wrote a second study summing up Wang's further discoveries in 1921. The two studies are reprinted as "Ō Gai" 王亥 and "Zoku Ō Gai" 續王亥 in *Naitō Konan zenshū*, 7:469–80 and 7:481–500, respectively.

16. Jao Tsung-i sums up this evidence in *Yindai zhenbu renwu*, 124–26.

There is a man named Wang Hai. In his two hands he holds birds, and eats their heads. Wang Hai entrusted to the Youyi and Hebo [Sire of the Yellow River][17] the harnessed oxen. The Youyi murdered Wang Hai and took the oxen.[18]

有人曰王亥，兩手操鳥，方食其頭。王亥託于有易河伯僕牛。有易殺王亥，取僕牛。

The Classic of Mountains and Seas was not really regarded as a proper "classic" on the level of the Confucian classics; it has been described as a "bestiary" of ancient China, full of fanciful stories about gods, monsters, and imaginary places.[19] Wang Hai's consumption of bird totems, though perhaps reflecting the authentic avian mythology of the Shang dynasty, does not encourage faith in the historical accuracy of this passage. Yet, as Wang Guowei shows, this text turned out to contain correct information about this figure from remote antiquity, who is also named in the oracle bone inscriptions.

Another of Wang Guowei's contributions to scholarship, which would turn out to be highly relevant to the study of the "Heavenly Questions," had to do with the *Bamboo Annals*, an ancient chronicle that had also traditionally been held in some suspicion. In particular, the Modern-Text version was long suspected of being a forgery by Yuan or Ming scholars. But Qing scholars had already engaged in careful study of the Modern-Text *Bamboo Annals* and shown that much of its content was authentic. Wang Guowei prepared a new edition of this text, the *Jinben zhushu jinian shuzheng* 今本竹書紀年疏證.[20] It contains a helpful reference to Wang Hai:

---

17. The Hebo (Sire of the Yellow River) is a god mentioned also in the *Chuci*'s "Nine Songs," but here may refer to another competing tribe. There is even a theory that the harnessed oxen (Puniu 僕牛) are actually the name of a third tribe. We will surely never know with certainty, but it is relatively natural to take Hebo as a proper name alongside Youyi.
18. Yuan Ke ed., *Shanhaijing jiaozhu*, 14.300.
19. Strassberg, *A Chinese Bestiary*. He translates *jing* 經 itself as "guideways," which better hints at its functional meaning, but I understand it as intended to compete with and complement the other classics.
20. Fang Shiming and Wang Xiuling conveniently included a newly-edited version of Wang Guowei's *Jinben zhushu jinian shuzheng* in their own *Guben Zhushu jinian jizheng*, 202–89.

> In the twelfth year, the Marquis of the Shang, Lord Hai, was a guest of the Youyi. The Youyi killed him and exposed his body.[21]
>
> 十二年，殷侯子亥賓于有易，有易殺而放之。

Considering all this evidence, Wang Guowei concludes that Shang ancestor Wang Hai was probably a historical personage who lived in remote antiquity.[22] He counts altogether nine references to Wang Hai in the oracle bone inscriptions, two of which have to do with offerings to the sun.[23] Like other Shang ancestors, his name is derived from one of the cyclical signs determining the date (other names are based on determinations of the hour as well).[24]

Indeed, later scholars have elaborated on this discovery to flesh out Wang Hai's story (which components are history and which are legend is of course unknowable). In particular, Li Xueqin's 李學勤 (1933–2019) analysis of related texts clarified the legend further.[25] First, Li explained that a puzzling line in the *Classic of Mountains and Seas* should be read as follows: "Wang Hai had entrusted to the Youyi the domesticated cattle of the Hebo" 王亥託于有易河伯僕牛, where Hebo 河伯 is the name of another tribe, not the god of the Yellow River.[26] This accords well with the story that the Hebo also helped Shangjia Wei, Wang Hai's son, to defeat the Youyi.[27] Moreover, Li shows that the same story is referenced in hexagram 56 or "Lü" 旅 (The wanderer) of the *Book of Changes* (*Yijing* 易經*)*:

---

21. Fang and Wang, eds., *Guben Zhushu jinian jizheng*, 219 (quoting here from Wang Guowei's *Jinben Zhushu jinian shuzheng*); *Zhushu jinian tongjian*, 4.1a. As Wang Guowei points out, though, this text is also found in Guo Pu's commentary to the *Shanhaijing*. See Yuan Ke, ed., *Shanhaijing jiaozhu*, 14.301.
22. Wang Guowei, "Yin buci zhong suo jian xiangong xianwang kao," 416–17.
23. Wang Guowei, "Yin buci zhong suo jian xiangong xianwang kao," 418.
24. Wang Guowei, "Yin buci zhong suo jian xiangong xianwang kao," 418.
25. See Li Xueqin, *Zhouyi suyuan*, 3–7.
26. Yuan Ke, ed., *Shanhaijing jiaozhu*, 14.300.
27. The story is preserved in Guo Pu's commentary to the same passage; Yuan Ke, ed., *Shanhaijing jiaozhu*, 14.301, n. 8.

Upper nine: birds set fire to their nest. The traveler first laughs and later cries and howls, losing the oxen at Yi. Inauspicious.[28]

上九: 鳥焚其巢, 旅人先笑後號咷。喪牛于易, 凶。

The line involving birds flocking may also relate to Wang Hai's name, since the Hai 亥 character can also be written as 鳥 or 隹.[29]

The precise nature of Wang Hai remains somewhat unclear, as his status is something like a demigod between the mortal and divine realms. According to David N. Keightley, he belonged to the class of "ex-humans whom the cultists now associated with the dynasty."[30] Nonetheless, although later scholars have added some refinements and there also remain points of uncertainty, Wang Guowei's analysis remains the definitive interpretation of quatrain 56. Wang concluded his discussion, with justifiable pride: "The text of the 'Heavenly Questions' for millennia has not been explained coherently, but now by means of the oracle bones I have done so. This is a matter in which researchers of both history and literature ought

---

28. See *Zhouyi zhengyi*, 6.271, and Li Daoping (1788–1844) and Pan Yuting, eds. *Zhouyi jijie zhuanshu*, 7.494, for some traditional interpretations of the same text. The "Da zhuang" 大壯 hexagram no. 34, also has a similar phrasing but it may not be directly related. Cf. Shaughnessy's translation (of an excavated version of the *Changes*, in this case identical) in *Unearthing the Changes*, 274.

29. Li Xueqin, *Zhouyi suyuan*, 7.

30. This is just one of six categories into which Keightley analyzes Shang objects of worship. The full scheme is as follows: "(1) Di 帝, the High God; (2) Nature Powers, like He 河 (the River Power), Yang 羊+山 (the Mountain Power) and Ri 日 (the sun); (3) Former Lords, like Nao 夒 and Wang Hai 王亥, who were apparently ex-humans whom the cultists now associated with the dynasty; (4) predynastic ancestors, like Shang Jia 上甲 (P1) and the three Bao 報 (P2–P4) who received cult ahead of Da Yi 大乙, the dynasty founder, in the Period V ritual cycle; (5) the dynastic ancestors, starting with Da Yi 大乙 (K1), who could be grouped in a number of ways . . . and (6) the dynastic ancestresses, the consorts of those kings on the main line of descent." Keightley, "Making of the Ancestors," reprinted in *These Bones Shall Rise Again*, 157. According to Keightley, "The P and K numbers indicate the regnal sequence of the Predynastic ancestors (P1 indicates the first predynastic ancestor) and the dynastic Kings (K1 indicates the first dynastic ancestor)." See *These Bones Shall Rise Again*, 192 n. 17.

to take much delight."³¹ Indeed, this was probably Wang Guowei's greatest contribution to *Chuci* scholarship.³²

All modern studies of which I am aware accept this discovery and its critical importance for reading the text. It is truly a remarkable new insight, and the further elaborations up to Li Xueqin even allow us to relate the original lines in "Heavenly Questions" to events of ancient history as represented in other early texts. The discovery demonstrates, as well as any single discovery could, the critical importance of applying recent archaeological findings to the study of ancient texts. It has enabled precise identification of a single individual in an ancient poem, even surpassing the insights available to Han-dynasty scholars from an imperial library.

The Need for Interpretation

If we took Wang Guowei at his word, however, we might think that the Han commentary provided the only interpretation of the passage on which all readers had had to rely throughout Chinese history; we might believe that no one in premodern China had ever questioned Wang Yi's reading of the passage; we might have trouble understanding who in past centuries had ever successfully parsed the text of "Heavenly Questions."

Yet a more careful examination of the intervening period between the Han dynasty and modernity shows that Wang Guowei was exaggerating his own achievement. Though the scholarship of Luo and Wang certainly improved our understanding of this ancient crux, premodern scholars had already questioned Wang Yi's interpretation long before the unearthing of the oracle bones. In the Tang dynasty, the inveterate skeptic and redoubtable philologist, Liu Zongyuan 柳宗元 (773–819), had already proposed

---

31. The Chinese text: 天問之辭，千古不能通其說者，而今由卜辭通之。此治史學與文學者所當同聲稱快者也. Wang Guowei, "Yin buci zhong suo jian xiangong xianwang kao," 422.

32. Although Wang was of course a prolific and transformative scholar, he devoted relatively little attention to the *Chuci* anthology, though he did express his admiration for it in an essay, "Quzi wenxue zhi jingshen" 屈子文學之精神. However, an argument for the importance of that essay and Wang's *Chuci* interpretation in general may be found in Liao Tung-liang, *Lingjun yuying*, 227–69.

that *gai* was a proper name, even though his identification of the person named was not convincing. And in the early Qing, the brilliant scholar Xu Wenjing 徐文靖 (1667–after 1756) already identified Gai as referring specifically to Wang Hai, based on his own rigorous studies of the *Bamboo Annals* and other ancient texts. In the later chapters of this book, I will elaborate further on each of these cases.

In other words, rather than a simple case of error clarified by modern research, the history of interpretation of "Heavenly Questions" tells a different and more complicated story of knowledge and doubt interacting, where questions are answered only to create further questions. But none of this would have surprised the author(s) of the "Heavenly Questions." For when we consider the lines quoted above as part of the full rhyming quatrain to which they belong, we read:

When Wang Hai upheld the virtue of Ming,	該秉季德
He showed the same excellence as his father.	厥父是臧
Why was he ultimately murdered by the Youyi Clan	胡終弊于有扈
While tending the cattle and sheep?[33]	牧夫牛羊

In other words, the original text was evidently not intended to provide information about Wang Hai or the historical events in which he was involved. Taking for granted certain knowledge about ancient history, the author wanted to ask a different question, namely, why a hero like Wang Hai had died ignominiously at the hands of an enemy clan.

In spite of all the scholarly investigations from the Han dynasty up to the present, no one has discovered an answer to this question in the text of the "Heavenly Questions." The basic query underlying most of the poem has to do with whether the rise and fall of states, and the life and death of individuals, is governed by any underlying order or cosmic justice; this is a question of ethics and political philosophy that remains open. But readers of different periods have attempted to use the text of the "Heavenly Questions" as a starting point to provide different answers. This volume will explore both the text of the "Heavenly Questions" itself and, equally importantly, how it has inspired and challenged later readers, from the Han to the Qing and beyond.

---

33. See commentary in the complete "Text Three" below.

Even limiting ourself to Wang Guowei alone, though, his extraordinary scholarship should not be seen as a scientific approach devoid of hermeneutical ramifications. To the contrary, Wang was throughout his life committed to his ideals of a Chinese cultural renaissance, and his identification of the correct dating and titles of ancient rulers was part of his own project of promoting "national quintessence" (guocui 國粹).[34] He knew as well as anyone that understanding is a communal and relativistic process, that the purposes and qualities of Heaven are ultimately comprehended only by examining man's actions.

In his own verse, Wang Guowei refers in several places to the "Heavenly Questions" and to dialogue with Heaven in several places. For example, in the second half of his regulated verse poem "Journey's Woes" ("Chen lao" 塵勞), he places "Heavenly Questions" within the tradition of protest and martyrdom associated with the person of Qu Yuan:

Till now men have clamored at the walls, but Heaven has not spoken;[35]	至今呵壁天無語
For eternity have buried their sorrows, but even Earth is not secure.	終古埋憂地不牢
Hurling themselves from towers, drowning in the abyss, striving for a moment—	投閣沈淵爭一間
Why again did Ziyun bother to "Refute 'Sublimating Sorrow'"?[36]	子雲何事反離騷

Like Wang Guowei, Yang Xiong was a formidable scholar as well as a creative writer. Here Wang aligns both of them with the figure of Qu Yuan, protesting in vain at the misfortunes ordained by Heaven and also the misbehavior of the sovereign.

---

34. Hu Qiuhua's monograph on Wang Guowei, *Konfuzianisches Ethos und westliche Wissenschaft*, is a compelling study of the various strands interwoven in his thought and scholarship.

35. This formulation derives from the preface to the poem in the Han commentary, to be discussed in chapter 2 below, but in particular from Li He's 李賀 (790–816) formulation in his poem "Lord Don't Go Out the Gate" 公無出門, highlighting a conception of Qu Yuan as a figure of madness and rebellion.

36. Xiao Ai, ed., *Wang Guowei shici jianjiao*, 20. Ziyun 子雲 refers to Yang Xiong 揚雄 (53 BCE–18 CE), who famously wrote a refutation of Qu Yuan's "Sublimating Sorrow" ("Lisao" 離騷); see Knechtges, Han shu *Biography*, 13–16, 66–76.

In Wang's characterization here, the tragedy of the "Heavenly Questions," as of the *Elegies of Chu* in general, is that protestations against injustice fall unheard before a silent, uncommunicative Heaven. After all, the questions posed within the "Heavenly Questions" never receive an answer within that poem. Even Wang's research establishing the meaning of the text only clarifies the questions, not their answers. But even if that is the case within the "Heavenly Questions" and the *Elegies of Chu* in general, it is not an absolute silence. For as Wang wrote in a *ci* song lyric:

"Sedge-stepping Song" ("Ta suo xing" 踏莎行)

The highest peak has no clouds	絕頂無雲
there was rain only last night.	昨宵有雨
I have come to this place to hear Heaven speak.	我來此地聞天語
Sparse bells in the twilight echo in muddled peaks,	疏鐘暝直亂峰回
a lone monk at dawn crosses the chill stream to depart.	孤僧曉度寒溪去
At these green hills	是處青山
my companions of a former life	前生儔侶
All are invited inside the gate of my calm garden.	招邀盡入閒庭戶
Every day harboring a smile, and also a scowl:	朝朝含笑復含顰
how could the flattery of men compare?[37]	人間相媚爭如許

In his isolated garden in the hills, Wang enjoys the clear air just after a rainstorm, and the faint sounds and images around him, hints of a Buddhist tranquility beyond individual suffering. For this is an idyllic place of such natural beauty and vividness that Heaven seems to speak to the observant mind. The vocabulary is exactly the reverse of the previous poem: *Tian yu* 天語 (Heaven speaks) rather than *Tian bu yu* 天不語 (Heaven does not speak). The higher powers of the universe are reluctant to disclose their intent upon the demand of querulous mortals. And yet, in the cosmic vision of reflective thinkers, all our thinking and writing does in some sense enact a dialogue with those same powers—for why else would have it meaning and inspiration? Why else would Yang Xiong have bothered to refute "Sublimating Sorrow" ("Lisao")?

---

37. Xiao Ai, ed., *Wang Guowei shici jianjiao*, III. Xiao Ai notes this was composed while Wang was in Nantong, Jiangsu.

In other words, as I will argue in this book, the rift in interpretive tradition is not one that can be repaired simply by identifying mysterious graphs or excavating new materials. Though these discoveries do play an important role, the foundation of our understanding of ancient texts ought to be the interpretive tradition that goes on generation after generation, continued by mortal poets and scholars, but carried out in the shadow of a Heaven who gives that dialogue a purpose and destination. The tricky details of particular characters are important, and evidence from archaeology, historical linguistics, and other sources extremely useful; but the application of all these resources is constantly directed and determined by broader ideological concerns.

In this project we can draw inspiration from the work of Hans-Georg Gadamer, who saw historical research in general as a dialogue of past and present.[38] Due to the way that texts are embedded in their own sociopolitical contexts, interpretation is not just a matter of reconstructing these contexts, which is never entirely feasible, but is also subject to the individual will of the interpreter in his or her own historical setting. In general, Gadamer sees our relationship with a text as one of question and answer; we must understand what other voices the text is responding to in order to appreciate its own message. As Gadamer points out, any speech act relies for its success on the infinity of what still remains unsaid:

> To say what one means, to be understood, is what holds a message together, and allows it to be so understood, with the infinity of the unsaid, together in one unity of meaning. Who speaks in this fashion, needs only to use the most familiar words for most familiar things, and then through them can bring into language what is unsaid and yet to say. Insofar as that which is expressed, the one who speaks is being speculative; his words then do not

---

38. My concern within this volume will lie solely with the practice of interpretation in China, *not* with the theory of Chinese hermeneutics. I borrow insights from Gadamer because I find them relevant to my own position as interpreter in the third decade of the twenty-first century. For the history of Chinese hermeneutics, a separate but important topic, helpful studies include Gu Ming Dong, *Chinese Theories of Reading and Writing*, and the various essays in Tu Ching-I, ed., *Interpretation and Intellectual Change*.

provide an image of what exists presently, but rather express a relation to the whole of Being and allow it to come into speech.[39]

Here we see a restatement of Gadamer's key insight, which is that any particular statement, message, or text cannot be interpreted properly in itself, but rather exists in a collaborative unity with its interpreters. We can speak only by relying on the "infinity of the unsaid." Thus for any ancient text, and particularly for a relatively opaque one like the "Heavenly Questions," proper understanding requires a careful examination of the original context in which the poem was composed. And this is true not just to understand the message itself, but also to appraise its "relation to the whole of Being," which, translated into the more prosaic language of American academia, we might describe as its "historical significance"; but Gadamer also sees the example of the poetic message as being distinct because its form itself expresses a different kind of relation to the whole of experience. Poetry touches on the realm of what is unsayable and beyond speech, while also maintaining its inherent bond to the nature of speech and language itself. It possesses its own relation to historical reality that needs to be interpreted as such. According to Gadamer, "it is truly meaningful and productive for the message of the poetic expression to be expressed in what is said as such, without having any occasional knowledge beyond that."[40]

---

39. Original text from Gadamer, *Wahrheit und Methode*, 444–45 (cf. translation, *Truth and Method*, 485–86):

> Sagen, was man meint, sich verständigen, hält im Gegenteil das Gesagte mit einer Unendlichkeit des Ungesagten in der Einheit eines Sinnes zusammen und läßt es so verstanden werden. Wer in dieser Weise spricht, mag nur die gewöhnlichsten in gewohntesten Worte gebrauchen und vermag doch eben dadurch zur Sprache zu bringen, was ungesagt ist und zu sagen ist. Insofern verhält sich, wer spricht, spekulativ, als seine Worte nicht Seiendes abbilden, sondern ein Verhältnis zum Ganzen des Seins aussprechen und zur Sprache kommen lassen.

The word "speculative" is a term of art here borrowing from its etymological root of speculum, "mirror," implying that "speculation" is an interaction between self and world.

40. Original text from Gadamer, *Wahrheit und Methode*, 445 (cf. translation, *Truth and Method*, 485–86): "... ist es wirklich sinnvoll und gefordert, daß der Sinn des dichterischen Wortes sich im Gesagten als solchem, ohne jede Hinzunahme okkasionellen Wissens, aussagt."

The mere fact that it is a poem, deprived of "occasional knowledge," is one aspect of its message and has its own irreducible significance. Or to restate with regard to the "Heavenly Questions": it is not enough just to understand the questions as a kind of rhetorical device; the interrogativity of the poem is itself a kind of poetical message, a voice speaking not just within its own literary context, but also offering something meaningful beyond that original occasion.

Gadamer's 1960 study *Truth and Method* focuses solely on the European hermeneutical tradition, but this is no reason for us to reject its relevance to the Chinese case. As Gadamer himself notes, his own particular understanding of the centrality of the question-and-answer relationship to humanistic inquiry is hardly common even in the European intellectual tradition—he cites only Plato and R.G. Collingwood as his two key predecessors in this respect.[41] Thus it is not implausible that aspects of Gadamer's hermeneutical thought would find resonance in intercultural hermeneutics as well. And within an awe-inspiringly vast philological realm of Chinese scholarship from the past two millennia, one chain of questions and answers stands out as singularly relevant to Gadamer's own "logic of the question" (Logik der Frage): the poem "Heavenly Questions" and the long history of attempts to answer its queries by means of historical research, exegetical ingenuity, and sheer literary bravado.

In this light the relation of the "Heavenly Questions" to the reality of ancient China needs itself to be reexamined. Not simply a litany of questions about ancient history, the poetic form of the text forces us to consider its relation to experience and interpretation themselves. When we consider the hidden protagonist Wang Hai, he is separated from us by several layers of historical distancing. It is not just that he is rarely mentioned in the transmitted historical records, for this is a lacuna that can be filled in partially by the evidence of the oracle bones. But "Heavenly Questions," even once we recover its original meaning, continues to ask yet further questions about his murder, questions that the text itself cannot answer. Even though philology may have resolved one challenge to our understanding of these lines, the poem reasserts the infinity of what is left unsaid, what is unsayable.

With this perspective in mind, the three main chapters of the book

---

41. Gadamer, *Wahrheit und Methode*, 352.

examine how the poem evolved along with its interpreters in different periods. Following each chapter, an appendix presents a translation of the poem in accordance with the dominant interpretation analyzed in the preceding chapter. Chapter 1 looks at "Heavenly Questions" in light of its earliest audience of whom we have any information, the scholars of the Han dynasty. It is by following their interpretations and misinterpretations that we can begin to gain a sense of the real scope and value of the poem, since they are historically the closest to the poem. The appendix presents "Heavenly Questions" along with a complete translation of the commentary to the poem compiled by Wang Yi.

Chapters 2 and 3 turn to later interpretations of the poem, and show how they have offered new insights on its meaning through exegetical creativity and interpretive insight. Chapter 2 is devoted entirely to Liu Zongyuan's verse response to the poem, "Heavenly Responses." Though this is a literary work, it is also full of technical and scholarly insights into the meaning of the original poem. Moreover, it offers one of the deepest interpretations of "Heavenly Questions" as a philosophical and moral reflection on the human condition. The appendix presents a complete translation of Liu Zongyuan's poem in tandem with the source text.

Chapter 3 turns to the scholarly tradition from the Song dynasty up to the present century. It does not aim for a comprehensive treatment of the hundreds of commentaries and editions of the poem that survive, but tries to identify some of the most innovative treatments of the poem and explain the reasons for their new discoveries. The chapter focuses on the coherent vision of the poem's message offered by Ming critics; Qing dynasty innovations in philological technique; and finally, the meticulous collation of all the relevant sources in modern scholarship. The appendix to this chapter presents a translation of "Heavenly Questions" reflecting many of these new approaches and insights.

Finally, the epilogue to the book suggests that scholarly interpretations of poetry are inherently limited in scope. "Heavenly Questions" contains questions that are unanswerable, and poetic images that pose challenges to any fixed interpretation. As we continue to grapple with the challenges of ancient texts, there will continue to be dynamic interactions between knowledge and forgetting, certainty and doubt, scholarship and poetry.

CHAPTER ONE

The Poem's Earliest Interpretations

> A word is not only a sign. In some sense that is hard to grapple with, it is also almost something like an image. One needs only to reflect upon the extreme alternative of a purely manmade language, to appreciate the relative correctness of such an archaic theory of language. In some puzzling manner there develops a bond between the word and what is "imaged" by it, a belonging to the Being of what is imaged.
>
> —Gadamer, *Truth and Method*[1]

One key challenge in approaching difficult old texts is to distinguish between two different types of misunderstanding. In one case, the text is truly difficult and the correct reading, if there is one, is not obvious, and has never been obvious. But in the other case, the text was originally straightforward and simple, but has become corrupt through scribal error, or for some other reason, or has been obscured by linguistic drift, or its original meaning is simply lost and forgotten. And yet some texts really were difficult from the very beginning, because reality can be complicated and humanity has sought to describe or master that difficulty in words. When dealing with an ancient text—in particular, in the case of Chinese texts, a work created before the standardization of the script in the Qin and Han Dynasties—it can be difficult to distinguish among the many varieties of ignorance and error.

"Heavenly Questions" is particularly challenging in this sense, even

---

1. Gadamer, *Wahrheit und Methode*, 394 (cf. translation, *Truth and Method*, 434): "Das Wort ist nicht nur Zeichen. In irgendeinem schwer zu erfassenden Sinne ist es doch auch fast so etwas wie ein Abbild. Man braucht nur die extreme Gegenmöglichkeit einer reinen Kunstsprache zu erwägen, um in einer solchen archaischen Sprachtheorie doch ein relatives Recht zu erkennen. Dem Wort kommt auf eine rätselhafte Weise Gebundenheit an das 'Abgebildete', Zugehörigkeit zum Sein des Abgebildeten zu."

within the *Elegies of Chu*, because there are two causes for our lack of comprehension. On the surface level, the text refers cryptically to figures of the remote past who are often hard to identify. Even in the Han dynasty, many of the ancient records had been lost, or transcribed incorrectly, so that readers already struggled to identify the subjects of quatrains. But even leaving aside historical distance, the poem is inherently challenging just because of its interrogative nature, its interrogativity. The entire poem is composed in the interrogative mood, not making statements but posing queries on hundreds of distinct topics. In other words, it is not accidentally opaque but rather intentionally open to interpretation, because it is discussing challenging topics and not resolving any of them explicitly. As Liu Chenweng 劉辰翁 (1232–1297) wrote: "In that mysterious haze, turbulent and tumultuous, the feelings can be pitied, even though the pattern cannot be found." 恍惚怳宕, 其情可憫, 其理不可求.[2] He was writing in reference to these lines from the "Heavenly Questions," quatrain 40 by my count:

The white nimbus winding around and spreading out,	白蜺嬰茀
Why has it / some person come upon this hall?	胡為此堂
How was that fine elixir obtained,	安得夫良藥
Which could not be used for good / kept secure?[3]	不能固臧

There are different identifications of the protagonist here (a legendary Daoist transcendent, or the moon goddess Chang'e 嫦娥, etc.). But Liu suggests that even if one cannot quite follow the logic, the poem holds together nonetheless and conveys a message full of pathos.

From this point of view, the interrogativity of "Heavenly Questions" is not superficial; the questions are not, in general, rhetorical questions, that is, assertions rephrased in the form of questions. Instead, most of the questions posed in this poem are truly questions, their answer uncertain even to the very first audiences for this poem, and hence in most cases

---

2. *Qishier jia*, 3.10b–11a. On this compilation of interpretive comments by seventy scholars, see the discussion below in chapter 4.

3. My translation of this quatrain is different from others below, since it aims to preserve the ambiguity of the text without adopting either the Han or a later interpretation. *Zang* 臧 is problematic, so I translate with both possibilities, which will be discussed further in translations of the quatrain below.

unknown to us as well. Though Warring States astronomy and geography have long been superseded, so that certain questions may appear primitive, the origins of the universe and man's ultimate destiny remain as problematic today as they have ever been, and it is these foundational questions that retain their point—even their sting—today. The reasons underlying success and failure remain uncertain, just as the poem suggests in quatrain 72:

> As the Mandate of Heaven revolves and reverses: 　天命反側
> Why does it punish and why does it aid?[4] 　　　何罰何佑

Though various answers were put forth in the Warring States period, and more robust explanations established to legitimize later dynasties, it is a fact of our human condition that none of these explanations can be final, and so a question regarding the Mandate of Heaven is not, and cannot be, simply rhetorical.

Indeed, the question of whether there is some kind of heavenly mandate or cosmic justice behind historical events is not just one of the topics covered in "Heavenly Questions," but its central theme. The importance of this theme was implicitly recognized by Sima Qian 司馬遷 (b. 145 BCE), who in his double biography of Qu Yuan and Jia Yi 賈誼 (200–168 BCE) in the *Shiji* 史記 (Records of the grand historian) wrote:

> The Grand Historian comments: When I read "Sublimating Sorrow," "Heavenly Questions," "Summons to the Soul," and "Lamenting Ying," I grieve for Qu Yuan's aspirations (*zhi*).[5]
>
> 太史公曰：余讀離騷、天問、招魂、哀郢，悲其志。

---

4. Translations from "Heavenly Questions" in this chapter generally follow my "Text One," which aims to present the poem as it was understood by the Han commentary. Since the *Chuci zhangju* does not correctly divide the poem into quatrains, I present the number of the quatrain, according to my own understanding, for ease of comparison, but keep it in brackets to remind the reader that this division into quatrains, following the rhyme scheme, was not, apparently, applied to the text in the Han dynasty.

5. *Shiji*, 84.3018. *Zhi* 志 is often translated as "intent," but is a capacious term that can mean also "thought," "ideal," "ambition," etc., all of which are equally relevant here and in its classic usage in the formula *shi yan zhi* 詩言志: "poems articulate thoughts," "poems express aspirations," etc.

I take this to mean that Sima Qian read all four of these poems on the model of the "Sublimating Sorrow" ("Lisao" 離騷), as expressions of Qu Yuan's frustrated aspirations. It is not easy to evaluate this judgment precisely since Sima Qian only quotes two texts attributed to Qu Yuan in his biography: "Embracing the Sand" ("Huai sha" 懷沙) and "Fisherman" ("Yufu" 漁父), and *not* any of the four pieces mentioned above.[6] So he did not have occasion to elaborate on his view that "Heavenly Questions" was an embodiment of Qu Yuan's "aspirations." Even so, his interpretation of the poem is easy to corroborate with lines such as those quoted just above, or alternatively, quatrain 67 below:

When all under Heaven had been allotted to the Yin,	授殷天下
By what authority did they rule?	其位安施
When in turn success met with destruction,	反成乃亡
By what crime was it incurred?	其罪伊何

These powerful lines simply ask why the Shang dynasty attained the mandate of Heaven, and how the rulers lost it. This question is a central concern of "Heavenly Questions," and other passages suggest some possible answers, particularly having to do with the tyrannical behavior of the final ruler of Shang, Zhow 紂.[7] The problem of a wicked ruler is of course one that Qu Yuan faces directly in "Sublimating Sorrow" and several of the "Nine Avowals" ("Jiuzhang" 九章) poems, including "Lamenting Ying" ("Ai Ying" 哀郢), so it is plausible to relate the poems with respect to this theme.[8] As a matter of literary criticism, then, Sima Qian's verdict is plausible. But one might ask separately how Sima Qian's statement makes sense as a matter of hermeneutics: that is, how did Sima Qian read the "Heavenly Questions" itself and come to understand its message in this way? How did he make sense of the text, identify its author and dating, and read the different questions in succession?

---

6. Both these pieces are also translated in Williams, *Elegies of Chu*, 61–63 and 83–84, respectively. The curious title "Embracing the Sand" seems to refer obliquely to Qu Yuan's suicidal intent; see note in Williams, *Elegies of Chu*, 210–11.

7. I romanize the name of this ruler as "Zhow" to distinguish him from the name of the Zhou dynasty, which was established by overthrowing him.

8. "Summons to the Soul" ("Zhao hun" 招魂) is another question and raises separate issues, treated in my monograph *Chinese Poetry as Soul Summoning*.

These questions may all be understood as belonging to the broader field of reception theory, in which one might ask: how did the learned and serious readers of the Han dynasty, so much closer in time and cultural milieu to the poem "Heavenly Questions" than anyone in the present time, read this poem? But this is not simply a historical question, nor is it a question with a definite answer. Instead, it is another way of representing the problem of interpreting "Heavenly Questions" that we ourselves confront. Understanding how Han readers read the poem will help people today to construct more sophisticated and accurate readings of the poem, because Han interpretations elicit key features of the poem that might otherwise be invisible to us.[9] Thus the goal is not to understand the Han reception *per se*, so much as to become more keenly aware of the questions and implicit messages already set forth in the original poem. As Paul de Man wrote in a preface to a collection of essays by *Rezeptionsästhetik* scholar Hans Robert Jauss: "A dialectic of understanding as a complex interplay between knowing and not-knowing, is built within the very process of literary history."[10] By engaging with that earlier dialectic, we can come closer to a correct reading of the "Heavenly Questions" itself.

Sima Qian's own view is only one possible vantage point on this broader issue. While we cannot know exactly what text of the poem he used, we have access to a comprehensive document on the anthology from the Han dynasty, namely the *Chuci zhangju* 楚辭章句 (Elegies of Chu with chapter-and-verse commentary) anthology, as compiled by Wang Yi two centuries after Sima Qian's time. The Han compilation has been the principal mediating force between the original poem and post-Han readers, so it is a critical work for understanding the reception of the "Heavenly Questions," and also an essential tool for understanding the poem itself. Even when more recent scholarship has shown the Han commentary to be erroneous, its highly influential interpretations may still be useful for understanding how "Heavenly Questions" came to be preserved in its current form. This chapter will be devoted to analyzing the interpretation and presentation of

---

9. There has already been good work on this subject with relation to the *Chuci* as a whole, and "Sublimating Sorrow" ("Lisao") in particular. See references cited below, but in particular Michael Schimmelpfennig, "Qu Yuans Weg," and Li Daming, *Han Chuci xue shi*.

10. de Man, "Introduction," xii.

the "Heavenly Questions" in the anthology, and will also argue that these aspects are representative of Han scholarship, rather than being singular to Wang Yi personally. They are not just artifacts of a single scholar of the Han, but suggest difficulties in the poem that were unavoidable for any Han reader, and thus were intrinsic to the establishment of the earliest text of the poem. That is to say that even early misreadings of "Heavenly Questions" can contribute to a clearer view of what the poem originally meant. The *Chuci zhangju* is probably a good representation of the consensus interpretation of Han readers; although they clearly struggled to grasp the meaning of many of the lines in the poem (just as we do), nonetheless they appreciated its essential theme, which they identified as a searching examination of history's moral significance for the present.

The "Wang Yi" Preface and Postface

Before examining the Han interpretation in detail, we need to identify as clearly as possible how that interpretation came into being. The *Elegies of Chu* as we know it was compiled by Wang Yi in the form of the *Chuci zhangju* in the Eastern Han dynasty (25–220 CE). The specific date is unknown, but it seems to have been completed in the early second century, and has been dated to around 120. Wang Yi served for a time as a collator (*jiaoshu lang* 校書郎), essentially an imperial librarian, so it makes sense that his role in forming the anthology was primarily that of editing texts and commentaries that had already been completed by earlier scholars.[11] After all, the original anthology had probably been compiled by Liu Xiang 劉向 (79–8 BCE), when he was charged with supervision of the imperial library in 26 BCE.[12] Meanwhile, it is unclear if even the *Chuci zhangju* was actually completed by Wang Yi himself, since the final

---

11. See the discussion in Timothy Chan, *Considering the End*, 9. Chan also carefully explains the argument for dating the work to 120, but I find the logic somewhat tenuous. Wang's title is identified in the *Chuci buzhu* (p. 1), but not in early texts of the *Chuci zhangju*. On the Eastern Han imperial library see Bielenstein, *Bureaucracy of Han Times*, 59.

12. Although it is not mentioned in his *Hanshu* biography, Liu Xiang is identified as the original editor in the *Chuci buzhu*, 1 and 48; see also Lin Weichun, "Liu Xiang bian Chuci chutan." For a succinct biography of Liu, see Loewe, *Biographical Dictionary*, 372–75.

fascicle contains his own poems along with a commentary which makes some obvious blunders. It is probably best to think of it as an accretive compilation that gathers in the various achievements of Han scholarship, with names like Liu Xiang and Wang Yi merely marking critical stages in that longer process.[13]

The "Heavenly Questions" seems to have been placed third or fourth in the anthology and attributed to Qu Yuan.[14] However, we do not have an original manuscript of this anthology, and the earliest surviving texts are from the sixteenth century and may have been reconstructed based on the *Chuci buzhu* 楚辭補注 text compiled by Hong Xingzu 洪興祖 (1090–1155). Hong distinguishes clearly between the original commentary and his own supplementary notes, and the original text of the *Chuci zhangju* commentary has also been carefully collated by Huang Linggeng 黃靈庚, so the text appears to be an authentic Eastern Han work, but certainly may have been rearranged or altered since.[15] Though the *Chuci zhangju* attributes about half of the contents of the anthology to Qu Yuan, these attributions are open to question. Some evidence suggests that originally "Sublimating Sorrow" was seen as canonical, and all other pieces, including "Heavenly Questions," were viewed as *zhuan* 傳, "commentary" or "tradition" subordinate to "Sublimating Sorrow."[16] As we have seen, Sima Qian seems to have read both the "Heavenly Questions" and "Summons to

---

13. To be more precise about the limits of this argument, since it resembles numerous other problems of authorship in early China and could be misunderstood: it is reasonable to think of the compilation as a collective process because of our lack of definite knowledge, but this should not be taken as evidence of some anonymous oral tradition underlying the work. It is entirely possible that there may have been just two or three distinct individuals who wrote most of the commentary; it is just that we have no way of assigning individual authorship to particular portions of the texts.

14. The *Chuci buzhu* places it third, but also provides an alternative table of contents from the *Chuci shiwen* 楚辭釋文, a lost version of the anthology, which places it fourth after "Sublimating Sorrow," "Nine Songs," and "Nine Phases" ("Jiubian" 九辯). Huang Linggeng restores the order of the *Shiwen* in his *Chuci zhangju shuzheng*. See also Timothy Chan, "The *Jing/Zhuan* Structure," 326.

15. This is Huang Linggeng's *Chuci zhangju shuzheng*, now an indispensable scholarly resource.

16. See Timothy Chan, "The *Jing/Zhuan* Structure," and Tang Bingzheng, "*Chuci* chengshu zhi tansuo."

the Soul" through the filter of "Sublimating Sorrow," inclining towards a reading of all these pieces as works of protest or plaint.[17]

Modern scholars have sometimes attempted to present an explicit agenda in the *Chuci zhangju*, and there certainly are biases and intentional framings of texts in the anthology. Michael Schimmelpfennig has examined the commentary to "Sublimating Sorrow" in considerable detail, and argues that Wang Yi intentionally tries to elaborate on the interpretation of Liu An centuries earlier, praising Qu Yuan's suicide as a noble act, while responding to the critique of Qu Yuan by Ban Gu and others.[18] Taking a broader view of Han political and religious trends, Timothy W. K. Chan shows how the emphasis on personal virtue in the commentary seems to reflect an Eastern Han concern with restoring correct values in a time of corruption.[19] As Chan writes, "Remonstration and allegiance were common themes in the official discourse throughout China's recorded history, but these themes had achieved a particularly prominent place in the political arena around the time that Wang Yi wrote his *Chuci zhangju*."[20]

Whatever the commentators' agenda was with regard to "Sublimating Sorrow" or the anthology in general, however, when one focuses solely on the "Heavenly Questions," there seems to have been no agenda at all. Instead, one can perhaps better understand the Han commentary to this poem as being no more than a flailing attempt to make sense of an appealing but cryptic source. Consider, for instance, the commentary to quatrain 46:

> When [Shaokang] capsized the vessels of Zhenxun, 覆舟斟尋
> By what route did he conquer them? 何道取之

---

17. See Du Heng's "The Author's Two Bodies," an account of how the authorial figure of Qu Yuan ramified across the poems in the anthology via paratexts by Sima Qian and other Han scholars.

18. Schimmelpfennig, "Quest for a Classic," for example, on p. 157: "Wang Yi fell back upon the earliest systematic reading of the 'Li sao' put down in writing more than two hundred years before him by Liu An, integrated it within his own commentary, and reinstated it with a variety of additional and highly sophisticated exegetical means."

19. Timothy Chan, "Wang Yi on Integrity and Loyalty," in *Considering the End*, 7–40. This is only one argument in Chan's rich article. Notably, he further places the commentary in the context of Han writings on omens and their significance in light of Yin-Yang correlative cosmology, in pp. 8–19.

20. Timothy Chan, "Wang Yi on Integrity and Loyalty," 31.

> *Han commentary*: When Shaokang destroyed the Zhenxun people, as if capsizing their vessels, by what route did he take them?[21]
> 言少康滅斟尋氏，奄若覆舟，獨以何道取之乎？

The "commentary" is essentially a paraphrase of the text, explaining the capsizing as being a metaphor, but failing to add much context or detail. It reads more like a student's notes than an authoritative interpretation, or even an attempt at such an interpretation. In other words, one essential fact about the Han reception of "Heavenly Questions" is that Han readers were frequently confused by the poem, and could only guess at its intended meaning.[22]

Nonetheless, the *Chuci zhangju* does offer some explicit guidelines for reading the poem outside of the line-by-line commentary itself. The anthology already presents an implicit interpretation of the "Heavenly Questions" merely by virtue of including it among other compositions attributed to Qu Yuan, an interpretation consistent with Sima Qian's remark quoted above. But the anthology also encapsulates the text of the poem between a preface and a postface, each of which are full of interest. The preface to "Heavenly Questions" gives us a sense of the motivation and content of the poem:

> "Heavenly Questions" was composed by Qu Yuan. Why is it not called "Questioning Heaven"? Because Heaven is revered and cannot be questioned, so instead the poem is titled "Heavenly Questions." Qu Yuan was

---

21. Huang Linggeng, ed., *Chuci zhangju shuzheng*, 4.1121. As generally in "Text One" below, I quote the interpretive discussion from the commentary, but omit the glosses of words that precede them. These are also important and I have tried to follow them in my English translations based on the Han commentary, but there is little point in translating sentences like "'boat' means 'ship'" 舟，船也 in the commentary to these lines. That said, these glosses do raise some interesting philological problems. Here Huang Linggeng points out that several texts have a variant 舩 for 船 in the first line. This is simply a regular graphic variant for *chuan* 船 with no special significance, but it may explain why the commentary has bothered to gloss such a common character: the regularization of the script has rendered the note redundant.

22. Another good example of this phenomenon is the way that the Han commentary frequently neglects to gloss difficult terms and instead simply repeats them verbatim in its paraphrases. Examples are *yingdu* 營度 (quatrain 4); *tu* 菟 (9); *yexian* 曳銜 (13); *huangxiong* 黃熊 (38).

banished, and his anxious heart was full of sorrow and suffering. Wandering at will amid the hills and lakes, he traversed much of the land. Sighing and exclaiming at the vast firmament, he looked up at Heaven and sighed aloud. He then saw that in Chu there was a temple of the ancestral kings, and an altar to the lords and officers, which was decorated with images of Heaven and Earth, mountains and rivers, and all the spirits, as well as precious things and strange marvels,[23] and the deeds of the sages of old and also of monsters. Surveying it all until he was exhausted, he rested below the painting, and then, looking up at them, he wrote upon the walls, asking about each of them, so as to express his frustration and anger, and to relieve and purge his sorrowful thoughts. The people of Chu grieved for Qu Yuan, so they continued to discuss and transmit these questions, and for this reason the meaning of the text is not in proper order.[24]

天問者，屈原之所作也。何不言問天？天尊不可問，故曰天問也。屈原放逐，憂心愁悴。彷徨山澤，經歷陵陸。嗟號昊旻，仰天歎息。見楚有先王之廟及公卿祠堂，圖畫天地山川神靈，琦瑋僪佹，及古賢聖怪物行事。周流罷倦，休息其下，仰見圖畫，因書其壁，何而問之，以渫憤懣，舒瀉愁思。楚人哀惜屈原，因共論述，故其文義不次序云爾。

This introduction has been extraordinarily influential in both premodern and modern scholarship, even though its authorship and genesis are unclear.[25] Numerous readers who have struggled with the poem have been gratified to learn that even Han readers found the text's arrangement to be confusing. Indeed, the problem of misplaced bamboo strips, which has caused many excavated and transmitted texts to come to us in confused arrangements, is a familiar one for modern scholars of early China, so the remark that the text is "not in proper order" rings true.[26]

---

23. The four-character term *qiwei jugui* 琦瑋僪佹 is a euphoniously alliterative expression, its Old Chinese pronunciation being OCM *kai-gai kwit-ŋoi ("OCM" refers to Axel Schuessler's Minimal Old Chinese, a simplified version of the reconstruction of William H. Baxter).

24. Huang Linggeng, ed., *Chuci zhangju shuzheng*, 4.995–98.

25. Notably, Lin Weichun argues that it was composed by Liu Xiang. This is not necessarily right but is as likely as anything else. See Lin Weichun, "Shilun *Chuci zhangju* 'xuwen,'" and Timothy Chan, "The *Jing/Zhuan* Structure," 306.

26. For an example of a "misplaced strip" (*cuojian* 錯簡) in early poetry, specifically the *Shijing*; see Shaughnessy, "Unearthed Documents," 350. As Matthias Richter points out,

Aside from the assertion that the poem is out of order, the "mural thesis," or the proposition that Qu Yuan composed the poem upon looking at actual murals in a temple, has inspired a considerable amount of secondary scholarship. This was the central conceit behind the earliest Western translation of the text in 1931, by August Conrady and Eduard Erkes: *Das älteste Dokument zur chinesischen Kunstgeschichte*. Conrady and Erkes translate the poem according to a convoluted scheme in which they read certain lines as the original captions to murals, and other lines as answers to the questions inscribed by Qu Yuan.

Although this "mural thesis" to me seems more like an etiological myth than a historical hypothesis, it is worth discussing why certain readers of the poem have found the art-historical approach so compelling, even though the original story has a legendary quality in its neglect of any verifiable factual basis. After all, an obvious critique of this art historical interpretation is that the very opening of the poem appears to describe a state of chaos that could not be depicted visually. Conrady and Erkes consider this criticism and attempt to refute it by citing Wang Yanshou's 王延壽 (fl. 163) "Rhapsody on the Hall of Numinous Blessings in Lu" ("Lu Lingguang dian fu" 魯靈光殿賦) and also the personification of Chaos (Hundun 混沌) in *Zhuangzi*.[27] The example of Chaos is not really *à propos*, since it does not relate to visual art, but the case of Wang Yanshou's rhapsody is highly suggestive, particularly as Wang Yanshou was also the son of commentator Wang Yi.[28] In particular, that rhapsody suggests an explanation for the popularity of the mural hypothesis in the Eastern Han: perhaps contemporary readers were accustomed to seeing this kind of mural art in their own lives.[29] Indeed, the rhapsody contains the following passage describing murals within the Hall of Numinous Blessings:

---

however, this concept may technically be misleading, if it causes us to neglect the potential for intentional rearrangement in the context of a broader textual fluidity (*The Embodied Text*, 97–98).

27. Conrady and Erkes, *Das älteste Dokument*, 26.

28. Kominami points out that the haunting fact that Wang Yanshou drowned at a young age in the Xiang River suggests that the Wang family, centuries later, still belonged to the same world of aquatic legend described in the *Chuci* poems; see *Soji to sono chūshakushatachi*, 363.

29. Tang Bingzheng points out similar examples in *Chuci leigao*, 292–94, but then goes on to show that "Heavenly Questions" has to be read as a broader work of cosmological speculation.

Last come the Three Tyrants.	下及三后
Depraved consorts, misguided rulers,	婬妃亂主
Loyal statesmen, filial sons,	忠臣孝子
Heroic knights, chaste women,	烈士貞女
Worthies and fools, the failed and accomplished,	賢愚成敗
None have gone unattested.	靡不載敘
The wicked are warnings to the world,	惡以誡世
The good are examples for posterity.[30]	善以示後

This passage seems to accord rather well with the content of "Heavenly Questions," particularly the examples of both good and wicked leaders placed in contrast with one another. Though this example is solely textual, one might cite also the famous murals from the Wu Liang shrine (Wu Liang ci 武梁祠) of 151 CE, which cover events similar to the "Heavenly Questions," and are even complemented by captions in tetrasyllabic verse.[31]

Both these examples of illustrative murals can be dated precisely, but not to Warring States Chu. Instead, they belong to the second century CE during the Han dynasty, and one of them is a poem authored by the very son of Wang Yi. As is often the case with the *Chuci*, then, we need to consider not just the text but the interpreter and text in tandem. It was reasonable for Eastern Han scholars like Wang Yi to read the "Heavenly Questions" as an ekphrastic response to temple paintings because this kind of textual project was so common in their own time. In other words, the mural thesis was a natural way for Han scholars to respond to the difficulties of the poem, even though it may not reflect the actual circumstances of composition of the text.[32] To show that the "Heavenly Questions" corresponded to visual art, we would like to see Warring States-era visual art depicting the Zhou conquest or related events in a parallel form, but for now, at least, this kind of evidence is lacking, although new archaeological discoveries might substantiate it better in the future.[33]

---

30. Knechtges, *Selections of Refined Literature*, 2:275; *Wenxuan*, 11.524–25.

31. See Wu Hung's study, *The Wu Liang Shrine*.

32. This is a natural and laudable human reaction, just as contemporary scholarship often deals with premodern literary phenomena by citing cinematic techniques like the montage, or practices from Internet culture. But it is then necessary to identify the ahistorical and anachronistic element in such a reaction.

33. There is a richly-documented recent study of the spiritual figures worshiped

Overall, the mural thesis cannot be relied on as a historical proposition, but it may nonetheless provoke important insights into the true meaning of the poem.[34] That is, it may still be valuable as an interpretation of the text. It would be foolish to read the commentarial insights of the *Chuci zhangju* as purely factual in nature; they are also rhetorical, like the poems themselves, and some of their claims are best interpreted metaphorically or allegorically. In this light, the real meaning of the mural thesis may be that the poem should be read as a contemplation of the principal historical traditions of Chu. Words are not images, but they are something like images, as Gadamer reminds us in the epigraph to this chapter. The "Heavenly Questions" are not simply questions meant to be answered in rote fashion; but also verbal enactments of historical drama that could also have been depicted visually.

Another important feature of the preface, of course, is its forceful insertion of the poem into Qu Yuan's biography. This again is a noteworthy feature of Han scholarship, what Martin Kern has called "the poetry of Han historiography."[35] However, no dates are given, and no quotations from the poem are supplied to corroborate this reading; nor does even the commentary to the poem itself, for the most part, attempt to substantiate this view. There is one bizarre moment at quatrain 40, in the middle of the poem, when the commentary interprets the line "Why has it come upon this hall?" 胡為此堂, as referring to the same temple decorated with murals where Qu Yuan composed the poem. But the commentary does not elaborate any further on this dubious reading, and there is only one sustained passage of commentary, following the cryptic final stanzas of the poem, which does tie the poem directly to Qu Yuan, albeit in a brazenly

---

during the Han dynasty, as depicted in contemporary murals and tomb art: Jiang Sheng, *Han diguo de yichan*. But the information there also does not seem to correspond too closely to the content of "Heavenly Questions," as best I can tell.

34. Cf. the brilliant, if ultimately unconvincing, argument of Zhang Shuguo that the poem describes Qu Yuan's reactions to murals at an ancestral temple not in Chu but in Wu 吳; see Zhang, "Cong Wu Zixu tuyong lun."

35. See especially Kern's conclusion that, "whether narratives were framed around songs attributed to historical heroes, or whether they were retrospectively enriched by ominous or judgmental ditties and sayings, Han song culture cannot be discussed in separation from Han historiographic culture." Kern, "Poetry of Han Historiography," 64.

ahistorical manner. Consider, then, the final four lines of the whole poem together with the original *Chuci zhangju* commentary:

| I warn Duao | 吾告堵敖 |
| That he will not long survive. | 以不長 |

Han commentary: Duao was a worthy man of Chu. When Qu Yuan was exiled, he told Duao: "The state of Chu is going to decline, and will not endure much longer."

堵敖, 楚賢人也。屈原放時, 語堵敖曰:「楚國將衰, 不復能久長也。」

| How could the trial of the sovereign accord myself | 何試上自予 |
| A reputation for loyalty more illustrious? | 忠名彌彰 |

Han commentary: Qu Yuan said, "How dare I test my sovereign, and so contradict my own reputation for loyalty and honesty, which will be prominent and glorious to later generations? Because we share a surname,[36] I am deeply distraught in my heart, and my loyalty to him cannot perish."

屈原言我何敢嘗試君上, 自干忠直之名, 以顯彰後世乎？誠以同姓之故, 中心懸惻, 義不能已也。

As far as we know, though, Duao is Xiong Jian 熊囏, an early ruler of Chu also known as Zhuang'ao 莊敖. His son killed him and usurped the throne to reign as King Mu 穆 (r. 626–614).[37] Many lines in the poem are opaque, but this one is not especially so, since it refers to a prominent figure in Chu history by his own distinctive name, Duao. Although he was a historical figure from Chu, he belonged to a different period of history than Qu Yuan himself.

There are a few ways we might make sense of this interpretation of the ending of the "Heavenly Questions." It might be that the commentary's author was mistaken about the historical background, and confused Duao

---

36. Qu Yuan was said to have one of the three surnames of the Chu royal family, the other two being Zhao 昭 and Jing 景. See, e.g., Jiang Liangfu, "*Shiji* Qu Yuan liezhuan shuzheng," 4–5.

37. Duao is mentioned in *Zuozhuan*, Duke Zhuang, year 16 (Durrant et al., *Zuo Tradition*, 175). There are numerous contradictions and alternate names in the sources, but I attempt to follow the account in Blakeley, "King, Clan, and Courtier," 6–10, based on the *Zuozhuan*. See "Text Three," quatrain 95.

with someone of Qu Yuan's own time; or alternatively, he might simply have invented the content of the commentary so as to relate the topic to Qu Yuan. But even though Han scholars were not motivated by the same demands for precision as modern ones, nonetheless, they could tell the Warring States apart from the Spring and Autumn period. Instead, we should not understand the commentary here as being intended as a historical record of the genesis of the poem. Instead, it is a forceful interpretation that inserts Qu Yuan into the story without regard to chronology or history, willfully ignoring the anachronism. The focus of interest here lies not on the circumstances of composition behind the poem, but rather on the "later generations" 後世 for whom all the questions are supposed to be significant. The issue of interest in the commentary is not why Qu Yuan wrote what he did, but what he intended to tell us.

Considering the preface, and its mural thesis, together with the commentary to the concluding passage of the poem, we find that, on one hand, the *Chuci zhangju* presents "Heavenly Questions" as a work addressed to the principal historical origins of the state of Chu as represented in the murals of the ancestral temple; but on the other, that its compilers are willing to conflate the events of different centuries when it seems effective for rhetorical purposes. Finally, of course, we note also that the text of the poem itself is frequently opaque to the commentators of the Han. In other words, the Han authors of the commentary believed that "Heavenly Questions" contained within it a message of considerable importance not just as a historical document, but as a caution and guide to future generations, yet that message frequently eluded them.

The postface to the poem provides an additional and important clue regarding the commentators' editorial procedure, as it discusses the history of the poem's exegesis since Sima Qian:

> Originally Qu Yuan's compositions numbered some twenty-five pieces. They were passed on and transmitted, but no one could explain them. Since the text of "Heavenly Questions" was not in order and referred to strange and marvelous events, few have penetrated its meaning since the Grand Historian's discussion. As for Liu Xiang and Yang Xiong, they cited various records and commentaries so as to explicate it, yet still could not be comprehensive. Many passages were omitted, and generally we heard nothing about them. Even when some explicated the words, that only made the

text more intricate, and muddied up the interpretation, so that its meaning became unclear, and its subtle referents were not made explicit. All those who perused it struggled and could not shed light on the poem. Now I compare the old sections and unite them with the classics and commentaries, so that they may display and illuminate one another, like the two halves of a tally that are reunited. Once the sections are separated and sentences are distinguished, the contents can be known so that later students will forever be without doubts.

昔屈原所作，凡二十五篇，世相教傳，而莫能說。天問以其文義不次，又多奇怪之事。自太史公口論道之，多所不逮。至於劉向、揚雄，援引傳記以解說之，亦不能詳悉。所闕者眾，日無聞焉。既有解□□□詞，³⁸乃復多連蹇其文，濛澒其說，故厥義不昭，微指不晢，自游覽者，靡不苦之，而不能照也。今則稽之舊章，合之經傳，以相發明，為之符驗，章決句斷，事事可曉，俾後學者永無疑焉。³⁹

The postface provides two key insights about the origin and function of the whole commentary. First of all, the commentary to "Heavenly Questions" seems to be based on previous work by Liu Xiang and Yang Xiong 揚雄 (53 BCE–18 CE), two of the preeminent scholars of the Han dynasty. Thus criticisms of Wang Yi as being an ignorant scholar who could not understand the true meaning of the poems in *Chuci zhangju* are misplaced, at least with regard to the "Heavenly Questions." Timothy W. K. Chan quotes the last lines of this postface and comments rightly that, "No one knows how much Wang Yi incorporated from earlier commentaries in his *Chuci zhangju* or how much interpolation there is in *Chuci buzhu*, but his claimed adoption of the preexisting commentaries shows that he must have had reason to align his own commentary with those that preceded his."⁴⁰ It would seem that the postface was composed by the final editor of the text and commentary, Wang Yi, but that otherwise the commentary to the poem is based on previous scholarship.

---

38. The *Chuci buzhu* indicates that three characters are missing here, but in fact the meaning is quite clear even without them, so it is not clear what has happened to the text.
39. Huang Linggeng, ed., *Chuci zhangju shuzheng*, 4.1258–60. I have borrowed from Timothy Chan's translation of the last two sentences in *Considering the End*, 16.
40. Timothy Chan, *Considering the End*, 16. A footnote (omitted here) introduces scholarship by Kominami Ichirō, which will be discussed further below.

The other key lesson here is the memorable phrase "like the two halves of a tally that are reunited." Wang Yi's particular contribution has been to make text and commentary conform like a "tally" (*fu* 符). What is distinctive about a tally is that it consists of two separate parts which can also be carried independently. Thus, Wang Yi seems to be saying that he has taken the text, on one hand, and various other commentaries and interpretations, and stuck them together. He does not pretend at any point that he is recovering the original meaning of the "Heavenly Questions." Instead, he has combined it—sometimes by an act of interpretive violence—with legends about Qu Yuan. With this editorial strategy in mind, the commentary about Duao at the end of the poem makes much more sense. Even the mural story in the preface may be playing a similar role, not so much explaining the actual origin of the poem as conjoining it with legends of Qu Yuan's life. The temple murals, again, are an important feature of the cultural scene in the Eastern Han, which can be juxtaposed with "Heavenly Questions" in a productive way, despite the lack of any specific evidence underlying the historical hypothesis.

It is worth noting that the method of the commentary is not generally what we might today regard as scholarly or philological. Though most of the entries paraphrase the meaning of the questions, with more or less detail, a few respond in an entirely different way, by quoting long anecdotes which look more like early forms of fiction, somewhat resembling the anecdotes of the *Hanshi waizhuan* 韓詩外傳, for instance. In response to quatrain 63, which mentions Yi Yin 伊尹, minister to the founder of the Shang dynasty, the Han commentary presents this story:

When Yi Yin's mother was pregnant, she dreamt that a goddess told her: "When a frog appears from the mortar oven, you must go right away and never look back."[41] Not much later, a frog appeared in the mortar oven. She departed for the east, and when she looked back at her home, it had been covered in a flood. She was drowned in the flood and then transformed into a hollow mulberry tree. After the water dried up, there was a little child crying out by the water's edge, and someone came to adopt him. Once he grew up,

---

41. This curious prophecy seems also to be a kind of "orthography riddle" (see Timothy Chan, "A New Reading of an Early Medieval Riddle," 56), since it plays with several characters that employ the radical *mian* 黽.

he was a unique talent. The Youshen hated Yi Yin for appearing from the tree, and so sent him off to escort a bride elsewhere.

小子, 謂伊尹。媵, 送也。言伊尹母姓身, 夢神女告之曰:「臼竈生
鼃, 亟去無顧。」居無幾何, 臼竈中生鼃, 母去東走, 顧視其邑, 盡為
大水, 母因溺死, 化為空桑之木。水乾之後, 有小兒啼水涯, 人取養
之。既長大, 有殊才。有莘惡伊尹從木中出, 因以送女也。

This was a traditional story also preserved in somewhat different form in the *Lüshi chunqiu*.[42] As it happens, this fascinating tale of a divine message, a mysterious omen, and an aquatic transfiguration, does incidentally explain Yi Yin's birth and his relation with the Youshen people, so it can be appreciated as a kind of exegesis. But the "Heavenly Questions" text does not itself refer to the omen at all. So this is a special kind of editorial intervention, providing an anecdote which conforms to the poem's text but also adds memorable new content.[43]

Thus, if we try to reconstruct what has happened, we might speculate as follows: the "Heavenly Questions" existed in some tangled, messy form, as an old poem from Chu, associated with Qu Yuan even though it does not touch explicitly on Qu Yuan's life. Wang Yi, or other scholars whom he quotes, have attempted to interpret the text by adducing relevant materials, many of them of uncertain provenance, and in some cases simply juxtaposed, without historical basis, memorable episodes to the text, some of them having to do with Qu Yuan himself. The editors have made all the pieces conform *like two halves of a tally* even though they may realize that this is not the original state of the text. Their goal has been to put the "Heavenly Questions" into order, and they have tied its conclusion to Qu Yuan's life. Western scholarship has sometimes represented this approach to early poetry as being a "nonfictional" sort of interpretation,[44]

---

42. See Knoblock and Riegel, *Annals of Lü Buwei*, 307 (14/2.2). The prophecy there lacks the ingenious orthography riddle mentioned above.

43. Some other examples where the commentary provides creatively-embellished narrative in response to the text are quatrains 35, 40, 41, 60, 65, 71, and 88.

44. For instance, Pauline Yu on the "Lisao" (*Reading of Imagery*, 116): "The assumption that poetry represented at base a nonfictional response to an experienced stimulus also fueled the overpowering impulse to take words, in the last analysis, at face value, as an actual historical document, erasing the formal differences between the substituted and the juxtaposed."

but that characterization may not apply to the "Heavenly Questions." To the contrary, the commentary seems happy to present Qu Yuan as writing about historical figures from the remote past as if they were his contemporaries, the opposite of non-fiction, a creative fiction of bold anachronism. Consequently, we need to understand this conflation of historical time periods in a different way, appropriate to its proper intent.

Our first inclination might be to say that the interpretations of the final stanzas are wrong, since there is no evidence that the poem is about Qu Yuan's life. But perhaps the commentary just quoted above, and the implausible story about writing down captions from the murals of the ancestral temple in Chu, were never intended to have a historical function. They may only have been intended to provoke particular lines of interpretation in the reader. The point of the poem can after all never have been to inform us about remote antiquity (given its interrogative mood). According to the commentary, the purpose was to caution future generations, and from that point of view, the circumstances of composition are not so important. Instead, we should see these various elements of the commentary as interpretive strategies used to make sense of a difficult text by means of historical analogy, and also to highlight the principal message of that text in the present. For this purpose, it is then essential to explain Qu Yuan's authorial intention for the whole piece, so as to clarify the meaning of particular lines. Perhaps, then, it is not Wang Yi but only we contemporary readers who are confused by the anachronisms in the commentary. Recall the couplet just quoted above, "I warn Duao / That he will not long survive," and its commentary. Huang Linggeng argues that this whole passage is corrupt, and that it is actually Ziwen 子文, chief minister of Chu, who speaks to Duao. This emendation would remove the anachronism. But alternatively, we might observe that the verb "speak" (*yu* 語) in classical Chinese can also take an indirect object and hence mean "to speak *about*," so that this passage could also be saying, "When Qu Yuan was exiled, he spoke about [historical figure] Duao, and commented, 'The state of Chu . . .'" In other words, once we are aware of the general exegetical strategy of the commentary, and cognizant of its primary purpose in highlighting the moral message of the "Heavenly Questions," it is possible to understand even seemingly anachronistic or inaccurate passages as contributing to its overarching interpretation in a reasonable and consistent manner.

With all these considerations in mind, it seems that the commentary to the "Heavenly Questions" and its presentation within the *Chuci* anthology reflect a complex set of motives and strategies, not necessarily including historical accuracy. Han scholars Liu Xiang, Yang Xiong, and Wang Yi—among others and in proportions that are impossible to identify precisely—collaborated to interpret the poem expounding Qu Yuan's moral critique of Chu's decadence by citing some of the most important figures of myth and history, just as one might peruse in the temple murals of their own day. Though there is not sufficient space here to consider the anthology as a whole and the other problems it raises, we need to devote a brief analysis to the authorship of the Han commentary to the *Chuci*, as preserved in the *Chuci zhangju*. The disparate nature of the contents of this commentary constitutes a problem that has often been overlooked in scholarship on the anthology.

On the Authorship of the Extant Han Commentary to the Chuci Anthology

Unresolvable questions of authorship and dating vex many works of early Chinese literature, but on at least one important issue we can be certain: Wang Yi, who compiled the *Chuci zhangju* or "*Elegies of Chu*, with chapter-and-verse commentary" did *not* write the entire commentary to the anthology by himself.

Though little is known about Wang's life, recent scholarship has helped to place his commentary in the context of his period. Wang Yi's biography in the *Hou Hanshu* 後漢書, at a mere fifty-eight characters, is far less informative or detailed than that of Qu Yuan, identifying just a few facts of his life.[45] In the past couple of decades, though, there has been excellent new scholarship

---

45. *Hou Hanshu*, 80A.2618. It starts with his name and native place of Yicheng 宜城 (south of modern Yicheng, Hubei) in the heart of ancient Chu. It mentions three of his official positions in the Yuanchu 元初 era (114–120) and under Shundi 順帝 (r. 125–144), as well as his compilation of the *Chuci zhangju*, 21 pieces of *fu*, *lei* 誄, letters, disquisitions, and miscellaneous writings, as well as 123 "Han poems" 漢詩 (perhaps another anthology). The *Wenxuan jizhu* 文選集注 also records that he later served as governor of Yuzhang 豫章. See *Tangchao Wenxuan jizhu huicun*, 1:788.

on Wang Yi that has much elucidated our understanding of his life and the commentary attributed to him.[46] Gopal Sukhu has argued that Wang Yi's affirmation of Qu Yuan was calculated to appeal to Empress Dowager Deng 鄧 (81-121).[47] As we have seen above, Michael Schimmelpfennig showed that Wang Yi's commentary to "Sublimating Sorrow" is a synthesis and reconciliation of the interpretative tradition up to his time,[48] and Tim Chan has presented a convincing case that Wang Yi's commentary takes pains to make Qu Yuan's poems conform to Confucian thought as it had developed by the Eastern Han.[49] While the work of these scholars is extremely informative, none of them confronts the question of authorship directly, even though all their arguments rely heavily on the dating of Wang Yi's book to ca. 120 CE. Though the dating of the *Chuci zhangju* as a whole is not problematic, large sections of the commentary were probably composed much earlier.

While it remains common to speak of the "Wang Yi commentary" or to say that Wang Yi interprets a particular verse in such a way, this is strictly incorrect. Traditional commentators did not pay much attention to this issue, perhaps because they took for granted the fact of multiple authorship, and would not necessarily have found much point in distinguishing between author and editor of a text. After all, although the editing of the *Chuci zhangju* anthology is explicitly ascribed to Wang Yi in the anthology's prefaces, the same cannot be said for its other contents. As Du Heng has rightly observed:

> Each of its chapters, consisting of a poem or a suite of poems, is introduced by a preface and annotated with detailed interlinear commentaries. Two of these chapters, chapter 1, "Li sao," and chapter 3, "Tianwen" 天問 (Heavenly Questions), are followed by postscripts. The Han period commentarial writings were finalized by Wang Yi, but likely include materials from earlier redactions, some of which could have been written by Liu Xiang and even Liu An. Since Wang Yi identifies himself in both postscripts,[50] I will refer

---

46. Beside the studies mentioned below, there is a useful overview in Knechtges and Chang, eds., *Ancient and Early Medieval Chinese Literature*, 1272–74.
47. Sukhu, *Shaman and the Heresiarch*, 55–69.
48. Schimmelpfennig, "The Quest for a Classic."
49. Timothy Chan, *Considering the End*, 7–40.
50. Du Heng's original note to this sentence states: "Less directly so in the 'Tianwen'

to them as Wang Yi's writings. I will refer to the rest of the Han period prefaces and commentaries as Zhangju 章句 or Zhangju commentaries.[51]

In other words, the anthology is a compendium not just of poems by various authors, but also of commentarial and paratextual content by different authors.

Of course, since Wang Yi is identified as the compiler of *Chuci zhangju*, text not attributed to other scholars is naturally ascribed to him. But there happens to be overwhelming stylistic evidence showing that he cannot have been the sole author of the commentary, namely that it can be classified into two different types, in prose and verse forms, as identified by Kominami Ichirō 小南一郎 and others.[52] The commentary appears in two distinct types: 1) the prose typical of other *zhangju* (chapter and verse) commentaries, and 2) rhyming verse punctuated by the character *ye* 也. The commentary to the first few poems is entirely in prose, but after that the form varies piece by piece. For example, similar lines in "Sublimating Sorrow" and "Unraveled Yearnings" ("Chousi" 抽思) receive totally different treatment in the Han commentary:

"Sublimating Sorrow," line 46:

But later he broke faith, was altered, chose another　　後悔遁而有他

Han commentary: Later [King Huai] accepted slanderous words, and midcourse regretted and resented [Qu Yuan], concealing his feelings, and then had another resolve.

後用讒言，中道悔恨，隱匿其情，而有他志也。

"Unraveled Yearnings," lines 16–17:

But reversing course he set another resolve.　　反既有此他志
He flaunted before me his beauty and goodness—　　憍吾以其美好兮

---

postscript, but it overlaps with the 'Li sao' postscript in wording." This is an important observation but not dispositive with respect to authorship, so it may be that only the "Lisao" postface alone should be attributed directly to Wang Yi.

51. Du, "The Author's Two Bodies," 268.

52. Kominami, "Ō Itsu *Soji shōku* to Soji bungei no denshō"; Cao Jianguo, "*Chuci zhangju* yuntizhu kaolun"; Zha Pingqiu, "Wenxue de chanshi yu chanshi de wenxue"; Chan Hung To, "Lun *Chuci zhangju* yunwen zhu de xingzhi yu shidai"; etc.

Han commentary:
This says that he was not loyal, 謂己不忠
and so exiled me to another place. 遂外疏也
Grasping a precious plaything, 握持寶玩
he caused my disgrace.[53] 以侮余也

My translation of the commentary to "Unraveled Yearnings" mirrors the XAXA rhyme scheme it employs (which does not rhyme with the poem itself). As this brief example shows, the two commentaries are doing entirely different things: the "Sublimating Sorrow" commentary explains the context of the verse in straightforward prose, while the "Unraveled Yearnings" commentary rewrites the lines in a new verse form, often inserting new imagery extraneous to the poem ("precious plaything"). If Wang Yi were the author of both types of commentary, only a psychedelic experience or psychotic break could explain the disjunction between them.

Another reason few scholars have focused on the Wang Yi authorship question is simply that that he has never been held in high regard as a poet, like Qu Yuan or Song Yu, even though he is the author of the "Nine Yearnings" ("Jiusi" 九思), a set of nine poems included as the final work in the anthology. It is normally thought that the "Nine Yearnings" were added to the anthology after his time, and its commentary is certainly not by him, since it contains a startling misreading.[54] Like several other Han poets, Wang has been regarded as a tedious imitator of Qu Yuan's poetry who lacked his political grievances, "groaning and moaning without being

---

53. Huang Linggeng, ed., *Chuci zhangju shuzheng*, 1.122–24 and 5.1447–48. Huang Linggeng's collation of the commentary to *Chuci zhangju* is a seminal work of scholarship essential to the future of *Chuci* studies, which is cited throughout this study and will be discussed again in chapter 4 below. On the "Chousi" ("Unraveled Yearnings"), see also Williams, "Tropes of Entanglement."

54. Based mainly on a statement in the postface to "Sublimating Sorrow": "Now I have further, based on my own knowledge and views, examined these old pieces, and combined them in this classic and commentary, composing this chapter-and-verse commentary in sixteen fascicles" 今臣復以所識所知, 稽之舊章, 合之經傳, 作十六卷章句 (Huang Linggeng, ed., *Chuci zhangju shuzheng*, 1.557). However, this has also been interpreted by Huang as referring solely to "Sublimating Sorrow" rather than to the *Chuci* as a whole. The error is interpreting Ding 丁 as a verb rather than a proper name, referring to Shang ancestor Wu Ding 武丁; see Huang Linggeng, ed., *Chuci zhangju shuzheng*, 17.2842.

sick" 無病呻吟.[55] Since he is seen as a mediocre poet whose work is rarely mentioned in the same breath with that of Qu Yuan or Song Yu, few have bothered to challenge the authenticity of his writings.

In the years since Kominami's work, several scholars writing in Chinese have discussed these issues as well.[56] In particular, Zha Pingqiu 查屏球 points out that the preface to the *Chuci zhangju* itself states clearly that Wang Yi incorporated previous commentaries, just as we have seen above—so it has always been clear that Wang Yi is not presenting his own individual interpretations. Zha thus concludes that the verse commentary is most likely to be Wang Yi's original contribution to the anthology as a whole, his idiosyncratic embellishment to a mostly traditional volume.[57] This view seems to me likely to be correct. A recent study of the problem by Chen Hung To 陳鴻圖 argues, to the contrary, that Wang Yi composed the prose commentary to supplement a preexisting verse commentary.[58] But this hypothesis seems to conflict with the fact that the commentary takes verse form only for relatively late pieces in the anthology, whereas all of the pieces with the strongest claims to historical priority, such as "Sublimating Sorrow," "Nine Songs," and "Heavenly Questions," have only prose commentary. It seems implausible that there would have previously existed, available for reuse by Wang Yi, old commentaries to pieces as recent as Wang Bao's 王褒 (ca. 84–ca. 53 BCE) "Nine Longings" ("Jiuhuai" 九懷) from the late Western Han, but not to "Sublimating Sorrow" itself.

As several scholars have pointed out in recent years, another reason to pay attention to the verse commentary is simply to appreciate the creativity in its verse expression, often not strictly tied to the content of the origi-

---

55. It is particularly striking how, ever since Zhu Xi compiled his *Chuci jizhu*, it has been standard practice to omit the works of these Han writers from new editions of the anthology, a practice that has continued up to the present, with rare exceptions such as the *Chuci xinzhu* edited by Tang Bingzheng et al. One thesis of this book is that we overlook these mediating interpretations at our peril.

56. Cao Jianguo follows Kominami in attributing the prose commentary to Wang Yi, and identifying the verse commentary as a later addition; see his "*Chuci zhangju* yunti zhu kaolun."

57. Zha Pingqiu, "Wenxue de chanshi yu chanshi de wenxue," 134.

58. Chan Hung To, "Lun *Chuci zhangju* yunwen zhu."

nal text. Chen Weisong 陳維松 has written enthusiastically of the verse commentary as a kind of literary interpretation or even free translation of the original poems.[59] Liao Tung-liang 廖棟樑 has argued for the complexity of the rhymed commentary as "double-voiced discourse" that comments on the original text while also setting forth its own claims.[60] For instance, Liao points out the following commentary to lines 11–12 in "Nine Phases" (Jiubian 九辯; the particle *xi* 兮 below is represented by an en dash):

Rough and ragged – a penniless gentleman,	坎廩兮貧士
No profession and ambitions unsettled.	失職而志不平
Han commentary:	
Often enduring disaster and suffering,	數遭患禍
I suffered the worst of griefs.	身困極也 (*dzək)
Deprived of wealth, my possessions lost,	亡財遺物
Since I ran into these thieves.[61]	逢寇賊也 (*gək)

As Liao comments, this can hardly be read as a simple gloss on the original text. Even while it is paraphrasing some of the content, it might be said to be reinterpreting the "Nine Phases" in terms of more ordinary experience of dealing with violent theft, rather than the disappointment of losing position at court. But if we take the rhyming commentary seriously as a form of discourse with its own distinctive voice, it becomes impossible to assimilate it to a single "Wang Yi commentary" for the entire anthology as a whole. It would be implausible to attribute both this style of writing and the far more prosaic commentary to "Heavenly Questions" to the same author.[62] The baroque and unconventional imagery are not unlike the style of Wang Yi's own poems, the "Nine Yearnings" placed at the end of the *Chuci zhangju*, in style. Consider, for instance, the remarkable ending of the second poem in that series (lines 35–42):

---

59. Chen Weisong, "Wang Yi zhujie *Chuci* de wenxue shijiao."
60. Liao Tung-liang, "Chuwei zhi shi." Cf. my analysis of the "double voice" of imitation poetry in *Imitations of the Self*, 1–20.
61. Liao Tung-liang, "Chuwei zhi shi," 397; Huang Linggeng, ed., *Chuci zhangju shuzheng*, 2.581.
62. Or, even if they were *ex hypothesi* compiled by the same person Wang Yi, it must have been under radically different circumstances and with radically different motives.

The mole cricket – chirps in the east,	螻蛄兮鳴東
The leafhoppers – shrill in the west.	蟊蠽兮號西
The centipede crawls – up my skirts,	蚑緣兮我裳
Hawk moth caterpillar enters – my bosom.	蜀入兮我懷
Insect and slinker – assault me on both sides.	蟲豸兮夾余
How miserable and melancholy – is my state!	惆悵兮自悲
Standing still here – doubtful and dismayed,	佇立兮忉怛
My heart is knotted and tangled – ravaged and ruined.[63]	心結縎兮折摧

This overwrought and repetitious mode of expression seems similar in spirit to the verse commentary within the *Chuci zhangju*, rather than the prosaic paraphrases of the prose portions attached to the "Heavenly Questions" and other poems.

In sum, the Han commentary to "Heavenly Questions" is unlikely to have been composed by Wang Yi alone. It likely represents an accretive tradition incorporating interpretations of Liu Xiang, Yang Xiong, Wang Yi himself, and others. It synthesizes the joint efforts of Han scholars to make sense of what must have been fiendishly difficult for them to read: the "Heavenly Questions" text which had been transmitted to them from before the Qin unification, in strange Chu characters. To that extent, we cannot blame Wang Yi alone for passages in the commentary that seem erroneous or misguided. Even if he introduced errors, he was most likely working with previous commentaries and materials by other scholars. Unless the specific evidence indicates otherwise, we may surmise that the commentary represents either a consensus or at least a relatively sophisticated understanding of the poem for its time. The commentary is thus a major document of the Han reception of the "Heavenly Questions," not simply a reflection of Wang Yi's personal biases. The primary cause of the commentary's errors and lacunae is not ideological bias or individual ignorance so much as the difficulties of understanding pre-Qin texts in the Han, particularly insofar as they pertained to the history of remote antiquity.

---

63. Huang Linggeng, ed., *Chuci zhangju shuzheng*, 17.2865–66; see also Williams, *Elegies of Chu*, 244–45.

The Chaotic Appearance of "Heavenly Questions" in the Han

Recent scholarship based on the excavated bamboo strips in the Shanghai Museum and Tsinghua University collections, among others, has given us concrete demonstrations of the kind of challenges that Han editors and scholars would have faced. Pre-Qin texts often survived in bundles of bamboo strips that could easily be misarranged, damaged, and confused.[64] So far, these recently excavated texts have not shed much light directly on the contents of the *Elegies of Chu*, though insights drawn from the Chu script as seen in the bamboo strips have been applied to new proposals about how to read the anthology.[65] They also raise important questions about whether our received text of "Heavenly Questions" was merely one possible version among many, having undergone unknown processes of selection, revision, and rewriting.[66]

It is impossible to know in exactly what form the "Heavenly Questions" appeared to Han readers, but, as we have seen, the *Chuci zhangju* described the text this way, as a relic of Qu Yuan's life that had not been preserved in its original and proper arrangement:

> The people of Chu grieved for Qu Yuan, so they continued to discuss and transmit these, and for this reason the meaning of the text is not strictly in order.[67]
>
> 楚人哀惜屈原，因共論述，故其文義不次序云爾。

This concluding judgment strongly suggests that the original form of the poem was a disordered pile of bamboo strips. Moreover, it seems to suggest that the poem was irretrievably disordered and that it was impossible to

---

64. Shaughnessy's *Rewriting Early Chinese Texts* gives a good survey of how these texts were edited and transcribed, both in ancient times and more recently.

65. See Zhang Shuguo's important article "Han chu libian *Chuci*," for a bold but stimulating alternative reading of the title "Lisao" and other issues, and Huang Linggeng, *Chuci yu jianbo wenxian*, for a survey of intersections and insights drawn from excavated manuscripts.

66. For a strong case that our received texts of ancient poetry represent only some possible versions among many, see Kern, "'Xi shuai' 蟋蟀 (Cricket) and Its Consequences."

67. Huang Linggeng, ed., *Chuci zhangju shuzheng*, 4.998.

make sense of it. This view has continued to reecho across the centuries and even been revived in modern times. Zheng Zhenduo 鄭振鐸 (1898–1958) wrote that it "was a piece composed of questions not arranged in any order" 是一篇無條理的問語.[68] Su Hsüeh-lin 蘇雪林 (1897–1999), while valuing the piece more highly, found that the bamboo strips had been disordered and devoted a massive, painstaking reconstruction of what she saw as the proper order in her book *Tianwen zhengjian* 天問正簡 ("Heavenly Questions" with corrected strips). Unfortunately, her revisions to the order of the questions also forced her to make radical alterations to the text itself, vitiating the original rationale of her project.[69]

By contrast, more recent scholarship has instead argued that "Heavenly Questions" in its received text actually does have a coherent structure, even if there may be some problematic passages. Numerous Chinese scholars, as well as Kominami Ichirō in Japan, have succeeded in reading the text as a coherent whole.[70] Moreover, this coherence was already becoming evident to late imperial scholars (a theme to which we return in the chapter 3 of this book). Sun Kuang 孫鑛 (1543–1613), for instance, commented:

> Some of it is written at length, other parts concisely. Sometimes it is intricately interwoven, while other sections are arranged in parallel. Here a single event is covered repeatedly and in cumulative fashion, elsewhere several events may be combined into a single line. The writing may be abrupt and obscure, or smooth and lucid, or rebarbative and arduous, or fluent and fine. With its full application of all the different styles, one can say that the text exhausts the transformative possibilities of writing.[71]
>
> 或長言，或短言。或錯綜，或對偶，或一事而累累反覆，或聯數事而鎔成片語。其文或峭險，或淡宕，或佶倔，或流利，諸法備盡，可謂極文章之變態。

---

68. Zheng Zhenduo, *Zhongguo wenxueshi*, 87.

69. Similar contradictions afflict the work of Sun Zuoyun 孫作雲 (1912–1978) in *Tianwen yanjiu* 天問研究.

70. See Kominami, "Tenmon hen no seiri"; Lin Geng, "Tianwen lunjian," among others. Tang Bingzheng has an insightful analysis of the poem's four different narrative structures, which may be another cause of confusion in innocent readers; see his *Chuci leigao*, 279–80.

71. He is quoted thusly in Jiang Zhiqiao's 蔣之翹 supplemented edition of Zhu Xi's text of the *Chuci*, *Qishier jia piping Chuci jizhu*. I quote from the 1626 woodblock print edition, available in *Chuci wenxian congkan*, vol. 27, 3.20b. On Sun Kuang's *pingdian* commentary, see Luo Jianbo, *Mingdai* Chuci *pingdian lunshu*, 146–58.

Sun Kuang's comment is particularly helpful in reminding us that a literary work may be intentionally difficult, and only the unreflective reader ascribes complexity to error in transmission before first considering the possibility that difficulty had its own artistic motivation from the start. Sometimes we imagine that ancient Chinese texts must once have been simple, and have only grown complicated due to corruption and obfuscation, but this assumption is hardly tenable in light of the difficulty of Aeschylus or Pindar—or "Heavenly Questions."

Later in this study, we will return to this issue by examining the achievements of the Qing philologists in interpreting the thorniest passages in the poem. But the point here is simply to ask why it was that Han readers might generally have found the "Heavenly Questions" so difficult and incoherent. On one hand, according to the standard historical narrative, the poem was composed by Qu Yuan less than a century before the Qin unification, so there would not necessarily have been much linguistic change between its composition and its reception. On the other hand, though, this interval saw the Qin standardization of the script, so the variations of the original Chu script would have become one major source of difficulty in interpretation.[72] However, this latter issue, important as it is, is more or less the same challenge that we ourselves face today in reading all early Chinese texts (not just the *Elegies of Chu* but the Confucian classics, Warring States philosophers, etc.), which originated before the unification of the script, and have been mistranscribed or misedited at various stages, or even just rewritten in new configurations.

In the case of the "Heavenly Questions," perhaps the gravest challenge to early readers of the text had to do with the prosodic structure, for it seems that the *Chuci zhangju* did not arrange the poem in quatrains following its intended prosody, but rather in separate couplets, obscuring the natural arrangement of the content as well.[73] Although we do not have direct access to the original Han version of the anthology, but only to Hong Xingzu's recension *Chuci buzhu* (it appears that received texts of the *Chuci zhangju* were produced by excising Hong's supplementary commentary), our transmitted texts of both the *Chuci zhangju* and the *Chuci buzhu*

---

72. Such as Zhang Shuguo, "Han chu libian *Chuci*," already mentioned above.

73. In the Han dynasty, *zhangju* commentaries probably only included the commentary itself, not the text being commented on. See Cao Jianguo, "*Chuci zhangju* yuntizhu kaolun."

generally present the "Heavenly Questions" couplet-by-couplet rather than quatrain-by-quatrain. Moreover, this is not just an accident or later reformatting, since the original commentary is almost uniformly composed in response to couplets, rather than entire quatrains.[74] The opening of the poem, for instance, has the verse as four separate couplets, with commentary interjected after each couplet:[75]

[I] asked, regarding the beginnings of remote antiquity,　　曰遂古之初
Who recorded and told us of these things?　　誰傳道之 *lû?-tə

Before all above and below had taken shape,　　上下未形
What way was there to investigate it?　　何由考之 *khû?-tə

Dark and light still hazy and indistinct,　　冥昭瞢闇
Who could fully comprehend them?　　誰能極之 *dzək-tə

In that homogeneous mass of semblances,　　馮翼惟像
How could anything be differentiated?　　何以識之 *śək-tə

This is the case even though we evidently have two rhyming quatrains here, as indicated above in the reconstructed Minimal Old Chinese (OCM) readings of Baxter and Schuessler for the rhyme words.[76] Moreover, in "Text One" below, I translate the entire "Heavenly Questions" with the *Chuci zhangju* commentary in precisely this arrangement. An examination of the full commentary shows that, even independent of the formal

---

74. Rare exceptions include quatrains 63 and 94. In the latter case, though, there does seem to be textual corruption that makes the original structure of the lines debatable even today.

75. Incidentally, Lin Geng presents the text as rhyming octasyllabic couplets: 冥昭瞢闇誰能極之, 馮翼惟像何以識之. The decision of most editors to treat the lines as 4-4, rather than a single line of 8 with caesura, is in a sense arbitrary, but a tetrasyllabic meter facilitates comparison with the *Shijing* and other early poetry.

76. Though the reconstruction was originally devised by William Baxter in his *Handbook of Old Chinese Phonology*, I rely on the convenient updating of that reconstruction by Axel Schuessler, *ABC Etymological Dictionary of Old Chinese*. A slight complication is that the rhyme here is feminine (i.e. rhyming the last two syllables of the line, with the final syllable being the identical character *zhi* 之). But this is a regular feature of rhyming in pre-Qin texts, including the *Shijing*.

arrangement of the text on the page, the commentary explicates each couplet independently, and often ignores the evidence of the other half of the quatrain in doing so. Yet, if we recognize the meter as a variant of the tetrasyllabic meter of the *Book of Odes*, and take account of the rhymes, we have instead two quatrains as follows:

> Regarding the beginnings of the primordial age, 遂古之初
> Who recorded the events and told us of them? 誰傳道之
> Before all above and below had taken shape, 上下未形
> What way was there to investigate it? 何由考之
>
> When light and dark were still hazy and indistinct, 冥昭瞢闇
> Who could fully comprehend them? 誰能極之
> In that homogeneous mass of semblances, 馮翼惟像
> How could anything be differentiated? 何以識之

The poem then becomes a sequence of ninety-five quatrains, most of which are devoted to a single topic or issue, and I have translated the poem in this form as "Text Three" below. The different arrangement of the *Chuci zhangju* text is not just an artifact of woodblock print formatting; the Han commentary seems from the beginning to have been arranged couplet by couplet, ignoring the rhyme scheme of the original poem.

This formal arrangement can make a considerable difference in the interpretation of the poem. A dramatic example is the case of quatrain 40, already mentioned above:

> The white nimbus winding around and spreading out, 白蜺嬰茀
> Why has it come upon this hall? 胡為此堂

Han commentary: There was a nimbus spreading out and winding around, and why is it in this hall? This is about the temple hall that Qu Yuan had seen.

言此有蜺茀, 氣逶移相嬰, 何為此堂乎? 蓋屈原所見祠堂也.

> How did [Cui Wenzi] obtain that fine elixir, 安得夫良藥
> Which turned out to be incapable of good? 不能固臧

Han commentary: Cui Wenzi studied to be a transcendent with Prince Qiao. Qiao transformed into a white nimbus spreading out and winding around, and brought the elixir to Wenzi. Cui Wenzi was startled and baffled, and drew his halberd to strike at the nimbus. When he hit it the elixir fell to the ground. He looked down at it and saw the body of Prince Qiao. That is why it says that the elixir is not good.⁷⁷

言崔文子學仙於王子僑，子僑化為白蜺而嬰茀，持藥與崔文子，崔文子驚怪，引戈擊蜺，中之，因墮其藥，俯而視之，王子僑之尸也。故言得藥不善也。⁷⁸

The Han commentary interprets the first couplet as referring to Qu Yuan's visit to the temple hall, and the second to the early transcendent Cui Wenzi, a follower of Prince Qiao.⁷⁹ Even leaving aside the validity of the bizarre interpolation of Qu Yuan, in this interpretation, the poem seems to leap abruptly from one situation and topic to another, without regard to historical chronology at all. Moreover, the preceding lines have to do with archaic hero Gun, the following ones with the rain god and other topics. If the reader of the "Heavenly Questions" must guess anew, without any context, at the subject of the lines, while selecting from any historical period up to the time of Qu Yuan, the poem does indeed become nearly unreadable.

In spite of the chronologically confused nature of the Han commentary, though, the poem already provides internal clues to its sense and order; in particular, there is no doubt that these two couplets rhyme. The last words,

---

77. This interpretation does not seem to take into account the contradiction of interpreting the elixir as *liang* 良 but not *shan* 善.

78. Huang Linggeng, ed., *Chuci zhangju shuzheng*, 4.1105–8. My translation here is that of "Text One," attempting to follow as closely as possible the interpretation stated or implied in the Han commentary. As is my practice throughout, translations of the Han commentary omit the glosses of individual words, even though occasionally they are surprising and deserving of further consideration. Here, it is notable that the commentary inserts strange similes, glossing *ni* 蜺 as colored clouds "like a dragon" 似龍 and *fu* 茀 as white clouds spreading out "like a snake" 若蛇.

79. It is curious that the biography of Cui Wenzi as preserved in Wang Shumin, ed., *Liexian zhuan jiaojian*, A.95–97, is entirely different and does not even mention Prince Qiao or his disappearance. Wang Shumin argues that Wang Yi's source was not the *Liexian zhuan* at all but some earlier text. But on the other hand, Ying Shao's 應劭 *Hanshu* commentary quotes a similar story and attributes it to the *Liexian zhuan*; see *Hanshu*, 25A.1204. The story as cited in *Chuci zhangju* would later be included in *Soushen ji* 搜神記; see Wang Shaoying, ed., *Soushen ji*, 1.4.

tang 堂 (OCM *thâŋ) and *cang* 藏 (*dzâŋ), actually rhyme in every period of the history of the Chinese language, from the age of the *Odes* all the way through the present day. Moreover, the rhyme words at the end of the preceding and succeeding couplets, *ying* 盈 (*jeng) and *si* 死 (*si?) respectively, do not match, showing that the surrounding lines do *not* participate in the same rhyme sequence. Formally, then, we have four lines in tetrasyllabic meter,[80] composing an independent subunit within the larger poem. They might address multiple topics, of course, but the formal structure implies that they should all relate to one overarching theme. Indeed, Zhu Xi 朱熹 (1130–1200) already recognized, on the basis of new analysis of the rhymes of antiquity by Wu Yu 吳棫 (ca. 1100–1154) and others, that the poem was composed in rhyming quatrains, and arranged his commentary suitably.[81] Though Zhu Xi could not explain this particular quatrain, Qing philologist Ding Yan 丁晏 (1794–1875) would later propose that the topic of the quatrain is the moon goddess Chang'e 嫦娥, which makes the quatrain cohere fully.[82]

Another reason it is so important to read the poem according to its formal structure in quatrains is that this shows that each line is one part of a question. That is, even when one or two lines do not contain an interrogative word, the quatrain as a whole invariably does. For example, in quatrain 69:

Lord Zhao completed his excursion,	昭后成遊
Reaching as far as the southern lands.	南土爰底
What was the benefit for him in the end	厥利惟何
From coming upon the white pheasant?	逢彼白雉

I have punctuated the stanza according to the *Chuci zhangju*'s arrangement

---

80. With the minor exception of the third line in five-character meter, which fits well into George Kennedy's classic account of the "irregularities" in the *Shijing* meter. See Kennedy, "Metrical 'Irregularity' in the *Shih-ching*," to be discussed again below.

81. Zhu Xi, in "Chuci bianzheng" 楚辭辯證, mentions that he has consulted Wu's analysis of the rhymes both for the *Chuci* and even more extensively for his edition of the *Shijing*; see his *Chuci jizhu*, 190.

82. *Chuci Tianwen jian*, 33a/b. This is a good example of the Qing philologists' brilliance at interpreting particular cruxes, to be discussed in chapter 3.

in which there is separate commentary after each couplet, so that we have one declarative statement, followed by a question, about Lord Zhao (King Zhao 昭 of Zhou). But the punctuation really ought to be:

When Lord Zhao completed his excursion,	昭后成遊
Reaching as far as the southern lands:	南土爰底
What was the benefit for him in the end	厥利惟何
From coming upon the white pheasant?	逢彼白雉

In other words, even if the content is the same, reading each quatrain as a quatrain makes clear that the declarative statements are always used to provide framing context for a question, and do not occur as independent statements.

The quatrain form of the poem may not seem of critical significance for understanding its content, but even a few problematic passages of this kind create discontinuities in "Heavenly Questions." The Han commentary seems to be basically correct with regard to much of the content of the poem, but this kind of anachronism, even if only appearing occasionally, makes the poem seem to be disordered and thereby lose its overall coherence. It is impossible to identify any chronological sequence when you have references to these recent transcendents appearing abruptly before even the midpoint of the poem. The case of Wang Hai, discussed already in the prologue, is especially severe, as the Han interpretation makes the whole passage appear to be jumping forward and back in time among the Xia, Shang, and Zhou.

Based on the results of more recent research, we can tell that the poem generally seems to follow a kind of chronological order, albeit complemented by thematic progression. The basic narrative advances chronologically through the primordial age, then Xia, Shang, the Zhou founding, and early Zhou. Once this narrative is understood, the "Heavenly Questions" can be recognized as a coherent, lengthy poem that has suffered some textual corruption. Its essential argument, just as Sima Qian stated clearly, has to do with the transitions between rule and anarchy across history.[83] As we have seen, moreover, we can even interpret the Han commentary's theory of the temple murals as being a plausible one with respect to the spirit of the work, even if we reject its detailed speculation about captions

---

83. For the overall themes of the poem, see also Takeji, *Soji kenkyū*, 823–60. Takeji emphasizes that the theme is *zhiluan* 治亂, "governance and anarchy," just as Sima Qian said (pp. 840–41).

to a temple mural. Han readers struggled with details and formal structure, but recognized some essential themes in the poem.

At the same time, of course, recognizing mythic elements would not always have been sufficient to identify a specific mythic narrative. As recent scholarship has emphasized, a myth is not a fixed and timeless archetype, but "a phenomenon of language."[84] Where one reader identifies a single substructure underlying several mythic variants, others may struggle "to distinguish the essential from the accidental, the objective from projections."[85] One might also think of Jonathan Z. Smith's classic demonstration that what had been regarded as a Maori cosmogonic myth paralleling that in the Hebrew Bible was in fact the artifact of cultural contact with Western missionaries around the turn of the twentieth century; not that the text itself is a forgery, exactly, but rather that mythic fragments were repackaged in new guise to suit that modern context.[86] The variability of myth is even more pronounced in the Chinese context, moreover, particularly after Confucian orthodoxy suppressed some of the weirder versions of ancient legend.[87] A good example is the legend of Gun 鯀 controlling the flood. In the *Shiji* it is stated explicitly that he failed in the project, but the poem hints instead at his effective labors being disregarded.[88] While Han readers appreciated the epic narrative of the poem, they may have disagreed—both among each other and certainly with its pre-Qin audience—about its exact referents.

One major question about the Han reception of the poem has to do with the connection to Qu Yuan. As always with the *Elegies of Chu*, the Qu Yuan question looms large in the traditional interpretation of the poem. In light of the overall structure, it becomes unlikely that there would be idle references to Qu Yuan in the middle of the poem, and so we are able to reject the Han commentary's interpretation of the beginning of quatrain

---

84. Burkert, *Structure and History*, 2.

85. As Burkert suggests that structuralists have not even attempted to do; see *Structure and History*, 12.

86. Smith, "The Unknown God," in *Imagining Religion*, 66–89.

87. Among many other examples, I would note the alternative legend that King Wen of Zhou murdered his own father Jili 季歷, to which Edward L. Shaughnessy has recently drawn our attention.

88. Quatrains 12–14 of the poem vs. *Shiji*, 2.64.

40 with some confidence. But the end of the poem is a different case. Leaving aside the pseudo-question of authorship, this issue nonetheless touches directly on the issue of perspective: is the poem written from the point of view of men reflecting on events from the distant past, or viewing the contemporary state of affairs with alarm? Here are several key passages from the conclusion of the poem, along with the Han commentary:

[91] A bolt of lightning in the twilight sky: 薄暮雷電
     What should I fear if I return?   歸何憂

Han commentary: This says that Qu Yuan finished writing all his questions on the wall, and as twilight fell he was ready to depart. Then there was a great storm with lightning, and his worries returned. He explained himself, saying, "What should I fear if I return?"

言屈原書壁，所問略訖，日暮欲去，時天大雨雷電，思念復至。自解曰：歸何憂乎？

[93] Guang [King Helu] of Wu contested the realm,   吳光爭國
     And was long victorious over us.   久余是勝

Han commentary: This says that when Wu and Chu were at war, by the time of King Helu (r. 594–496), Wu soldiers invaded the capital at Ying, and King Zhao (r. 515–489) took flight. Thus [these two lines] say that they won a great victory over us.

言吳與楚相伐，至於闔廬之時，吳兵入郢都，昭王出奔。故曰「吳光爭國，久余是勝」，言大勝我也。

[94] Why did she pass by all the lanes and cross the altars,   何環閭穿社
     Even so far as the grave mounds?   以及丘陵
     Such wantonness, such wildness,   是淫是蕩
     So that she gave birth to Ziwen.   爰出子文

Han commentary: Ziwen was the chief minister (*lingyin*) of Chu [from 664 to 637].[89] Ziwen's mother was the daughter of a lord of Yun.[90] Roaming around the altars in the country, and committing adultery among the grave

---

89. See Durrant et al., *Zuo Tradition*, 610–11 (Lord Xuan, Year 4).

90. Ziwen was the illegitimate son of Dou Bobi 鬬伯比 and the wife of a lord of Yun 鄖. According to the Zuozhuan, his father was a "Viscount of Yun" 鄖子. See Durrant et al., *Zuo Tradition*, 612–13 (Duke Xuan, year 4). The state of Yun 鄖 was later conquered by Chu.

mounds, she gave birth to Ziwen. She abandoned him in Yunmeng, where a tiger nursed him. Thinking it a miracle of divine origin, she took him back and raised him herself. The people of Chu called nursing *gou*, and called the tiger *wutu*, so he was given the name Dou Gouwutu, styled Ziwen, and when he grew older, he was a talented and upstanding man.[91]

子文，楚令尹也。子文之母，鄖公之女，旋穿鄖社，通於丘陵以淫，而生子文，弃之夢中，有虎乳之，以為神異，乃取收養焉。楚人謂乳為穀，謂虎為於菟，故名鬭穀於菟，字子文，長而有賢仁之才也。

[95] I warn Duao   吾告堵敖
 That he will not long survive.   以不長
 How could the trial of the sovereign accord myself   何試上自予
 A reputation for loyalty more illustrious?   忠名彌彰

Han commentary: Qu Yuan said, "How dare I test my sovereign, and so contradict my own reputation for loyalty and honesty, which will be prominent and glorious to later generations? Because we share a surname, I am deeply distraught in my heart, and my loyalty to him cannot perish."

屈原言我何敢嘗試君上，自干忠直之名，以顯彰後世乎？誠以同姓之故，中心懇惻，義不能已也。

What will strike the reader about these selections from the commentary to the final passages of the poems is that there are several references to Spring and Autumn-period Chu history, in particular the assault on Chu by King Helu of Wu, and the birth of Ziwen who would become chief minister. Nor does the Han commentary gloss over these references, but provides substantial historical information regarding them (see "Text One" below for additional details). And yet, even though the commentary fully affirms the content of these historical allusions, it combines them with references to Qu Yuan's personal life, like two halves of a tally.

There are two ways we might resolve this problem. Perhaps the Han commentary is simply wrong, and the poem is not referring to Qu Yuan

---

91. This story generally agrees with the account given in *Zuozhuan*, quoted in the previous note. I follow the variant text provided in the Han commentary which seems to fit better with the prosodic scheme of the poem as a whole. The alternative reading is 何環穿自閭社丘陵，爰出子文. See *Chuci buzhu*, 4.118. This is a rare case where the commentary also seems to respond to the entire quatrain rather than just one couplet.

at all. In this case, the latest historical references in the poem are to King Helu of Wu, so we might speculate that the poem was composed around 500 BCE. The Han commentary has interpolated references to Qu Yuan, so as to fit the poem into the structure of the *Chuci zhangju* as a whole. Alternatively, perhaps the Han commentary is right that, even though the poem does not refer to the events of Qu Yuan's own time, it was compiled during the reign of King Huai of Chu or even later. The author had in mind contemporary circumstances around 300 BCE, but used events of the remote past from Chu history to illustrate his thought.

Either of these strategies would be a reasonable scholarly approach. There is nothing in the "Heavenly Questions" itself to indicate that it was intended to refer to any contemporary events. Instead, as the preface suggests, the poem may be a reflection on representations of historical events; even if not necessarily murals *per se*, certainly on the images and afterimages of history, and how they continue to hold out meaning for the present. To find Qu Yuan in conversation with figures from centuries earlier is an anachronism, but not necessarily an error, if it is a way of getting at the deeper meaning of the poem, the way that it is meant to find modern significance in the past.

But what does "the past" represent in "Heavenly Questions"? If we want to have an accurate appraisal of what constitutes pastness either for the authors, or readers, or commentators to the poem, it is worth considering, then, the actual dating of the "Heavenly Questions." While one cannot be confident of dating based on internal evidence, given the issues of historical significance already raised, it is impossible to disregard the question of dating in relation to the Han readership of the poem. The traditional view is of course that the poem was composed by Qu Yuan, but we can bracket the thorny question of Qu Yuan's involvement, and consider simply the dating of the materials of the poem. The question our study has led us to is thus, how ancient—how difficult, how foreign—would the "Heavenly Questions" have seemed to Han dynasty readers?

A Linguistic Analysis of Archaicity in "Heavenly Questions"

As David Hawkes observed: "There is one aspect of this text about which everyone is agreed: the antiquity of its style."[92] There are indeed many archaic features of the poem, and yet it is hard to be any more precise than that about its origins. There is, however, suggestive evidence that the contents of the "Heavenly Questions" are ancient in relation to the other poems in the *Elegies of Chu*. Conrady and Erkes already made two key points about the uniqueness of the poem in their anthology.[93] Firstly, the "Heavenly Questions" is fundamentally different from the other Qu Yuan poems in its narrative mode, being composed in the third person; in their terminology, it lacks "das persönliche Element" of those poems.[94] One might add the "Summons" poems "Summons to the Soul" ("Zhaohun" 招魂) and "Great Summons" ("Dazhao" 大招) to this category of impersonal works as well, but even leaving that aside, certainly the "Heavenly Questions" is markedly different from "Sublimating Sorrow" and "Nine Phases" in its lack of first-person statements and very slight reference to slandered ministers of the Qu Yuan type. Another differentiating feature is the tetrasyllabic meter of "Heavenly Questions," which distinguishes it from nearly all the other poems in the *Elegies of Chu*.[95]

Secondly, Conrady and Erkes also point out the use of archaisms, namely the use of *shi* 是, *jue* 厥, *yuan* 爰, *nai* 乃, and *hu* 胡.[96] One also finds in the poem a significant number of lines that employ syntactic inversion, with the verb at the end of the clause and the object represented by the pronominal *shi* 是 (quatrain number in parentheses):

---

92. Hawkes, *Songs of the South*, 126. He then further proposes that Qu Yuan was the "adapter" of what had "started as an ancient, priestly riddle-text." This is a fair proposal, with the qualification that I do not see anything distinctively "priestly" in the poem, especially relative to "Sublimating Sorrow" or "Nine Songs."
93. Conrady and Erkes, *Das älteste Dokument*.
94. Conrady and Erkes, *Das älteste Dokument*, 30.
95. This is obscured because the "Summons" poems and the "Encomium to the Tangerine" ("Ju song" 橘頌) both have a pseudo-tetrasyllabic meter which is actually closer to heptasyllabic: XXXX-XXXR, where R is a rhythmic particle such as *suo* 些.
96. They describe these as cases of "altertümelnde Imitation." Conrady and Erkes, *Das älteste Dokument*, 69.

60   Chapter One

- In order to perpetuate himself (31) 厥身是繼
- And succeeded in imprisoning him? (32) 而能拘是達
- The giant boar which he shot dead (36) 封豨是射
- There they planted only reeds and cresses (39) 蒲藿是營
- Territory ending at the Southern Marchmount (52) 南嶽是止
- Yi Zhi made offering to his Sovereign Lord (53) 后帝是饗
- He showed the same excellence as his father. (56) 厥父是臧
- And so obtain a propitious consort (62) 而吉妃是得
- And surrender to slanderous gossip? (73) 讒諂是服
- Though he was long victorious over us. (93) 久余是勝

And cases where the object is placed first with *jue*:

- If his authority they did not respect (91) 厥嚴不奉

There are also more than a few lines employing the adverbial particle *yuan*:

- That beguiling consort conspiring with him (37) 眩妻爰謀
- Why did they share lodgings in the same house? (45) 而館同爰止
- Until he arrived at the Youshen Clan (62) 有莘爰極

The syntax in the above cases resembles examples in the *Odes* such as:[97]

- Which cover this sublunary land (29/2) 下土是冒
- But other men shall enjoy it (115/1) 他人是愉
- It is only shallow words which they heed (195/4) 維邇言是聽
- That debt they do not repay (236/3) 厥德不回
- Indeed they lodge and stop there (252/7) 亦集爰止

These are distinctively archaic syntactic formations. As the rule is stated by Pulleyblank, "In the *Shījīng* and comparatively early texts of the classical period, such as the *Zuǒzhuàn* and *Guóyǔ*, an exposed object is regularly recapitulated by a pronoun, most often *zhī* 之 or *shì* 是, which is also placed in front of the verb."[98] Similarly, the usage of *jue* and *yuan* in the

---

97. Cited by poem number and stanza. For related examples of object-subject order (or inversion), see discussion in Xiang Xi, *Shijing yuyan yanjiu*, 356–67.
98. Pulleyblank, *Outline of Classical Chinese Grammar*, 14.

poem conforms to Pulleyblank's "preclassical" syntax.[99] This kind of syntax is of course possible to imitate, or rather to retain in a traditionalist, archaicist fashion, and so cannot be used to date the production of a text with certainty, but it does suggest that the "Heavenly Questions" was composed in an archaicizing manner.

Much of the evidence is ambiguous, though. There is also a tendency in the "Heavenly Questions" to monosyllabic expression without parallelism, but this is rare in any period of Chinese poetry. The "Heavenly Questions" contains hardly any of the descriptive compounds (*lianmian ci* 連綿辭), familiar from the *Odes*, other poems in the *Elegies of Chu*, the Han *fu*, and even the bronze inscriptions. In quatrain 2, *ping yi* 馮翼 might qualify, although it is an unusual separable compound, apparently short for *pingping yiyi* 馮馮翼翼 as in *Huainanzi* 淮南子.[100] Still, it is notable that even in this rare case of a term that is best explained as a descriptive compound, "Heavenly Questions" does not include the entire reduplicative term of the *Huainanzi*, which in the form *pingping yiyi* would easily fit into the tetrasyllabic meter of the poem, but instead condenses it into a two-character expression.

A simple kind of parallelism occurs in quatrains 74 and 75 between the proper names of Bi Gan 比干 and Lei Kai 雷開, and Sire Mei 梅伯 and Master Ji 箕子. But a more typical example of the syntactic structure of "Heavenly Questions" would be, for instance, quatrain 6:

Regarding the margins of the Nine Heavens:	九天之際
Where are they placed and where do they connect?	安放安屬
Though corners and interstices are many,	隅隈多有
Who can know their number in full?	誰知其數

There is no syntactic parallelism between any of the lines, although we do have intralinear repetition in the second line, *an fang an shu* 安放安屬, reminiscent of internal repetition in the *Odes*, such as in 35/1: "gathering

---

99. Pulleyblank, *Outline of Classical Chinese Grammar*, 80, 56, respectively.

100. "Before Heaven and Earth had formed, there was a chaotic congeries, shapeless and seamless, hence it was called the Supreme Brightness. The Way originated in this empty void, the empty void produced the universe, and the universe produced energy (*qi*)" 天墜未形，馮馮翼翼，洞洞灟灟，故曰太昭。道始于虛霩，虛霩生宇宙，宇宙生氣。See Liu Wendian, ed., *Huainan honglie jijie*, 3.79.

the turnips, gathering the radishes" 采葑采菲. By contrast, the structure of the other poems in the *Elegies of Chu*, including "Sublimating Sorrow," consistently tends towards the parallel couplet.

One function of parallelism in classical Chinese is to clarify syntax, since both halves of the parallel couplet typically share syntactic structure. The use of monosyllables without parallelism thus produces an effect which may have been cryptic even in the Warring States period. In quatrain 73, *wu* 惡 may be a normal verb, meaning "loathe," and used to describe how Zhow treated his underlings:

> Why did he loathe his own aides and assistants,   何惡輔弼
> And employ instead the men of slanderous gossip?   讒諂是服

> *Han commentary*: This says that Zhow hated his own aides and assistants, and did not put into practice their loyal and direct counsel, but instead employed the men who offered slanderous gossip.
>
> 言紂憎輔弼, 不用忠直之言, 而事用諂讒之人也。

As the quotation shows, the Han commentary understood *wu* here as a verb. But alternatively, and also quite plausibly, *wu* might be short for the proper name Wulai 惡來, who was one of Zhow's ministers, so that the lines would mean something like:

> Why is it that Wulai was his aide and assistant,   何惡輔弼
> Employing such slanderers and gossips?   讒諂是服

Similarly, in quatrain 80, *shou* 受 is the personal name of Zhow rather than having its ordinary significance as a common verb, but either reading of the line makes sense: "When Zhow presented the bloody paste / When this bloody paste was received as a gift" 受賜茲醢. I take these cases as most likely being intentional acts of wordplay, intended to give the poem multiple layers of significance. So far as I am aware, this kind of riddling language is rather unusual in pre-Qin poetry, so it does not particularly help with dating but rather confirms the exceptionality of the poem.

Turning from these isolated examples to the overall prosody and form of "Heavenly Questions," the poem is composed in rhyming tetrasyllabic lines. Though some lines are longer or shorter than four characters, the rhythm is essentially tetrasyllabic and conforms well to the pattern discussed by George Kennedy in his classic article "Metrical Irregularity in the *Shih-ching*." In that article Kennedy points out that 91% of the lines in the *Odes* are in fact four-character, with only 9% being exceptional or irregular. Kennedy provides the following chart showing the relative proportions of different irregular line lengths:[101]

Table 1. Prosodic irregularity in the *Shijing*		
Number of syllables in line	Number of lines	Percentage of total "irregularity"
2	7	1.0%
3	160	23.0%
5	397	58.0%
6	100	14.0%
7	22	3.0%
8	3	.5%

By contrast, for the "Heavenly Questions," I identify 95 quatrains, but two of them are corrupt and survive only as couplets, which leaves us with just 376 lines in total. Out of these, 88 lines are either shorter or longer than four characters, so 23.4% are irregular, a proportion considerably higher than the *Odes*, from which it seems that "Heavenly Questions" is, relatively speaking, less tetrasyllabic. Nonetheless, upon examining "Heavenly Questions" in the manner of Kennedy, I identify the following proportions:

Table 2. Prosodic irregularity in the "Heavenly Questions"		
Number of syllables in line	Number of lines	Percentage of total "irregularity"
3	20	22.7%
5	53	60.2%
6	14	15.9%
7	1	1.1%

There is debate and textual variance with regard to some of the lines (the ending of the poem in particular). But collectively, since line length is stable in the vast majority of cases, these figures are reasonably reliable.

101. Kennedy, "Metrical 'Irregularity' in the *Shih-ching*," 285.

Although the proportion of regular lines is considerably lower than Kennedy's figures for the *Odes*, the distribution of irregular lines is astonishingly similar. Kennedy found that 58.8% of the irregular lines in the *Odes* were five-character, and the figure for "Heavenly Questions" is almost exactly the same: 60.2% of the irregular lines are five-character. Kennedy writes that this pattern suggests, for the case of the *Odes*, that "the metrical 'irregularity' was only on the surface."[102] He further shows that most of the variation from the tetrasyllabic meter is regular within a poem, i.e., if one line has a length shorter or greater than four characters, the corresponding lines in other stanzas of the poem have the same length. By this method he reduces the number of truly "irregular" lines even further, and finds that five-character lines occupy 75% of the residue.[103] Kennedy then proposes that these lines are meant to have the same rhythm as the other lines, but that since they include an "unstressed" word like *xi* 兮, *yi* 矣, *ye* 也, *zhi* 之 "or some similar element," five characters can have an overall rhythmic effect similar to four.[104]

If we apply this principle to the irregular lines in the "Heavenly Questions," the results are mixed. "He descended to watch over all four parts of the earth" 降省下土四方 in quatrain 30 seems to contain no grammatical particle likely to be unstressed. On the other hand, it is easy to imagine some kind of copying error with either "the earth below" 下土 or "four parts" 四方 being a gloss on the other that has been erroneously included in the main text, which would bring us back to four characters in the original line.[105] Then again, the last line of this quatrain is "and mate with her at the Platform of Mulberries" 而通之於台桑, in which we have three syntactical words that might be unstressed. Or again, in quatrain 33 we have the line "and so his body was unharmed" 而無害厥躬, in which we might speculate again that the conjunction *er* 而 is unstressed. Thus it is possible to treat many of these lines as regular exceptions to tetrasyllabic meter, but not obvious how to do so in all these cases. Moreover, even as applied to the *Odes*, Kennedy's argument is not fully convincing, since he is ultimately

---

102. Kennedy, "Metrical 'Irregularity' in the *Shih-ching*," 285.
103. Kennedy, "Metrical 'Irregularity' in the *Shih-ching*," 287.
104. Kennedy, "Metrical 'Irregularity' in the *Shih-ching*," 294.
105. If *sifang* 四方 were the interpolation, it would disturb the rhyme, but *tu* 土 actually would rhyme well with *nü* 女 ending the third line of the quatrain.

forced to speculate about three distinct levels of stress, which would seem to require considerably more knowledge of Old Chinese phonology than we have, even today. Regardless of the full explanation for the prosodic variation in early Chinese verse, "Heavenly Questions" exhibits a very similar tendency to the tetrasyllabic prosody of the *Odes*. The exceptions might in large part be explained by rules of ancient prosody of which we remain uncertain, whether Kennedy's hypothesis or some other factors.

The rhyme scheme of "Heavenly Questions" is also relevant to the discussion.[106] In general, the phonology of the Warring States period remains obscure, because there is no single document that we can use to recover it (such as the *Book of Odes* or the *Qieyun* 切韻 rhyme book). The standard treatment of rhymes in the *Elegies of Chu* is the *Chuci yundu* 楚辭韻讀 by the great linguist Wang Li 王力. Wang Li's work seems to demonstrate that the rhymes in the "Heavenly Questions" are more or less consistent with Old Chinese as reflected in the *Odes*. Some of the exceptions are consistent with sound changes having taken place since the time of the *Odes*. For instance, the rhymes in quatrains 7 and 16, respectively, are as follows:

Table 3. Analysis of rhymes in two quatrains of "Heavenly Questions"				
	Rhyming word	OCM	Wang Li reconstruction	Wang Li rhyme
Quatrain 7	分	phən	piuən	文
	陳	drjin*	dien	真
Quatrain 16	寘	dins	dyen	真
	墳	bən	piuən	文
*Schuessler has *drən but the main vowel should clearly be *i in Baxter's system.				

Wang Li identifies each of these as cross rhymes between the Wen 文 and Zhen 真 rhyme groups. They also appear to be cross rhymes in Baxter's system as modified by Schuessler. But all four of these words are found in the Zhen 真 group of the Han dynasty in Lo and Chou's system.[107] The Zhen group words of Old Chinese have undergone the sound change Baxter calls "hi > mid," in which the high front vowel *i is lowered to a

---

106. I am extremely grateful to Zhu Xi of Pacific Lutheran University for help and discussion on this issue.

107. Luo and Zhou, *Han Wei Jin Nanbeichao yunbu yanjiu*, 199–203.

mid-front vowel *e.[108] So these two quatrains might provide confirmation that the "Heavenly Questions" is from a somewhat later period than the *Odes*. However, they are just as easily understood as a case of lax rhyming, which is very common in pre-Tang verse of all kinds, so this analysis is hardly conclusive.[109]

Galal Walker has made the most thorough study in English of rhyming in the *Elegies of Chu*, but of course he was working without the benefit of Baxter's treatise, and followed the older proposals of Li Fang-kuei. While Li had important innovations in reconstruction over Bernhard Karlgren's system, he did not make major modifications to the vowel system, which is fundamental to rhyming. Based on his comparison with the other works in the anthology, Walker observes:

> The degree of variance (rime-group 14%, tone category 7%) places Tian wen with pieces from the early period. However, there are sections in the late period which approximate this degree of variance (cf. Qi jian, Jiu huai). The most common variant rime, /e/~ /i/, is seen in sections belonging to the late period. Also, the variant rime /-ng/ ~ /-m/ is seen only in the late period of the major tradition. From these observations we may tentatively conclude that Tian wen belongs to the later period of the tradition.[110]

This argument does not entirely accord with the results of more recent research. In particular, the cross rhyme of -ng/-m is seen commonly both in the *Odes* and in Han rhyming, not to mention in song lyrics of the present, so it may be a form of lax rhyming to which poets were prone.[111] Walker's point about the cross rhyme between *-e and *-i refers to the same issue I have raised above with regard to Wang Li's reconstruction, though, and probably reflects an actual sound change.

Though William Baxter achieved extremely compelling results with his statistical analysis of the rhymes of the *Odes*, he was able to do so only based on the combination of a rigorous statistical methodology, and a large

---

108. Baxter, *Handbook of Old Chinese Phonology*, 184.
109. See Williams, "The Half-Life of Half-Rhyme."
110. Walker, "Towards a Formal History of the *Chuci*," 393.
111. See Baxter, *Handbook of Old Chinese Phonology*, 549: "the rhyming of *-m with *-ng can be regarded either as a dialect phenomenon or as poetic license."

body of rhyming data which can be treated as synchronic.¹¹² Since the main purpose of analysis of rhyming in the *Elegies of Chu* is not to improve our reconstruction of Old Chinese, but rather to analyze the dating and formation of the anthology, the assumption of synchronicity would be circular, and the body of data itself is too small and idiosyncratic to be adapted to a rigorous analysis.

The mixed linguistic evidence for dating the "Heavenly Questions" leaves us back where we began, with Hawkes' "the antiquity of its style." Though the poem indeed possesses formal features consistent with early Chinese poetry as represented by the *Book of Odes*, and which might suggest it was composed earlier than the other poems in the *Elegies of Chu* itself, the rhyming evidence, even though limited, seems to suggest a later date. So, the true dating of the poem might potentially reflect a chronological ambivalence, with an author at a later date making stylistic choices so as to exaggerate the archaicity of the text. For instance, in one hypothetical scenario, the same author might have composed both "Sublimating Sorrow" and "Heavenly Questions" while choosing intentionally to write "Heavenly Questions" in a more archaic form. Whatever the actual circumstances of authorship—a topic on which it would be rash to speculate further—"Heavenly Questions" is pointedly archaic in style, *even relative to the other poems in the* Elegies of Chu, and in content concerned intimately with remote antiquity from the early Zhou, Shang, and even before. The poem's archaic qualities were probably one reason that Han readers had trouble comprehending the work as a whole or recognizing its prosodic form accurately. But the essential quality of archaicity may also be a key to understanding the poem itself and the reason that Sima Qian and others nonetheless admired its poetic power.

From History to Archetype in "Heavenly Questions"

Apart from the ambiguous linguistic evidence, there is another point of evidence for the antiquity of "Heavenly Questions." As we have seen, the poem contains no explicit references to Qu Yuan or his times, and only

---

112. See his discussion of his statistical model in *Handbook of Old Chinese Phonology*, 97–117.

a few passages relate directly to other poems in the *Elegies of Chu*.[113] The poem seems to conclude with references to events of the late sixth century, and one recent hypothesis from Ishikawa Misao is that it was composed in response to the reign of King Zhao of Chu 楚昭王 (r. 523–489).[114] Ishikawa points out that the poem contains no references to any historical events after that reign period, while it may allude to the Wu invasions that took place under King Zhao. Moreover, he sees the poem generally as reflecting a contemporary view of King Zhao as a tyrannical ruler, which we can also see in recent excavated manuscripts from the Warring States era that center on the figure of King Zhao.

Ishikawa's argument is inspiringly original, but it fails for two reasons. First, he does not really demonstrate any specific references to the same events of King Zhao's reigns that are presented in the excavated manuscripts. That is, his most powerful evidence is the *argumentum ad ignorantiam*, the absence of specific references to events post-Zhao. Second, it is unclear whether the recently excavated texts do present a negative portrait of King Zhao. To the contrary, a major recent study of the representation of historical events in the excavated manuscripts asserts that the portrayal of Chu kings in these anecdotal texts is uniformly after the model of the sagely ruler.[115] To take one representative example, in the text "Zhao wang huishi" 昭王毀室 (King Zhao razes the palace), King Zhao builds a new palace and is celebrating its installation, when someone explains that his father was buried in that same location, so the King razes the palace and moves it elsewhere.[116] It is conceivable that this episode might have once formed part of a broader critique of King Zhao, of course, but in its present fragmentary form it does not support such a reading. What Ishikawa is right about is that the "Heavenly Questions" presents numerous archetypes of tyrants and their downfall, but he lacks sufficient evidence when he tries to tie these to a single, specific reign period. This may properly remind us of the *Chuci zhangju* interpretation of the text as Qu Yuan's responses to murals at the ancestral temple.

113. See examples in Kominami, "Tenmon hen no seiri," 236–42.
114. Ishikawa, "So Shō ō no jinbutsu jiseki kō."
115. Yang Bo, *Zhanguo Chu zhushu shixue jiazhi tanyan*, 186.
116. See transcription and notes in Cao Fangxiang, "Shangbo jian suo jian Chuguo," 193–203.

There too, as we saw above, it is hard to find the argument compelling as a historical account.

There is no way today to know precisely when "Heavenly Questions" was composed and completed. But considering all the ambiguous evidence for the antiquity of its content and style, perhaps the commentary's anachronistic references to Qu Yuan provide us the path to a better interpretation. These references may be intended to affirm the authentic and indisputable nature of the poem: that it presents the perspective of a Chu noble reflecting back on history. After all, most of the historical references in the poem belong to even earlier epochs, that of legendary heroes who shaped the very landscape, the ancestors who lived even before the Shang founding, and the founders of the Western Zhou. If we take the poem seriously as a literary work, history is an integral part of its subject matter. And yet the historical contents of the poems are also intended to be pertinent to present matters; perhaps the most passionate sections of the poem are those having to do with Gun's cruel punishment after striving to stem the Great Flood, because the real concern of the poem is something like Heavenly justice, which is equally relevant to past and to present. Perhaps the protagonists of the poem are ultimately meant to belong to the present and to history at the same time. Antiquity relative to the third century BCE may or may not be an attribute of the poem as a historical matter; it is certainly part of the structure and theme of the poem, and furthermore a trope by which the content is frequently transformed, with its various protagonists being represented as agents and victims within a broader vision of the past. For "poems trope their own schemes, allegorize their own arrangements":[117] we need to look at the archaic features of the poem as matter of form, not just content.

"Heavenly Questions" may not be archaic relative to the third century BCE, but it is surely archaicizing, taking the past as a theme, removing and displacing its subjects from their own contexts, and arranging them within different layers of pastness at various removes from its own present moment. Similarly, its main subject is not so much history as the archetypes that recur throughout history. That is why Nü Qi 女歧, whom I call "Lady Tangent" in my translation, appears twice, once as an astral goddess

---

117. See Hollander, *Melodious Guile*, ix.

and once as the mere sister-in-law of strongman Ao 澆. If we take the commentary seriously, perhaps even Qu Yuan is supposed to be a mythical figure who recurs in different historical periods to chastise the tyrannical rulers of different centuries. That is why the poem employs cryptic and polysemous references to historical figures that could be read as referring to several different historical figures. That is why the poem does raise specific events from history but then responds to them with generalizing questions about contingency, fate, and justice.

One's overall view of the text has a certain impact on the approach one takes in investigating the meaning of its lines. Since the Han dynasty, much commentary has taken the form of providing answers to the questions presented. If, however, one admits that at least some of the questions are intended to be unanswerable, then this method becomes suspect. When the poem presents a question about human relations or royal succession, the problem that needs to be solved is not to identify the specific historical event about which the question is posed, but rather, to understand the ongoing significance of the question in relation to historical archetypes and themes that reverberate across the centuries. Though it may be useful to identify one or more events which might have prompted the question, the more important task is simply to understand the meaning of the text, and to recognize the kind of answer thereby implied.

For example, quatrain 31 refers to a ruler who takes a concubine, and then asks why his tastes changed:

Caring for that maiden, he made a match with her,	閔妃匹合
In order to have a successor;	厥身是繼

Han commentary: The reason Yu was worried about lacking a consort was that he wanted to establish a successor for himself.

言禹所以憂無妃匹者，欲為身立繼嗣也。

Why did Yu, relishing such unlike flavors,	胡維嗜不同味
Yet hasten for a single day's consummation?	而快朝飽

Han commentary: Thus Yu married on the *xinyou* day [58th in the sexagenary cycle] and departed on the *jiazi* day [first in the sexagenary cycle, three days later], and so there was [his son and heir] Qi.

故以辛酉日娶，甲子日去，而有啟也。

Following the previous quatrain, this passage seems to allude to the myth-istoric figure Yu, sage emperor of remote antiquity, and the Han commentary interprets it accordingly. At the same time, the question as posed here might apply with equal pertinence to countless kings, strongmen, dictators, and taipans throughout human history.

Similarly, the word *shou* 受 appears four times throughout the poem. This can be a common verb meaning "received," but in context it must sometimes be understood as the personal name of the wicked King Zhow at the end of the Shang dynasty (as mentioned above in connection with quatrain 80). This ambiguity could be accidental, but is more likely a punning usage that is at once confusing and tantalizing to the reader. The author or transcriber of the poem is employing paronomasia to hint at alternative meanings, to create bridges across historical eras and episodes according to thematic similarities, using the logic of dream and myth.

Another example where the poem takes on a deeper significance, if we are cautious to identify any particular historical referent, is in quatrain 88. According to the modern interpretation, this stanza first asks about the regent Earl Gong (Gong Bo 共伯), who, according to the *Bamboo Annals*, governed in place of the wicked King Li 厲 of Zhou (r. ?–ca. 841 BCE):[118]

When the central states were governed by Earl Gong,	中央共牧
Why was the sovereign angered?	后何怒
How could the paltry lives of bees and ants	蠭蛾微命
Possess the strength to endure?	力何固

But then it goes on to ask a general question in metaphorical terms, which is how petty men or lesser leaders can manage to maintain their power. The "Heavenly Questions" does not answer either of these questions, but instead raises profound matters of political strategy and historical justice. It brushes lightly past the actual events, referred to obliquely or even cryptically as here, but then uses them as a framework to interrogate the nature of power through history.

Considering the cryptic, allegorical, and archetypal nature of the poem, then, it cannot be dated based on internal evidence with any more specificity than the *terminus post quem* of King Zhao's reign, and a *terminus ante*

---

118. See discussion in "Text Three" for more detail.

quem of Sima Qian. The methods of modern philology are simply not able to provide definite conclusions in this realm, nor to offer strong evidence either way in regard to Qu Yuan's relation with the text.[119] Even if we cannot determine how the "Heavenly Questions" was produced, it would certainly appear that it was composed by an author or authors rather like Qu Yuan, a learned and opinionated noble of Chu, but one can cannot reject the hypothesis of an extended compilation process, involving multiple authors and much older materials. The poem is one that traffics in the ancient material of myth, and keeps its own authorial identity well veiled (even more so than "Sublimating Sorrow"). And yet, just as it appears to be, the "Heavenly Questions" is an ambitious, philosophical poem about the nature of Heaven-determined fate, and how different historical actors have chosen to respond to it—a poem that speaks to the present while gazing into the remote past.[120]

This chapter is not intended, however, to resolve questions of interpretation surrounding the "Heavenly Questions." Instead, we have set out a framework for analyzing the text of the poem in relation to its Han commentary. If my interpretation is correct, after all, the poem is intended

---

119. Nowadays the tendency is for scholars writing in Chinese to accept Qu Yuan's authorship of most of the pieces traditionally attributed to him, and for scholars writing in English or other language to be suspicious of Qu Yuan's authorship. This was not always the case; one of the most brilliant and inspiring critiques of the Qu Yuan legend is Hu Shi's "Du *Chuci*," which is always worth rereading. My own view, for what it is worth, is that both sides take too much for granted. Certainly there is nothing in "Heavenly Questions" to tie it directly to Qu Yuan's life, let alone to date it to a particular period of that life. Yet on the other hand, the reasons given by modern scholars for questioning the traditional narrative often sneak in unwarranted assumptions. To take one relatively reasonable example, Du Heng, whose insightful analysis of the *Chuci zhangju*'s structure has been cited above, writes later in the same study of the way that the commentaries in the anthology relate the different poems to Qu Yuan's life: "This reading strategy allows the commentaries to rationalize how poems as different as 'Li sao' and 'Tianwen' can be the work of one poet" ("The Author's Two Bodies," 299). But how unusual is it for a single author to write works of very different kinds? Literary historians of the forty-first century will doubtless regard with scorn the ancient legend they find alluded to in some fossilized blog post, according to which the authors of *The Waste Land* and *Old Possum's Book of Practical Cats* were one and the same person.

120. One of the more sophisticated interpretations of the poem in this vein is Lu Jui-ching, "Qu Yuan de tian-ren-shi ming guan," in *Fengjian shuqing yu shenhua yishi*, 433–89.

to be "interrogative"; it does not declaim answers to its many questions, but poses problems and puzzles for the understanding of history and the origins of the cosmos. For the most part, the Han commentary attempted to set out the correct context for these questions. It was not composed by Wang Yi alone, but consists rather of a compilation of Han scholarship attempting to explain the poem. It does not have much of a polemical agenda, even if some other parts of the Han *Chuci zhangju* commentary do. That said, both the preface and the commentary to the final lines of the poem do explicitly contextualize the poem in Qu Yuan's biography. No evidence survives today to contradict these claims, but it is nonetheless right to treat them with some skepticism. To a certain extent, it is likely that Han scholars read the poem in light of their own contemporary concerns, assimilating it to the contemporary tradition of historical mural art with verse captions. With respect to certain historical identifications such as that of Duao, though, the commentary proposes outright anachronisms. These cannot be accepted as literal interpretation. Nonetheless, they very much can form part of a meaningful and coherent interpretation of the poem as a whole.

This interpretation would be as follows: the author, a Qu Yuan-like critic of the contemporary regime, is asking pointed questions about what makes a just ruler, drawing attention to many aspects of injustice or error from the past. He is interested in excess and tyranny generally, as well as concupiscence, greed, and other sins, but takes special notice of cases where the efforts of loyal servants have not been appreciated. In the perspective of Heaven, *sub specie aeternitatis*, the flaws and weaknesses of past heroes and sages become clear, even if there are also heroes like the Duke of Zhou who may serve as our models. And the inquiry as a whole illuminates some of the processes by which ordinary human protagonists end up as figures of reverence or of reproach. The value of the historical examples, then, lies in their transhistorical significance as archetypes of good or evil with continuing relevance to the present.

We have reached this view of the meaning of the text partly by examining the content and linguistic features of the poem, but also by passing through the Han commentary, by a close reading of the preface and postface, not neglecting the "mural thesis," and not regarding the anachronistic Qu Yuan references with contempt. For the Han commentary provides much material by which readers may begin to build a sophisticated interpretation of the poem as a whole. At the same time, there were severe obstacles to interpretation in the Han, namely the problems of recognizing the prosodic form of the poem, interpreting mistranscriptions of Warring States bamboo strips, or identifying allusions to Shang and other history that was not well understood. Because of the obstacles to interpretation that already existed in the Han, the *Chuci zhangju* commentary is erroneous on many questions of detail.

It would not be until much later, when scholars had resolved some of these cruxes in the poem, that it would be possible to achieve a more definitive interpretation of the poem as a whole. But this would require not just advances in philology, but also the application of critical scrutiny to the principal themes of the poem, above all the question of Heaven's justice.

APPENDIX TO CHAPTER ONE

Text One: "Heavenly Questions" as Read by Han Scholars

The correct way to read the "Heavenly Questions" is in light of its prosodical structure as a series of rhyming quatrains, and my own translation as "Text Three" below, based on modern scholarship, is arranged accordingly. But this was not generally how texts of the poem were presented historically, perhaps due to pressure to add commentary more frequently (after every couplet), or due to a lack of interest in linguistic form.

Thus, presenting the translation in its traditional arrangement (as a loosely arranged series of couplets) has an important heuristic function, in that it helps us to appreciate why a number of readers have regarded it as a jumble without any internal logic, and why some modern scholars further thought to rearrange the text to suit their own pet theories.

For purposes of comparison, quatrain numbers are identified in brackets, but it is important to recall that the early texts do not distinguish quatrains in any way, let alone number them in sequence.

Quotations from the Han commentary appear between the couplets. Glosses of individual words are generally omitted, but otherwise the commentary is translated in full, since its longueurs and redundancies contribute to its full effect. I have also left untranslated the word *yan* 言 ("it says") which is used to divide the glosses and the commentary proper.

I prefer to eschew brackets in my translations, but here I make use of them sparingly as a convenient way to indicate how certain ambiguities in the poem are resolved by the commentary.

[1] [I] asked   曰
    Regarding the beginnings of remote antiquity,   遂古之初
    Who recorded and told us of these things?   誰傳道之

This says that:[1] In the remote past, at the very origin of the primordial age,

---

1. The commentary opens its paraphrase and discussion with the word *yan* 言, "[this] says." The effect is like that of a punctuation mark introducing the commentary. For simplicity I generally omit it below.

the void was vast and formless, and neither spirits nor living beings had been created.² Who would have recorded or told us of these matters?
言往古太始之元, 虛廓無形, 神物未生, 誰傳道此事也。

> Before all above and below had taken shape, 上下未形
> What way was there to investigate it? 何由考之

Before Heaven and Earth had been divided, all was an amorphous muddle without any limits. Who then investigated and assessed things so as to know all this?
言天地未分, 涸沌無垠, 誰考定而知之也?

> [2] Darkness and brightness, murk and obscurity, 冥昭瞢闇
> Who could fully comprehend them? 誰能極之

Who could fully comprehend the sun and moon, day and night, pure and muddy, dark and bright?
言日月晝夜, 清濁晦明, 誰能極知之?

> In that homogeneous mass of semblances, 馮翼惟像
> How could anything be differentiated? 何以識之

Once Heaven and Earth were divided, and Yin and Yang were changing in turn, all was a homogeneous mass. How could one differentiate the forms and semblances?
言天地既分, 陰陽運轉, 馮馮翼翼, 何以識知其形像乎?

> [3] The brightest brightness, the darkest dark, 明明闇闇
> How were they then created? 惟時何為

Pure Yin and pure Yang, one dark and one bright, who created them?
言純陰純陽, 一晦一明, 誰造為之乎?

> Yin and Yang combine [with Man] to form the triad; 陰陽三合
> What was the origin, what the transformation? 何本何化

---

2. The *locus classicus* for *shenwu* 神物 is the "Appended Statements" commentary to the *Changes*, "Thus Heaven created divine objects, and the sages patterned themselves on these" 是故天生神物, 聖人則之 (see *Zhouyi zhengyi*, 17.341). There it seems to refer to the various signs and portents produced by natural processes. Here I take *shenwu* instead as two parallel nouns.

Heaven, Earth, and Man join together in a trinity, perfecting their virtue. How was their origin transformed so as to create them?
謂天地人三合成德，其本始何化所生乎？

[4] The Heavenly Sphere's nine layers:　　　　　　圜則九重
　　Who could construct and measure them?³　　　孰營度之

Heaven is round and divided in nine layers. Who could "construct and measure" them?
言天圜而九重，誰營度而知之乎？

　　What craft was responsible for it?　　　　　　惟兹何功
　　Who could have created it in the beginning?　　孰初作之

Heaven has nine layers. Whose craft and power could first have created it?
言此天有九重，誰功力始作之邪？

[5] Where are the axle and mainstays attached?　　斡維焉繫
　　Where is the fulcrum of Heaven placed?⁴　　　　天極焉加

Since Heaven revolves day and night, how could there be a mainstay tying it down? At its edges where would the fulcrum be attached?
言天晝夜轉旋，寧有維綱繫綴，其際極安所加乎？

　　How do the Eight Pillars support it?　　　　　　八柱何當
　　Why is the Southeast truncated?　　　　　　　東南何虧

Heaven is held up by the Eight Mountains as its pillars.⁵ How do they support it? Since it is insufficient in the southeast, who caused it to be lacking there?

---

3. The Han commentary simply quotes the original text for the difficult term *yingdu* 營度 here, so in the translation I use my own interpretation based on You Guoen (see "Text Three"). To follow the commentary more literally one might render the line "Who can *yingdu* it?" The Han commentary also explicitly connects the latter couplet here to form the quatrain following the rhyme scheme (but this is a rare exception, as we have seen above).

4. According to the commentary these are rhetorical questions, because nothing can stay the heavens in their circular motion.

5. There seems to be little documentation of these Eight Mountains/Pillars outside of this passage. See the interesting but inconclusive speculations in Huang Linggeng, ed., *Chuci zhangju shuzheng*, 4.1013–15; Jiang Liangfu, ed., *Qu Yuan fu jiaozhu*, 3.268.

言天有八山為柱,皆何當值?東南不足,誰虧缺之也?

[6] Regarding the margins of the Nine Heavens:　　九天之際
    Where are they placed and where do they connect?　　安放安屬

The Nine Heavens are Luminescent Heaven in the East, Sunlit Heaven in the Southeast, Crimson Heaven in the South, Vermilion Heaven in the Southwest, Complete Heaven in the West, Shaded Heaven in the Northwest, Mystic Heaven in the North, Transformed Heaven in the Northeast, and Harmony Heaven in the Center. How are the borders between them distinguished, and to what are they themselves attached?
九天,東方皞天,東南方陽天,南方赤天,西南方朱天,西方成天,西北方幽天,北方玄天,東北方變天,中央鈞天。其際會何分,安所繫屬乎?

　　Though corners and interstices are many,　　隅隈多有
　　Who can know their number in full?　　誰知其數

Heaven and Earth are vast, their corners and interstices are numerous; how can one know their number?
言天地廣大,隅隈眾多,寧有知其數乎?

[7] How is Heaven composed?　　天何所沓
    How were the Twelve Stations differentiated?[6]　　十二焉分

In what place do Heaven and Earth combine? By whom were the Twelve Stations differentiated?
言天與地合會何所?十二辰誰所分別乎?

　　To what entity are subjoined the sun and moon?　　日月安屬
　　How were the various constellations set in place?　　列星安陳

The sun and moon and myriad stars, to what are they subjoined? Who has placed them in order?
言日月眾星,安所繫屬,誰陳列也。

[8] Rising out of Sunny Vale in the East　　出自湯谷
    And lodging at the bank of the Meng River in the West,　　次于蒙汜

---

6. The Twelve Stations are the twelve regions of the sky through which the sun passes on its course, the elliptic, and which in turn correspond to the twelve months.

The sun rises from Sunny Vale in the East, and in the evening sets on the banks of the Meng River in the far West.
言日出東方湯谷之中,暮入西極蒙水之涯也。

> From dawning all the way to dusk, 自明及晦
> How many miles does [the sun] travel? 所行幾里

The sun rises at dawn and stops to rest in the evening. How many miles does it travel in between?
言日平旦而出,至暮而止,所行凡幾何里乎?

> [9] What power has the nocturnal radiance of the moon, 夜光何德
> That it may die and then grow back again? 死則又育

What power does the moon have in Heaven, such that it can die and then be reborn?
言月何德於天,死而復生也。

> What sort of singularity does it possess, 厥利維何
> That a rabbyt peers out from its belly? 而顧菟在腹

In the moon there is a rabbyt.[7] What desire or singularity does it possess, so as to abide in the belly of the moon and look down?
言月中有菟,何所貪利,居月之腹,而顧望乎?

> [10] Lady Tangent never had a mate, 女歧無合
> So how could she obtain Nine Sons? 夫焉取九子

Lady Tangent was a goddess who bore nine sons without a husband.
女歧,神女,無夫而生九子也。

> Where does the Sire of Might reside? 伯強何處
> Where do the gentle airs abide? 惠氣安在

---

7. I translate "rabbyt" because the character used here, *tu* 菟, is almost but not quite the same as *tu* 兔, "rabbit," leaving uncertain how Han scholars interpreted this line. As discussed below in "Text Three," one modern interpretation has it as a "tadpole" instead of a "rabbit." But the Han commentary seems to have chosen to leave the matter unresolved. As it does frequently, the commentary simply cites and repeats the most difficult word in the text.

The Sire of Might, Dali, is the great spirit of those injured by violence. He goes wherever people have been wounded... When Yin and Yang are properly balanced, the gentle airs appear, but if not, then the spirits of violence thrive. Where are these two located?
伯強, 大厲, 疫鬼也, 所至傷人。……言陰陽調和則惠氣行, 不和調則厲鬼興, 二者當何所在乎?

[11] What is it that closes when darkness falls? 何闔而晦
What is it whose opening brings light? 何開而明

By what means does Heaven close up and become dark? By what means does it open up and brighten with dawn?
言天何所闔閉而晦冥, 何所開發而明曉乎?

When the Horn Portal constellation has not yet dawned, 角宿未旦
Where does the radiant spirit conceal itself?[8] 曜靈安藏

Before the sun has dawned in the East, where does the sun conceal its luminous essence?
言東方未明旦之時, 日安所藏其精光乎?

[12] Were [Gun] not appointed to control the floods, 不任汨鴻
Why would the masses have elevated him? 師何以尚之

Gun's talent was not sufficient to be appointed to control the mighty floods, so why did the masses appoint him?
言鯀才不任治鴻水, 眾人何以舉之乎?

They all responded [to Yao's doubts]: "Why be anxious? 僉答何憂
"Why not test him with the challenge?" 何不課而行之

The masses appointed Gun to control the floods. Yao knew he was not capable, but the masses said, "Why be anxious? Why not first try him out?"
言眾人舉鯀治水, 堯知其不能, 眾人曰: 何憂哉? 何不先試之也。

---

8. "Radiant spirit" as kenning for the sun can be found in *Guangya*. See *Guangya shuzheng*, 9A.10a.

[13] With the owls and turtles leading and following, 鴟龜曳銜
      How did Gun obey [Yao's] instructions?²⁹ 鯀何聽焉

When Gun was controlling the flood, his task could not be completed. So Yao had him banished to Mount Plume. "Leading and following" the birds and water insects, he ate them. How could Gun ever refrain to obey again?
言鯀治水,績用不成,堯乃放殺之羽山,飛鳥水蟲,曳銜而食之。鯀何能復不聽乎?

   When he had fulfilled our desires and completed   順欲成功
      the task,
   Why did the Lord [Yao] then punish him?   帝何刑焉

Gun fulfilled the desires of the masses and completed his task. So why did Yao then punish and execute him?
帝,謂堯也。言鯀設能順眾人之欲,而成其功,堯當何為刑戮之乎?

[14] Perishing after long durance at Plume Mountain, 永遏在羽山
      Why was he not granted favor even after three years?¹⁰ 夫何三年不施

Yao for a long period banished Gun to Mount Plume. He perished in that desolate place, and even after three years his crime was not pardoned.
言堯長放鯀於羽山,絕在不毛之地,三年不舍其罪也。

   Since Prince Yu regarded Gun as obstinate,   伯禹愎鯀
   How could he have achieved such a transformation?   夫何以變化

Gun was extremely foolish. He was obstinate and bore the son Yu, who would disdain his father's deeds. How could he then transform so as to have sagely virtue?
言鯀愚很,愎而生禹,禹小見其所為,何以能變化而有聖德也?

[15] Continuing the legacy of his predecessors,   纂就前緒
      Yu ultimately accomplished the task of his father.   遂成考功

---

9. The commentary does not gloss but instead simply repeats the difficult phrase *yexian* 曳銜, so there is no way to be sure how it is interpreting the phrase. My interpretation as "leading and following" borrows from Wen Yiduo's reading in "Tianwen shuzheng," 543.

10. Later scholars would propose various alternative interpretations of the main verb *shi* 施. The Han commentary seems to understand its sense here as an extension of a root meaning of "give, supply," a strained but not impossible reading.

Yu was able to succeed and inherit the task bequeathed by Gun, and complete the work of his deceased father.
言禹能纂代鯀之遺業，而成考父之功也。

> Why, to further the effort and advance the work, 何續初繼業
> Did he use such different stratagems? 而厥謀不同

How could Yu continue Gun's work, although his stratagems and concerns were different?
言禹何能繼續鯀業，而謀慮不同也。

> [16] The source of the floodwaters was most deep, 洪泉極深
> So how could [Yu] block the flow? 何以寘之

The abyssal source of the flood waters was most deep and vast. How could Yu fill it in and make it level?
言洪水淵泉極深大，禹何用寘塞而平之乎？

> The earth is square and divided into nine sections, 地方九則
> How could he distinguish among them?[11] 何以墳之

The territory of the nine provinces has nine classes in all. How was Yu able to differentiate among them?
謂九州之地，凡有九品，禹何以能分別之乎？

> [17] How did the winged dragon demarcate them? 應龍何畫
> How did it pass over the rivers and oceans? 河海何歷

The rivers and oceans have their source very far away. But the winged dragon passes over them and roams among them, penetrating to every place. Another [commentary? text?] reads: "When Yu regulated the great flood, a divine dragon came to measure the earth with its tail, leading the waters to pour out into a place where they could be blocked and hence regulating the flood."
言河海所出至遠，應龍過歷遊之，而無所不窮也。或曰：禹治洪水時，有神龍以尾畫地，導水所注當決者，因而治之也。

---

11. The commentary notes a variant 分 for 墳, perhaps used to justify its reading. Since the two are homophonous, it is likely that one is a phonetic loan for the other. See also discussion of Wang Niansun's analysis in chapter 3.

[18] What did Gun himself construct and measure?　　鮌何所營
　　　What did Yu accomplish?　　　　　　　　　　　禹何所成

When Gun controlled the mighty flood, what did he construct and measure? What did Yu accomplish?
言鮌治鴻水，何所營度，禹何所成就乎？

　　　When Kanghui [Gonggong] was angered,　　　康回馮怒
　　　Why did the earth sink down to the southeast?　墬何故以東南傾

Huainanzi says: "When Gonggong and Zhuanxu were vying to become High Lord and Gonggong lost, he was angered and struck the Broken Mountain. The mainstays of Heaven were severed, the Pillars of Earth cracked, and so the southeast sank downward."[12]
《淮南子》言共工與顓頊爭為帝，不得，怒而觸不周之山，天維絕，地柱折，故東南傾也。

[19] How did [Yu] arrange the Nine Continents?　　九州安錯
　　　How deep are the rivers and valleys?[13]　　　　川谷何洿

The Nine Continents were arranged in interlocking fashion. How did Yu distinguish them? The rivers and valleys were placed in the earth, but why were they uniquely deep?
言九州錯廁，禹何所分別之？川谷於地，何以獨洿深乎？

　　　Flowing to the east they do not overflow:　　　東流不溢
　　　Who knows the reason behind all this?　　　　孰知其故

The hundred rivers flow eastward, and it is unknown if they fill and overflow. Who is there that knows the reason?
言百川東流，不知滿溢，誰有知其故也。

[20] East and west, south and north:　　　　　　　東西南北
　　　Which direction extends the farthest?　　　　其修孰多

---

12. This is an unusually apposite citation, one which is also used frequently by modern scholars in interpreting "Heavenly Questions." The episode can be found, with slight differences, in Liu Wendian, ed., *Huainan honglie jijie*, 3.95–96; Major et al., *Huainanzi*, 115.

13. The commentary glosses *wu* 洿 as *shen* 深, and then uses the two words as a compound in its paraphrase of the text.

Heaven and Earth have their east, west, south, and north; which one of these is the longest?
言天地東西南北，誰為長乎？

> South and north bulge outward; 南北順橢
> How much further do they extend? 其衍幾何

South and north bulge further outward. How much do they differ in their extent?
言南北墮長，其廣差幾何乎？

> [21] The Hanging Garden of Kunlun's peaks: 崑崙縣圃
> Where is it located? 其居安在

Kunlun is the name of a mountain in the northwest, the source of the primal pneuma. Its peak is called the Hanging Garden, and at its highest point it connects to Heaven.
崑崙，山名也，在西北，元氣所出。其巔曰縣圃，乃上通於天也。

> The nine tiers of those elevated walls: 增城九重
> How many leagues high do they stand? 其高幾里

Huainanzi says that the mountains of Kunlun are nine-tiered, and twelve thousand li in height.[14]
《淮南》言崑崙之山九重，其高萬二千里也。

> [22] Who is it who passes through 四方之門
> The Gates of the Four Directions? 其誰從焉

Heaven has four quarters, and each one has its own gate. Who uses them to go up or down?
言天四方，各有一門，其誰從之上下？

> When the northwestern gate opens up wide, 西北辟啓
> What kind of air blows through it? 何氣通焉

---

14. These questions are answered in the received text of the *Huainanzi* as well: Major et al., *Huainanzi*, 4.156; Liu Wendian, ed., *Huainan honglie jijie*, 4.159 and 162. Curiously *Huainanzi* gives a height of eleven thousand *li* instead. The commentary ignores the key term here, *zengcheng* 增城, which seems to identify a specific peak in the received *Huainanzi*, and I translate as a proper noun, "Tiered Palisade," in "Text Three."

Whenever the northwestern gate of Heaven opens up, how does the primal pneuma pass through it?
言天西北之門, 每常開啓, 豈元氣之所通?

[23] Why does the sun not reach its mark? 日安不到
　　　What does the Torch Dragon illumine?[15] 燭龍何照

The northwest part of heaven has a kingdom of profound darkness and no sun. But there is a dragon there that bears a torch in its mouth to illuminate it all.
言天之西北, 有幽冥無日之國, 有龍銜燭而照之也。

　　　Till Xihe lifts the reins [of the sun carriage] 羲和之未揚
　　　What gleams on the blossoms of the Dimming Wood? 若華何光

Before the sun has risen, how can the Dimming Wood already have bright crimson flowers that gleam?
言日未出之時, 若木何能有明赤之光華乎?

[24] What place is warm in the wintertime? 何所冬暖
　　　What place will chill in the summer? 何所夏寒

Regarding the airs of Heaven and Earth, what place can be warm in the winter, or cool in the summer?
言天地之氣, 何所有冬溫而夏寒者乎?

　　　Where is there a forest of stone? 焉有石林
　　　What beast is capable of speech? 何獸能言

What place under Heaven has a forest of stone trees? Or in the forest, a beast that can speak?[16] *The Book of Rites* says: "The orangutan can speak, but is not distinct from the birds and beasts."[17]
言天下何所有石木之林, 林中有獸能言語者乎? 《禮記》曰: 猩猩能言, 不離禽獸也。

　　15. These lines would have to be rearranged to make the rhyme scheme conform. The kingdom of darkness is an invention of the commentary to make sense of the received text, and thus a useful indication of the hermeneutical principles at work.
　　16. It is noteworthy that the commentary seems to conflate the subject of the two lines, placing the beast in the same forest.
　　17. See *Liji zhengyi*, 1.17.

86 Text One

[25] How could there be a hornless dragon　　　焉有虺龍
　　　That roams with a bear-creature on its back?　負熊以遊

How could there be a hornless dragon that carries a bear-creature on its back and roams playfully?
有角曰龍,無角曰虺。言寧有無角之龍,負熊獸以遊戲者乎?

[26] The fierce hamadryad of nine heads[18]　　　雄虺九首
　　　That moves like lightning—where is it?　　儵忽焉在

There is a fierce hamadryad with nine heads on one body. It is as fast as lightning. Where are all these located?
言有雄虺,一身九頭,速及電光,皆何所在乎?

　　　What place is there without death?　　　　何所不死
　　　Where do the giant men abide?　　　　　　長人何守

Images of Terrestrial Demarcation reads: "There is a country without death."[19] The "giant men" are the "giant barbarians." The *Spring and Autumn Annals* reads: "Regarding the Fangfeng Clan, when Yu gathered the various feudal lords, the Fangfeng arrived late, so he enfeoffed them with Mounts Feng and Yu."[20]
《括地象》曰：有不死之國。長人,長狄。《春秋》云：防風氏也。禹會諸侯,防風氏後至,于是使守封嵎之山也.

[27] Waterlily on the nine-branched road,　　　靡蓱九衢
　　　And hemp blossoms: where can they be found?　枲華安居

---

18. I translate the special term *hui* 虺 with another rare term for a serpent, "hamadryad," synonymous with the king cobra. The commentary does not explain the term.

19. *Kuodi xiang* 括地象 seems to be an abbreviation of the title of a weft text from the Han dynasty, the *Hetu kuodi xiang* 河圖括地象. It does not survive intact but is quoted frequently in the Li Shan commentary to the *Wenxuan* (e.g. 1.11) and other sources. Mounts Feng and Yu were located near modern Mount Mogan 莫幹 in Zhejiang, and guarded by Fangfengshi 防風氏, ancestor of the Changdi. See Xu Yuangao, ed., *Guoyu jijie*, 5.202–3. Liu Zongyuan also mentions Feng and Yu in his response below in "Text Two."

20. This text is actually closer to the received text of the *Guoyu* (see Xu Yuangao, ed., *Guoyu jijie*, 5.202–3).

How could there be waterlilies that grow on the water without a root, and then spread out onto the nine-branched road? And also hemp plants dangling gorgeous flowers? Where do these things exist?
言寧有薜草，生於水上無根，乃蔓衍於九交之道，又有枲麻垂草華榮，何所有此物乎?

> When a snake swallowed an elephant, 一蛇吞象
> How gigantic must it have been? 厥大何如

The Classic of Mountains and Seas reads: "In the south is a numinous snake. It swallowed an elephant for three years, and only then expelled the bones."[21]
《山海經》云：南方有靈蛇，吞象，三年然後出其骨．

> [28] Blackwater and Mystic Base 黑水玄趾
> And Mount Triperil: where are they found? 三危安在

Mystic Base and Triperil are mountains in the west. The Blackwater flows from Mount Kunlun.
玄趾、三危，皆山名也，在西方，黑水出崑崙山也．

> Though years without dying may be prolonged, 延年不死
> When must longevity come to an end? 壽何所止

The transcendents hold onto life and do not die. When does their longevity ever come to an end?
言仙人稟命不死，其壽獨何所窮止也?

> [29] Where is the home of the hill-fish? 鯪魚何所
> Where do the griffins abide? 魃堆焉處

The hill carp has four feet, and comes from the south.[22] The griffin (*qidui*) is a legendary creature.
鯪鯉也，有四足，出南方．魃堆，奇獸也．

---

21. The quotation in the received text is somewhat different. For details see "Text Three."
22. I understand *ling* 鯪 as representing the homophone 陵. This is probably equivalent to the *lingyu* 陵魚 or merman described in *Shanhaijing*; see Yuan Ke, ed., *Shanhaijing jiaozhu*, 12.280.

> How did Archer Yih shoot down the suns?[23]
> How were the suncrows then deplumed?

羿焉彃日
烏焉解羽

Huainanzi says that in the time of Yao, ten suns rose simultaneously, so the plants and trees were scorched and barren. Yao commanded that Yih shoot down the ten suns. He hit nine of them, and the nine crows in the suns all died. Their feathers fell off, and he just left one sun.[24]

淮南言堯時十日並出，草木焦枯。堯命羿仰射十日，中其九日，日中九烏皆死，墮其羽翼，故留其一日也。

> [30] Yu exerted himself to complete the task,
> He descended to watch over all four parts of the earth.

禹之力獻功
降省下土四方

Yu used his diligent effort to advance his achievement, so Yao sent him to observe and visit the four quarters of the earth below.

言禹以勤力獻進其功，堯因使省造下土四方也。

> How did he find that lady of Tushan,
> And mate with her at the Platform of Mulberries?[25]

焉得彼嵞山女
而通之於台桑

When Yu was managing the flood, on his way he married the lady of the Tushan Clan. He fulfilled the way of husband and wife at the site of the Platform of Mulberries.

言禹治水，道娶塗山氏之女，而通夫婦之道於台桑之地。

> [31] Caring for that maiden he made a match with her,
> In order to have a successor;

閔妃匹合
厥身是繼

The reason Yu was worried about lacking a consort was that he wanted to establish a successor for himself.

言禹所以憂無妃匹者，欲為身立繼嗣也。

> Why did [Yu], relishing such unlike flavours,
> Yet hasten for a single day's consummation?

胡維嗜不同味
而快鼂飽

---

23. I write the name of the Archer as Yih 羿 rather than Yi to distinguish from the ruler Yi 益 mentioned below.

24. There is indeed a similar, but far more detailed, account in *Huainanzi*; see Liu Wendian, ed., *Huainan honglie jijie*, 8.305–6.

25. Yu is said to have found his mate, mother of Qi, at Tushan, perhaps in Dangtu 當塗 (*Shiji*, 2.100). On these terms see notes to "Text Three."

Thus Yu married on the *xinyou* day [58th in the sexagenary cycle] and departed on the *jiazi* day [first in the sexagenary cycle, three days later], and so there was [his son and heir] Qi.
故以辛酉日娶，甲子日去，而有啓也。

[32] When Qi replaced the minister Yi as sovereign,   啓代益作后
        All of a sudden [Yi] met with disaster.   卒然離蠥

This is about when Yu abdicated the realm to Yi. Yi then banished Qi to the south of Mount Ji. But all the people under heaven rejected Yi and turned their allegiance to [Yu's natural son] Qi as ruler. Thus Yi ultimately could not be established as sovereign, which is why the text says "met with disaster."
言禹以天下禪與益，益避啓於箕山之陽。天下皆去益而歸啓，以為君。益卒不得立，故曰遭憂也。

    Why was it that Qi was still beset by anxiety,   何啓惟憂
    And was able to overcome his captivity?[26]   而能拘是達

The reason all the people under Heaven rejected Yi in favor of Qi was that he was able to consider anxiously the way of virtue, and also was able to escape his captivity and sequestration. His captivity and sequestration refers to when the Youhu Clan rebelled against Qi, and Qi led the six armies to conquer them.
言天下所以去益就啓者，以其能憂思道德，而通其拘隔。拘隔者，謂有扈氏叛啓，啓率六師以伐之也。

[33] Since all [the Youhu] did was make trouble,[27]   皆歸射鞠
        [Qi punished them] and so his body was unharmed.   而無害厥躬

What the Youhu Clan had done amounted to the gravest evil, so Qi punished them, and for a long time had no harm to his own body.

    26. For Qi's conquest of the Youhu, see *Shiji*, 2.104, but the account there does not mention Qi's captivity. This is why my interpretation in "Text Three," following from the previous couplet which belongs with this question in a single quatrain, understands this as referring to Qi's defeat of Yi.
    27. This line is practically impossible to read without emendation. The commentary seems only to provide a rough guess.

言有扈氏所行, 皆歸於窮惡, 故啟誅之, 長無害於其身也。

> How was it that Lord Yi was overthrown, 何后益作革
> While Yu had helped the people cultivate the land? 而禹播降

The reason Qi could overturn Yi, and replace Yi as ruler, was that Yu had calmed and controlled the waters and land, so the common people were able to plant the hundred grains. So they all longed to be subjects of Qi. 言啟所以能變更益, 而代益為君者, 以禹平治水土, 百姓得下種百穀, 故思歸啟也。

> [34] Qi set forth and arranged the notes of [Gong and] 啟棘賓商
>   Shang,[28]
>   The "Nine Phases" and the "Nine Songs." 九辯九歌

The "Nine Phases" and "Nine Songs" were the music composed by Qi. Qi was able to achieve and make famous the task of Yu, and to arrange the tones of Gong and Shang, so as to prepare the ritual music. 〈九辯〉、〈九歌〉, 啟所作樂也。言啟能修明禹業, 陳列宮商之音, 備其禮樂也。

> Why did his diligent son rupture his mother, 何勤子屠母
> Who, dying, made new division in the earth?[29] 而死分竟地

Yu divided and ruptured his mother's back when he was born. His mother's body was scattered across the earth. How was it that he could have sagely virtue, but also cause all under Heaven worry and trouble? 言禹腷剝母背而生, 其母之身, 分散竟地, 何以能有聖德, 憂勞天下乎?

> [35] The Lord [of Heaven] sent down Archer Yih of 帝降夷羿
>   the Yee tribe,[30]

---

28. I follow the commentary's reading that Shang refers to the notes of Gong and Shang, synecdoche for proper music. This reading requires very strained glosses of *ji bin* 棘賓 as "set forth and arrange" 陳列.

29. What appears to be a remarkable legend about the birth of Qi, with its Freudian resonances, is unfortunately not well attested. See comments on stanza 35 in "Text Three" below.

30. This line is harder to follow in English than in Chinese because the name of both

> And he brought new evils to the people of Xia. 革孽夏民

Yih killed the house of Xia and occupied the position of the Son of Heaven. Dissipated and filling his time in hunting, he upset the way of Xia, and caused much grief and anguish for the myriad peoples.
言羿弒夏家，居天子之位，荒淫田獵，變更夏道，為萬民憂患。

> But why did he shoot at the Sire of the Yellow River, 胡射夫河伯
> And take the nymph of the Luo River as his wife? 而妻彼雒嬪

A commentary [another tradition?] reads:[31] "The Sire of the Yellow River transformed into a white dragon and roamed along the edge of the water. Yih saw him and shot him in the left eye. The Sire of the Yellow River complained to the Lord of Heaven, saying, 'Kill the archer Yih for me.' The Lord of Heaven said, 'How was it that he could shoot you?' 'At that time I had transformed into the guise of a white dragon and was out roaming.' The Lord of Heaven replied: 'If you had deeply guarded your own divine power, how would Yih have been able to violate it? If you now turn into an insect or beast, you will be shot at by men, and so it must be. What fault is it of Yih's?'" "Deeply" has a variant "protect." Yih also dreamed of copulating with the goddess of the Luo River, Fu Fei.
傳曰：河伯化為白龍，遊于水旁，羿見躲之，眇其左目。河伯上訴天帝，曰：為我殺羿。天帝曰：爾何故得見躲？河伯曰：我時化為白龍出遊。天帝曰：使汝深守神靈，羿何從得犯？汝今為虫獸，當為人所躲，固其宜也。羿何罪歟？深，一作保。羿又夢與雒水神宓妃交接也。

> [36] With his nacre-inlaid bow and keen gauntlet 馮珧利決
> The giant boar [Yih] shot dead. 封狶是射

---

the protagonist, archer Yih 羿, and the Yee 夷 tribe, are written Yi in pinyin romanization. So I distinguish both with slightly distinctive spellings.

31. The source of this story is unclear, since it is only identified as a *zhuan*, "commentary" (or perhaps just "verbal tradition"), but it is one of the most fascinating texts quoted in the Han commentary. It should be understood as a mythologized equivalent of a more straightforward story in which Yih merely shot at the leader of a tribe called the Hebo (Sire of the Yellow River) Clan. For more context on Hebo, compare the myths and rituals discussed in Lai, "Looking for Mr. Ho Po."

Yih did not cultivate his own virtue, but instead, bearing his bow and arrows and quiver, went hunting to capture divine beasts, and satisfy his own passions.
言羿不修道德，而挾弓躱韝，獵捕神獸，以快其情也。

> Why, when [Yih] presented the rich offering of meat, 何獻蒸肉之膏
> Did the High Lord [of Heaven] not approve? 而后帝不若

Yih went hunting and shot the giant boar, and made of its meat an offering to the Lord of Heaven. The Lord of Heaven still did not approve of what Yih had done.
言羿獵躱封狶，以其肉膏祭天帝，天帝猶不順羿之所為也。

[37] When Han Zhuo seduced Pure Fox, 浞娶純狐
That beguiling consort conspired with him. 眩妻爰謀

When Zhuo married the lady of the Pure Fox Clan, he was dazzled and blinded into loving her. With Zhuo she conspired to murder Yih.
言浞娶於純狐氏女，眩惑愛之，遂與浞謀殺羿也。

> Why was it that the hide-piercing Archer Yih 何羿之射革
> Was destroyed altogether by [Han Zhuo's] 而交吞揆之
>   intervention?

Yih loved hunting and ignored the regulations and measures of governance, so [Han] Zhuo intervened in the affairs of the state, distributing his beneficence and bestowing rewards, until Zhuo swallowed up and destroyed Yih.[32]
言羿好躱獵，不恤政事法度，浞交接國中，布恩施德而吞滅之也。

[38] When blocked and thwarted while traveling westward, 阻窮西征
How was it that [Yao] managed to cross those cliffs? 巖何越焉

When Yao banished Gun to Mount Plume, he traveled west and crossed over the perilous cliffs and crags, perishing there.
言堯放鯀羽山，西行度越岑巖之險，因墮死也。

---

32. The reading offered by the commentary here does not appear to follow the original syntax at all.

> When Gun was transformed into a *huangxiong*, 化為黃熊
> How did the shaman bring him back to life? 巫何活焉

After Gun died he was transformed into a *huangxiong*,[33] and entered the Plume Abyss. How could the shaman-physician then resurrect him?
言鯀死後化為黃熊，入於羽淵，豈巫醫所能復生活也？

> [39] Then all could sow the black millet and sticky millet, 咸播秬黍
> Where they had planted only reeds and cresses. 莆雚是營

When Yu had calmed and put in order the waters and land, the myriad peoples were all able to plant black millet and sticky millet in the land of reeds and cresses, so that it all became good farmland.
言禹平治水土，萬民皆得耕種黑黍於雚蒲之地，盡為良田也。

> How could they plant all the crops? 何由并投
> Gun's fault only greatened and expanded. 而鯀疾脩盈

It was not because Yao hated Gun that he killed him, but Yu could not manage to continue the prosperity, so how could people plant the five grains? Then he knew that Gun's evil had expanded to fill all under Heaven.
言堯不惡鯀而戮殺之，則禹不得嗣興，民何得投種五穀乎？乃知鯀惡長滿天下也。

> [40] The white nimbus winding around and spreading out, 白蜺嬰茀
> Why has it come upon this hall? 胡為此堂

There was a nimbus spreading out and winding around, and why is it in this hall? This is about the temple hall that Qu Yuan had seen.
言此有蜺茀，氣逶移相嬰，何為此堂乎？蓋屈原所見祠堂也。

---

33. The *huangxiong* 黃熊, which might appear to mean "brown bear," is mentioned in *Zuozhuan*, Duke Zhao, year 7 (Durrant et al., *Zuo Tradition*, 1423), as the spirit into which Gun transformed after death. But it is reasonably clear that *huangxiong* represents an aquatic spirit-animal and hence *xiong* 熊 should actually be read *nai* 能, "turtle" (terrapin). See the Tang commentary in *Chunqiu Zuozhuan zhengyi*, 44.1433; Huang Linggeng, ed., *Chuci zhangju shuzheng*, 4.1102. The Han commentary to "Heavenly Questions" does not gloss this term, however, but instead simply recapitulates it, perhaps suggesting that Han scholars recognized there was something mysterious in the term already.

| | How did [Cui Wenzi] obtain that fine elixir, | 安得夫良藥 |
| | Which turned out to be incapable of good? | 不能固臧 |

Cui Wenzi studied to be a transcendent with Prince Qiao. Ziqiao transformed into a white nimbus spreading out and winding around, and brought the elixir to Wenzi. Cui Wenzi was startled and baffled, and drew his halberd to strike at the nimbus. When he hit it, the elixir fell to the ground. He looked down at it and saw the body of Prince Qiao. That is why it says that the elixir is not good.[34]

言崔文子學仙於王子僑，子僑化為白蜺而嬰茀，持藥與崔文子，崔文子驚怪，引戈擊蜺，中之，因墮其藥，俯而視之，王子僑之尸也。故言得藥不善也。

[41] Heaven is configured horizontal and vertical: 天式從橫
　　　When Yang energy disperses then you die. 陽離爰死

The Law of Heaven has its own Ways: good and evil, Yin and Yang, horizontal and vertical. When a person loses Yang energy he dies.

言天法有善惡陰陽從橫之道。人失陽氣則死也。

　　　Why did the great bird cry out, 大鳥何鳴
　　　And how did the man's body disappear? 夫焉喪厥體

When Cui Wenzi obtained the body of Prince Qiao, he placed it in a chamber, and covered it with offerings in bamboo baskets. In just an instant, the body transformed into a great bird and cried out. When he opened up [the coffin] and looked at it, it soared up and departed. How could Wenzi lose the body of Ziqiao? This tells us that the transcendents cannot be killed.

言崔文子取王子僑之尸，置之室中，覆之以幣篚，須臾則化為大鳥而鳴，開而視之，翩飛而去，文子焉能亡子僑之身乎？言仙人不可殺也。

[42] When Ping cries out to summon the rain, 萍號起雨
　　　How does he get it to start? 何以興之

---

34. For this story, which presumably was popular in the Han but likely has nothing to do with the original poem, see Wang Shumin, ed., *Liexian zhuan jiaojian*, A.95–97. This interpretation seems unlikely, but You Guoen nonetheless follows it as the best among bad options.

The Master of Rains cries out, and then the clouds gather and the rain falls. But how does he cause it to be created?
言雨師號呼,則雲起而雨下,獨何以興之乎?

> Having created those bodies possessing two torsos, 撰體協脅
> How could deer assume them? 鹿何膺之

Heaven created the twelve sacred deer, with each body having eight feet and two heads. How did they obtain bodies in such a shape?
言天撰十二神鹿,一身八足兩頭,獨何膺受此形體乎?

[43] When the mighty mountain-bearing turtles clap,[35] 鼇戴山抃
How do they hold them steady in place? 何以安之

The *Biographies of the Transcendents* states: "There are gigantic, magic turtles, who carry on their backs the Penglai mountains and dance rhythmically, playing in the midst of the azure seas. But how do they keep them in place?"[36]
《列仙傳》曰:有巨靈之鼇,背負蓬萊之山而抃舞,戲滄海之中,獨何以安之乎?

> Releasing the ships to go by land instead, 釋舟陵行
> How are they kept moving through space? 何以遷之

The boats depart the water and travel by land, then how can they be moved along? This says that the reason the turtles can carry the mountains is just as with boats, because they are in the water. If the turtles could escape the water to travel on land, then how could they cause the mountains to move along?
舟釋水而陵行,則何能遷徙也?言龜所以能負山若舟船者,以其在水中也。使龜釋水而陵行,則何以能遷徙山乎?

[44] When Ao arrived at the doorstep, 惟澆在戶
What was he seeking from his brother's wife? 何求于嫂

---

35. The commentary specifies that *bian* 抃 means "to clap" 擊手, even though it is even harder to visualize turtles clapping than "dancing," another meaning of the same word.

36. The *locus classic* of this legend seems to be in the transmitted text of *Liezi* rather than *Liexian zhuan*, but we do not have an intact received text of the *Liexian zhuan*, and the precise dating of *Liezi* is controversial. See Yang Bojun, ed., *Liezi jishi*, 5.161.

Ao was a strongman of in ancient times. The *Analects* says: "Ao pushed boats over dry land."[37] This says that Ao lacked propriety, and engaged in immoral relations with his sister-in-law. He went right to her door pretending that he was seeking something else, and in this way carried out his adultery.[38]
浇, 古多力者也。《論》曰：浇盪舟。言浇無義, 淫佚其嫂, 往至其戶, 佯有所求, 因與行淫亂也。

| Why did Shaokang, while on the chase with hounds, | 何少康逐犬 |
| End up decapitating his head? | 而顛隕厥首 |

Shaokang of Xia in his hunting let his hounds chase the prey. Then he killed Ao and cut off his head.
言夏少康因田獵放犬逐獸, 遂襲殺浇而斷其頭。

| [45] When Lady Tangent [Ao's sister-in-law] was sewing an undershirt, | 女歧縫裳 |
| They shared lodgings in the same house. | 而館同爰止 |

Lady Tangent was the sister-in-law of Ao.... While they were engaged in adulterous relations, she sewed an undershirt for him.
女歧, 浇嫂也。……言女歧與浇淫佚, 為之縫裳。

| Why did Shaokang behead that other one, | 何顛易厥首 |
| So that the lady met with harm instead? | 而親以逢殆 |

Shaokang attacked at night and took the head of Lady Tangent, thinking it was that of Ao, and cutting it off. Thus this says "behead the wrong one," that is, he met with harm.
言少康夜襲得女歧頭, 以為浇, 因斷之, 故言易首, 遇危殆也。

---

37. In broader context, the statement reads, according to *Analects* 14/6: "Nan-kung K'uo asked Confucius, 'Both Yi who was good at archery and Ao who could push a boat over dry land met violent deaths, while Yü and Ji who took part in planting the crops gained the Empire.'" 南宮适問於孔子曰：「羿善射, 浇盪舟, 俱不得其死然。禹、稷躬稼而有天下。」. See Lau, *Analects*, 133; *Lunyu zhushu*, 14.207.

38. This interpretation, which is surely wrong, takes the text here with exceeding literalness and so reads it as a kind of satire of Ao's bad behavior.

[46] When Tang plotted to transform the people [of Xia], 湯謀易旅
　　How did he treat them generously? 何以厚之

When Tang of Yin wanted to transform the people of Xia, and make them follow himself, how then did he treat them generously?
言殷湯欲變易夏眾，使之從己，獨何以厚待之乎？

　　When [Shaokang] capsized the vessels of Zhenxun, 覆舟斟尋
　　By what route did he conquer them? 何道取之

When Shaokang destroyed the Zhenxun people, capsizing their vessels, by what means did he capture them?
言少康滅斟尋氏，奄若覆舟，獨以何道取之乎？

[47] When Jie assaulted Mount Meng, 桀伐蒙山
　　Whom did he obtain there? 何所得焉

Jie of Xia went to attack the country of Mengshan, where he obtained Moxi.
言夏桀征伐蒙山之國，而得妹嬉也。

　　Why was Moxi taken advantage of [by Jie], 妹嬉何肆
　　And how did Tang destroy him for it? 湯何殛焉

When Jie obtained the concubine Moxi and behaved wantonly, Tang then banished him to Nanchao.
言桀得妹嬉，肆其情意，故湯放之南巢也。

[48] While Shun was anxious about the household, 舜閔在家
　　Why did his father keep him a bachelor? 父何以鰥

Shun was a commoner who was deeply concerned for his household. His father was stubborn and his mother garrulous. They did not let him marry a wife, so he had to remain a bachelor.[39]
言舜為布衣，憂閔其家。其父頑母囂，不為娶婦，乃至于鰥也。

---

39. The story of Shun's abuse by his father and wicked stepmother is set forth in *Shiji*, 1.38.

98   Text One

> Why did sagely Yao not inform the groom's own clan Yaw[40]
> When marrying off to Shun his two daughters?

堯不姚告
二女何親

Yao did not tell Shun's parents before allowing him to marry [his daughters]. If he had told them, they would not have agreed, and then to whom would Yao's daughters have joined as family?[41]
言堯不告舜父母而妻之，如令告之，則不聽，堯女當何所親附乎？

> [49] When the sprouting of events is at its start,
> How can one even speculate upon it?

厥萌在初
何所億焉

When the sages anticipate the earliest sprouting of future events, they already know how life and death, good and evil will end up. This is not empty speculation.
言賢者預見施行萌牙之端，而知其存亡善惡所終，非虛億也。

> The agate-studded tower had ten stories;
> Who was it who completed it?

璜臺十成
誰所極焉

Zhow made chopsticks out of ivory and Sir Ji lamented, knowing that once there were ivory chopsticks, surely there would be jade goblets; and once there were jade goblets, surely there would be feasts of bear paw and leopard fetus, and ultimately he would build great palaces and halls.[42] Zhow ended up building a ten-story tower of agate, a mound out of ale lees, and a pool of ale, and so the dynasty fell.[43]
言紂作象箸，而箕子歎，預知象箸必有玉杯，玉杯必盛熊蹯豹胎，如此，必崇廣宮室。紂果作玉臺十重，糟丘酒池，以至于亡也。

> [50] When [Fuxi] ascended to the throne as Lord,
> By what path was he elevated to it?

登立為帝
孰道尚之

---

40. Here again I distinguish two apparent homonyms in pinyin romanization, Yao 堯 and Shun's family name Yaw 姚, with slightly different spellings.
41. The problem of Yao's failure to notify Shun's parents is mentioned in *Mencius*. See *Mengzi zhushu*, 5A.290–91; Lau, *Mencius*, 100.
42. This description is similar to the passage about Sir Ji's complaint in *Shiji*, 38.1933–34, including the famous ivory chopsticks.
43. Zhow's dissipation is described with these and other examples at *Shiji*, 3.135. The ten-story tower may be what is there called "Deer Tower" 鹿臺.

When Fuxi first made the eight trigrams, cultivating virtue, the masses had him ascend to become emperor. Who prepared the way to elevate him thus?
言伏羲始畫八卦,脩行道德,萬民登以為帝,誰開導而尊尚之也.

> As for the body possessed by Nü Wa, 女媧有體
> Who crafted and constructed it? 孰制匠之

It is said that Nü Wa had a human head and snake's body, and transformed seventy times in a day. By whom was such a body constructed and designed?
傳言女媧人頭蛇身,一日七十化,其體如此,誰所制匠而圖之乎?

> [51] Shun served his younger brother, 舜服厥弟
> But ultimately met with harm. 終然為害

When Shun's younger brother Xiang was behaving viciously, Shun still obeyed and served him, but Xiang nevertheless attempted to harm Shun.
言舜弟象,施行無道,舜猶服而事之,然象終欲害舜也。

> When Xiang acted wantonly in his cur-like body, 何肆犬體
> Why was Shun's person not endangered or ruined? 而厥身不危敗

When Xiang was behaving viciously, and acting wantonly as if with the mind of cur or swine, he set fire to the granary and dug out the well, attempting to murder Shun, but in the end was unable to destroy Shun's person.
言象無道,肆其犬豕之心,燒廩窴井,欲以殺舜,然終不能危敗舜身也。

> [52] When the state of Wu was obtained by Lord Gu, 吳獲迄古
> Then [his son Taibo] stopped only at the Southern Marchmount. 南嶽是止

Gu refers to Lord Gu, Danfu [early ruler of Zhou, grandfather of King Wen]. This says that when the state of Wu obtained a sagely ruler, at the time of Lord Gu, it was ruled by Taibo [son of Lord Gu], who had modestly yielded the throne of Zhou to Wang Ji [Jili 季歷], and departed for the Southern Marchmount, seeking to gather herbs. Then he stopped [in Wu] and did not return.[44]

44. See the opening of the "Hereditary House of Wu Taibo" chapter, *Shiji*, 31.1747.

古,謂古公亶父也。言吳國得賢君,至古公亶父之時,而遇太伯,陰讓避王季,辭之南嶽之下,求采藥。於是,遂止而不還也。

> Who was it that they encountered, after departing　孰期去斯
> [Zhou],
> And who then obtained these two young noblemen?　得兩男子

Originally Lord Gu had a younger son named Wang Ji, who later was the father of King Wen. Lord Gu wanted to enthrone Wang Ji, causing the mandate of Heaven to reach on to King Wen. The eldest son Taibo and his younger brother Zhongyong departed off to Wu. Wu then enthroned Taibo as ruler. Who was it who met with them and obtained these two young noblemen? The two noblemen were Taibo and Zhongyong.
昔古公有少子,曰王季,而生聖子文王,古公欲立王季,令天命及文王。長子太伯及弟仲雍去而之吳,吳立以為君。誰與期會,而得兩男子,兩男子,謂太伯、仲雍也。

> [53] With crane-flavored broth and jade-ornamented　緣鵠飾玉
>   tripods,
> Yi Yin made offering to his Sovereign Lord [Tang].　后帝是饗

This is about when Yi Yin began to serve [Tang]. Because he prepared broth from boiled crane and ornamented tripods with jade, to serve Tang, Tang regarded him as a talented official, and made him his chief minister.
言伊尹始仕,因緣烹鵠鳥之羹,脩玉鼎,以事於湯。湯賢之,遂以為相也。

> Why did [Tang] employ stratagems against Jie of Xia,　何承謀夏桀
> Which ultimately resulted in death and destruction?　終以滅喪

Tang thus employed Yi Yin's stratagems to attack Jie of the Xia, ultimately destroying them.
言湯遂承用伊尹之謀,而伐夏桀,終以滅亡也。

> [54] The supreme Lord [Tang] descended to observe,　帝乃降觀
>   And below among the people encountered Yi Zhi.[45]　下逢伊摯

---

45. Here Yi Yin is referred to by the name Yi Zhi, which helps to conform to the rhyme scheme for this quatrain.

Tang went out to observe the customs, and worried about the people below. Making a wide selection from among the people, he encountered Yi Yin, and elevated him to be his minister.
言湯出觀風俗, 乃憂下民, 博選於眾, 而逢伊尹, 舉以為相也。

> Why was it that when [Jie] was punished by exile 　何條放致罰
>   to Tiao,
> The people did rejoice greatly?[46]　　　　　　　而黎服大說

When Tang applied the punishment of all under Heaven to discipline Jie, he banished him to the wilds of Mingtiao, and all the people under Heaven rejoiced greatly.
言湯行天之罰, 以誅於桀, 放之鳴條之野, 天下眾民大喜悅也。

> [55] While Jian Di was at the altar, why did High　簡狄在臺嚳何宜
>   Lord Ku find it proper?
> At the gift proffered by the dark bird, why was　玄鳥致貽女何嘉
>   she so gratified?[47]

Jian Di was the concubine of the High Lord Ku. The dark bird is the swallow...[48] This says that Jian Di served High Lord Ku at the altar, when a flying swallow dropped an egg there. She was delighted and swallowed it, upon which she gave birth to Xie [Shang ancestor].
簡狄, 帝嚳之妃也。玄鳥, 燕也。…… 言簡狄侍帝嚳於臺上, 有飛燕墮遺其卵, 喜而吞之, 因生契也。

> [56] Embracing and maintaining the virtue of his legacy,　該秉季德
>   [Tang] showed the same excellence as his father.　　厥父是臧

Tang embraced and maintained the virtue remaining [=inherited] from his ancestors, and cultivated the excellent endeavors of his forefathers, so that Heaven aided him to become the ruler of the people.[49]
言湯能包持先人之末德, 脩其祖父之善業, 故天祐之以為民主也。

　　46. Variant has *fu* 伏 for *fu* 服.
　　47. The traditional commentaries treat this quatrain as a single unit or couplet, perhaps because they immediately recognize the intimate link between Jian Di and the dark bird.
　　48. The founding myth of the Shang identified their origin in the egg laid by the mysterious dark bird, a totem of the Shang people; see Chen Zhi, "A Study of the Bird Cult of the Shang People."
　　49. Difficulties with this interpretation have been discussed already in chapter 1.

> Why was [Ao] finally murdered among the Youhu Clan　　胡終弊于有扈
> [By Shaokang] who was tending the cattle and sheep?　　牧夫牛羊

The Youhu was the name of Ao's kingdom. When Ao defeated Xiahou Xiang, Xiang's unborn son named Shaokang later became the Chief Herdsman of the Youreng, charged with managing all the cattle and sheep. Then Shaokang attacked and killed Ao, defeated the Youhu, and restored the past traces of Yu, making offerings to Xia and matching the blessings of Heaven.

有扈, 澆國名也。澆滅夏后相, 相之遺腹子曰少康, 後為有仍牧正, 典主牛羊, 遂攻殺澆, 滅有扈, 復禹舊跡, 祀夏配天也。

> [57] Seeking to pacify with timely tasks,[50]　　干協時舞
> How did [Shaokang] cause [the people] to obey him?　　何以懷之

After Xiahou Xiang had lost the realm, Shaokang was still young and immature. How could he obtain additional duties at that time? Pacifying and calming the common people and causing them to obey him, how could he cause them to draw closer?

言夏后相既失天下, 少康幼小, 復能求得時務, 調和百姓, 使之歸己, 何以懷來之也？

> [Zhow's] full figure and lustrous skin:[51]　　平脅曼膚
> How did he fatten himself up so?　　何以肥之

Since Zhow was vicious and unprincipled, all the feudal lords rebelled against him, and the realm was thrown into anarchy, and the people were emaciated and ravished by fear and worry. Why then to the contrary did he still have a plump, attractive body, and how could he alone have a full figure and lustrous skin?

言紂為無道, 諸侯背畔, 天下乖離, 當懷憂癯瘦, 而反形體曼澤, 獨何以能平脅肥盛乎？

---

50. The commentary arbitrarily reinterprets *wu* 舞 as *wu* 務. In a sense this is anticipating the phonological method of Qing and modern philologists, attentive to the possibility of phonetic loans, but here without any clear justification.

51. The commentary here shuttles abruptly back and forth between Xia and late Shang events.

[58] The lowly oxherds among the Youhu Clan:　　　有扈牧豎
　　　How was it that they obtained favor?　　　　云何而逢

The Youhu Clan were originally a people of oxherds. How was it that they obtained favor and became feudal lords?
言有扈氏本牧豎之人耳，因何逢遇而得為諸侯乎？

　　　When [Qi] ambushed [Youhu] upon the couch,　　擊床先出
　　　How was it that the mandate had gone?　　　　其命何從

When Qi attacked [the leader of the] Youhu, he approached him on the couch, and slew him at a stroke.[52] What was the cause that his ancestors had lost their kingdom?
言啓攻有扈之時，親於其牀上，擊而殺之。其先人失國之原，何所從出乎？

[59]　Ever upholding the virtue of his legacy,　　　恆秉季德
　　　How did [Tang] obtain that large ox?　　　　焉得夫朴牛

This says that Tang was ever able to maintain and uphold the remnant [inherited] virtue of Xie [minister of Yao, ancestor of the Shang], to cultivate and to broaden it, so Heaven acclaimed his intent, and when he set out to hunt, was able to attain the auspicious sign of a large ox.[53]
言湯常能秉持契之末德，脩而弘之，天嘉其志，出田獵，得大牛之瑞也。

　　　How is it that [Tang] distributed his takings as　　何往營班祿
　　　　bounty,
　　　Not only [racing all over] in vain?　　　　　不但還來

When Tang went out to hunt, he not only raced back and forth, but also used the birds and beasts he had caught to distribute rewards and gifts all around among the common people.
言湯往田獵，不但驅馳往來也，還輒以所獲得禽獸，徧施祿惠於百姓也。

　　52.　Normally Youhu is understood as the name of a clan, but the commentary seems to treat it instead as an individual person.
　　53.　Here again the commentary identifies Tang, the Shang founder, as the subject, rather than Wang Heng 王恆, brother of Wang Hai.

[60] Men followed the paths through the darkness and obscurity, 昏微遵跡
So that the Youdi were not content. 有狄不寧

There were people following dark and obscure paths, licentious travelers from the Yi and the Di,[54] and a man could not find a place to rest there. This refers to the grandee of Jin, Xie Jufu.
言人有循闇微之道，為姪妷夷狄之行者，不可以安其身也。謂晉大夫解居父也。

Why, like the myriad owls flocking together in the brambles, 何繁鳥萃棘
Did [Xie Jufu] betray his son with untrammelled passions? 負子肆情

When Xie Jufu went to marry in Wu, he passed the gate of a cemetery in Chen, and saw a lady carrying her child. He wanted to engage in licentious deeds with her and give way to his own sensual desires. But the lady quoted the *Odes* to criticize him, saying: "There are brambles growing by the gates of the cemetery, / And there are owls that gather there." Thus the text tells of "Many owls flocking together in the brambles."[55] This means that since there are brambles on the gates of the cemetery, even though there may be no people [who would observe us], in the brambles there will be owls, so how can you not be ashamed?
言解居父聘吳，過陳之墓門，見婦人負其子，欲與之淫泆，肆其情欲。婦人則引《詩》刺之曰：墓門有棘，有鴞萃止。故曰繁鳥萃棘也。言墓門有棘，雖無人，棘上猶有鴞，汝獨不愧也。

[61] The confused younger brother [Xiang], joining in adultery, 眩弟並淫
Endangered and injured his brother [Shun]. 危害厥兄

---

54. The commentary may be confusing the Youdi (possibly identical with the Youyi 有扈) with Yi and Di, the barbarians. For details see its explanation of the following couplet.

55. This is an actual passage in the *Book of Odes* poem 141, stanza 1; citations to the *Odes* below will be in this form: [poem #]/[stanza #]. The interpretation seems to belong to the Lu tradition, but the specific content seems unrelated to the original text. The Han commentators struggle to make sense of the abrupt reference to the "myriad birds (or owls)" 繁鳥 without more context. Since we have so little information about these Shang ancestors, though, we cannot do much better. See *Shi sanjia yi jishu*, 10.470–71. In the *Lienü zhuan* passage quoted there, the protagonist's name is written Xie Jufu 解居甫.

Xiang was the younger brother of Shun, who confused and misled his father and mother, and together with them engaged in drastic, dissolute evils, intending to endanger and kill Shun together.
言象為舜弟，眩惑其父母，並為淫泆之惡，欲共危害舜也。

> When [Xiang] transformed his shape to dissimulate and deceive, 何變化以作詐
> Why did [Shun's] progeny enjoy rapid increase? 後嗣而逢長

When Xiang wanted to kill Shun, he transformed his own shape and plotted perfidious intrigues within the family, causing Shun to build a granary, and then setting fire to it from below; then he told him to dig out a well, and filled it in from above, but throughout he could not damage Shun. When Shun became the Son of Heaven, he enfeoffed Xiang at Youbi,[56] and later the sons and grandsons of his lineage all became noble lords.
言象欲殺舜，變化其態，內作姦詐，使舜治廩，從下焚之；又命穿井，從上寘之，終不能害舜。舜為天子，封象於有庳，而後嗣子孫，長為諸侯也。

> [62] Cheng Tang journeyed east 成湯東巡
> Until he reached the Youshen. 有莘爰極

Tang went on a hunting expedition to the east, and reached the kingdom of the Youshen, where he was married.
言湯東巡狩，至有莘國，以為婚姻也。

> What did he request of lesser official [Yi Yin], 何乞彼小臣
> And so obtain a propitious consort? 而吉妃是得

Tang went on a hunting expedition to the east, following the Youshen, and importuned Yi Yin, and so obtained a propitious consort, to be his helper within the household.
言湯東巡狩，從有莘氏乞匄伊尹，因得吉善之妃，以為內輔也。

> [63] It was by a tree at the water's margin 水濱之木
> That the little child [Yi Yin] was found; 得彼小子

---

56. Youbi 有庳 was located in modern Dao 道 County, Hunan.

> So why did [the Youshen], detesting him,　　　夫何惡之
> Send him off escorting a bride of their own clan?[57]　　媵有莘之婦

When Yi Yin's mother was pregnant, she dreamt that a goddess told her: "When a frog appears from the mortar oven, you must go right away and never look back." Not much later, a frog appeared in the mortar oven. She departed for the east, and when she looked back at her home, it had been covered in a flood. She was drowned in the flood and then transformed into a hollow mulberry tree. After the water dried up, there was a little child crying out by the water's edge, and someone came to adopt him. Once he grew up, he was a rare talent. The Youshen hated Yi Yin for having appeared from the tree, and so they sent him off to escort a bride elsewhere.[58]

言伊尹母姙身，夢神女告之曰：「臼竈生鼃，亟去無顧。」居無幾何，白竈中生鼃，母去東走，顧視其邑，盡為大水，母因溺死，化為空桑之木。水乾之後，有小兒啼水涯，人取養之。既長大，有殊才。有莘惡伊尹從木中出，因以送女也。

> [64] When Tang emerged from Double Springs,　　湯出重泉
> Of what crime had he been found guilty?　　　　夫何辠尤

When Jie captured Tang at Double Springs, and then released him, why did he employ the criminal law in unscrupulous fashion?
言桀拘湯於重泉，而復出之，夫何用罪法之不審也?

> [Tang] could no longer refrain from attacking the　不勝心伐帝
>   Sovereign [Jie];
> Who was it that had provoked him [Jie]?　　　　夫誰使挑之

Tang could no longer check the will of the people, and so assaulted Jie. Who caused Jie first to provoke him?[59]

---

57. Also the clan to which Tai Si 太姒, consort of King Wen of Zhou, was said to belong.

58. This is one of the rare passages where the Han commentary responds to a quatrain as a whole, apparently because the quatrain so obviously refers to events in Yi Yin's life. As mentioned in chapter 2, this story can also be found in Knoblock and Riegel, *Annals of Lü Buwei*, 307 (14/2.2). But although the gist is the same, the prophecy there lacks the orthographic play with the frog in the oven.

59. There is more to say about these events, and I cite some sources in "Text Three," but the Han commentary is content to explicate the surface meaning, straining to make Jie the object in the final line.

言湯不勝眾人之心，而以伐桀，誰使桀先挑之也？

[65] When they met at dawn to make the war compact, 會晁爭盟
    Who was it that accomplished their common oath? 何踐吾期

When King Wu was going to attack Zhow, Zhow sent Jiao Ge to examine the armies of King Wu. Jiao Ge asked, "On what date do you intend to reach Yin?" King Wu replied, "On the *jiazi* day [i.e. the first in the sexagenary cycle]." Jiao Ge returned and reported to Zhow. On that day there was heavy rain and the paths were hard to traverse, but King Wu proceeded day and night. Someone advised him that the rain was too heavy, and the soldiers were suffering, and pleaded with him to rest. King Wu said, "I promised Jiao Ge that I would reach Yin on the *jiazi* day, and now he has reported that to Zhow. If I do not arrive on the *jiazi* day, Zhow will surely kill him. Therefore, I dare not rest, since I aim to rescue a worthy man from death." Thus, on the morning of the *jiazi* day he attacked Zhow, and did not miss the appointed date.⁶⁰

言武王將伐紂，紂使膠鬲視武王師。膠鬲問曰：欲以何日至殷？武王曰：以甲子日。膠鬲還報紂。會天大雨，道難行，武王晝夜行。或諫曰：雨甚，軍士苦之，請且休息。武王曰：吾許膠鬲以甲子日至殷，今報紂矣。吾甲子日不到，紂必殺之。吾故不敢休息，欲救賢者之死也。遂以甲子日朝誅紂，不失期也。

    When the gray-black birds assembled in flight⁶¹ 蒼鳥群飛
    Who was it that caused them to flock together? 孰使萃之

When King Wu attacked Zhow, the generals were bold and fierce as a convocation of eagles. Who caused King Wu to assemble them in such fashion? The *Odes* say: "The grand-master Shangfu [Lü Wang] / Was like a goshawk on the wing."⁶²

    60. This enjoyable story, which seems not directly related to this passage of "Heavenly Questions," can also be found in the *Lüshi chunqiu*; see Knoblock and Riegel, *Annals of Lü Buwei*, 365–66 (15/7.3). The commentary again doubles as a repository of early narrative texts.
    61. The Han commentary also glosses *cangniao* 蒼鳥 as *ying* 鷹, "goshawk." This gloss is accepted and quoted in modern dictionaries, but actually seems to be no more than a guess based on the *Odes* quotation cited for the line.
    62. *Odes* 236/8; *Maoshi zhengyi*, 16B.1144; Legge, *She King*, 436, modified. The reference is odd but not entirely irrelevant. The next line following this quotation is "Aiding that King Wu" 涼彼武王. This poem "Great Brightness" 大明 extols the conquest of Shang, and here

言武王伐紂，將帥勇猛如鷹鳥羣飛，誰使武王集聚之者乎？
《詩》曰：惟師尚父，時惟鷹揚也。

[66] Arriving they struck fiercely at the body of Zhow, 到擊紂躬
But Uncle Dan [Duke of Zhou] did not approve the act. 叔旦不嘉

When King Wu first reached Meng Ford, the eight hundred feudal lords had arrived there unexpectedly as well, and they all said that Zhow ought to be attacked. A white fish fell into the king's boat, and all the ministers said in unison: "Let us rest!" But the Duke of Zhou said: "Though we want to rest we cannot rest." Therefore it says that Uncle Dan did not approve the act.

言武王始至孟津，八百諸侯不期而到，皆曰紂可伐也。白魚入于王舟，羣臣咸曰：休哉。周公曰：雖休勿休。故曰：叔旦不嘉也。

Why did [the Duke of Zhou] survey and initiate [the return], 何親揆發足
While [the people] sighed in admiration at the mandate bestowed upon Zhou? 周之命以咨嗟

When the Duke of Zhou surveyed the mandate of Heaven at Meng Ford, he initiated the return of the army to gather together [in advance of the attack on the Shang],[63] and at this time, the commands of Zhou were already promulgated throughout the whole realm, and the people sighed in admiration at them.[64]

---

employs an avian metaphor for the prowess of King Wu's famous adviser Lü Wang 呂望. If one looks at the quatrain as a whole, the poem might simply be understood as wondering which individual was able to unite King Wu's allies. The answer might nonetheless be Lü Wang again.

63. *Shiji*, 4.156. But the references both in the original poem and the commentary do not seem to align perfectly with the received story about the famous gathering at Meng Ford (here 孟津, also written 盟津, i.e. "the ford where the great compact was made"). This is also said to be where King Wu made the "Great Declaration" 泰誓. See Legge, *Shoo King*, 281–83.

64. I believe this commentary is garbled, but is based in various stories about the conquest. For instance, the feudal lords told King Wu it was time to attack Zhow, but he made them wait (*Shiji*, 3.108); here this decision is attributed to the Duke instead. This

言周公於孟津揆度天命,發足還師而歸,當此之時,周之命令已行天下,百姓咨嗟歎而美之也。

[67] When all under Heaven had been allotted to the Yin, 授殷天下
　　　By what authority did they rule?[65] 其位安施

When Heaven first bestowed all under Heaven unto the Yin house, how was it that their royal authority was administered? It was administered as excellently as under Tang.
言天始授殷家以天下,其王位安所施用乎?善施若湯也。

　　　When success in turn met with destruction, 反成乃亡
　　　What was the fault that caused it? 其罪伊何

When the sovereign authority of the Yin was established, and then after reversals and defeats was lost, what was the fault? The fault refers to such as Zhow.
言殷王位已成,反覆亡之,其罪惟何乎?罪若紂也。

[68] Contending to dispatch the weapons of aggression, 爭遣伐器
　　　How did [King Wu] accomplish it? 何以行之

When King Wu attacked Zhow, he distributed spears and halberds, the weapons of aggressive war. They all vied to be in front: how did King Wu accomplish it?[66]
言武王伐紂,發遣干戈攻伐之器,爭先在前,獨何以行之乎。

　　　Advancing in stride, striking on both flanks, 並驅擊翼
　　　How did he take command of all this? 何以將之

The three armies of King Wu were eager for battle, and they charged forward at a gallop, competing to be in the vanguard as they reached the enemy. Those in front sang and those behind danced, and all exclaimed with joy like ducks amid pondweed, flapping and beating their wings. How did he lead them all alone?

---

may also refer in part to the story in *Shuoyuan* about King Wu's generous conduct after the victory. See Xiang Zonglu, *Shuoyuan jiaozheng*, 15.377.

65. Here the commentary directly answers the question of the main text.

66. *Shuoyuan* explains various measures that King Wu took to demonstrate that the army had no intention of reversing course on its path. See *Shuoyuan jiaozheng*, 13.329.

言武王三軍,人人樂戰,竝載驅載馳,赴敵爭先,前歌後舞,鳧藻讙呼,奮擊其翼,獨何以將率之也?

[69] Lord Zhao completed his excursion, 昭后成遊
  Reaching as far as the southern lands, 南土爰底

When King Zhao turned his back upon the rule of King Cheng and set off on his excursion, he travelled south as far as Chu. The people of Chu drowned him and so he did not return.[67]
言昭王背成王之制而出遊,南至於楚,楚人沈之,而遂不還也。

  What was the benefit for him in the end 厥利惟何
  From coming upon the white pheasant? 逢彼白雉

When King Zhao set off on his southern excursion, how did it benefit Chu? Because the Yueshang people offered him a white pheasant. But because King Zhao's favor could not be obtained, he wanted to set off personally to meet them.[68]
言昭王南遊,何以利于楚乎?以為越裳氏獻白雉,昭王德不能致,欲親往逢迎之。

[70] Why did King Mu, so clever and covetous, 穆王巧梅
  Choose to pursue his world-spanning journey? 夫何為周流

King Mu was clever with regard to the verbal commands.[69] He was greedy for conquest and went on a distant campaign against the Quanrong. There he obtained four white wolves and four white deer. From this time on the

---

67. According to *Diwang shiji*, when he reached the Han River, the boat people built him a boat out of soluble glue, which dissolved while he was crossing the river and drowned him. See *Diwang shiji*, 5.44, as also quoted in *Shiji*, 4.134n.

68. This episode is only preserved in fragmentary form in other historical sources. See, for instance, the short poem on the "White Pheasant" that concludes Ban Gu's 班固 "Eastern Capital Rhapsody" ("Dongdu fu" 東都賦), in *Wenxuan*, 1.43; Knechtges, *Selections of Refined Literature*, 1:179, citing *Han shi waizhuan*, 5.7a/b (Hightower, trans, *Han shi wai chuan*, 172).

69. As Qu Yuan was said to be in his *Shiji* biography. The commentator is evidently struggling with *mei* 梅 "plum." Wang Fuzhi proposes it is a loan for *mei* 枚 or "bridle," so the line just means that he excelled at riding, which fits since King Mu was a legendary traveler.

Yi and Di peoples did not submit, and the feudal lords did not attend court. King Mu then made further attempts to disseminate his exquisite speeches, and went to persuade them, intending to cause them all to submit to his rule.
言穆王巧於辭令,貪好攻伐,遠征犬戎,得四白狼、四白鹿。自是後夷狄不至,諸侯不朝。穆王乃更巧詞周流,而往說之,欲以懷來也。

> Putting in order all under Heaven, 環理天下
> What was it that he was searching for? 夫何索求

The one who rules should nurture his virtue so as to cause the four quarters to come submit to him. So why did he instead roam all around the realm seeking them out?
言王者當脩道德以來四方,何為乃周旋天下,而求索之也?

> [71] When the uncanny couple were selling goods, 妖夫曳衒
> What did they call out in the marketplace? 何號于市

Long ago in the past age of King You of Zhou there was a children's ditty saying: "Mulberry bow and willow quiver / Will surely mark the end of the Zhou state!" Later on, a couple were selling these items, and so people thought they must be demonic. They were caught, and dragged out into the market to be humiliated.[70]
昔周幽王前世有童謠曰:檿弧箕服,實亡周國。後有夫婦賣是器,以為妖怪,執而曳戮之於市也。

> Who was it that King You of the Zhou would execute, 周幽誰誅
> So that he obtained his concubine Bao Si? 焉得夫褒姒

Bao Si was the consort of King You of Zhou. Once when the lords of Xia were in decline, there were two divine dragons that stopped in the Xia court and said, "We are the two lords of Bao." The lord of Xia distributed silk and grains and reported to them. The dragons disappeared but their spittle remained, and it was preserved in a wooden casket. When the Xia perished, they passed it on to Yin, and when the Yin perished, they passed

---

70. Another source for this curious tale can be found in *Guoyu* (Accounts of the states); see Xu Yuangao, ed., *Guoyu jijie*, 16.473.

it on Zhou, but throughout the three dynasties no one dared to open it. By the end of the reign of King Li, people opened and examined it. The spittle flowed through the court and transformed into a dark turtle, which entered the rear chambers of the royal palace. In the rear chambers there was a serving lady who came upon it and got pregnant. She gave birth to a child, though she had no husband, and so was afraid and abandoned it. At that time the couple who had been left in the market fled in the night. On the road they heard the crying of the daughter of the lady in the rear palace. Feeling pity, they took care of her, and then fled to Bao. The people of Bao later committed a crime, and so King You was going to punish them, but they presented this girl to atone for their crime. This was Bao Si. She was made royal consort and the king was beguiled by love for her. Later on, she was killed by the Quanrong.[71]

襃姒，周幽王后也。昔夏后氏之衰也，有二神龍止於夏庭而言曰：余襃之二君也。夏后布幣糈而告之，龍亡而漦在，櫝而藏之。夏亡傳殷，殷亡傳周，比三代莫敢發也。至厲王之末，發而觀之，漦流于庭，化為玄黿，入王後宮。後宮處妾遇之而孕，無夫而生子，懼而弃之。時被戮夫婦夜亡，道聞後宮處妾所放女啼聲，哀而收之，遂奔襃。襃人後有罪，幽王欲誅之，襃人乃入此女以贖罪，是為襃姒，立以為后，惑而愛之，遂為犬戎所殺也。

[72] As the Mandate of Heaven revolves and reverses:	天命反側
How does it punish and how does it aid?	何罰何佑

The way of Heaven is that spiritual powers descend and determine the fates of men. It revolves and reverses and is not fixed. Those who are good are aided, and those who are villainous are punished.

言天道神明，降與人之命，反側無常，善者佑之，惡者罰之。

Duke Huan of Qi convened the lords nine times,	齊桓九會
But he too was murdered in the end.	卒然身殺

When Duke Huan of Qi [d. 643 BCE] appointed Guan Zhong, and convened all the lords nine times, he managed to put the whole realm in order at once. When he appointed Shu Diao and Yi Ya as his advisors,

---

71. Aside from the *Guoyu* passage cited in the previous note, this story is similar to the account in the *Shiji*; see *Shiji*, 4.186.

though, the next generations slaughtered one another, and vermin swarmed from the houses. In one man's person there is both good and bad, and the mandate of Heaven is not fixed, but punishes or aids with no fixed rule.
言齊桓公任管仲，九合諸侯，一匡天下。任豎刁、易牙，子孫相殺，蟲流出戶。一人之身，一善一惡，天命無常，罰佑之不恆也。

[73] As for that Zhow the King himself:　　　　　彼王紂之躬
　　　Who set him into disturbance and confusion?　孰使亂惑

The source of the confusion was Da Ji.[72]
惑，妲己也。

　　　Why did he loathe his own aides and assistants,　何惡輔弼
　　　And employ instead the men of slanderous gossip?　讒諂是服

Zhow hated his own aides and assistants, and did not put into practice their loyal and direct counsel, but instead engaged the gossips and slanderers.
言紂憎輔弼，不用忠直之言，而事用諂讒之人也。

[74] Why did his adviser Bi Gan revolt,　　　　比干何逆
　　　Only to be crushed and destroyed?　　　　而抑沈之

Bi Gan was a sage and one of the elders of Zhow. He admonished Zhow, and Zhow was angered and killed him by cutting out his heart.
比干，聖人，紂諸父也。諫紂，紂怒，乃殺之剖其心也。

　　　Lei Kai was obsequious and obedient,　　　雷開阿順
　　　And yet received enfeoffment.　　　　　　而賜封之

Lei Kai was a toady who was obsequious to Zhow, and thereupon received gold and jade, and was enfeoffed as a noble.
雷開，佞人也，阿順於紂，乃賜之金玉而封之也。

[75] Why does the virtue of the sages, though constant,　何聖人之一
　　　Achieve success in different places?　　　　　　卒其異方

72. Various accounts in both received and excavated texts identify Zhow's concubine Da Ji as the cause of his tyranny; see discussion in Huang Linggeng, ed., *Chuci zhangju shuzheng*, 4.1200.

King Wen was humane and wise, and was constant in his virtue, so the various parts of the realm were ultimately submissive to him.
言文王仁聖，能純一其德，則天下異方，終皆歸之也。

> Sire Mei was ground into meat paste,　　梅伯受醢
> And Master Ji feigned madness.　　　　　箕子詳狂

Sire Mei was loyal and honest, and repeatedly admonished Zhow, so Zhow was angered and killed him, grinding his body into meat paste. Master Ji saw this, and let down his hair to feign madness.
梅伯，紂諸侯也。言梅伯忠直，而數諫紂，紂怒，乃殺之，葅醢其身。箕子見之，則被髮詳狂也。

> [76] Hou Ji was the primary son already;　稷維元子
> Why did the Lord of Heaven honor him?　帝何竺之

Hou Ji's mother was Jiang Yuan. She went out and saw the footprint of the Great Man. She was startled and stepped in it, and then became pregnant and bore Hou Ji. Hou Ji from birth was humane and worthy. Why did the Lord of Heaven honor him specially?[73]
言后稷之母姜嫄，出見大人之迹，怪而履之，遂有娠而生后稷。后稷生而仁賢，天帝獨何以厚之乎？

> When [Hou Ji] was discarded on the ice,　投之於冰上
> Why did the birds keep him warm?　　　鳥何燠之

Since Jiang Yuan gave birth to Hou Ji without a father, she discarded him on the ice. There were birds that covered him up and warmed him, so he was thought to be divine, and so she took and raised him. As the *Odes* say: "He was placed on the cold ice, / And a bird screened and supported him with its wings."[74]

---

73. Hou Ji is Lord Millet, inventor of agriculture, culture-hero of the Zhou people. The birth of Hou Ji from Jiang Yuan and these events are also referred to in the poem "Giving Life to the People" 生民 (#245) in *Shijing*. The commentary cites two lines from it for the next couplet, but the opening stanza could also be cited here. See *Maoshi zhengyi*, 17A.1239–40; Legge, *She King*, 465–68.

74. *Odes* 245/3, as cited in previous note. But note that the poem does not answer this question.

言姜嫄以后稷無父而生，弃之於冰上，有鳥以翼覆薦溫之，以為神，乃取而養之。《詩》曰：誕寘之寒冰，鳥覆翼之。

[77] Why was [Hou Ji], with mighty bow and 　　　何馮弓挾矢
　　　bearing arrows,
　　Able beyond all others to lead them? 　　　殊能將之

When Hou Ji grew to maturity, he carried a great and strong bow, and bore a quiver of arrows. He was mighty in appearance and exceptional, having the talent of a great general.
言后稷長大，持大強弓，挾箭矢，桀然有殊異，將相之才。

　　Since [King Wu] had fiercely startled the sovereign 　　既驚帝切激
　　　[Zhow],
　　How did he arrive at enduring success? 　　何逢長之

King Wu was able to uphold and continue the task of Hou Ji. He carried out the retribution of Heaven by punishing Zhow. Abrupt and brutal, repeatedly erring, how did he end up as the leader of succeeding ages?
帝，謂紂也。言武王能奉承后稷之業，致天罰，加誅於紂，切激而數其過，何逢後世繼嗣之長也。

[78] When Prince Chang exclaimed upon the decline, 　　伯昌號衰
　　He wielded the whip and became master. 　　秉鞭作牧

The whip is used as a metaphor for governance. This says that when Zhow's command had disintegrated, King Wen [Prince Chang or Ji Chang 姬昌] wielded the whip and controlled the government, and served as ruler of Yongzhou.[75]
鞭以喻政。言紂號令既衰，文王執鞭持政，為雍州之牧也。

　　Why did [King Wu] take over all the Qi altars, 　　何令徹彼岐社
　　And the mandate for the dynasty of Yin? 　　命有殷國

Once King Wu had defeated Zhow, he commanded that the altars of Bin and Qi be destroyed,[76] saying that he had already received the mandate

---

75. There was a tradition in the Han that King Wen was governor (or prince, *bo* 伯) of Yongzhou. See, e.g., the commentary in *Shangshu zhengyi*, 10.307.

76. The ancient sites of worship of Heaven at Mount Bin 邠 (also written 豳) and Mount Qi 岐, in the Zhou homeland and modern Shaanxi province.

of Heaven and possessed the Yin realm. So he transferred them to be the supreme altars of all under Heaven.
言武王既誅紂，令壞邠岐之社，言己受天命而有殷國，因徙以為天下之太社也。

[79] When he transported prized possessions   遷藏就岐
      towards Mount Qi,
  Why did people follow along with him?   何能依

When King Tai [Gugong Danfu 古公亶父] and the people first moved precious belongings to occupy Qi, how did he persuade the people to follow along with him?
言太王始與百姓徙其寶藏，來就岐下，何能使其民依倚而隨之也？

  That bewitching lady in Yin: 殷有惑婦
  Why was she so vilified?   何所譏

Da Ji beguiled and misled Zhow, so he could no longer be remonstrated with.
言妲己惑誤于紂，不可復譏諫也。

[80] When Zhow presented the bloody paste,   受賜茲醢
  The Prince of the West [King Wen] protested to   西伯上告
      Heaven.

Zhow ground up Sire Mei into meat paste, and presented it to the feudal lords. King Wen received it, and made an offering reporting this to Heaven above.
西伯，文王也。言紂醢梅伯，以賜諸侯，文王受之，以祭告語於上天也。

  Why did the High Lord [of Heaven] personally   何親就上帝
  Revoke the mandate of Yin and not preserve it?   罰殷之命以不救

The "Lord on High" refers to Heaven. This says that the Lord of Heaven personally caused the punishment of Zhow. So the mandate of Yin could not have been restored.
上帝，謂天也。言天帝親致紂之罪罰，故殷之命不可復救也。

[81] When Master Wang was in the market,   師望在肆
  How did Chang [King Wen] recognize him there?   昌何識

When Lord Tai was working as a butcher in the market, how did King Wen recognize him there?
師望, 謂太公也。昌, 文王名也。言太公在市肆而屠, 文王何以識知之乎?

> When [Lü Wang] was wielding a knife and raising his cry, 鼓刀揚聲
> Why did the sovereign rejoice therein? 后何喜

When Lü Wang was wielding the knife in the market, King Wen personally went to visit him, and Lü Wang responded: "The inferior butcher is a butcher of cows; the superior butcher is a butcher of kingdoms." King Wen was pleased and brought him back home with him.
后, 謂文王也。言呂望鼓刀在列肆, 文王親往問之, 呂望對曰:「下屠屠牛, 上屠屠國。」文王喜, 載與俱歸也。

[82] When Wu set forth to assault Yin, 武發殺殷
What was it that had infuriated him? 何所悒

When King Wu wanted to defeat Zhow of Yin, why was he so infuriated that he could not bear it?
言武王發欲誅殷紂, 何所悁悒而不能久忍也?

> When he bore his spirit tablet to join in battle, 載尸集戰
> What was it that spurred him on? 何所急

This says, when King Wu attacked Zhow, bearing the spirit tablet of King Wen, he told his prince to set out, wanting to carry out Heaven's punishment swiftly, and eliminate the harm to the people.
言武王伐紂, 載文王木主, 稱太子發, 急欲奉行天誅, 為民除害也。

[83] The elder prince hung himself: 伯林雉經
What was the reason for it? 維其何故

The crown prince of Jin, Shensheng, was slandered by his stepmother Lady Li, and so hung himself.[77]
謂晉太子申生為後母驪姬所譖, 遂雉經而自殺。

---

77. The commentary here offers the almost incomprehensible gloss, "'Forest' means 'prince'" 林, 君也. It understands these lines as referring to the famous story of Shensheng

> Why did it disturb the Heavens and convulse the Earth, 何感天抑墜
> And who was still afraid of [Lady Li]? 夫誰畏懼

Lady Li slandered Shensheng, resulting in his death. That injustice stirred Heaven. She also slandered and drove away the various lords, so who was left to fear her?[78]
言驪姬讒殺申生,其冤感天,又讒逐羣公子,當復誰畏懼也?

> [84] When awesome Heaven located its Mandate, 皇天集命
> Why was [the King] so circumspect? 惟何戒之

Awesome Heaven gathered rewards and the mandate and bestowed them on the King, so why was the King not permanently reverent and fearful?
言皇天集祿命而與王者,王者何不常畏慎而戒懼也?

> When the rites were offered to all under heaven, 受禮天下
> Why did this result in [the King's] own overthrow?[79] 又使至代之

Since the King had cultivated the rites, he received the mandate of Heaven and so ruled all under Heaven. Why should someone of another surname then replace him?
言王者既已修行禮義,受天命而有天下矣,又何為至使異姓代之乎?

> [85] At first the minister of Tang was Zhi [Yi Yin], 初湯臣摯
> But later this one took on the responsibility of counsellor. 後茲承輔

---

and Lady Li, recounted in detail in the *Guoyu*; see Xu Yuangao, ed., *Guoyu jijie*, 8.275–81. Though it is probably coincidence, it is worth noting that that story features a character named Boshi 伯氏, the style name of Hutu 狐突, Shensheng's chariot driver. The commentary's explanation may be a wild guess, but also links to mythic archetypes well known to Western readers from the story of Hippolytus and Phaedra.

78. The story cited in the previous note concludes with Lady Li having Shensheng killed, and then slandering the heroic statesmen Chonger 重耳 and Guan Zhong 管仲 (Xu Yuangao, ed., *Guoyu jijie*, 8.281).

79. It might be suspected here that the authors of the commentary were baffled at the topic, and so identify the subject simple as "the King" 王者.

Tang first elevated Yi Yin to be an ordinary minister. Later, appreciating his value, he made him one of [his four prime counselors,] the Aide, Adjutant, Assistant, and Auditor, and employed his stratagems.[80]
言湯初舉伊尹，以為凡臣耳。後知其賢，乃以備輔翼承疑，用其謀也。

> Why did he ultimately serve as officer for Tang, 何卒官湯
> To honor the offerings of the ancestral succession? 尊食宗緒

Yi Yin aided Tang's rule, so he ultimately became Son of Heaven, and honored his ancestors, and carried out the rites of the King, so that his great accomplishments were passed on to his descendants.
言伊尹佐湯命，終為天子，尊其先祖，以王者禮樂祭祀，緒業流於子孫。

[86] The meritorious scion Helu was born of Meng, 勳闔夢生
But was cast away in his youth. 少離散亡

Shoumeng died, and his heir Zhufan become king. Zhufan died, and the throne was passed on to his younger brother Yuji. Yuji died, and the throne passed on to his younger brother Yiwei. Yiwei died, and his heir became King Liao. Helu [a.k.a. Helü 闔閭] was the oldest son of Zhufan. He did not become king, but in his youth was banished from the kingdom, and sent Zhuan Shezhu to kill King Liao. Thus Helu became King of Wu instead, and his descendants flourished. He made Wu Zixu his minister, and so achieved great merit.[81]
壽夢卒，太子諸樊立。諸樊卒，傳弟餘祭。餘祭卒，傳弟夷未。夷未卒，太子王僚立。闔廬，諸樊之長子也。次不得為王，少離散亡放在外，乃使專設諸刺王僚，代為吳王。子孫世盛，以伍子胥為將，大有功勳也。

---

80. *Yi cheng fu bi* 疑承輔弼 are the "four advisors" 四輔 according to the *Shangshu dazhuan* 尚書大傳, quoted in *Liji zhengyi*, 20.743. This account differs slightly.
81. The vexed succession of the Wu kings is discussed in *j.* 31 of *Shiji*. The commentary adds a mention of Wu Zixu, Helu's minister, presumably because his life story anticipates that of Qu Yuan, since he was also a talented native of Chu who was slandered by a rival at court.

> Why was [Helu] so mighty and practiced in arms, 何壯武厲
> That he could spread his reputation far and wide? 能流厥嚴

When Helu was young he was exiled, so how could he become mighty and heroic in arms, and so spread his reputation far and wide?
言闔廬少小散亡，何能壯大厲其勇武，流其威嚴也。

> [87] When Peng Keng brewed the pheasant soup, 彭鏗斟雉
> Why did the Lord consume it? 帝何饗

Peng Keng refers to Peng Zu. Modulating the flavors, he excelled in preparing the pheasant soup on behalf of Emperor Yao. Yao was pleased and partook of it.
彭鏗，彭祖也。好和滋味，善斟雉羹，能事帝堯，堯美而饗食之。

> When he achieved extraordinary longevity, 受壽永多
> How was it that it extended for such a long time?[82] 夫何久長

Peng Zu offered the pheasant soup to Yao, and Yao partook of it in order to enjoy longevity. Peng Zu reached the age of eight hundred years, but still regretted he could not live longer, complaining of "the pillow too high and the spittle too far."[83]
言彭祖進雉羹於堯，堯饗食之以壽考。彭祖至八百歲，猶自悔不壽，恨枕高而唾遠也。

> [88] When the central provinces shared the pasture, 中央共牧
> Why was the Sovereign angered? 后何怒

In the central provinces, there are bicephalous snakes that vie to eat the grasses of the pasturage, and bite and gnaw at one another. This is a metaphor for how the Yi and Di battle one another, so why should the sovereign by angered?[84]

---

82. The text is easier to understand if we read *chang* 長 as a loan for *chang* 悵, "to be distressed." See my discussion of this hypothesis from Wen Yiduo in "Text Three." But it is unclear whether the commentary reads it this way or not.

83. Huang Linggeng shows that the complaint about the pillow and spittle is related to nascent Daoist practices from the Han dynasty; see Huang Linggeng, ed., *Chuci zhangju shuzheng*, 4.1237–39.

84. This curious interpretation may relate to the maxim quoted in *Han Feizi*: "Among the vermin there is a serpent with two mouths on its body, which snap at each other as they

言中央之州，有歧首之蛇，爭共食牧草之實，自相啄嚙。以喻夷狄相與忿爭，君上何故當怒之乎？

> How could the paltry lives of bees and ants 蠭蛾微命
> Possess the strength to endure? 力何固

Insects with venomous sting like bees and ants follow the mandate of heaven and keep themselves in a stable position by means of force. Qu Yuan uses this as a metaphor for how the Man and Yi poison one another and keep doing so forever, when they ought only to worry about Qin and Wu.
言蠭蛾有蠚毒之蟲，受天命，負力堅固。屈原以喻蠻夷自相毒蠚，固其常也。獨當憂秦吳耳。

[89] When a girl was startled while gathering vetch, 驚女采薇
   Why did a deer protect her? 鹿何祐

Long ago there was a girl who went to gather vetch. Somebody surprised her and she ran away, and so obtained a deer. Her family then thrived, and was blessed by Heaven.[85]
言昔者有女子采薇菜，有所驚而走，因獲得鹿，其家遂昌熾，乃天祐之。

> North as far as the Winding Waters, 北至回水
> In meeting there, why did they delight nonetheless? 萃何喜

The girl was startled and fled north all the way to the Winding Waters. She stopped there and obtained a deer, and so was delighted and happy.
言女子驚而北走，至於回水之上，止而得鹿，遂有禧喜也。

[90] When the elder brother had a keen-toothed hound, 兄有噬犬
   Why did the younger seek it? 弟何欲

---

vie for food. Ultimately they murder each other, which is the same as committing suicide. When ministers vie with one another such that they cause the ruin of their own kingdom, it is just like this serpent." 蟲有虺者，一身兩口，爭食相齕也。遂相殺，因自殺。人臣之爭事而亡其國者，皆虺類也。See Wang Xianshen, ed., *Han Feizi jijie*, 23.189–90.

85. The poem may be referring to a legend about Bo Yi 伯夷 and Shu Qi 叔齊, but the Han commentary does not connect these lines to any named individuals at all.

The older brother is the Prince of Qin ... the younger brother is the prince's younger brother Qian. The Prince of Qin had a keen-toothed hound, and his younger brother Qian asked for it.
兄,謂秦伯也。……弟,秦伯弟鍼也。言秦伯有齧犬,弟鍼欲請之。

> Though bartering it for a hundred in gold,   易之以百兩
> Why was he ultimately without any estate?   卒無祿

The Prince of Qin was unwilling to give Qian the dog, so Qian traded one hundred in gold for it. He was still unwilling, so he chased Qian and stole all his emoluments and titles.[86]
言秦伯不肯與弟鍼犬,鍼以百兩金易之,又不聽,因逐鍼而奪其爵祿也。

> [91] A bolt of lightning in the twilight sky: 薄暮雷電
> What should I fear if I return?   歸何憂

Qu Yuan finished writing all his questions on the wall, and as twilight fell he was ready to depart. Then there was a great storm with lightning, and his worries returned. He explained himself, saying, "What should I fear if I return?"
言屈原書壁,所問略訖,日暮欲去,時天大雨雷電,思念復至。自解曰:歸何憂乎?

> If we do not respect his authority,   厥嚴不奉
> How can we importune the Lord [of Heaven]?   帝何求

The King of Chu was befuddled and trusted in slanderous counsel. As his authority and repute were collapsing daily, he could no longer be served dutifully. Though he requested blessings from the Lord of Heaven, the spirits would do nothing for him.

---

86. The Han commentary offers an explanation of this quatrain based on a story about the Duke of Qin and his younger brother Qian 鍼. It has no other extant source, but corresponds in part to *Zuozhuan*, Duke Zhao, year 1, which mentions that Qian fled to Jin with one thousand chariots: "Qian of Qin had been a favorite son of Lord Huan [r. 604–577] and was like a second ruler under Lord Jing [r. 576–537]. Their mother said to Qian, 'If you do not depart, I fear that you will be sent away.' In the fifth month, on the *guimao* day (25), when Qian went to Jin, his chariots numbered one thousand." Durrant et al., *Zuo Tradition*, 1319.

言楚王惑信讒佞,其威嚴當日墮,不可復奉成,雖從天帝求福,神無如之何。

[92] Hiding and skulking in cavernous places, 伏匿穴處
What more is there to say? 爰何云

I will retreat to the riverbanks, taking refuge by hiding in cavernous places. What more is there to say?
吾將退於江濱,伏匿穴處耳,當復何言乎?

The army of Jing achieved a meritorious deed, 荊師作勳
But how was it to endure? 夫何長

In the beginning, a maiden from a village near the border of Chu was competing with a maiden from a village near the border of Wu to harvest the mulberry, and the two wounded each other. Their families were angered and attacked each other. Then Chu's armies began an assault, conquering the border town of Wu, so their anger began to achieve something. At that time Qu Yuan remonstrated again, saying, "It was we who first acted improperly; I fear we cannot long endure thusly."[87]
初,楚邊邑之處女,與吳邊邑處女爭采桑於境上,相傷,二家怒而相攻,於是楚為此興師,攻滅吳之邊邑,而怒始有功。時屈原又諫,言我先為不直,恐不可久長也。

[93] May he see his faults and change his ways— 悟過改更
What more have we to say? 我又何言

He wants to make the King of Chu perceive the truth, so he cites his faults, such as surrendering to Wu, when he did not follow counsel and was attacked. This says that the disaster began with trivialities.
欲使楚王覺悟,引過自與,以謝於吳,不從其言,遂相攻伐。言禍起於細微也。

Guang [King Helu] of Wu contested the realm, 吳光爭國
And was long victorious over us. 久余是勝

---

87. This amusing episode can be found in *Shiji*, 31.1462, but there it is dated to the rule of King Liao 僚 (r. 526–515), long before Qu Yuan was born.

When Wu and Chu were at war, by the time of King Helu, Wu soldiers invaded the capital at Ying, and King Zhao took flight. Thus the text says that they won a great victory over us.
言吳與楚相伐，至於闔廬之時，吳兵入郢都，昭王出奔。故曰「吳光爭國，久余是勝」，言大勝我也。

[94] Why did she pass by all the lanes and cross the altars, 何環閭穿社
    Even so far as the grave mounds? 以及丘陵
    Such wantonness, such wildness, 是淫是蕩
    So that she gave birth to Ziwen.[88] 爰出子文

Ziwen was the chief minister (*lingyin*) of Chu. Ziwen's mother was the daughter of Duke Yun. Roaming around the altars in the country, and committing adultery among the grave mounds, she gave birth to Ziwen. She abandoned him in Yunmeng, where a tiger nursed him. Thinking it a miracle of divine origin, she took him back and raised him herself. The people of Chu called breastfeeding *gou*, and called the tiger *wutu*, so he was given the name Dou Gouwutu, styled Ziwen, and when he grew older, he became a talented and upstanding man.
子文，楚令尹也。子文之母，鄖公之女，旋穿閭社，通於丘陵以淫，而生子文，弃之夢中，有虎乳之，以為神異，乃取收養焉。楚人謂乳為穀，謂虎為於菟，故名鬭穀於菟，字子文，長而有賢仁之才也。

[95] I warn Duao 吾告堵敖
    That he will not long survive. 以不長

Duao was a worthy man of Chu. When Qu Yuan was exiled, he said to [of?] Duao, "The state of Chu is going to decline, and will not endure much longer."[89]
堵敖，楚賢人也。屈原放時，語堵敖曰：「楚國將衰，不復能久長也。」

---

88. I follow the variant text provided in the Han commentary, which seems to fit better with the prosodic scheme of the poem as a whole. This is a rare case where the commentary also seems to respond to the entire quatrain rather than just one couplet. The alternative reading is 何環穿自閭社丘陵，爰出子文. See *Chuci buzhu*, 4.118; Wen Yiduo, "Tianwen shuzheng," 634–35.

89. Again the commentary is anachronistic, as discussed in chapter 1 above.

> How could the trial of the sovereign accord myself   何試上自予
> A reputation for loyalty more illustrious?   忠名彌彰

Qu Yuan said, "How dare I test my sovereign, and so contradict my own reputation for loyalty and honesty, which will be prominent and glorious to later generations? Because we share a surname, I am deeply distraught in my heart, and my loyalty to him cannot perish."
屈原言我何敢嘗試君上，自干忠直之名，以顯彰後世乎?誠以同姓之故，中心懇惻，義不能已也。

CHAPTER TWO

Liu Zongyuan's Critique and Affirmation of "Heavenly Questions"

> Understanding in a dialogue is not simply an acting out and assertion of one's own standpoint, but a transformation into something shared, in which one does not remain as one was to begin with.
>
> —Gadamer, *Truth and Method*[1]

As Gadamer observes, our use of language and our strategies of interpretation are not one-sided acts under our direction. Instead, we participate in and construct ongoing dialogues with other voices past and present. In exchange with an interlocutor, we do not just receive or transmit information, but rather participate in an event, an experience, that assumes its own significance. In order to read an ancient text, one has to construct a shared language, in the sense of creating a body of translational equivalents to the source text; one has to be able not just to identify the original meaning but also to be able to comment on it. Reading has a productive component in conjunction with its receptive component—and how much more apparent this is in the case of a text that consists of a series of questions!

We are not the first readers of the "Heavenly Questions." The classical commentators also are participating in a dialogue with it. We have noted above that the Han commentary to the poem often neglects a proper explanation of what the text is saying in favor of answering the questions in its own creative ways. Even the sober and reticent interpretations of more recent scholarship are in their own way putting forth a response and indicating their own views on the issues at hand, not simply the mean-

---

1. Gadamer, *Wahrheit und Methode*, 360 (cf. translation in *Truth and Method*, 387): "Verständigung im Gespräch ist nicht ein bloßes Sichausspielen und Durchsetzen des eigenen Standpunktes, sondern eine Verwandlung ins Gemeinsame hin, in der man nicht bleibt, was man war."

ing of the text. Our understanding of the "Heavenly Questions" and other classic works is likely to be more sophisticated if we integrate this element of literary response into our view. In fact, I would make the stronger claim that it is necessary to incorporate some of the traditional exegesis of the text into our own interpretation. An attempt to strike directly at the original meaning, skipping beyond any of the traditional commentators, is doomed to fail, not simply because the traditional commentators provide a glimpse at interpretive worlds no longer available to us; but also because the traditional exegesis has already transformed the meaning of the text. That is, whatever "Heavenly Questions" means, the commentary of the *Chuci zhangju* is part of that meaning as well, even if in many cases one can correct or reject it, just as with other interpretations and responses.

To take a parallel case, "Sublimating Sorrow" ("Lisao") was of course the most imitated and most closely studied poem in the *Elegies of Chu*. Depending on one's guesses about dating and authorship, it may be that a majority of the contents of the anthology consists of imitations and responses to "Sublimating Sorrow" from Han or late Warring States (positing that the Song Yu poems, for instance, might be from Chu students of the poem). Numerous poems from the Han were explicitly modeled on "Sublimating Sorrow," even if they presented different points of view.[2] All these responses take for granted that "Sublimating Sorrow" is a document of Qu Yuan's biography. One might criticize this interpretation as history; there has always been some uncertainty about how "Sublimating Sorrow" relates, exactly, to Qu Yuan's suicide. But they belong in some sense to the comprehensive meaning of "Sublimating Sorrow" today, because they are examples of meanings that well-informed readers have discovered within the poem.

Even the "Summons to the Soul" ("Zhaohun" 招魂), apparently one of the more esoteric pieces in the original anthology, can be shown to have exerted considerable influence and have been a source of inspiration throughout the ensuing history of Chinese literature.[3] Its famous envoi with its lament for the "pity of spring" originally must refer to the soul of the individual being mourned in the poem, and yet in medieval literature it

---

2. One of the finest examples, by Zhang Heng 張衡 (78–139), is discussed in Knechtges, "A Journey to Morality."

3. See Williams, *Chinese Poetry as Soul-Summoning*, for a further consideration of this topic.

is continually reused and reworked for new situations.⁴ But we should not think of this situation as one of misreading or forgetting. When readers discover new meanings in old texts, they are participating in a dialogue *in which both participants are changed*. The change may be only infinitesimal, but to the extent that we are speaking of poetic subtleties, it cannot therefore be disregarded.

From this point of view, Liu Zongyuan's 柳宗元 (773–819) "Heavenly Responses" ("Tiandui" 天對), to be considered in this chapter, is one of the most important interpretations of "Heavenly Questions" from any period. Liu already evinces a critical consciousness towards the poem and its Han commentary, even if he can only make some modest steps at revising the earlier understandings of the poem. But at the same time, he goes further than almost any reader or commentator in exploring the essential themes of the poem. His own deep consideration of the theme of Heaven's justice leads to him to elaborate on this as the key message of both the source poem and his own response to it. But at the same time, by responding to the poem in his own knotty, archaicizing verse, which often adds further questions rather than answering the original ones, Liu truly participates in a dialogue with the source text, achieving one of the most important premodern interpretations of any poem in the *Elegies of Chu*.

A Predecessor to Liu's Response

By contrast with the other key poems in the anthology, the "Heavenly Questions" was rarely imitated directly in literary form. Medieval poets referred to Qu Yuan's daring in questioning Heaven (*wen tian* 問天),⁵ but few thought of copying the form and nature of the original poem. It seems likely that it was simply too difficult for readers in the medieval period to make sense of the poem as the Han commentary had presented it, and they had trouble engaging with it in its entirety. This was not just a matter of scholarship *per se* but also of the technological context. After

---

4. Williams, "The Pity of Spring."
5. For example, Liu Zhangqing 劉長卿, in *Quan Tang shi*, 151.1563; Fang Gan 方干, in *Quan Tang shi*, 650.7470; Jiaoran 皎然, in *Quan Tang shi*, 820.9250; most famously Li He 李賀, in *Quan Tang shi*, 393.4429.

all, woodblock printing only appeared in the late Tang; for most of the medieval period, texts were circulating solely in handwritten copies, and it would have been difficult to do the kind of textual criticism that gradually established standard editions of both the poem itself and all the historical sources needed to correct and evaluate it. The great imperial project of collation and commentary for the Five Classics (*Wujing zhengyi* 五經正義) is the exception that proves this rule. Another great medieval commentary was Li Shan's 李善 commentary to the *Wenxuan* 文選 anthology, but even this seems to have circulated in multiple versions, and has itself been restored to us by the work of Qing and modern philologists.[6] In general, medieval poetry circulated in fluid and unstable forms, and it was rare that readers and scholars were able to devote themselves to painstaking examination of ancient texts (outside the Classics).[7]

Even Jiang Yan 江淹 (444–505), a Six Dynasties poet renowned for his creative imitations—poems composed in the style of earlier works—did not quite manage it. Jiang's greatest achievement was the set of thirty "Poems in Diverse Forms" ("Zati shi" 雜體詩), a suite of poems that provides not just an outline history of pentasyllabic verse up to his own time, but also a model of criticism and interpretation, identifying distinctive styles and personalities but also skipping freely among them, resolving the interactions of reader and text in thirty different ways, each characteristic of Jiang himself.[8] Among Jiang's other numerous poems of imitation are several important pieces borrowing from the imagery, style, and prosody of the *Elegies of Chu*, notably the "*Chuci* in the Mountains" ("Shan zhong Chuci" 山中楚辭).[9] "Verses on the Remote Past" ("Suigu pian" 遂古篇), by contrast, is avowedly modeled after the "Heavenly Questions," the first two words of which are "remote past" (*suigu*), and may also be a sequel to another piece of this type, Jiang's nonextant "Verses on the Creator of Transformations" ("Zaohua pian" 造化篇).

---

6. See Fu Gang, *Wenxuan banben yanjiu*, 210–39.

7. On the fluidity exhibited in circulation of poetry in the Tang, see Nugent, *Manifest on Words, Written on Paper*.

8. Williams, *Imitations of the Self*.

9. Ding Fulin, ed., *Jiang Wentong ji jiaozhu*, 1705–16. For a study of these poems and others relating to the *Chuci*, see Williams, *Imitations of the Self*, chap. 6, "Allusive and Illusive Journeys."

Unlike his achievement in his other imitations, though, Jiang Yan seems to have missed the point of the "Heavenly Questions," since his version is composed solely in the declarative mode. The following passage in the middle of the poem describes some of the deities of the cosmos:

Below the nine levels of Earth,	九地之下
just as in Heaven –	如有天兮
The Earthking has a nine-crooked body,[10]	土伯九約
who would go there first? –	竁若先兮
In the West is the god Reaper of Rushes,[11]	西方蓐收
charged with the Metal Gate –	司金門兮
At the Northern Pole is Yuqiang,[12]	北極禺強
who endures there ever –	為常存兮
The two daughters of the High Lord	帝之二女
roam by the Xiang and Yuan rivers –	遊湘沅兮
Nightbright and Candleflame	宵明燭光
face you glittering and gleaming –[13]	向煌煌兮
Grand Unity and the Controller of Destinies,	太一司命
first among the spirits there –	鬼之元兮
"Mountain Spirit," "Lament for the Fallen,"[14]	山鬼國殤
are composed for those roaming spirits –[15]	為遊魂兮

In spite of his chosen subject matter, Jiang Yan is diverted by the gravity of the other Chuci poems back to pieces other than "Heavenly Questions." In just this short space, he references "Summons to the Soul," "Far Roaming," and especially the "Nine Songs," actually naming two of its poems explicitly. But it is evident that he asks no questions, instead remarking in some

---

10. "Summons to the Soul," line 85; Williams, *Elegies of Chu*, 89. But here I follow the *Chuci zhangju* interpretation of *jiuyue* 九約 as referring to the god's body, rather than to Nine Gates.

11. For the "Reaper of Rushes" see "Far Roaming," line 120; Williams, *Elegies of Chu*, 78.

12. Yuqiang is a divinity of the North and descendant of the Yellow Emperor. Jiang Yan perhaps identified him with Bo Qiang 伯強 in "Heavenly Questions," quatrain 10, but this is different from the interpretation of the Han commentary.

13. According to Guo Pu, the style names of the two daughters of Shun; see Yuan Ke, ed., *Shanhaijing jiaozhu*, 12.277.

14. Two of the poems in the "Nine Songs." Grand Unity and the Greater and Lesser Controllers of Destinies also feature in the titles of other songs.

15. Ding Fulin, ed., *Jiang Wentong ji jiaozhu*, 1766–68.

awe at the pantheon of spirits mentioned within the old poetic corpus. Even the meter, as we can see here, is closer to that of the "Summons to the Soul," being XXXX/XXXP, where P is a prosodic particle, in this case *xi* 兮 (in the "Summons to the Soul," *suo* 些). What might seem oversights for a dedicated reading of the "Heavenly Questions" are probably not accidents or errors, but merely reflect that it was the "Summons" and "Nine Songs" that drew Jiang's attention with their vivid pictorial imagination, and which he attempted to recall by his meter.

The succeeding passage introduces a new element to the *Chuci* tradition:

At Kapilavastu,[16]	迦維羅衛
the Way was most revered –	道最尊兮
His body made of gold,	黃金之身
who could trace its origin? –	誰能原兮
The fixed stars were not visible then,	恆星不見
a matter beyond any discussion –[17]	頗可論兮
His sayings scintillated and shone,	其說彬炳
rich in sagely phrases –	多聖言兮
Within the six corners of the cosmos,	六合之內
human hearts are ever muddled –	心常渾兮
Men both dim and brilliant are beguiled in nature,	幽明詭性
ruling both wise and foolish –	令智惛兮

Here Jiang Yan inserts a brief encomium to the Buddha to match the native Chinese divinities mentioned previously. Only a few of Jiang Yan's poems touch explicitly on Buddhism, but they are enough to show that he found a lasting consolation in its teachings, particularly after the death of his son.[18]

---

16. Birthplace of the historical Budda, Siddhartha Gautama.

17. Some Buddhists identified 687 BCE as the year of the Buddha's birth based on the omen reported in that year of stars falling from Heaven. See *Bianzheng lun* 辯正論: "Of old, in the seventh year of Duke Zhuang [of Lu], in the fourth month, on the *xinmao* day [March 23, 687], during the night the stars were not visible. The stars fell like rain during the night. And some interpreted this as being the moment on the eighth day of the fourth month when the Buddha was born." 昔春秋莊公七年四月辛卯。夜恆星不見, 夜中星 隕如雨。而意說者, 以為四月八日佛生時也。*T* 2110: 52.520a/b. See also Franke, "On Chinese Traditions Concerning the Dates of the Buddha," 444.

18. See translation and discussion of one such piece in Kroll, "Huilin on Black and White, Jiang Yan on Wuwei."

Jiang Yan's elegant response to the "Heavenly Questions" adds a new and philosophical layer of Buddhism to this poetic tradition.

Jiang Yan's imitations of other *Chuci* poems manage to convey the keen sense of loneliness and longing that he finds in the original poems, yet somehow strained into a more delicate filament of Six Dynasties poeticism. But in the case of "Verses on the Remote Past," Jiang Yan's creative imitation is generally less successful, matching the obscurity of the source but not its plaintive questioning. "Verses on the Remote Past" has never been one of Jiang's more popular poems, and was even excluded from the *Sibu congkan* edition of his collected works. Though it remains an intriguing work, it misses the essence of the "Heavenly Questions," the interrogation of Heaven's intent, the inquiry into the justice of historical events. This is an element of the poem that might be called "uranodicy," after Leibniz's coinage "theodicy," since the issue is the justice of Heaven rather than of a single creator god. One might have expected Jiang Yan to be interested in this theme as well, based on his "Rhapsody on Bitter Regret" ("Hen fu" 恨賦) and other works of protest and sorrow. But cosmic justice is a theme that requires not just passion and eloquence, but also a certain philosophical bent which Jiang Yan does not seem to have possessed. In particular, he missed the formal feature of interrogativity, which is so indispensable to the original poem. To perpetuate the dialogue in another age, a poetic response would need not only to follow the model of the source, but also to ask new questions.

Liu Zongyuan's Heavenly Responses

By contrast with Jiang Yan, Liu Zongyuan composed a different kind of response to "Heavenly Questions" that explicitly highlights the interrogativity of the original poem. The need for this interrogativity was clear in Liu's time, in context of his own broader reflections on state power and political history from a position of marginality. Like most of Liu's major works, this was likely written during his period of rustication to the south in Yongzhou 永州 (modern Lingling 零陵 county, Hunan). Liu had been involved in the reform efforts of the Wang Shuwen 王叔文 (753–806) clique as a precocious scholar at the court of Emperor Shunzong 順宗

(r. February–August 805). When Shunzong suffered a stroke, Liu and his friends were expelled to remote parts of the realm, in Liu's case to be administrator of Yongzhou. He seemed in 815 to have been reprieved when he was recalled to the capital, but in fact, upon his return, he was immediately sent away to an even more remote locale, Liuzhou 柳州 (in modern Guangxi province), where he died a few years later: poor, isolated, and a total failure in politics, his only hope that his writings would win him immortal fame.[19]

During his ten years in Yongzhou, Liu wrote a vast number of poems and essays on different topics, in various ways expressing his dissatisfaction with current modes of thought, his longing for the capital, and above all his longing for restitution from the ruler. Many of these writings naturally borrowed from the themes and forms of the *Elegies*. If Liu had not identified with Qu Yuan before his demotion, he certainly found reason to empathize with Qu Yuan's story as he composed critical and theoretic works some seven hundred miles from the capital. Among other works, he occasionally wrote *fu* 賦 (rhapsodies) and other extended poems in the vein of "Sublimating Sorrow" and "Summons to the Soul." As one might expect, even in these pieces he found opportunities to adopt a searching examination of heaven's justice; Liu was not a man to take justice for granted.[20]

---

19. William H. Nienhauser's edited volume *Liu Tsung-yuan* offers valuable insights but is quite brief and unfortunately has not been followed by much scholarship in English. Stephen Owen keenly noted at the time of its publication that "this forcing Liu into a biographical mold to fit which all the inconsistencies and irregularities have been pressed away, leaves one with the feeling that there is much more to him." (Review of Nienhauser, 520). Chen Jo-shui's *Liu Tsung-yüan and Intellectual Change in T'ang China, 773–819* is a valuable survey but focuses on intellectual history and somewhat neglects Liu's literary originality. Moreover, Chen represents Liu as essentially a conventional Confucian thinker, which seems to me true at the level of ideas but not so much with regard to style and expression. In Chinese, we are fortunate to have Sun Changwu's two splendid studies, *Liu Zongyuan zhuanlun* (a more traditional biography arranged by chronology) and *Liu Zongyuan pingzhuan* (containing a traditional biography but also thematic studies of Liu's theory of Heaven, relations with the Three Teachings, etc.). See also the fine biography by Shimosada Masahiro, *Ryū Sōgen: Gyakkō o ikinuita utsukushiki tamashii*.

20. See also Williams, *Chinese Poetry as Soul Summoning*, chap. 3, "Summoning Wronged Souls in the Tang."

While these other pieces may have touched on questions of justice and man's fate, in one poem Liu dealt in great detail with the problems raised by "Heavenly Questions." In fact, he wrote a poem the same length of the original in the *Elegies*, responding to it almost line by line: this is the "Heavenly Responses" ("Tiandui" 天對). Liu's response is such a complex work, containing the entire "Heavenly Questions" with Liu's patient and elaborate verse responses, that it requires a detailed examination here. No preface survives, unfortunately, although there are occasional annotations, often criticizing the Han commentary.[21] Because, as our discussion below will demonstrate, Liu's poem is composed at least in part in the voice of Heaven responding to the queries of the original poem, its title might also be translated as "Heaven Responds," but for consistency with usage throughout this book I will use instead the straightforward rendering "Heavenly Responses."

Liu wrote the poem at a momentous time in his life and also in Chinese history; half a century after the An Lushan rebellion, when the Tang dynasty was still struggling to resume its former glories, ultimately unsuccessfully, while Liu's own teachers and friends, as well as Liu himself, were actively working to rebuild a Confucian order, and to reconceive the role of writing in relation to political and religious order.[22] "Heavenly Responses" does not quite fit into the picture of Liu Zongyuan as a reformer, though, and instead exhibits the paradoxical, self-questioning, agonizingly self-reflective interrogation of traditional culture; it may be Liu's highest achievement.[23] The poem received relatively little attention until the waning days of the Great Proletariat Cultural Revolution, when it was the subject of detailed commentaries in Chinese.[24] Though this reflected

---

21. See Tozaki, "*Ryū Sōgen shū* chū ni mirareru 'jichū,'" to be discussed in more detail below.

22. Much of Sun Changwu's work has examined this topic from various angles, in particular, *Liu Zongyuan pingzhuan*, 139–284. For a discussion of Liu and Han Yu on *guwen* in particular, see DeBlasi, *Reform in the Balance*, 115–45.

23. This has not been explored as fully in either English or Chinese scholarship as it deserves, but there are numerous suggestive discussions in Japanese, notably Matsumoto Hajime's chapter on "The Grammar of Self-Castigation" (Jiko shobatsu no bunpō 自己処罰の文法), in *Ryū Sōgen kenkyū*, 295–365.

24. Specifically, *Tianwen Tiandui zhu* and *Tianwen Tiandui yizhu*. I have relied heavily on the former, compiled collectively by the Chinese department at Fudan University, which

a general boom in Liu Zongyuan studies, it is striking that the "Heavenly Responses," of all pieces, received special attention—perhaps because the Cultural Revolution had made newly relevant the existential questioning of both the ancient poem and Liu's medieval response to it.

"Heavenly Responses" makes the most of Liu's varied talents as poet, scholar, and politician. What is critical to recognize, in reading the poem, is that Liu was not a rebel; he would not willingly have adopted the persona of the "madman of Chu" railing in his exile, desperation, and blindness against the ruling authority. To the contrary, Liu conceived of himself as a born administrator; he was eager to participate in governing the state, and thought deeply about policy questions. Thus, when the Wang Shuwen clique was defeated and he was sent to rural Hunan, instead of writing self-pitying verses or turning against his former self, to the contrary, he wrote even more passionately and earnestly about how to make sense of history and politics.[25] The first goal of his "Heavenly Responses" is very much to rationalize the text, to explain its errors, to reject its superstition and mystification.

At the same time, Liu was also a dedicated rhetorician. He did not think about policy and justice in abstract terms but rather by means of history, genres, and literary expression. A key element in his overall thought was his advocacy of reforming modes of literary expression and restoring the best aspects of ancient writing. Though recent scholarship tends to treat the term "*guwen* movement" 古文運動 with some caution, it is certainly true that Liu himself was a *guwen* writer and thinker. In particular, he singled out Western Han writings as a model for his own time, and was

---

at the time included Wang Yunxi 王運熙, Zhang Peiheng 章培恆, and other luminaries. So far as I am aware, the "Tiandui" has never before been translated in its entirety into a foreign language. It has been used extensively in Chinese scholarship, even going back to the *Chuci buzhu*, which cites it frequently. You Guoen's *Tianwen zuanyi*, to be discussed more in the fourth chapter, patiently cites Liu's poem stanza by stanza after the original text and the Han commentary.

25. Chen Jo-shui's overview of Liu's "Declaration of Principles: *Tao* and Antiquity" (*Liu Tsung-yüan and Intellectual China in T'ang China*, 81–98) gives a good sense of his positive thought in this regard, expounding the centrality of the Confucian Way of governance, though it must be said that Liu (and hence by necessity his interpreters) was often vague on the details here.

in this sense a conscious archaicist.²⁶ He was never a doctrinaire moralist, though. Even though he frequently avowed the necessity of employing literature to Confucian ends, as Chen Jo-shui remarks, "His literary practice was at times incongruous with his theory. It appears that he often treated writing as a form of art in its own right."²⁷ With regard to specific literary genres, indeed, we see Liu both borrowing archaic elements from Han or pre-Qin writing, and also innovating in creative ways, or indeed often doing both of these at the same time.

The "Heavenly Responses" itself is classified within Liu's collected works not as one of the primary poetic genres (*fu* 賦, *shi* 詩, etc.) but instead as a *dui* 對, "response" or "dialogue." While not a classical genre precisely, Liu's understanding of the *dui* seems to derive from the "hypothetical discourse" (*shelun* 設論) and perhaps above all from "Fisherman" ("Yufu" 漁父) and "Divination" ("Buju" 卜居) in the *Chuci*.²⁸ For instance, in Liu's concise "Responding to One Who Congratulated Me" ("Dui hezhe" 對賀者), someone from the capital comes upon Liu in his reclusion, and says that he had come to commiserate (*yan* 唁) with him, but that upon seeing Liu's serene countenance, he should rather congratulate (*he* 賀) him. Liu then responds with a philosophical explanation of how his eremitic detachment is actually the superficial expression of his deep sorrow.²⁹ While this kind of short essayistic composition looks entirely different from "Heavenly Responses" in either prosody or substance, these *dui* works together constitute a vivid tableau of Liu's dedication to the creative revival of ancient literary forms.

Even in the context of Liu's generic and stylistic originality, though, it remains unclear why he would pick out the "Heavenly Questions," in

---

26. Liu Zongyuan's explicit and sophisticated thought in this area is encapsulated, among other places, in his remarkable "Liu Zongzhi *Xihan wenlei xu*" 劉宗直西漢文類序. See *Liu Zongyuan ji*, 21.575–775; discussion in Sun Changwu, *Liu Zongyuan pingzhuan*, 261.

27. Chen, *Liu Tsung-yüan and Intellectual China*, 133.

28. On the former, the definite resource is Declercq, *Writing against the State*. The latter works have not been sufficiently studied because they are hard to fit into either a biographical analysis of Qu Yuan (since they are obviously fictionalized) or a literary study of his works (since they include him as a protagonist), but see Timothy Chan on "Fishermanism" in *Considering the End*, 191ff.

29. *Liu Zongyuan ji*, 14.361–62.

particular, to engage with so closely. This choice has to reflect not just matters of style and technique, but also of content. And with regard to the content of the poem, it is clear that even if Liu did object to certain features of the original poem as being overly supernatural or credulous, he certainly did not reject its content in totality. After all, there would be no point in writing such a long and detailed response to a poem for which he had little regard. Thus, his response has to be understood in light of his fascination and deep concern with many of the historical episodes and even—*pace* his historical materialist admirers in contemporary China—legendary archetypes from the remote past.

The appeal of "Heavenly Responses" lies in this ambivalent set of impulses within Liu's own mind; his admiration and criticism for the text, each reacting to one another in turn in a kind of creative perpetual motion machine. And yet all of this action takes place against the background of Heaven itself, awesome and yet imperturbable, the source of cosmic order and yet never intervening in the affairs of men. On one hand, Liu rejects simplistic ideas of a Heavenly mandate passing from one ruler to the next; but the comprehensive effect of his long response to "Heavenly Questions" must ultimately convey a certain awe for Heaven's power. The poem returns over and over to a critique of certain superstitions and legendary accounts, but the critique is framed in the voice of Heaven itself, and superstition is seen more than anything as a kind of slander against a supreme Heavenly power that neglects to interfere with humanity primarily out of disdain for human frailty and ignorance. In appreciating this ultrahuman, even cosmic perspective, it is also useful to keep in mind Liu's abiding fondness for Buddhist thought and practice: while denying any direct intervention from a higher power, Liu searched for an underlying principle, which he sometimes seems to identify with a Buddhist concept of emptiness (śūnyatā).[30] In places within his "Heavenly Responses," as we have seen, Liu writes in the voice of Heaven, and he is able to imagine himself looking down on history *sub specie aeternitatis* because he is well acquainted, both in mind and body, with some kind of transcendent power.

The opening lines of "Heavenly Responses" can give one sense of its overall agenda:

---

30. See Sun Changwu's enlightening discussion in *Liu Zongyuan zhuanlun*, 236–37; I also return to this topic at the end of this chapter.

The so-called chaos at the very beginning	本始之茫
Is only something transmitted by fabulists.	誕者傳焉
Magnific numinosity divided in darkness:	鴻靈幽紛
What can even be said of it?	曷可言焉

In response to the vague speculations of the original poem, Liu points out that only liars, "fabulists," would invent stories about a phase of history before any human observer was present. Indeed, one theme of the poem is Liu's consistent, lifelong skepticism of the superstitious stories of fables and omens that were incorporated into the Confucian canon. But when Liu goes on to comment, "What can be said of it?" he is, curiously enough, returning to the interrogative mode of the source poem rather than concluding with his own critique. This is the bizarre and paradoxical aspect of his response as a whole. On one hand, he is clearly critiquing the "Heavenly Questions," but at the same time, he is also carefully retracing the rhetoric of the original poem and presenting his own ideas in a variation on that same poetic voice.

For Liu's poem is written in a remarkable, archaicizing pastiche of the original, in keeping with the diction, syntax, and prosody that he found in his *Chuci* source. In that sense, "Heavenly Responses" turns out to be a relatively comprehensive Tang-era demonstrations of *guwen* ideology in practice. Many passages borrow from the original "Heavenly Questions" while adding stylistic layers from the *Odes*. Consider the following passage on the legendary ancestor of the Zhou dynasty, Lord Millet (Hou Ji 后稷). Here, as elsewhere throughout this chapter, I present the original text of "Heavenly Questions" first before Liu's responses, since they are very often incomprehensible without the full context of the original questions (not to mention, often difficult to comprehend even with that context included):[31]

[76] *Hou Ji was the primary son already;*	稷維元子
Why did the Lord of Heaven honor him?	帝何竺之
When he was discarded on the ice,	投之於冰上
Why did the birds keep him warm?	鳥何燠之

---

31. *Liu Zongyuan ji*, 14.392. Throughout this chapter and the translation of Liu's entire poem in "Text Two," I present my translation of the original text of "Heavenly Questions" in italics, to distinguish it from my translation of Liu's original Tang-era verses.

[77]　Why was [Hou Ji], with mighty bow and bearing arrows, 何馮弓挾矢
　　　Able beyond all others to lead them? 殊能將之
　　　Since [King Wu] had fiercely startled the sovereign [Zhow], 既驚帝切激
　　　How then did he arrive at enduring success? 何逢長之

　　　Qi [the Discarded One] was charmed and deserving; 棄靈而功
　　　But why did [the Lord's] favor make itself evident? 篤胡爽焉
　　　Warmed by the birds' wings on the ice, 翼冰以炎
　　　What kind of honor or elevation was this? 盍崇長焉
　　　Since he was both majestic and intelligent, 既岐既嶷
　　　He was capable of taking charge of them. 宜庸將焉
　　　Zhow's harshness was such a provocation 紂凶以啓
　　　That King Wu was able long to continue his reign. 武紹尚焉

The Han commentary here is not very satisfactory, since it identifies both the subjects of the first quatrain and of the first half of the second quatrain as being Hou Ji, but then abruptly switches to King Wu, founder of Zhou, at the end of quatrain 77.[32] Liu Zongyuan has no choice but to follow along in this interpretation, treating the main subject as the Moses-like myth of Hou Ji being discarded on the ice as a baby, only later to rise to prominence. Liu's response, as one might expect from his skeptical bent, is to cast doubt on the original myth, but to identify the kernel of the story as being Hou Ji's exceptional prowess, described in the notable line "Since he was both majestic and intelligent" (*ji qi ji ni* 既岐既嶷). Here *qi ni* 岐嶷 is a rhyming descriptive compound that can also be divided, and it occurs in this same form in *Odes* 245, "The Birth of the People" ("Sheng min" 生民), describing the young Hou Ji.[33] Thus Liu is striving to be "more classical than thou," quoting an even earlier canonical poem in response to the already ancient "Heavenly Questions." Meanwhile, the passage rhymes regularly with a feminine, two-character rhyme (*-aŋ ʔian* in Middle Chinese), ending each

---

32. This is yet another example of the Han commentary's failure to analyze the poem by quatrain, as discussed in chapter 1.

33. See Legge's translation: "He looked majestic and intelligent" 克岐克嶷 (*She King*, 468).

time with the repeated final particle *yan* 焉.³⁴ These eight lines thus constitute a dense homage not just to the substance of history but also to the very language of antiquity. Moreover, although they quibble on the significance of the original legend, they affirm the substance of the traditional historical narrative.

In general, Liu's poem is written in tetrasyllabic verse, but as with the original "Heavenly Questions," there is some irregularity in his prosody.³⁵ The rhymes can be regular as in the example just cited, but can also be irregular. For instance, he responds to quatrain 8 as follows (rhymes in Pulleyblank's reconstruction):³⁶

[8]   *Rising out of Sunny Vale in the East*   出自湯谷
       And lodging at the bank of the Meng River in   次于蒙汜
       the West,

    While the spokes are disposed southward,   輻旋南畫
    The axle is fixed in the north.   軸莫於北   puək
    How could that one "rise" or "lodge" itself?   孰彼有出次   tsʰẓ
    It is your own viewpoint that is askew.   惟汝方之側   tʂəək
    Moving horizontally and revolving orthogonally,   平施旁運
    *How could it have a "vale" or a "riverbank"?*³⁷   惡有谷汜   sfiẓ

Since in the original Tang-era pronunciation, *bei* 北 and *ce* 側 rhyme and so do *ci* 次 and *si* 汜, we have a rhyme scheme of XABAXB, which is intricate and compelling. On the other hand, in response to quatrain 39, Liu writes:³⁸

    Yao was brutal to that man's father,   堯酷厥父   ffiuə̂
    So the son was provoked to his achievement.   厥子激以功   kəwŋ
    He was able to magnify the ancestral offerings,   克碩厥祀   sfiẓ
    That later generations establish suburban   後世是郊   kja:w
    *sacrifices for him.*³⁹

---

34. For this chapter I generally use the reconstructions of Late Middle Chinese in Edwin G. Pulleyblank's *Lexicon of Reconstructed Pronunciation*.
35. See discussion in chapter 1.
36. *Liu Zongyuan ji*, 14.367.
37. In other words, Liu denies that there are such geographical features in Heaven.
38. *Liu Zongyuan ji*, 14.379.
39. As mentioned in *Zuozhuan*, Duke Zhao, year 7. According to Zichan 子產 from

This appears to be a non-rhyming quatrain, even if perhaps there is some other kind of phonetic patterning that is not obvious. It is unclear why Liu would rhyme inconsistently, but my guess is that he is scrupulously imitating the original. For a Tang reader unaware of the phonology of Old Chinese, it would seem that the "Heavenly Questions" itself rhymed frequently but inconsistently.

Just as Liu Zongyuan's poem is an archaistic response that borrows ancient-style prosody to reply to the "Heavenly Questions," in content it also works with the original poem as in a dialogue, responding but also posing further questions, criticizing in part but also agreeing with and reasserting the message of the earlier poem:[40]

[88] When the central states shared the pasture, 中央共牧
    Why was the Sovereign angered? 后何怒
    How could the paltry lives of bees and ants 蠢蛾微命
    Possess the strength to endure? 力何固

    The vipers chomped on their own poison, 螝蠚已毒
    It was not that it had spread to the outside.[41] 不以外肆
    A thin-waisted rabble of stingers— 細腰群螫
    What cause for worry should they be? 夫何足病

My translation follows the *Chuci zhangju* commentary, which refers to a preposterous legend about two-headed snakes that bite at themselves, used as a metaphor for the foreign nomadic enemies of the Han people.[42] But there is really no need for this ingenuity when the surface meaning of the lines is comprehensible too: if some enemies (not necessarily two-headed

---

the state of Zheng, Gun received the suburban sacrifices in recognition of his achievement, even though he ultimately failed; see Durrant et al., *Zuo Tradition*, 1423.

40. *Liu Zongyuan ji*, 14.396.

41. The Han commentary's interpretation may be based on a brief parable preserved in *Han Feizi*, as mentioned above in the note to "Text One." On the other hand, since the Han commentary goes on to interpret the passage of "Heavenly Questions" as referring to foreign enemies, it diverges from the message of the *Han Feizi* allegory about strife between ministers (which, ironically, would have a more obvious link to the Qu Yuan narrative).

42. Modern scholars generally understand it as referring specifically to King Li 厲 of Zhou (fl. 9th c. BC). King Li was a famously incompetent ruler whose disastrous reign had to be saved by a joint regency of two nobles.

snakes) shared pasture land in the central plain, that would not in itself be a threat to the state. But the Han commentary refers to two-headed vipers, and many later readers have followed this interpretation, as one may observe even in the seventeenth-century illustration of the text by Xiao Yuncong 蕭雲從 (1596–1673) (fig. 1).

Liu Zongyuan follows the same interpretation, so far as we can guess from the responding quatrain in which he continues to refer to vipers. This passage, in which Liu Zongyuan uses just one quatrain to answer one, suggests how his poem often functions in the same way as a commentary. By naming the viper clearly instead of using the periphrasis "Zhongyang," Liu helps to explain the original meaning. The first couplet seems essentially to be confirming the sense of the original text, while the latter couplet questions the premise (that the bees, even assembled as a single force, could be at all formidable). Thus, even when Liu criticizes implausible claims in the source text, he is essentially copying the method of the "Heavenly Questions" itself. Using a mixture of explicatory remarks, rhetorical questions, and probing questions, he elaborates on the original text in ways that can deepen its original effect, creating an even more complex reflection on myth and history. Rather than resolving the questions fully, Liu leaves a residue of doubt and mystery as well.[43]

Liu's relationship with many texts from antiquity is neither that of a commentator simply explicating the source, nor that of an independent critic asserting an original and freestanding point of view. His attitude is in-between, tentative, and agnostic, but in his more ambitious compositions he achieves a bold transformation of the source. He is willing to participate in a dialogue with the source text,[44] indeed in a rich enough dialogue that he might achieve the Gadamerian ideal of "a transformation into something shared, in which one does not remain what one was to begin with." Since this kind of dialogue does not consist of replacing

---

43. It is telling that Zhu Xi objected to Liu's work for its inclusion of "interpretations that are exaggerated, conceited, or intricate" 誇多衒巧之意; see *Chuci jizhu*, 3.49, and Xie Jun, *Zhu Xi Chuci xue yanjiu*, 103.

44. Liu Yuxi, by contrast, also alludes to the "Heavenly Questions," but sees these questions as to a large extent having been resolved by subsequent philosophy. In his *fu* on "Questioning the Great Potting Wheel" 問大鈞賦, he finds that his query is answered to his satisfaction. See Qu Tuiyuan, ed., *Liu Yuxi ji jianzheng*, 1.3.

Fig. 1: Bees and vipers. Illustration from *Chuci tuzhu* 楚辭圖注 (1645) by Xiao Yuncong 蕭雲從. Courtesy of Harvard-Yenching Library, Harvard University.

the source text with one's own point of view, we might think also of Liu's famous conviction that he was not qualified to be a teacher of other men, that indeed no one in his age was so qualified.[45] For him writing is not so much a matter of a sage setting forth an authoritative text as a process of interpretation and criticism.

Liu Zongyuan's "Heavenly Responses" cannot be understood as an independent work, nor as a commentary to the earlier poem. Like the source, it is partially interrogative in form and intention, and continues an oscillating dialogue with Chinese tradition. Thus, Liu's work has to be interpreted in tandem with its many layers of interaction with the original "Heavenly Questions." From this point of view, we can examine it from three different angles: Liu's view of the source text; his view of superstition in that text and its relation to real history; and finally, his attitude towards Heaven, as a force that does not intervene directly in human affairs, but stands beyond it, transcendent and awesome.

Liu's Understanding of the Source Text

Liu's "Heavenly Responses" needs to be read, first of all, with some attention to the textual transmission of the poem itself, and in relation to the "Heavenly Questions." We do not have Liu's "Heavenly Responses" in its original form. Early editions such as the *Sibu congkan* edition from the Shaoxi 紹熙 (1190–1194) period or the *Wubaijia zhu* 五百家注 edition of 1200 make clear that Liu's poem was originally preserved as an independent work, and that the Song editors have inserted the text of the source

---

45. This reluctance is set forth in detail in his "Da Wei Zhongli lun shidao shu" 答韋中立論師道書, *Liu Zongyuan ji*, 34.871–74; *Liu Hedong ji*, 34.541–43. It is worth noting that Liu's oft-cited claim that "the purpose of writing is to illuminate the Dao" 文者以明道 comes in the middle of this very same letter in which he refuses to serve as a teacher, and that this letter concludes: "You're lucky enough if you can obtain the truth and discard the appearance, without causing the hounds of Yue and Shu to bark at you as a monstrosity, or the outer court to guffaw at you" 取其實而去其名，無超越、蜀吠怪，而為外廷所笑，則幸矣. One must be cautious about summing up Liu Zongyuan's views even within a single document.

"Heavenly Questions" alongside it.[46] Similarly, in the 1177 *Liu Hedong ji* 柳河東集 version of his collection included in the *Siku quanshu*, the text of the original "Heavenly Questions" is not included, and only cited in the notes compiled by Han Chun 韓醇 in the Song dynasty.[47] Most editions since then include both Liu's and the source text, but that creates a different problem of where to break stanzas. Modern editions tend to arrange the poem quatrain by quatrain, like the source text itself. Some early editions present Liu's poem (and the corresponding passages of the "Heavenly Questions") in longer continuous sections of a dozen or more lines. Whether or not this is the earliest form of the poem, which seems impossible to determine, I find it illuminating regarding the internal structure and so have followed the divisions as in *Zengguang zhushi yinbian Tang Liu xiansheng ji* from the *Sibu congkan*.

Aside from the arrangement of Liu's text in relation to the source, another problem has to do with the commentary. Commentary to the "Heavenly Responses" was added by numerous scholars in the Song and later, but occasionally they distinguish Liu's own "autocommentary" 自注 or "original commentary" 元注. As Tozaki Tetsuhiko 戶崎哲彥 has shown in a masterful article, however, the treatment of this commentary to the "Heavenly Responses" varies considerably in different editions, and in some cases seems itself to be an interpolation by later scholars. Tozaki identifies eleven notes that might appear to belong to Liu himself, but in most cases it seems dubious whether they were actually composed by Liu. For instance, in quatrain 90 there is a note explaining that "hundred *liang*" 百兩 in the "Heavenly Questions" should be referring to one hundred chariots, not one hundred pieces of gold, as the *Chuci zhangju* indicates. But since this interpretation is clear from Liu's poem, the note seems redundant, and moreover ought to belong with the source text (which

---

46. Tozaki, "*Ryū Sōgen shū* chū ni mirareru 'jichū' ni kansuru shohonkan no idō ni tsuite," 46. See note in *Zengguang zhushi yinbian Tang Liu xiansheng ji*, 14.5a; a note by the Southern Song scholar Cai Mengbi 蔡夢弼 also explains this in *Wubaijia zhu Liu xiansheng ji*, 14.11a.

47. The modern punctuated edition by Shanghai guji chubanshe, however, prints the text of "Tianwen" in large characters.

146 Chapter Two

was originally separate from Liu's poem).⁴⁸ In any case, even accepting all eleven of these notes, this would be all the paratextual information we have for the "Heavenly Responses," since it lacks an introduction.

As a result, we have to evaluate the "Heavenly Responses" primarily based on its implicit relationship with the source text, the "Heavenly Questions," and as an example of Liu Zongyuan's hermeneutical approach to traditional texts. Stepping back to consider Liu's broader attitude to classics, we find that Liu Zongyuan was a painstaking reader. He was not a skimmer; he did not read to identify an ideological position and then evaluate the text based on that simplification. He struggled with the obscure details and odd particularities of texts. In his ancient-style poem "On Reading" ("Dushu" 讀書), inspired by the work of Tao Yuanming 陶淵明 (365?–427?), Liu presents reading as an activity with moral heft, perhaps partly because he thinks that morality is only fully realized in history, i.e., in books:⁴⁹

Buried in obscurity and turning away from the world's affairs	幽沈謝世事
Peering down in silence, I perceive Tang and Yu [Yao and Shun].	俯默窺唐虞
Above and below, observing past and present,	上下觀古今
Thousands of paths rise and plummet down in turn.	起伏千萬途
If I encounter joy, I might find myself smiling,	遇欣或自笑
And stirred by sorrow, I might sigh as well.	感戚亦以吁
The blue-bound volumes lie open and scattered,	縹帙各舒散
Overlapping with one another before and after.	前後互相踰
Miasma and disease disturb my spirit chamber [the mind];⁵⁰	瘴癘擾靈府

---

48. See Tozaki, "*Ryū Sōgen shū* chū ni mirareru 'jichū' ni kansuru shohonkan no idō ni tsuite," 50. The *Siku quanshu* edition of *Liu Hedong ji* prefaces this comment, "According to the original note, the 'Question' reads" 元注問云 (*Liu Hedong ji*, 14.60b). The modern punctuated edition does not even identify a source for this note (*Liu Hedong ji*, 14.265).

49. *Liu Zongyuan ji*, 43.1254.

50. In *Zhuangzi* "spirit chamber" 靈府 is employed as a kenning for the heart-mind, *xin* 心, according to Early Tang commentator Cheng Xuanying 成玄英. See *Zhuangzi jishi*, 5.212–13.

And every day is yet more different from the past.	日與往昔殊
Facing the text I'm suddenly entirely lucid;	臨文乍了了
Putting away the scrolls at once I'm as if nothing.	徹卷兀若無
All night who is there for me to speak to?	竟夕誰與言
I have only the bamboo and silk for company.[51]	但與竹素俱
Tired to death, I lie down to rest again,	倦極更倒卧
And after a deep rest I start to recover.	熟寐乃一蘇
Yawning and stretching out my limbs,	欠伸展肢體
I chant what I had read and my mind is relieved.	吟詠心自愉
Intent satisfied, what was to be fulfilled having been fulfilled,	得意適其適
I have no desire to become one of those vulgar scholars.	非願為世儒
When my way is ended, I will close my mouth at once,	道盡即閉口
Relaxed and at ease, discard all my bonds and chains.	蕭散捐囚拘
The clever ones may think me dull,	巧者為我拙
The wise may find me foolish.	智者為我愚
But books and histories are enough to satisfy me,	書史足自悅
So what need to strive and labor?	安用勤與劬
You must treasure your six-foot frame,[52]	貴爾六尺軀
And not be driven by pursuit of fame!	勿為名所驅

In the opening of the poem Liu seems to think of reading as a way of turning away from the world, and again throughout the poem he refers to a kind of escapist satisfaction that he can find there regardless of what is going on around him. But he also makes clear that what he is reading is not simply idle entertainment, but rather history, the records of great deeds in the past. Moreover, he disdains the vulgar scholars who exploit learning for pursuit of fame. For Liu Zongyuan, the reading of history is an activity that is meaningful in itself, even if the vulgar may consider it foolish to pursue something without tangible profit.

51. I.e. his writing implements.
52. Since the conventional expression was "seven-foot frame" (*qi chi qu* 七尺軀), the commentaries suggest that "six" is an error for "seven." But the length of a "foot" varied over time. In the Warring States era it was closer to nine Western inches, so "seven feet" would have meant a height of merely 5'3". By the Tang a "foot" was twelve inches just as in its modern English meaning, so "six feet" would be a reasonable height for a tall man.

In light of Liu Zongyuan's general remarks in "On Reading," we can better appreciate how he actually read "Heavenly Questions." He was not a philologist aiming to recover the original meaning of the text, nor a pragmatic politician thinking of how to apply its lessons to the present; he was a reflective person examining the way that good and evil have worked themselves out in history. Thus, Liu Zongyuan's understanding of "Heavenly Questions" as a poem is generally based on the *Chuci zhangju* version, and he does not attempt to improve or transform the text, aside from pointing out a few errors. With regard to identification of names and historical events, he tends to follow the Han commentary. He would be forced to, of course, in the Tang dynasty; the Song alternatives of Zhu Xi and Hong Xingzu had not yet appeared, so the *Chuci zhangju* would have been the primary edition in which readers encountered the anthology.[53] As we will see below, Liu was still able to identify a considerable number of errors in the text and commentary, but this was not his primary goal, which seems instead to have been to reflect on the questions and assumption of the source in *Chuci zhangju*.

Liu's method of responding to the text is clearly demonstrated by his treatment of the poem's original title, "Tianwen." It seems that Liu follows the *Chuci zhangju* preface's explanation that it means "questioning Heaven" (*wen tian* 問天), but that the order of the two words has been reversed out of a kind of respect for Heaven. But Liu's own title, "Tiandui" 天對, does not mean "responding to Heaven," exactly, but rather, following the literal order of the words, means "Heavenly Responses"—answers to the original poem, that is. So Liu puts himself in a position of superiority towards Qu Yuan, who merely sent up his queries in the direction of Heaven; Liu can assume the mantle of Heaven answering back down to him.

Thus, in response to a question about Kang Hui changing the orientation of the earth's landmass (from quatrain 18), Liu responds almost with disdain towards the original questioner Qu Yuan, or perhaps towards ignorant humanity in general, which so pathetically mistakes its own primitive mythmaking for the actual power of Heaven:[54]

---

53. There was also the Tang-era *Chuci shiwen* 楚辭釋文, but for whatever reason, Liu does not seem to have used it. See Timothy Chan, "The *Jing/Zhuan* Structure of the *Chuci* Anthology," 294–95; Takeji Sadao, *Soji kenkyū*, 209–51.

54. *Liu Zongyuan ji*, 14.371; *Liu Hedong ji*, 14.234.

| When Kanghui [Gonggong] was angered, | 康回馮怒 |
| Why did the earth sink down to the southeast? | 墜何故以東南傾 |

That petty man, Hui:	彼回小子
How could the toppling be his effort alone?	胡顛隕爾力
Ah, who has scared you to such an extent,	夫誰駭汝為此
That you would confuse him with the axis of Heaven?	而以恩天極

And when Liu mocks the practice of giving animal sacrifices, he presents his satire in the voice of Heaven, speaking in the archaic first-person pronoun *yi* 台 (quatrain 36):⁵⁵

With his nacre-inlaid bow and keen gauntlet	馮玼利決
The giant boar [Yih] shot dead.	封豨是射
Why, when [Yih] presented the rich offering of meat,	何獻蒸肉之膏
Did the High Lord [of Heaven] not approve?	而后帝不若

That immoderate man took pleasure in killing,	夸夫快殺
And cooked the boar in a tripod to feed his hunger.	鼎豨以慮飽
Taking the savory fat as offering to the Lord on High	馨膏腴帝
Only offended proper virtue by using force to excess.	叛德恣力
Why should stuffing Our tongue and throat with fat	胡肥台舌喉
Make someone else's blessings more bountiful?	而濫厥福

The "blessings" Liu Zongyuan refers to here are the blessings enjoyed by humanity. His response asserts that they are entirely dependent on humanity itself, and that Heaven will not be swayed by any crass bribes from human priests or sovereigns. One might easily take the message as that of the rationalist who dismisses "the opiate of the masses"; and yet the message is placed in the very mouth of an omnipotent Heaven. Thus Liu's poem is designed to throw cold water on the easy consolations and cheap spirituality of his contemporaries; but it is designed to do so by manipulating a faith in the power of Heaven's own voice, which is shared by his audience and—I would suspect on account of his frequent reliance on it—himself.

Incidentally, this is also one of many cases where Liu adopts an even more archaic style and diction than the original poem, from a millennium

---

55. *Liu Zongyuan ji*, 14.378; *Tianwen Tiandui zhu*, 37.

earlier, that is his model. As we have seen in chapter 1, the archaic style was already a distinctive feature of "Heavenly Questions," but Liu attempts to outdo even that model with archaic vocabulary such as this ancient first-person pronoun, *yi* 台, which, while common in the *Book of Documents*, does not even appear once in the original "Heavenly Questions." The use of obscure and outmoded vocabulary is just one stylistic tool by which Liu conveys his own stance of critical response to the earlier text and to the whole legendary discourse of antiquity. Yet it is a critical attitude that has been hard for later readers to appreciate or comprehend, since it is rather different from the well-known *fugu* 復古 template of returning to the model of Han prose or Jian'an 建安 poetry. Liu Zongyuan is going further back to the archaic models of the *Book of Documents*, the *Book of Odes*, and the bronze inscriptions. As we have seen above, a certain degree of archaicism seems to be a formal feature of the "Heavenly Questions," but Liu takes this even further.[56]

Thus, elsewhere in the poem he again adopts the voice of Heaven itself, reminding the human questioner that astronomy is a science invented by humans, not intrinsic to the celestial bodies themselves:[57]

[7]	How is Heaven composed?	天何所沓
	How were the Twelve Stations differentiated?	十二焉分
	Carving the bamboo strips, whittling the bamboo tokens,	折篿剡筳
	Crisscrossing horizontally and vertically,	午施旁豎
	They explored the brilliance and investigated the dark,	鞠明究曛
	Themselves obtaining Twelve Stations.	自取十二
	This was not accomplished by me,	非予之為
	So how can I explain it to you?	焉以告汝
	To what entity are subjoined the sun and moon?	日月安屬
	How were the various constellations set in place?	列星安陳

---

56. A different but parallel case of fidelity to the source text is when Liu refers to the historical figures by different names than in "Heavenly Questions," creating challenges for an incautious reader. For instance, he identifies King Helu of Wu simply as "Guang" 光 after quatrain 86.

57. *Liu Zongyuan ji*, 14.367.

Circular flame and crescent vortex	規燧魄淵
Both belong to the supreme void:	太虛是屬
Where myriad fires, arrayed like a chessboard,	棋布萬熒
All are lodged in place there.	咸是焉託

Liu closely imitates the archaic form of the original text, with compressed tetrasyllabic lines. The comic tone of the response is not immediately apparent through the archaic and arcane language, but becomes noticeable in the third couplet, when Heaven itself speaks: "So how can I explain it to you?" The division of Heaven into twelve stations and the location of the sun and moon, it turns out, are not the responsibility of Heaven at all. The arrangement of the twelve lunar stations is not a fact of nature ordained by Heaven, but merely a human invention for the convenience of astrologers and magicians. Liu does elaborate on the following lines with the simple assertion of fact that the sun, moon, and stars are all in the sky. But regarding the principal "why" question, the teleology, he responds in the voice of Heaven itself only to abjure all responsibility.[58] Liu seems to have conceived his own poem as a creative response adopting the voice of Heaven, in some cases to answer the questions directly, but in others to debunk the myths to which they refer, or to point out the false assumptions behind them. Liu Zongyuan's work presents his own critical views while also employing an impersonation of Heaven in the rhetorical mode of prosopopoeia.

From his own position as a learned scholar who can see through the false assumptions of the text, Liu is also able to identify errors in the *Chuci zhangju* commentary, as with the vexed quatrain 56:

[56] *Embracing and maintaining the virtue of his legacy,*	該秉季德
[Tang] showed the same excellence as his father.	厥父是臧
Gai had virtue inherited from his ancestors,	該德胤考
Such that he could be Reaper of Rushes in the West.	蓐收於西
Claws like a tiger's, battle-axes at hand,	爪虎手鉞
Charged with punishments, he corrects misdeeds.	尸刑以司愆

Liu had discovered that the original Han commentary is mistaken here: *gai* was not a verb meaning "to embrace, encompass," but instead a proper

---

58. This is also Yang Wanli's interpretation: Heaven is responding to Qu Yuan's question. See *Tianwen Tiandui jie*, 5a.

noun. But Liu made a bold and original identification of the personage to whom it referred. As an "original note" (*yuanzhu* 元注) explains: "*Gai* refers to Rushou [Reaper of Rushes]. The Wang Yi note is incorrect" 該為 蓐收。王逸注誤.⁵⁹ Though Liu does not explain the chain of reasoning that led him to propose this new identification, it may be that he guessed that the syntax proposed by the *Chuci zhangju*, with the first two characters being coordinate verbs, was unlikely, and hence that *gai* 該 ought to represent a person. However, he was unable to recognize the figure of Wang Hai here, and instead proposed that the subject was Rushou 蓐收 (Reaper of Rushes), in early Chinese cosmology one of the spirits of the four directions, namely that corresponding to autumn.⁶⁰

Liu's hypothesis, that the subject here is Rushou, is actually very plausible because Gai was in fact an alternative name for Rushou.⁶¹ Unfortunately, Liu failed to recognize that the prosodic form of the poem, with its division into quatrains, implies that the succeeding couplet should also refer to the same protagonist or at least to the same episode. But there is no historical episode involving both Rushou and the Youhu Clan, who come up in the second half of this same quatrain, so even Liu's creative and insightful guess is not really tenable, and this passage of the "Heavenly Responses" ends up sharing the discordant quality of the "Heavenly Questions" as read in the Han. On the other hand, it seems to have been influential enough that Xiao Yuncong illustrated this same quatrain with the divine figure of Rushou, as shown here (fig. 2).

That Liu Zongyuan would be able to notice the error in the Han commentary and make a partial step to resolving it is already, however, an impressive demonstration of his searing insights into the poem. Though Liu, as a voracious reader of history, was generally sympathetic to Qu Yuan, he was disappointed by any sign of ignorance or self-contradiction, and

---

59. *Liu Zongyuan ji*, 14.384; *Wubaijia zhu Liu xiansheng ji*, 42.14b. In light of Tozaki's argument, we should not assume that this "original" note was actually part of Liu Zongyuan's text. It might have been added by later scholars. Nonetheless, it clearly accords with the intent of Liu's poem, which mentions Rushou explicitly.

60. The god is also mentioned in the "Far Roaming" (Yuanyou 遠遊) poem of the *Chuci*; see Williams, *Elegies of Chu*, 120.

61. As identified in the passage of *Zuozhuan* (Duke Zhao, year 29) that introduces the gods of the four directions; see Durrant et al., *Zuo Tradition*, 1698–99.

Fig. 2: Rushou. Illustration from *Chuci tuzhu* 楚辭圖注 (1645) by Xiao Yuncong 蕭雲從. Courtesy of Harvard-Yenching Library, Harvard University.

unlike many other Qu Yuan fans throughout history, Liu was unwilling simply to ignore these. Liu finds errors in the assumptions of the poem and also in the Han commentary to "Heavenly Questions," as we have seen. But he also objects to the very spirit of the poem, which he interprets, as with the traditional Han reading, as being one of vehement personal protest. Thus Liu's response to the concluding stanzas of the poem, understood by the Han commentary as referring back to Qu Yuan's own circumstances, is rather stern:[62]

Singing your lament in the wilds:[63]	咨吟於野	jia´
Why is your resentment so fierce?	胡若之很	xfiən`
Prestige fallen, duty destroyed, you fulfill your responsibility,	嚴墜誼殄丁厥任	rim`
If appropriate behavior is violated, you must hide yourself where you are;	合行違匿固若所	ʂəð´
Ah, oh, in the poison of your fury who will you find to join you?	咿嚘忿毒意誰與	jiă´
Reviling Qi and turning to Qin, [the King] swallowed the bait:	醜齊徂秦啗厥詐	tʂa:`
Slanderers ascended, schemers were employed, all advances set in reverse;	讒登狡庸咈以施	ʂi
Taking pleasure and ease in disaster and peril, all were weeded out;	甘恬禍凶亟鋤夷	ij
That stubbornness cannot be transformed, so let all your deeds be in vain.	愎不可化徒若罷	pfia:j`

I have indicated the rhyme scheme here according to Pulleyblank's reconstruction of Late Middle Chinese, as above. The rhyme scheme of Liu's responses is irregular, and in this passage is not entirely clear, but these nine lines seem to divide naturally into two separate stanzas of four lines each (treating the first two tetrasyllabic lines as a variant of a single heptameter). The first stanza is then largely unrhymed and the second has an ABBA rhyme scheme. With regard to content, the

---

62. *Liu Zongyuan ji*, 14.397–98.
63. Just as Qu Yuan was doing when he encountered the Fisherman. See Huang Linggeng, ed., *Chuci zhangju shuzheng*, 8.1897.

first turns the questions back on Qu Yuan himself, challenging him for violating norms and acting alone. The second stanza then looks at the disastrous results of the poor rulership of King Huai and King Qingxiang of Chu, who ignored Qu Yuan's advice and led the state to ruin and eventually the conquest by Qin. This miniature "poem within a poem" ranges further away from the original "Heavenly Questions" than most of Liu's response, rather in the same way that the Han commentary, as we saw above, also inserted Qu Yuan forcefully into its interpretation here.

The final stanza of "Heavenly Responses," based on quatrains 94 and 95 of the original poem, goes even further, explicitly criticizing Qu Yuan's verbosity:

But if you did not cherish fame above all,	誠若名不尚
Why expire producing speeches?[64]	曷極而辭

This criticism applies better to Qu Yuan's other writings than to "Heavenly Questions," which is surely the least self-pitying of works in the whole Qu Yuan corpus. But it is impossible for Liu—just as it was impossible for the authors of the Han commentary—to resist elaborating further on his thoughts about Qu Yuan at the conclusion of the poem. The sardonic tone here is worth noting too, incidentally. It is not easy to detect humor in archaic tetrasyllabic verse, but there are several places in the poem where I read Liu's tone as satirical.[65]

In sum, the relation of Liu's "Heavenly Responses" to the source text results in a complex balance. On one hand, Liu is striving to be "more orthodox than

---

64. If taken as a criticism of the solipsism of literature this might seem to apply to Liu Zongyuan as well. On the other hand, Liu did not write anything like "Sublimating Sorrow," which was understood as a direct criticism of the current regime. So perhaps this can be understood as an objection to Qu Yuan's disloyalty, following in the tradition of similar criticisms.

65. My favorite is the response to quatrain 45, asking about the ancient episode when Shaokang of Xia revenges himself on his wife's infidelity, but kills his wife Lady Tangent rather than Ao. Liu comments simply, but in mock-classical language: "Because of the undershirt, because of the lodging, / It would have been right to remove both their heads at once."

thou," but on the other, he is pursuing an imitative archaicism in style even further than the "Heavenly Questions." In spite of his admiration for Qu Yuan as poet, his affinity with the style and themes of the *Chuci*, and deep interest in "Heavenly Questions" itself, Liu is critical of Qu Yuan's oppositional stance, and particularly resistant to the note of unqualified protest. Qu Yuan may have become legendary, to be sure, but what was the result of this sound and fury in his own time, and what were the consequences for his own state of Chu? Liu finds the correct response to troubled times to be instead the serenity of quiet scholarship. Accordingly, he reads the "Heavenly Questions" from the point of view of a Heaven untouched by human disappointments and agonies. We might even regard this as one further piece of his wide-ranging critique of moralizing superstition from the past, which is one of the principal themes of the "Heavenly Responses."

Liu's Critique of Superstition and Affirmation of Virtue

Liu's critical stance towards Qu Yuan's political record also makes sense in context of his broader attack on the superstitious and fanciful elements of the poem, which he generally rejects or treats with some suspicion. This aspect of his creative interpretation of "Heavenly Questions" has to be seen in context of the transformation of classical scholarship in his time.[66] A critical attitude toward antiquity was typical of scholarly trends post-An Lushan, and Liu's approach was inspired by recent classical scholarship; specifically, that of Dan Zhu 啖助 (724–770), Zhao Kuang 趙匡 (n.d.), and Lu Chun 陸淳 (?–805), who were famous for their careful readings of the *Chunqiu* 春秋 (Spring and autumn annals) and the three commentaries to it.[67] Liu Zongyuan explicitly praises these three for their work in clar-

---

66. Pulleyblank's classic article, "Neo-Confucianism and Neo-Legalism in T'ang Intellectual Life," remains revelatory. There is an important recent study by Zha Pingqiu, *Tangxue yu Tangshi*, pointing out, for instance, how scholars of the mid-Tang were active in devising new formats and modes of scholarship (p. 79ff).

67. Lu Chun completed three works on the *Chunqiu*, all of which integrate the insights of his colleagues: *Chunqiu jizhuan bianyi* 春秋集傳辨疑, *Chunqiu jizhuan weizhi* 春秋集傳微旨, and *Chunqiu jizhuan zuanli* 春秋集傳纂例. All three of these were included in the *Siku quanshu*. See also Pulleyblank, "Neo-Confucianism and Neo-Legalism," 88–91.

ifying the meaning of the *Chunqiu*.⁶⁸ Neither the three earlier scholars nor Liu himself were wholesale opponents of the *Chunqiu*, of course.⁶⁹ Rather, the innovation of this school, as admired by Liu, was in a sophisticated new approach that aimed to preserve the moral core of the *Chunqiu* while at the same time critiquing earlier interpretations, and inaccuracies within the classic commentaries. Liu was consistently interested in conserving some moral essence of the tradition while at the same time critiquing huge swathes of its substance.

This attitude is demonstrated most fully in "Against the *Accounts of the States*" ("Fei *Guoyu*" 非國語). Like the "Heavenly Responses," this is an intricate work, engaging with dozens of episodes in the classic historical text *Guoyu* 國語 (Accounts of the states). The *Guoyu* has traditionally been regarded as an "informal" equivalent to the *Zuozhuan*, likewise being a commentary to the *Chunqiu* classic, though "commentary" in both cases can only be understood loosely.⁷⁰ It was traditionally attributed, like *Zuozhuan*, to Zuo Qiuming 左丘明, but is more likely to have been composed by several authors.⁷¹ Liu Zongyuan may have picked out the *Guoyu* as his target because it was not normally regarded as part of the central Confucian canon, and yet, since much of its content actually overlaps with the *Zuozhuan*, he could attempt an "indirect criticism" of the *Zuozhuan*, which was itself of course understood as a canonical commentary to the *Chunqiu* classic.⁷² In the preface to his critique, Liu Zongyuan states clearly the dilemma he sees in confronting the text: "I fear that scholars of the world [vulgar scholars] may be besotted with its literary appeal and lose sight of whether it is true or false" 余懼世之學者溺其文采而淪於是非.⁷³ In the body of the text, just as with "Heaven Responds," Liu quotes a short passage from the *Guoyu*, and then criticizes implausible, inaccurate, or

---

68. See "Tang gu jishizhong huang taizi shidu Lu Wentong xiansheng mubiao" 唐故給事中皇太子侍讀陸文通先生墓表 in *Liu Hedong ji*, 9.132.
69. As David McMullen sums up, Liu Zongyuan "perpetuated precisely the school's paradoxical and basically conservative orientation." McMullen, *State and Scholars in T'ang China*, 104.
70. Chang I-jen et al., "Kuo yü," 265.
71. Chang I-jen et al., "Kuo yü," 263.
72. Chen Jo-shui, *Liu Tsung-yüan and Intellectual Change in T'ang China*, 141.
73. *Liu Zongyuan ji*, 44.1265.

158 Chapter Two

supernatural elements. He seeks to point out examples of "falsity" in the text that readers might otherwise miss.

One episode touches on content that is referred to in "Heavenly Questions" too:

> The Marquis of Jin dreamed about a yellow bear entering his bedchamber door. Zichan said, "Gun perished at Mount Plume, then was transformed into a tawny bear, entered the Plume Abyss. This was actually the suburban altar of Xia (etc., etc.).[74]
> 晉侯夢黃熊入於寢門，子產曰：鯀殛於羽山，化為黃熊以入於羽淵，實為夏郊。（云云）

> The critique: Gun becoming the object of worship at the suburban altar of Xia was because he was the father of Yu, not because he was a bear. The story of the bear was invented by busybodies (*haoshizhe*). In general, when a person becomes ill, the earthsoul stirs and the vital spirit becomes disturbed, so vision and hearing dissipate. Thus in sleeping you can have weird dreams. This happens to everyone, so what is marvelous about it?[75]
> 非曰：鯀之為夏郊也，禹之父也，非為熊也。熊之說，好事者為之。凡人之疾，魄動而氣蕩，視聽離散，於是寐而有怪夢，罔不為也，夫何神奇之有？

In the original story, the Marquis of Jin is cured of his illness because Zichan identifies the cause as the spirit of the ancient hero Gun, who famously transformed into a *huangxiong* 黃熊, "tawny bear."[76] Liu's critique exemplifies his metaphysics and theory of history. Gun, he argues, is indeed an important historical figure because he was the father of the great ruler Yu. His achievement has nothing to do with any kind of animal metamorphosis. Similarly, the Marquis's illness is not due to some kind of spirit haunting, but rather some kind of disturbance in his inner body and spirit. One of the side effects of illness can be unstable vision and hearing,

---

74. This episode is in "Jin yu 8" 晉語八 in *Guoyu*. See Xu Yuangao, ed., *Guoyu jijie*, 14.437.

75. *Liu Zongyuan ji*, 45.1319.

76. I render this animal as "terrapin" in "Text Three," however, because all evidence suggests that it was originally an aquatic creature of legend.

so it is perfectly understandable that he might have been haunted by bad dreams which he interpreted as representing a visitation by Gun.

Curiously, in the passage of "Heavenly Questions" that relates this same story, Liu's comment is unusually brief and uncritical:[77]

[38] When blocked and thwarted while traveling westward,	阻窮西征
How was it that he managed to cross those cliffs?	巖何越焉
When Gun was transformed into a tawny bear	化為黃熊
How did the shaman bring him back to life?	巫何活焉
Gun perished at Plume Cliff;	鯀殛羽巖
Turning tawny, he fell into the abyss.	化黃而淵

Although Liu does not directly criticize the original text, his assertion that Gun simply died and fell into the abyss does implicitly reject the notion of resurrection.[78] But this is an unusually restrained response. In other passages of "Heavenly Responses," Liu sets forth a powerful critique of the superstitious elements in legends about Gun, as here:[79]

[13] With the owls and turtles pulling and dragging,[80]	鴟龜曳銜
How could Gun obey [Yao's] instructions?	鯀何聽焉
When he had fulfilled our desires and completed the task,	順欲成功
Why did the Lord [Yao] then punish him?	帝何刑焉
[14] Perishing after long durance at Mount Plume,	永遏在羽山
Why was he not forgiven even after three years?	夫何三年不施
He stole the augmenting soil to dam the flood,	盜堙息壤
Incurring the grievous anger of the Lord.	招帝震怒
Enduring the punishment while living below,	賦刑在下

---

77. *Liu Zongyuan ji*, 14.378.

78. Sun Changwu compares these two passages but seems to me to ignore the notable point that Liu Zongyuan's reaction to the legend in the "Heavenly Responses" is surprisingly tepid; see Sun Changwu, *Liu Zongyuan pingzhuan*, 174.

79. *Liu Zongyuan ji*, 14.369.

80. The Han commentary does not gloss but instead simply repeats the difficult phrase *yexian* 曳銜, so there is no way to be sure how it is interpreting the phrase. But Liu seems to interpret it as being part of Gun's punishment so I try to render it appropriately here.

160　Chapter Two

> He was then exiled and abandoned at Plume.　而投棄於羽
> Then his prime son was properly advanced,　方陟元子
> So as to inherit the task, and determine the territory.　以胤功定地
> Why would he abandon his own late father,　胡離厥考
> To let owls and turtles satisfy their hunger?　而鴟龜肆喙

The original text of "Heavenly Questions" asks about why Gun failed to control the flood, why he was punished, and why he was kept captive at Mount Plume but still not forgiven. The Han commentary does not shed much further light on these questions, simply paraphrasing the original text. But Liu offers various responses to these questions: he points out that Gun was punished for stealing the soil he used to dam up the floodwaters, and then replaced by his proper son and heir Yu. In the end, while he could not reverse his father's punishment, Yu could at least protect Gun's body from the ravages of wild animals, such as owls and turtles. Liu implies that events proceeded in an orderly way, since the principle of merit was satisfied by Gun's punishment, while the principle of heredity was satisfied by Yu's succession.[81]

But the conclusion here is not like the "Against the *Accounts of the States*" at all. For Liu concludes not by rejecting the stories, but by reaffirming the moral order behind the original stories, even while rejecting the supernatural and legendary elements within them. He is hesitant to present his conclusion explicitly, leaving it in the form of an ambiguous question, but the implication comes through nonetheless. Liu has a good explanation for why Gun had to be punished in spite of his efforts to control the flood, namely, that he had to commit larceny to do so. The final question must be a rhetorical one, since it is inconceivable that the sage Yu would simply abandon the body of his father. In general, Liu's attitude is not so peremptory and one-sided here as in the "Against the *Accounts of the States*" case. Liu is profoundly fascinated by the passage of "Heavenly Questions" to which he is responding, and his response builds on the core narrative that is referred to therein, even while it rejects some of the figurative embellishments upon it.

Another passage demonstrates Liu's ambivalent attitude to the more implausible stories in "Heavenly Questions." The interpretation of the two

---

81. As in Sarah Allan's account of these events in *The Heir and the Sage*, 62–66.

quatrains of "Heavenly Questions" is difficult, but my rendering follows Wang Yi's interpretation, which seems to be the basis for Liu Zongyuan's objections as well:[82]

[40] The white nimbus winding around and spreading out, 白蜺嬰茀
　　　Why has it come upon this hall? 胡為此堂
　　　How did [Cui Wenzi] obtain that fine elixir, 安得夫良藥
　　　Which turned out to be incapable of good? 不能固臧
[41] Heaven is configured horizontal and vertical: 天式從橫
　　　When Yang energy disperses then you die. 陽離爰死
　　　Why did the great bird cry out, 大鳥何鳴
　　　And how did the man's body disappear? 夫焉喪厥體

The Prince [Qiao] was startled and shocked, 王子怪駭
At the nimbus-like form that enfolded his robes. 蜺形茀裳
Wen wore borrowed robes and wielded the halberd, 文襐操戈
So he was unaware of how fine was the elixir. 猶憯夫藥良
Ultimately the bird cried out as it wandered, 終鳥號以游
And rose out of the bamboo cases square and round. 奮厥筐筐
He was unable to glean from the tenebrous gloom 窅漠莫謀
Where the form was present and where absent. 形胡在胡亡

Wang Yi reads these eight lines as referring to a story about the transcendent Prince Qiao (Wangzi Qiao 王子僑). Prince Qiao appeared wrapped in wisps of cloud, offering his student Cui Wenzi 崔文子 a potion of longevity. Cui was startled and struck at the clouds around Prince Qiao with an axe, scattering the medicine on the ground. Thinking that Qiao had died, he covered up his body in a bamboo coffin, but Qiao then transformed into a great bird that cried out and flew away.[83] From a modern point of view informed by the historical study of Daoism, the story seems irrelevant and also likely to have originated only in the Han dynasty, but Liu nonetheless follows this tradition in his response. In his first quatrain he seems to be answering the original question in a straightforward manner, merely pointing out that Cui Wenzi was unaware of what was going on.

---

82. *Liu Zongyuan ji*, 14.379.

83. More plausibly, the former quatrain refers to Chang'e, the moon goddess who stole a potion of longevity, while the latter simply employs the bird as a totem of transfiguration. See You Guoen's comments in *Tianwen zuanyi*, 247–48.

But the second quatrain retains the bird from the original legend, treating it as the cause of the mistake, and thereby not fully contradicting that story, and merely trying to interpret it without any supernatural action. Liu concludes with a question of its own: in the darkness, how can you tell whether a body is present or not? How could anyone evaluate whether the story was true or not?

Liu's skepticism towards superstition was rooted in a deeper belief in human responsibility, as we can see in his critical analyses of other works beyond the *Chunqiu* and its companion texts. His skeptical attitude is stated clearly in his famous essay on "Determination of the Tallies of Divination" ("Zhenfu" 貞符").[84] This is a remarkable piece in the traditional genre of "Fu ming" 符命 (lit. "portents for the Mandate [of Heaven]") panegyrics.[85] Even though Liu borrows the form of the genre dating back to classic works of the Han dynasty, including the extended parallel prose preface and tetrasyllabic verse, he employs it in order to contradict the traditional notion of auspicious omens verifying Heavenly authority for a dynasty's legitimacy. As Liu writes, "Receiving the mandate is not determined by Heaven, but by the human being; being blessed by portents is not determined by good fortune, but rather by humaneness" 受命不于天, 于其人, 休符不于祥, 于其仁.[86] In other words, the stability and righteousness of a dynasty are simply a function of their human leadership, not of some supernatural mandate.[87]

More broadly, Liu Zongyuan was deeply concerned with the question of whether there is an underlying justice and logic to historical events: the question of uranodicy, or whether Heaven is just. Though "Heavenly Questions" probably already contains an underlying theme of moral questioning, Liu Zongyuan elucidates and emphasizes it in his responses. For instance, in response to a series of questions all relating to the founding of Zhou and the conquest of Shang, inquiring both why the conquest was

---

84. *Liu Hedong ji*, 1.17–23.

85. For a detailed study of one such precedent, see Travis Chan, "Writing for the Empire."

86. *Liu Hedong ji*, 1.22.

87. For a detailed study of Liu's position, see Tozaki Tetsuhiko, "Tōdai chūki ni okeru jukyō shingaku e no teikō."

originally justified and whether the actual execution of the war was proper, Liu presents a powerful, extended response. As mentioned above, while modern editions tend to divide up Liu's poem into shorter sections, a few early editions divide it into longer passages, and clearly in this case that is the correct treatment:[88]

[65] When they met at dawn to make the war compact, 會晁爭盟
  Who was it that accomplished their common oath? 何踐吾期
  When the gray-black birds assembled in flight 蒼鳥群飛
  Who was it that caused them to flock together? 孰使萃之
[66] Arriving, they struck fiercely at the body of Zhow, 到擊紂躬
  But Uncle Dan [Duke of Zhou] did not approve the act. 叔旦不嘉
  Why did [the Duke of Zhou] survey and initiate [the return], 何親揆發足
  While [the people] sighed in admiration at the mandate bestowed upon Zhou? 周之命以咨嗟
[67] When all under Heaven had been allotted to the Yin, 授殷天下
  By what authority did they rule? 其位安施
  When success in turn met with destruction, 反成乃亡
  What was the fault that caused it? 其罪伊何
[68] Contending to dispatch the weapons of aggression, 爭遣伐器
  How did [King Wu] accomplish it? 何以行之
  Advancing in stride, striking on both flanks, 並驅擊翼
  How did he take command of all this? 何以將之

88. *Liu Zongyuan ji*, 14.388–89; but formatted as a single coherent response in *Zengguang Zhushi yinbian Tang Liu xiansheng ji*, 14.81a. At the same time, it is worth nothing that Liu's response is divided naturally into two sections based on the rhyme scheme. The first four lines deal with the figure of Jiao Ge, not identified at all in "Heavenly Questions" but introduced by the Han commentary in the first half of quatrain 65; the remainder of Liu's response deals with the second half of quatrain 65 all the way through 68, maintaining a feminine -*i-tsi* (X-之) rhyme throughout. This kind of feminine rhyme, like that of *declaration-separation-sublimation* in English, was gradually banned from formal *shi* poetry, but was common in early verse, including this very passage of the "Heavenly Questions." The transition is actually even more subtle because the rhyme in the opening quatrain is also *-i*, a formal hint that the whole passage is meant to be read as a coherent whole.

Jiao Ge was close to being vivisected,[89]	膠鬲比䐧
So [King Wu] acted in the rain, to meet the deadline.[90]	雨行踐期
Just like hurling forth a pot of water to prevent a burn,	捧盎救灼
When humaneness advances then all follow in its wake.	仁興以畢隨

The goshawks all shared the same intent,	鷹之咸同
And so were caused to flock together there.	得使萃之
Slicing Zhow's neck with a gold battleaxe:	頸紂黃鉞
Why would Dan [Duke of Zhou] delight in that?	旦孰喜之
The father of the people had received his blessing,	民父有聲
So they sighed in admiration of him.	嗟以美之
Authority is meant to protect the people,	位庸庇民
Only the humane can assume it.	仁克蒞之
Zhow was dissipated and destructive,	紂淫以害
So the people murdered and overthrew him.	師殛圮之
They all chased after his death,	咸逭厥死
Striving to seize weapons of their own.	爭徂器之
As both flanks were incited to overcome and resist,	翼鼓顛樂
With delighted dances they overswept him.	謹舞靡之

The questions in the original poem generally concern the Mandate of Heaven, given to the Yin-Shang dynasty by the Lord of Heaven, but then withdrawn. But they also fixate on several stories about specific omens that encouraged Zhou to conquer the Shang and to believe they possessed the Mandate. According to the Han commentary, the first two lines refer to a story about King Wu striving to fulfill his promise to Jiao Ge 膠鬲 that his armies would arrive on the first day of the sexagenary cycle, so as to prevent him from being executed by Zhow. Liu Zongyuan seems to interpret this as a straightforward proof of King Wu's humane approach to governance. With regard to the gray birds, which the Han commentary had read as auspicious omens after "The Great Illumination" ("Da ming" 大明; *Odes* 236) Liu again finds moral significance as a symbol of communal harmony: the birds represent the consensus among the Zhou warriors. Finally, when the original poem asks why King Wu distributed the weapons of war, Liu answers that the army was united in its desire to

---

89. I take *li* 䐧 as an error for *li* 脟.

90. According to the legend in the Han commentary, King Wu attacked at the appointed time so as to save the life of Zhow's advisor Jiao Ge.

punish Zhow. In general, Liu Zongyuan answers the questions by reducing the problem of the Mandate of Heaven to the moral relationship between government and the people: "Government is used to protect the people"; but if the sovereign fails in his duties, it may be equally just that the people destroy him.

Liu's response thus amounts to a critique of a superstitious faith in a heavenly mandate that is granted only in response to human offerings or ritual obeisance. And he places the ultimate onus of human action determinedly in human minds and hearts: humane behavior that attracts the support of the whole people will naturally lead to success. But in spite of what in many ways seems a pragmatic and even enlightened view of political history, Liu does not eschew the judgmental tone of antiquity, but instead proclaims in the monosyllabic language of the *Odes*: "Zhow was dissipated and damaging" 紂淫以害, the two attributes separated by the particle *yi* 以 which in early Chinese frequently serves as a conjunction. Though Liu affirms that Heaven does not intervene in human events in any simple way, his strident judgments of praise and blame reassert the absoluteness of moral standards in the view of Heaven. After all, as we have seen, the poem is composed from the vantage point of Heaven, so the indictment of Zhow as "dissipated" possesses the full authority not just of the historian or poet but also of Heaven itself. In the end, Liu Zongyuan's "Heavenly Responses" refers to the authority of an awesome Heaven so as to cast doubt upon some of the lesser idols that have been established by ignorant humanity.

Regarding Liu's critique of superstition, we cannot pass over his response to quatrain 8 on the sun's journey from east to west:[91]

[8] *Rising out of Sunny Vale in the East*   出自湯谷
    And lodging at the bank of the Meng River in the West,   次于蒙汜

    While the spokes are disposed southward,   輻旋南畫
    The axle is fixed in the north.   軸奠於北
    How could that one "rise" or "lodge" itself?   孰彼有出次
    It is your own viewpoint that is askew.   惟汝方之側

---

91. I analyzed the rhyme scheme above, since it is particularly interesting (perhaps intended to highlight the theoretical importance of this passage as well?).

> Moving horizontally and revolving orthogonally,   平施旁運
> How could it have a "vale" or a "riverbank"?[92]   惡有谷汜

Liu is arguing here that the "Sunny Vale" and "Meng River," said to be the two resting places of the sun, are pure fantasy, vague human attempts to describe the mathematical motion of the sun with words. As for the fourth line, "It is your own [humanity's] viewpoint that is askew," since it might be implying that the appearance of the sun's motion is an illusion created by the earth's motion, the Fudan commentary argues that Liu is asserting the heliocentric theory of the cosmos here.[93] As always, Liu's language is somewhat obscure, but even if he is not quite asserting heliocentrism, he would seem at least to be relying on the *xuanye* 宣夜 theory of cosmology, with heavenly bodies floating in infinite space, and the earth capable of motion, even if not necessarily revolving around the sun.[94] The intended meaning is perhaps only that the disappearance of the sun is an illusion created by moving astronomical bodies. But whatever level of astronomical knowledge it reflects, this stanza certainly demonstrates Liu's skeptical attitude at work.

In Dialogue with Heaven

Perhaps the most surprising thing about "Heavenly Responses" is that, in spite of its apparent intention as a critique, it ends up reaching a similar position to that of "Heavenly Questions." The logic of question and answer, and the trajectory of responses building into dialogue, ultimately lead to a similar end state.[95] It would be wrong to say that either poem has a message, exactly, but one might describe their shared attitude as something like wonder before the workings of the cosmos and fate, awe at the terror and tragedy of human history, and doubt with regard to heavenly justice.

Yet with regard to this essential problem, *uranodicy*, the justice of

---

92. In other words, Liu denies that there are such geographical features in Heaven.
93. *Tianwen Tiandui zhu*, 8.
94. For details on this theory, see Needham, *Science and Civilisation in China*, 3: 219–24.
95. This is also pointed out in Zhang Guodong, "Cong 'Tianwen' 'Tiandui' kan Qu Yuan yu Liu Zongyuan."

heaven, it is hard to state Liu Zongyuan's position precisely. Indeed, the sense of Liu Zongyuan's poem has sometimes been obscured by attempts to sum up his thought in a single ideology or attitude. This is clearly not appropriate in the case of a refined mentality like Liu's, which responds to many slogans and systems with skepticism. For Liu's general attitude towards Heaven, the most convenient resource in English is Lamont's "An Early Ninth Century Debate on Heaven," translating Liu Zongyuan's "Tianshuo" 天說 and Liu Yuxi's 劉禹錫 (772–842) "Tianlun" 天論.[96] But whereas Liu Yuxi's piece is an elaborate philosophical argument, Liu Zongyuan's is a caustic response to a quotation from Han Yu, and by no means a systematic theory of heaven.

In general, Liu Zongyuan is dismissive of notions of an interventionist divine power. Apart from his "Determination of the Tallies of Divination" ("Zhenfu" 貞符), discussed above, two other treatises make his position clear. In the "Disquisition on Seasonal Statutes" ("Shiling lun" 時令論), he discusses the traditional "monthly statutes" (*yueling* 月令) prescribing different activities to be performed by the common people in different seasons. He challenges the notion that these have any kind of divine warrant: "According to the way of the sages, one should not pursue anomalies and treat them as divine, should not rely on heaven as supreme. To be beneficial to people, and prepared for events, that is all it is" 聖人之道, 不窮異以為神, 不引天以為高, 利於人, 備於事, 如斯而已矣.[97] Similarly, in his "Disquisition on Abolishing Punishments" ("Duanxing lun" 斷刑論), Liu mocks the idea that there are rules ordained by Heaven on when to apply punishments or rewards: "For when in ancient times they spoke of Heaven, it was in consideration of those who were foolish and naïve, and not established for those who were intelligent and discerning" 且古之所以言天者, 蓋以愚蚩蚩者耳, 非為聰明睿智者設也.[98] In other words, Liu seems to accept that there may be some practical need to talk about Heaven and the supernatural so as to persuade the ignorant, but seems confident that this would be necessary only for pedagogical reasons, and that for wise literati like himself there is no need to justify matters with reference to Heaven.

96. Lamont, "An Early Ninth Century Debate on Heaven."
97. *Liu Zongyuan ji*, 3.85.
98. *Liu Zongyuan ji*, 3.91.

It is worth noting, though, that both these pieces probably date to early in his career, and there is some evidence that Liu's stance moderated during his period of rustication in Yongzhou.[99] Even the last line quoted employs the term *yu* 愚, "foolish," in etic fashion referring to the uneducated commoners, but Liu Zongyuan would reappropriate this concept to refer to himself in his Yongzhou poetry. Moreover, even in his polemical essays, Liu's key point is just that there is no mechanical, simplistic intervention by Heaven, no way of predicting the future by means of omens. But this does not mean that he did not believe in any kind of transcendent authority or divine fate. As Edward Schafer has written, "He was a teleologist, but not a superficial one."[100] What is more, any treatment of Liu Zongyuan and Heaven needs to take into account the "Heavenly Responses," his most sustained treatment of these issues. And when we consider his portrayal of Heaven here, the poem guides in a different direction, towards appreciating Liu's view of Heaven as a source of transcendent authority, even if it is reticent and refrains from any direct and visible intervention in human affairs.

Perhaps, then, in reading the "Heavenly Responses" we need to look not for a cosmology or ideology but rather for an apophatic theology, that is, a religious conception that can only be communicated negatively. This is, after all, fundamental to Daoism, and is common in Buddhism (not to mention religious discourse of all kinds). It is merely the habit of dividing Chinese thought into the Three Teachings, or into elite secularism vs. popular superstition, and so on, that makes it easy to miss what Liu is doing. But it should be clear enough by now that the author of a tremendous poem of several hundred lines on the topic of Heaven is not totally innocent of some kind of religious awe. After all, as we have seen, this is a poem where Heaven speaks in scorn of man's ignorant pretentions. What Liu's poem communicates in the end is a kind of awe at the power of Heaven, but an awe that can be communicated only by describing how

---

99. For the likely dating of these political essays, see Sun Changwu, *Liu Zongyuan pingzhuan*, 63–64. For Liu's more questioning attitude towards Heaven, see Williams, *Chinese Poetry as Soul Summoning*, 122.

100. Schafer, "The Idea of Created Nature," 153. I have previously quoted this wonderful and profound evaluation of Liu's work in *Chinese Poetry as Soul Summoning*, 122. In its balanced appraisal, it strikes the right note on Liu's writing as a whole, in a way rarely matched in modern scholarship in any language.

Liu Zongyuan's Critique and Affirmation 169

remote, unapproachable, and incomprehensible Heaven is to the perception of mortals.

Considered as a religious work of an apophatic kind, Liu's poem takes Heaven seriously in its own way. His responses are frequently longer than the questions, suggesting he invests these issues with even greater weight than the author of "Heavenly Questions" had. Consider this exchange on the moon:

[9]	*What power has the nocturnal radiance of the moon?*	夜光何德
	That it may die and then grow back again?	死則又育
	It is no peer of the blazing conflagration [the sun];	燉炎莫儷
	When approaching the depths it is just a crescent;	淵迫而魄
	But when veering farther then it grows complete.	遝違乃專
	How could it die or grow?	何以死育
	What sort of singularity does it possess,	厥利維何
	That a rabbyt peers out from its belly?	而顧菟在腹
	When the dark Yin is mostly absent,	元陰多缺
	Then it comes to look like a rabbit.	爰感厥兔
	The form of formlessness	不形之形
	Itself resembles the divine.[101]	惟神是類

This quatrain of "Heavenly Questions" is neither a sort of catechism recording lunar mythology, nor a skeptical challenge to received wisdom, but merely a symmetric pair of questions examining and reflecting on the moon myth. The two questions mirror the mythic significance of the moon itself, which is both celestial body and rabbit at the same time.

Liu's responses demonstrate a characteristic philosophical depth. First, he answers the original questions with a rhetorical one casting doubt on the premise, and implying that if the moon appears to die or to grow, this is merely an illusion created by its movement in relation to the sun (not far off from the astronomical fact as we know it today). In the second quatrain, likewise, he interprets the rabbit observers have found in the moon as an illusion created by the area of its surface covered in darkness. Thus far, the response fits Liu's reputation for skepticism well, as in writings like

---

101. *Liu Zongyuan ji*, 14.367–68.

"Against the *Accounts of the States*."[102] But the final couplet here is even more subtle: the divine is the form of the formless. This suggests a more profound layer of meaning not obvious in the original quatrain. Moreover, it seems to complement Liu Zongyuan's appreciation of the difficulty of stating any fixed principle underlying phenomena. It is impossible for anything in the world to be literally "formless"; instead, Liu Zongyuan seems to say here, humans misinterpret the transitory and perplexing impressions they receive from celestial forces. Our impressions of the world can only be provisional, and even the impression that something has no fixed form is itself shaped by the tricks of vision.

But if that is true, perhaps our new insight into the moon's shape is itself an illusion; Liu does not go so far as to present any final answers here. Instead, Liu's "Heavenly Responses" elaborates in such detail on the myths and stories of the source poem, rather than simply attempting to refute their mistakes, that it ends up leaving the reader with a sense of unfathomable mystery. Another of Liu's responses suggests that the metaphysical grounding for his beliefs is a kind of agnosticism which accepts the existence of imponderable questions. To the first half of quatrain 5 on the composition of the universe, Liu responds:[103]

[5]	*Where are the axle and mainstays attached?*	斡維焉繫
	Where is the fulcrum of Heaven placed?	天極焉加
	Why should Heaven have mainstays attached	烏俟繫維
	To keep its position fixed?	乃糜身位
	Its farthest limits being limitless,	無極之極
	It wafts ineffably towards infinity.	漭瀰非垠
	And were one to impose on space a shape,	或形之加
	How would one even measure the size?	孰取大焉
	How do the Eight Pillars support it?	八柱何當
	Why is the Southeast truncated?	東南何虧
	Its august majesty ceaselessly swelling,	皇熙亹亹
	Where is the ridgepole and where the eaves?	胡棟胡宇

102. Yang Wanli explains him as identifying the rabbit as simply the shape of the absent or hidden part of the moon; see his *Tianwen Tiandui jie*, 6a.
103. *Liu Zongyuan ji*, 14.366.

Widely distributed and not dependent,	宏離不屬
Why would it rely on Eight Pillars?	焉恃夫八柱

The first two questions here refer to the geometry of a revolving heaven, while the latter two have to do with traditional understandings of Eight Sacred Mountains, and an earth set atilt by the great battle between Zhuanxu and Gonggong. Liu here seems to mock the physical assumptions of "Heavenly Questions," and to rebut them by asserting the vastness and formlessness of Heaven. In other words, he contradicts overly simplistic notions of the cosmos, rebutting superstition with philosophy. In a sense, though, he is also repudiating the possibility of any finite description of the cosmos by means of infinity. Moreover, Stephen Field has argued that the questions posed here reflect not just ancient mythology but also Warring States-era innovations in astronomy.[104] If that is right, it may be better to say that Liu is elaborating on and refining the same inquisitive spirit that is already present in the original text. Liu honors the cosmic ambitions of the "Heavenly Questions" while objecting to its naiveté with regard to the scale of cosmic dimensions.

One of the central concepts expounded in Liu's "Heavenly Responses" is indeed the view that Heaven's awesome scale simply cannot be comprehended by humanity:

[72] *As the Mandate of Heaven revolves and reverses:*	天命反側
How does it punish and how does it aid?	何罰何佑
Heaven is remote and obscure,	天邈以蒙
Man is miniscule and set apart.	人么以離
How could their two paths intersect	胡克合厥道
To punish someone's errors or transgressions?	而詰彼尤違

The original "Heavenly Questions" had asked, some three-quarters of the way through its length, why the Mandate of Heaven changed so frequently; what logic underlay the strange saga of Gun and Yu; how the final rulers of Xia and Shang had somehow lost their moral authority. The poem provided no answer, only this question, which can be interpreted in various ways. In Liu's response, he points out that the question seems to

---

104. See Field, "Cosmos, Cosmograph," especially pp. 93–100 on the "cosmograph."

be presupposing that Heaven had punished errors directly, with the trajectories of Heaven and Man intersecting, and he criticizes the presumption here that such interference is even possible. But it is important to observe his justification for this argument. It is not that "man is the measure of all things," but rather that humanity is too miniscule, *yao* 么 (a character whose modest and unprepossessing form seems to recapitulate its semantic value). Moreover, Liu does not claim that Heaven is impotent but instead only that it is remote and difficult to comprehend. After all, there is no possibility of being an atheist with respect to Tian 天—the sky is there whether one likes it or not.

Liu's cosmological breadth of vision borrows from the tools and insights of "Heavenly Questions" to demonstrate the insignificance of humanity. On a philosophical level, this issue ought also to be considered in light of Liu's views of the Three Teachings, not just Confucianism.[105] In particular, one might consider his sympathetic writings on Buddhism.[106] In his numerous inscriptions, prefaces, and poems touching on Buddhism, Liu expresses admiration for its concepts of *prajñā* and *nirvāna*, and writes that, while it is founded like Confucianism on filial piety, nonetheless it "finishes in emptiness" 歸於空無.[107] Perhaps because Liu is an outsider with respect to Buddhism, he is willing to write a bit more clearly and straightforwardly in his critique of Buddhist doctrine, and as with Confucianism, he admires the doctrines but worries about their being misused by the venal and vulgar.[108] But at the same time, he shares with the most devout Buddhists a quest for the reality of emptiness, as when he writes in a poem about reading the sutras:[109]

---

105. This has been the subject of important recent scholarship such as the monograph by Zhang Yong, but the standard work remains Sun Changwu's *Liu Zongyuan pingzhuan*.

106. For Liu's overall attitude towards Buddhism, perhaps the decisive text is his preface sending off Haochu 浩初, in which he painstakingly distinguishes his own approbation of Buddhism from his friend Han Yu's opposition to it; see *Liu Zongyuan ji*, 25.673–75.

107. In the opening sentence of his "Song Jun shangren gui Huainan jinsheng xu" 送濬上人歸淮南覲省序. See *Liu Zongyuan ji*, 25.683–84. Liu even reiterates this sentiment again later in the preface.

108. A good example comes in the "Song Chen shangren nanyou xu" 送琛上人南遊序, *Liu Zongyuan ji*, 25.680.

109. The poem is "Chen yi Chaoshiyuan du chanjing" 晨詣超師院讀禪經. *Liu Hedong ji*, 42.686–87; *Liu Zongyuan ji*, 42.1135; Wang Guoan, ed., *Liu Zongyuan shi jianshi*, 2.219.

> The font of truth we can scarcely draw from at all,[110] 真源了無取
> But instead the world hurries after the tracks of delusion. 妄跡世所逐

Thus we see once again that Liu's conception of the ultimate is apophatic, hard to define except negatively. Perhaps, then, the ultimate lesson to which the entire "Heavenly Responses" leads steadily but slowly is that of Liu's immortal poem "Snow on the River" ("Jiang xue" 江雪):[111]

> Over a thousand hills the birds fly past and vanish, 千山鳥飛絕
> On ten thousand paths the tracks of men are effaced: 萬徑人蹤滅
> An old man in straw coat and hat on a lonely boat 孤舟蓑笠翁
> Fishing alone in the snow of the chill river. 獨釣寒江雪

This is a bleak view of human existence where consolation lies in a kind of reconciliation with an infinity inaccessible to ordinary human perception. But for someone like Liu, who rejects the facile anthropomorphism of interpreting natural phenomena as if they had human agency, there is no refuge but an uncompromising, philosophical worldview in which humanity stands alone within a vast cosmos.[112]

What is remarkable about Liu's "Heavenly Responses" is that he is able to elicit the same profound implications from the "Heavenly Questions" itself. While frequently critical, his responses are still based on that ancient material, making use of it as both inspiration and provocation. Liu's poem is a scholarly response, engaging both with the poem itself and its dominant commentary, so it is a response to the text by someone who has intimately understood its message and also noted its lacunae and obfuscations. But it is also a cosmological response, personifying Heaven so as to point out the absurdity of human speculations about the limits of the universe or Heavenly intention, so as to reaffirm the fundamentally incomprehensible quality of the transcendent. And certainly it is a moral

---

110. The "font of truth" is a phrase beloved by Liu Zongyuan to connote the truth of Buddhism. See also *Liu Zongyuan ji*, 6.161; 7.167–68. The *locus classic* seems to be in "Huayan yicheng jiaoyi fen qi zhang" 華嚴一乘教義分齊章, T 1866: 45.501c.

111. *Liu Hedong ji*, 43.725; *Liu Zongyuan ji*, 43.1221.

112. The use of numbers to evoke the vastness of the universe in contrast to the individual consciousness may also owe something to Buddhism, as pointed out in Chen and Zhao, "Liu Zongyuan shige Foxue yuanyuan tanxi," 17.

response, which affirms over and over again the fact of human agency and personal responsibility. Finally, it may be fair to call it a religious response as well, even if the religious conception implied by the poem is unique to Liu Zongyuan himself. As singular and personal as his views sometimes seem, he finds some precedent for them in classic poetry, and so creates a dialogue with the "Heavenly Questions" in which neither reader nor text remains unchanged.

APPENDIX TO CHAPTER TWO

Text Two: "Heavenly Questions" as Read by Liu Zongyuan

My translation of Liu Zongyuan's "Heavenly Responses" is presented in tandem with my translation of the original "Heavenly Questions," the latter being set in italics. The translation of "Heavenly Questions" generally follows the *Chuci zhangju* commentary as in "Text One" above, but omitting the commentary unless necessary. As discussed above, it seems that Liu's original text was one continuous poem without the quotations from "Heavenly Questions," and that it was only later editors who compiled the composite text, but it is sometimes difficult to identify the best arrangement, particularly since Liu's rhyme scheme is often unclear. Liu Zongyuan does not seem to follow the rhyme scheme of the original text closely, and tends to respond directly to topics rather than to quatrains in their entirety. Modern editors often rearrange into quatrains, but I have instead followed the arrangement in the *Zengguang zhushi yinbian Tang Liu xiansheng ji* from the *Sibu congkan*, which seems to represent the structure of Liu's argument best by keeping together extended passages on the same topic, even if they respond to two or three quatrains from the source at once.[1]

I have relied heavily on the Fudan commentary, *Tianwen tiandui zhu*, for my interpretation of Liu's often obscure writing.

[1]　*[I] asked, regarding the beginnings of remote antiquity,*　曰遂古之初
　　　Who recorded and told us of these things?　誰傳道之
　　　Before all above and below had taken shape,　上下未形
　　　What way was there to investigate it?　何由考之
[2]　*Darkness and brightness, murk and obscurity,*　冥昭瞢闇
　　　Who could fully comprehend them?　誰能極之
　　　In that homogeneous mass of semblances,　馮翼惟像
　　　How could anything be differentiated?　何以識之
[3]　*The brightest brightness, the darkest dark,*　明明闇闇
　　　How were they then created?　惟時何為

---

1. There are also numerous variants in the *Quan Tang wen* text; see *Quan Tang wen*, 585.5908b–5916a.

176　Text Two

The so-called chaos at the very beginning	本始之茫
Is only something transmitted by fabulists.	誕者傳焉
Magnific numinosity diffused in darkness:	鴻靈幽紛
What can even be said of it?	曷可言焉
The dim and dusky, along with the distinct and bright,[2]	眒黑晣眇
Alternate back and forth, swarming and swelling,[3]	往來屯屯
Renewed and transformed in the massive murk.	龐昧革化
Only primal pneuma endures;	惟元氣存
But what could have produced it?	而何為焉
Yin and Yang combine [with Man] to form the triad;	陰陽三合
By what transformation is the origin formed?	何本何化
The elements constitute a triad,	合焉者三
With a single one to rule and regulate.	一以統同
Exhaling heat and breathing the cold,	吁炎吹冷
The interaction of the two makes the effect.[4]	交錯而功

[4]　*The Heavenly Sphere's nine layers:*　　　　　　　圜則九重
　　Who could construct and measure them?　　　　孰營度之

Complete without being manufactured,　　　　　　無營以成
Overlapping Yang powers make nine.　　　　　　　沓陽而九
The whole mass revolving like a carriage wheel　　運輠渾淪
Is what earned it the description as round.　　　　蒙以圜號

What craft was responsible for it?　　　　　　　　惟茲何功
Who could have created it in the beginning?　　　孰初作之

---

2. Both *huhei* 眒黑 and *ximiao* 晣眇 are not transparent at all, but the Fudan commentary's suggestion that they simply oppose darkness and daylight seems to fit.

3. It is difficult to find a gloss of *zhunzhun* 屯屯, but it seems most likely that Liu is inspired by the third hexagram in the *Book of Changes*, Zhun 屯. The "Sequence of the Hexagrams" (Xu gua 序卦) commentary explains: "After heaven and earth have come into existence, individual beings develop. It is these individual beings that fill the space between heaven and earth. Hence there follows the hexagram of DIFFICULTY AT THE BEGINNING. Difficulty at the beginning is the same as filling up" (Wilhelm, *I Ching*, 398). I translate the line loosely but inspired by this sense of beings filling "the space between heaven and earth."

4. In other words, Liu denies the premise of the question and asserts that Yin and Yang have a dialectical relation in which both participate to produce the effect.

The mystic coheres and the primal is modified, 冥凝元釐
Without any effort, without any creation. 無功無作

[5] Where are the axle and mainstays attached? 斡維焉繫
Where is the fulcrum of Heaven placed? 天極焉加

Why should Heaven have mainstays attached 烏俟繫維
To keep its position fixed? 乃縻身位
Its farthest limits being limitless, 無極之極
It wafts ineffably towards infinity, 漭瀰非垠
And were one to impose on space a shape, 或形之加
How would one even measure the size? 孰取大焉

How do the Eight Pillars support it? 八柱何當
Why is the Southeast truncated? 東南何虧

Its august majesty ceaselessly swelling, 皇熙壘壘
Where is the ridgepole and where the eaves? 胡棟胡宇
Widely distributed and not dependent, 宏離不屬
Why would Heaven rely on Eight Pillars? 焉恃夫八柱

[6] Regarding the margins of the Nine Heavens: 九天之際
Where are they placed and where do they connect? 安放安屬

Neither green nor yellow, 無青無黃
Neither red nor black, 無赤無黑
Without center, without periphery: 無中無旁
What borders alongside Heaven?[5] 烏際乎天則

Though corners and interstices are many, 隅隙多有
Who can know their number in full? 誰知其數

---

5. Liu is responding primarily to the Han commentary here: "The Nine Heavens are Luminescent Heaven in the East, Sunlit Heaven in the Southeast, Crimson Heaven in the South, Vermilion Heaven in the Southwest, Complete Heaven in the West, Shaded Heaven in the Northwest, Mystic Heaven in the North, Transformed Heaven in the Northeast, and Harmony Heaven in the Center." 九天，東方皞天，東南方陽天，南方赤天，西南方朱天，西方成天，西北方幽天，北方玄天，東北方變天，中央鈞天。He denies that there are multiple heavens of different colors.

With cunning deception and abundant falsehood, 巧欺淫詭
Dark and light Heavens were distinguished;[6] 幽陽以別
But Heaven has no corners, no interstices: 無限無隅
Why confuse its ranks thusly? 曷憒厥列

[7] *How is Heaven composed?* 天何所沓
How were the Twelve Stations differentiated? 十二焉分

Carving the bamboo tablets, whittling the bamboo tokens,[7] 折筭剡筳
Crisscrossing horizontally and vertically, 午施旁豎
They explored the brilliance and investigated the dark, 鞠明究曛
Themselves obtaining Twelve Stations. 自取十二
This was not accomplished by me 非予之為
So how can I explain it to you? 焉以告汝

To what entity are subjoined the sun and moon? 日月安屬
How were the various constellations set in place? 列星安陳

The circular flame and crescent vortex 規燬魄淵
Both belong to the supreme void, 太虛是屬
Where myriad fires, arrayed like a chessboard, 棋布萬熒
All are lodged in place there. 咸是焉託

[8] *Rising out of Sunny Vale in the East* 出自湯谷
And lodging at the bank of the Meng River in the West, 次于蒙汜

While the spokes are disposed southward, 輻旋南畫
The axle is fixed in the north. 軸莫於北
How could that one "rise" or "lodge" itself? 孰彼有出次
It is your own viewpoint that is askew. 惟汝方之側
Moving horizontally and revolving orthogonally, 平施旁運
How could it have a "vale" or a "riverbank"?[8] 惡有谷汜

---

6. Again, this is based on two of the Heavens identified in the Han commentary to quatrain 6.

7. This is a clever reuse of the rare term *zhuan* 篿 from "Sublimating Sorrow" ("Lisao"), line 257: "I gathered jade-like rushes along with bamboo strips and *tablets* –" 索藑茅以筳篿兮.

8. In other words, Liu denies that there are such geographical features in Heaven.

"Tianwen" as Read by Liu Zongyuan 179

> From dawning all the way to dusk, 自明及晦
> How many miles does the sun travel? 所行幾里
>
> What faces it will then be bright; 當焉為明
> Where it does not reach, that place is dark. 不逮為晦
> Measuring its extent will have no limit,[9] 度引無窮
> You cannot mark it out in miles. 不可以里

[9] What power has the nocturnal radiance of the moon? 夜光何德
That it may die and then grow back again? 死則又育

> It is no peer of the blazing conflagration [of the sun], 熾炎莫儷
> When approaching the depths it is just a crescent; 淵迫而魄
> But when veering farther then it grows complete. 退違乃專
> How could it die or convalesce? 何以死育
>
> What sort of singularity does it possess, 厥利維何
> That a rabbyt peers out from its belly? 而顧菟在腹
>
> When the dark Yin is mostly absent, 元陰多缺
> Then it comes to look like a rabbit. 爰感厥兔
> The form of formlessness 不形之形
> Itself resembles the divine. 惟神是類

[10] Lady Tangent never had a mate, 女歧無合
So how could she obtain Nine Sons? 夫焉取九子

> When the Yang force is healthy, the Yin excessive, 陽健陰淫
> Descending they diffuse, increasing create friction. 降施蒸摩
> Tangent was numinous and so had sons, 歧靈而子
> What need that they be produced by a husband?[10] 焉以夫為
>
> Where does the Sire of Might reside? 伯強何處
> Where do the gentle airs abide? 惠氣安在
>
> When the weird surges and the dark expands, 怪瀰冥更
> Then the Sire of Might appears.[11] 伯強乃陽

9. There is a variant 久 for 無.
10. The Fudan commentary interprets this as an example of Liu's atheism (*Tianwen tiandui zhu*, 11), but in fact he reasserts the "numinous" quality of Lady Qi. So it seems he is merely pointing out that unmarried women can also give birth.
11. Since the Sire of Might is the god of pestilence, Liu responds with the explanation

When all is harmonious and well-modulated,	順和調度
The gentle airs proceed in motion.	惠氣出行
Sometimes they advance, sometimes contract,	時屈時縮
But they have no fixed abode.	何有處鄉

[11] What is it that closes when darkness falls? 　　何闔而晦
What is it whose opening brings light? 　　何開而明

When it is bright—this is not a matter of opening; 　　明焉非闔
When dimmed—this is not a matter of hiding. 　　晦兮非藏

When the Horn Portal constellation has not yet dawned, 　　角宿未旦
Where does the radiant spirit [of the sun] conceal itself? 　　曜靈安藏

What dawns and what darkens? 　　孰旦孰幽
They are overlapping on their pathways. 　　繆躔於經
The Azure Dragon has its location, 　　蒼龍之寓
And it advances towards the Horn and Neck.[12] 　　而迋[13]彼角亢

[12] Were [Gun] not appointed to control the floods, 　　不任汩鴻
Why would the masses have elevated him?[14] 　　師何以尚之
They all responded [to Yao's doubts]: "Why be anxious? 　　僉答何憂
"Why not test him with the challenge?" 　　何不課而行之

Truly Gun was quarrelsome, 　　惟鯀詵詵
Facing the Sage he was recalcitrant. 　　鄰聖而犟
For a long time the masses were confused and chaotic, 　　恆師龐蒙

---

that pestilence rises when "weird" and "dark" airs and forces stir.

12. Horn and Neck are the first and second constellations within the Eastern Quadrant or Azure Dragon. They represent the Horn and Neck of the Dragon (see Schlegel, *Uranographie chinoise*, 87, 93). I take this stanza to mean that the Horn constellation and sun are not coordinated; the sun traverses its own path, the elliptic, which may or may not intersect with the Horn.

13. *Tianwen tiandui zhu* commentators (p. 12) read *guang* 迋 as meaning to "deceive," but I fail to comprehend how Liu could regard the existence of constellations themselves as a fraud.

14. The Han commentary glosses *shi* 師 as the "masses."

So they elevated this worthless wretch. 乃尚其妃
The Sovereign was caused trouble by the masses, 后惟師之難
So with furrowed brow he sent Gun to be tested. 瞶頌使試

[13] *With the owls and turtles pulling and dragging,*[15] 鴟龜曳銜
How did Gun [not] obey [Yao's] instructions? 鯀何聽焉
When he had fulfilled our desires and completed 順欲成功
the task,
Why did the Lord [Yao] then punish him? 帝何刑焉
[14] *Perishing after long durance at Mount Plume,* 永遏在羽山
Why was he not granted favor even after three years? 夫何三年不施

Gun stole the self-replenishing soil to dam the flood,[16] 盜堙息壤
Incurring the devastating anger of the Lord. 招帝震怒
Suffering punishment while living below, 賦刑在下
He was then exiled and abandoned at Plume. 而投棄於羽
Then the prime son was properly advanced, 方陟元子
So as to inherit the task and determine the territory.[17] 以胤功定地
Why would he abandon his own late father, 胡離厥考
And let owls and turtles indulge their hunger?[18] 而鴟龜肆喙

Since Prince Yu regarded Gun as obstinate, 伯禹愎鯀
How he could have achieved such a transformation? 夫何以變化
[15] *Continuing the legacy of his predecessors,* 纂就前緒
Yu ultimately accomplished the task of his father. 遂成考功
Why, to further the effort and advance the work, 何續初繼業
Did he use such different stratagems? 而厥謀不同

[Gun's] disposition was wicked, he deserved 氣孽宜害
destruction,
But his successor [Yu] was able to attain sagehood. 而嗣續得聖

15. The Han commentary does not gloss but instead simply repeats the difficult phrase *yexian* 曳銜, so there is no way to be sure how it is interpreting the phrase. But Liu seems to interpret it as being part of Gun's punishment, so I try to render it appropriately here.

16. Liu follows the account in the *Shanhaijing*; see Yuan Ke, ed., *Shanhaijing jiaozhu*, 18.395.

17. *Quan Tang wen* has 允 for 以胤.

18. Liu's question here is ambiguous. It could be a rhetorical question, casting in doubt the assumptions of the original text; or it could be a serious question in the vein of the original. In any case, he seems to prefer the Confucian orthodoxy on Gun to the questions raised by the "Heavenly Questions."

Out of muck and mire comes the lotus;	汙塗而蕖
But even so, the two should not be likened.	夫固不可以類
Callused body, hobbling gait,	胝躬躄步
By sledge [over mud] and clogs [up mountains], tired and lame,[19]	橇楯勩踏
His work lasted thirteen years.	厥十有三載
And so he covered for his late father's ugliness,	乃蓋考醜
And formed the model for the nine categories of regulations.	宜儀刑九疇
Having received the mystic treasure,[20]	受是玄寶
Darkness was completed by that one's wickedness,	昏成厥孽
And brilliance born out of the other's virtue.	昭生於德
Though Yu continued the legacy of his clan,	惟氏之繼
Why follow the model of that man's schemes?	夫孰謀之式
[16] The source of the floodwaters was most deep,	洪泉極深
So how could [Yu] block the flow?	何以寘之
He created the channel, plummeting downwards,	行鴻下隤
So that from the hillocks the water descended.[21]	厥丘乃降
And thus he filled in the extreme abyss,	焉填絕淵
So that from then on it was level with the earth.	然後夷於土
The earth is square and divided into nine sections,	地方九則
How could he distinguish among them?	何以墳之
According to the needs of the people,	從民之宜
He divided ninefold the wild lands.	乃九於野
And distinguished the revenues and the plantings,	墳厥貢藝
So there was the upper, the mid-range, and the lower.[22]	而有上中下

19. This line references the account of Yu quelling the flood in *Shiji*, 29.1687, in which he is said to have employed carriage and boat to cross land and water, but a sledge (*qiao* 毳 or 橇) to cross mud, and clogs (*jiao* 橋, also written *ju* 欙) to climb mountains. Written somewhat differently in *Shiji*, 2.98.

20. Yu received a mystic jade tablet from Shun in reward for quelling the flood; see *Shiji*, 2.96.

21. Alternatively, the *Tianwen tiandui zhu* commentary interprets these "hillocks" (*qiu* 丘) as peaks of flood water (p. 17).

22. This passage follows the account in the "Tribute of Yu" ("Yu gong" 禹貢) chapter in the *Book of Documents*.

[17] *How did the winged dragon measure them?* 應龍何畫
How did it pass over the rivers and oceans? 河海何歷

How could a sage be so lacking 胡聖為不足
That he needed to consult a dragon's wisdom? 反謀龍智
Shovels and spades they exerted to the utmost, 畚鍤究勤
But you hoodwink us with a dragon's surveying tail! 而欺畫厥尾

[18] *What did Gun himself construct?* 鯀何所營
What did Yu accomplish? 禹何所成
When Kanghui [Gonggong] was angered, 康回馮怒
Why did the earth sink down to the southeast? 墬何故以東南傾

The round canopy of Heaven is vast, 圜煮廓大
But it stands up without support. 厥立不植
As the earth is in the southeast, 地之東南
So it is in the northwest. 亦已西北
That petty man, Hui: 彼回小子
How could the toppling be his effort alone? 胡顛隕爾力
Ah, who has scared you to such an extent, 夫誰駭汝為此
That you would confuse him with the axis of Heaven? 而以恩天極

[19] *How did [Yu] arrange the Nine Continents?* 九州安錯
How deep are the rivers and valleys? 川谷何洿

The continents are arranged across the Fertile Earth,[23] 州錯富媼
And then fixed on its base. 爰定於趾
The turbid rivers and the quiet valleys 躁川靜谷
Have forms there lofty, forms here low. 形有高庳

Flowing to the east they do not overflow: 東流不溢
Who knows the reason behind all this? 孰知其故

Eastward flowing all the way to the Hollow 東窮歸墟
 of Return,[24]
Then circling back to fill in the West, 又環西盈
Opening up channels and cavities in the 脈穴土區
 earthen spaces,

---

23. Technically the goddess of the earth, Ao 媼.
24. The "Hollow of Return" (Guixu 歸墟) is mentioned in *Liezi* as the valley where waters gather; see Yang Bojun, ed., *Liezi jishi*, 5.158.

Here turbid and there clear:	而濁濁清清
The rocky soil of the plateau, dry and loose,	墳壚燥疏
Soon absorbs the irrigated waters and so rises up.	滲渴而升
Swelling and surging to excess,	充融有餘
Once the moisture leaks out it flows again.	泄漏復行
When the vessel continues to churn, ever gushing and rushing;	器運液液
How should it ever overflow?[25]	又何溢為

[20] East and west, south and north:	東西南北
Which direction extends the farthest?	其修孰多

East and west, south and north:	東西南北
There are no limits to their extent.	其極無方
Why take that immeasurable vastness	夫何鴻洞
And quibble or compare the discrete lengths?	而課校修長

South and north bulge outward;	南北順橢
How much further do they extend?	其衍幾何

Without any measure of the infinite and imperceptible,	茫忽不準
How to protrude? How to conclude?	孰衍孰窮

[21] *The Hanging Garden of Kunlun's peaks:*	崑崙縣圃
Where is it located?	其居安在

Lifted up high in the northwestern region,	積高於乾
That is where Kunlun is located.	崑崙攸居
With disheveled head and tiger jaws,	蓬首虎齒
There she burrows, there she abides.[26]	爰穴爰都

The nine tiers of those elevated walls:	增城九重
How many leagues high do they stand?	其高幾里

The elevated walls [of Kunlun] have a height	增城之高
Of thirteen thousand *li*.[27]	萬有三千

---

25. Liu compares the system of waterways to a great vessel; though the waters keep shifting in position the quantity is constant and so does not overflow the container.

26. The Spirit Mother of the West (Xiwangmu 西王母) is described this way in *Shanhaijing*; see Yuan Ke, ed., *Shanhaijing jiaozhu*, 2.45, 16.344. On this goddess's name, see Goldin, "On the Meaning of the Name *Xi wangmu*."

27. The Han commentary says that they are twelve thousand *li* tall, and the received text

[22] *Who is it who passes through* 　　四方之門
　　The Gates of the Four Directions? 　其誰從焉

　　Cool or warm, scorching or chill, 　　清溫燠寒
　　Follow one another by season. 　　　迭出於時
　　The seasons' mighty transformations 　時之丕革
　　By this means establish their own gates. 由是而門

　　When the northwestern gate opens up wide, 西北辟啓
　　What kind of air blows through it? 　　何氣通焉

　　What passes through when these are opened wide 辟啓以通
　　Is no more than the element of air. 　　茲氣之元

[23] *Why does the sun not reach its mark?* 　日安不到
　　What does the Torch Dragon illumine?[28] 燭龍何照

　　The slender dragon's mouth is aflame, 修龍口燎
　　And its head faces northward. 　　　爰北其首
　　Though Ninefold Yin is utterly dark, 　九陰極冥
　　Yet the North is illumined thereby. 　厥朔以炳

　　Till Xihe lifts the reins of the sun carriage, 羲和之未揚
　　What gleams on the blossoms of the Dimming Wood? 若華何光

　　The blossoms of the Dimming Wood 　惟若之華
　　Receive their incandescence from the passing Xihe.[29] 稟羲以耀

[24] *What place is warm in the wintertime?* 　何所冬暖
　　What place will chill in the summer? 　何所夏寒

　　The Mountain of the Mad is fully frozen over,[30] 狂山凝凝
　　And ice covers the northernmost point. 　冰於北至

---

of *Huainanzi* eleven thousand (Liu Wendian, ed., *Huainan honglie jijie*, 4.159). Either Liu Zongyuan has a different text of *Huainanzi*, or he is playing a metascholarly game with us.

　28. As noted in "Text Three," these lines would have to be rearranged to make the rhyme scheme conform.

　29. Xihe is the name of the charioteer of the sun. Liu seems effectively to be reframing the question rather than answering it.

　30. The Mountain of the Mad, Kuangshan 狂山, is mentioned in the *Shanhaijing* as a place that remains cold in the summertime; see Yuan Ke, ed., *Shanhaijing jiaozhu*, 3.73.

Then there is also the Isle of Fire:	爰有炎洲
The Master of Cold finds no employment there.[31]	司寒不得以試
Where is there a forest of stone?	焉有石林
What beast is capable of speech?	何獸能言
How should stone not become a forest?	石胡不林
Go observe the Western Pole.	往視西極
One creature speaks, gabbing and chatting,	獸言嘐嘐
And perfectly cognizant of men's names.[32]	人名是達
[25] How could there be a hornless dragon	焉有虯龍
That roams with a bear-creature on its back?	負熊以遊
A hornless dragon writhes and scrithes,	有虯蜿蛇
It has no horns and has no scales.	不角不鱗
When it sported with the dark bear,	嬉夫玄熊
The spectacle was treated as something divine.[33]	相待以神
[26] The fierce hamadryad of nine heads;	雄虺九首
Like Shu and Hu, where does it abide?[34]	儵忽焉在
In the south there is a monstrous hamadryad,	南有怪虺
Which bites with all its heads at once.	羅首以噬
Where Shu and Hu abide,[35]	儵忽之居

31. Liu proposes an answer to the question based on a geographical miscellany, *Shi zhou ji* 十洲記, which mentions an island in the southern ocean called "Isle of Fire"; see *Yiwen leiju*, 80.1364. Amusingly, though, he points out that the deity associated with cold weather would be out of a job there.

32. The orangutan is said to recognize people's names, in Yuan Ke, ed., *Shanhaijing jiaozhu*, 10.243.

33. It is unclear exactly what the original poem is asking about here (see "Text Three" where I speculate about water deities). Liu demythologizes the legend anyway; the dragon and bear were just two animals playing together, not any kind of supernatural event that requires further explanation.

34. I translate this line differently from that in "Text One," based on Liu Zongyuan's interpretation. See next note.

35. There is a note here, perhaps Liu's own, saying that the meaning of Shuhu 儵忽 is quite clear from the parable in *Zhuangzi* (see *Zhuangzi jishi*, 7.309) where they bore nine holes into Hundun, thereby killing him. Liu thinks that Wang Yi has misunderstood *shuhu* as a compound referring to lightning. It is interesting to see another case where Liu

They are the Supreme Lords of Oceans South 帝南北海
and North.

What place is there without death? 何所不死
Where do the giant men abide? 長人何守

In the country of Yuanqiu, 員邱之國
The local people die later than elsewhere. 身民後死
The Guardian of Mounts Feng and Yu 封嵎之守
Is some three miles wide.[36] 其橫九里

[27] Waterlily blossoms on the nine-branched road, 靡蓱九衢
And hemp blossoms, where can they be found? 枲華安居

There is a duckweed with nine forks, 有萍九歧
So the image described here is a fraud.[37] 厥圖以詭
What is produced by the Floating Mountain? 浮山孰產
The hemp that flowers with crimson blossoms.[38] 赤華伊枲

When a snake swallowed an elephant, 一蛇吞象
How gigantic must it have been? 厥大何如

A snake of Ba engorged an elephant: 巴蛇腹象
That is sufficient to perceive its size. 足覿厥大
After three years it disgorged the bones, 三歲遺骨
Which has verified its full length. 其修已號

[28] Blackwater and Mystic Base 黑水玄趾
And Mount Triperil: where are they found? 三危安在

---

disagrees with the Han interpretation of the poem, but Liu's interpretation makes it impossible to make sense of the couplet as a unit, so the Han interpretation is likely superior.

36. Liu refers to a story in the *Guliang zhuan* (*Chunqiu Guliang zhuan zhushu*, 11.201) about an enemy tribe called the "Changdi" 長狄 ("tall barbarians") whose bodies were nine acres (*mu* 畝) wide. Instead of criticizing the exaggeration, Liu doubles down on it. Mounts Feng and Yu were located near modern Mount Mogan 莫幹 in Zhejiang, and guarded by Fangfengshi 防風氏, ancestor of the Changdi; see Xu Yuangao, ed., *Guoyu jijie*, 5.202–3. The connection is also made in Lu Chun's guide, *Chunqiu jizhuan zuanli*, 10.19b.

37. The note here (perhaps by Liu himself) remarks that Wang Yi has misunderstood *qu* 衢 as road rather than fork.

38. Liu identifies the reference here as being to the entry on Fushan 浮山 in Yuan Ke, ed., *Shanhaijing jiaozhu*, 2.23.

The Blackwater gushes forth in abundance,	黑水淫淫
And exhausts itself only at Bujiang.[39]	窮於不姜
Mystic Base then is to the north,	玄趾則北
And Triperil to the south.	三危則南。

Though years without dying may be prolonged,	延年不死
When must longevity come to an end?	壽何所止

Those transcendents are remote and indiscernible,	僊者幽幽
Their longevity who would envy?	壽焉孰慕
Though all will vary as to length of life,	短長不齊
Each has his own termination.	咸各有止
Why embellish into the murky and measureless,	胡紛華漫汗
And dissemble by saying they do not die?[40]	而僊謂不死

[29] Where is the home of the hill-fish? 鯪魚何所
Where do the ravenous birds abide? 鬿堆焉處

The hill-fish have the appearance of men,	鯪魚人貌
And are located near Lieguyi.	邇列姑射
The ravenous birds stand upon Mount Beihao,	鬿雀峙北號
And what they feed on there is men.[41]	惟人是食

How did Archer Yih shoot down the suns?	羿焉彈日
How were the suncrows then deplumed?	烏焉解羽

How could there be ten suns?	焉有十日
They would incinerate the hundred living things.	其火百物
Yih would have had to make flaming charcoal of his body,	羿宜炭赫厥體

---

39. According to the *Shanhaijing*, Bujiang is a legendary place out in the wastelands; see Yuan Ke, ed., *Shanhaijing jiaozhu*, 15.313.

40. As Stephen Bokenkamp has pointed out, Daoist practices generally aimed at longevity and transcendence, but not precisely "immortality" in the sense of unchanging eternal life. See Bokenkamp, *Early Daoist Scriptures*, 21–23.

41. A note possibly original to Liu Zongyuan (*Zengguang zhushi yinbian Tang Liu xiansheng ji*,14.78b) criticizes Wang Yi's commentary for locating the hillfish in the south, rather than out near Mount Lieguyi 列姑射 in the oceans; see Yuan Ke, ed., *Shanhaijing jiaozhu*, 12.279–80. I also translate *qidui* 鬿堆 merely as "ravenous birds" rather than "griffin" because Liu's note seems to dispute the Han identification as a legendary beast.

So how could he then bend his limbs?　　　　　　胡膺以枝屈
The great lake hundreds of miles wide　　　　　　大澤千里
Is where the birds all deplumed themselves.　　　群鳥是解

[30] Yu exerted himself to complete the task,　　　禹之力獻功
He descended to watch over all four parts of the earth.　降省下土四方
How did he find that lady of Tushan,　　　　　　焉得彼嵞山女
And mate with her at the Platform of Mulberries?　而通之於台桑
[31] Caring for that maiden he made a match with her,　閔妃匹合
In order to have a successor;　　　　　　　　　厥身是繼
Why did Yu, relishing such unlike flavors,　　　　胡維嗜不同味
Yet hasten for a single day's consumption?　　　　而快晁飽

Yu had been cautioned about progeny,　　　　　　禹懲於績
Hence he promptly mated with the Lady of
　Mount Soil.　　　　　　　　　　　　　　　嵞婦亟合
His skin had been depilated by his labors,[42]　　　胈離厥膚
And thrice passing the gate, he did not go in to look,[43]　三門以不眄
And did not even heed the wailing of an infant:　　呱呱之不盡
Why would he crave that other flavor?[44]　　　　　而孰圖厥味
When he had fully exsiccated the wild lands,　　　卒燥中野
The people could reside there, could abide there.[45]　民攸宇攸曁

[32] When Qi replaced the minister Yi as sovereign,　啓代益作后
All of a sudden [Yi] met with disaster.　　　　　　卒然離蠥

---

42. This odd fact is mentioned by *Zhuangzi*. Yu worked until "his calves were hairless, his shins were without hair" 腓无胈, 脛无毛. See *Zhuangzi jishi*, 33.1077.

43. Here Liu borrows the description of Yu's industriousness from Mencius. See *Mencius*, 3A.4; *Mengzi zhushu*, 5B.174; Legge, *Works of Mencius*, 252; Lau, *Mencius*, 102. Yu is said to have spent eight years away from home, and three times to have passed his own house without entering it.

44. See the "Yi Ji" 益稷 chapter of *Shujing* (Book of documents): "When my son Qi was wailing and weeping, I did not regard him, but kept planning with all my might my labor on the land." 啓呱呱而泣, 予弗子, 惟荒度土功. Text and translation from Legge, *Shoo King*, 85. Throughout this passage Liu defends Yu, a hero of Confucian virtue, against potential slander.

45. My translation preserves the intralinear repetition of Liu's idiosyncratic Chinese, employing the archaic relative pronoun *you* 攸.

That wailing child [Qi] was worthy of praise. 彼呱克臧
And his clan of Ni came to rule the Xia. 俾姒作夏
Yi was presented for honor by the Sovereign Lord 獻后益於帝
    [of Heaven],
Reverent and respectfully declining the mandate 諄諄以不命
    himself.[46]
After that he became no more than an old codger: 復為叟者
What to worry about, what to call disaster?[47] 曷戚曷孽

Why was it that Qi was still beset by anxiety, 何啓惟憂
And succeeded in imprisoning him? 而能拘是達
[33] *Since all [the Youhu] did was accomplish trouble,* 皆歸射鞠
[Qi punished them] and so his body was unharmed. 而無害厥躬

That wailing one was diligent in the work of virtue, 呱勤於德
So the people were able to live and thrive. 民以乳活
The Youhu then were opposed to his proper rule, 扈仇厥正
So the Lord bestowed the weapon to smite the 帝授柄以摣兇窮
    worst foe.[48]
What ordinary man could have harmed that sage? 聖庸夫孰克害

How was it that Lord Yi was overthrown, 何后益作革
While Yu had helped the people cultivate the land? 而禹播降

Yi had eliminated the hardships of the people, 益革民艱
And they all polished their grains to the finest white. 咸粲厥粒
For Yu had bestowed them with the soil, 惟禹授以土
So they could seed the myriads and millions. 爰稼萬億
Avoiding the soggy places, stepping on firm ground, 違溺踐坰
They could abide in prosperity and eat in plenty. 休居以康食
Not even for a moment did he depart from sagehood, 姑不失聖
Nor go any place under Heaven not according to 天胡往不道
    the Way.[49]

46. Liu here borrows from *Mencius*, which says that "Yu commended Yi to Heaven" 禹薦益於天, but that when the time came to succeed Yu, Yi declined the succession in favor of Yu's son Qi; see *Mencius*, 5A.6; *Mengzi zhushu*, 9B.304; Legge, *Works of Mencius*, 358.

47. In other words, Yi declined the throne and was able to retire in peace, so why should the original question refer to that happy outcome as a disaster? There is indeed some lack of clarity in the question as interpreted by the Han commentary.

48. The Fudan commentary identifies Di here as Qi, but this seems implausible.

49. The words *sheng tian* 聖天 are absent from some texts, and omitted from the Fudan

[34] *Qi hurried to arrange the marriage rites of Shang,*　　啟棘賓商
　　　With the "Nine Phases" and the "Nine Songs."　　　九辯九歌

　　Qi let his voice pass far and wide;　　　　　　　　　啓達厥聲
　　Chanting according to the way of Heaven and Earth.　堪輿以呻
　　Distinguishing and aligning the order of performance, 辨同容之序
　　His Lordship [Qi] then arranged the marriage rites.⁵⁰　帝以賀嬪

　　Why did his diligent son rupture his mother,　　　　何勤子屠母
　　Who, dying, made new division in the earth?　　　　而死分竟地

　　It was Yu's mother who produced that sage;　　　　禹母產聖
　　Why would he split her spine?⁵¹　　　　　　　　　　何龘厥旅
　　Such rumor of corruption from anarchic voices　　　彼淫言亂噣
　　Perceptive eardrums will not let abide.　　　　　　聰職以不處

[35] *The Lord [of Heaven] sent down Archer Yih for*　　帝降夷羿
　　　the Yee tribes,
　　　And he brought new evils to the people of Xia.　　革孽夏民
　　　But why did he shoot at the Sire of the Yellow River,　胡射夫河伯
　　　And take the nymph of the Luo River as his wife?　而妻彼雒嬪

　　Archer Yih of the Yee was haughty and wild,　　　夷羿滔荒
　　So he usurped the rulership of the Xia.　　　　　割更后相
　　Who then was responsible for all his crimes?　　　夫孰作厥孽
　　Yet they slander the Lord for "sending him down."⁵²　而誣帝以降
　　Shaking the scales of the white serpent,　　　　　震皦厥鱗
　　Yih gathered his arrows in its pupils.⁵³　　　　　集矢於皖
　　Claiming without compunction that the Lord was　肆叫帝不諶
　　　untrue,

---

edition, but preserved in, e.g., *Liu Hedong ji*, 14.242. Accordingly, there are also various ways of punctuating the couplet. Though retaining them makes the couplet more awkward, I preserve them as the *lectio difficilior*.

50. The meaning of the "Heavenly Questions" is unclear here and has been the topic of much scholarly debate. Liu creatively interprets 賓 as the equivalent with the woman radical, 嬪.

51. The Fudan commentators read *lü* 旅 as a variant of *lü* 膂; see *Tianwen tiandui zhu*, 35.

52. In other words, Yih was responsible for the punishment he received, and Heaven should not be blamed. I leave a line break here to mark the rhyme change within Liu's answer.

53. *Wan* 皖 seems to be a graphic error for *huan* 睆; see *Tianwen tiandui zhu*, 36.

He then lost his position and was bathed in scorn.	失位滋嫚
There was indeed a beauty of the Luo River,	有洛之嫛
But why should she have mated with this madman?	焉妻於狡

[36] With his nacre-inlaid bow and keen gauntlet　　馮珧利決
The giant boar [Yih] shot dead.　　封狶是射
Why, when [Yih] presented the rich offering of meat,　　何獻蒸肉之膏
Did the High Lord [of Heaven] not approve?　　而后帝不若

That immoderate man took pleasure in killing,　　夸夫快殺
And cooked the boar in a tripod to feed his hunger,　　鼎豨以厭飽
Taking the savory fat as offering to the Lord on High;　　馨膏腺帝
He offended proper virtue, using force to excess.　　叛德恣力
Why should stuffing Our tongue and throat with fat　　胡肥台舌喉
Make someone else's blessings more bountiful?[54]　　而濫厥福

[37] When Han Zhuo seduced Pure Fox,　　浞娶純狐
That beguiling consort conspired with him.　　眩妻爰謀
Why was it that the hide-piercing Archer Yih　　何羿之射革
Was destroyed altogether by that intervention?　　而交吞揆之

Han Zhuo's calumnies and his wife's stratagems　　寒讒婦謀
Resulted in Archer Yih's assassination.　　后夷卒戕
While he was idly cast out in the wilderness,[55]　　荒棄於野
Those villains were able to be rewarded.　　俾奸民是臧
All throughout the land were his enemies;　　舉土作仇
He had only his bow to guard himself.　　徒怙身孤

[38] When blocked and thwarted while traveling westward,　　阻窮西征
How was it that he managed to cross those cliffs?　　巖何越焉
When Gun was transformed into a tawny bear,[56]　　化為黃熊
How did the shaman bring him back to life?　　巫何活焉

54. The speaker is Heaven so I translate in the royal (celestial?) first-person plural.
55. "Cast out in the wilderness" echoes the "Cai Zhong zhi ming" 蔡仲之命 chapter in the *Shujing*: "Do not idly throw away my charge!" 無荒棄朕命. See Legge, *Shoo King*, 491.
56. Apparently, Liu Zongyuan is unaware of the evidence that this should be a sea turtle rather than a bear.

Gun perished at Plume Cliff; 鯀婞羽巖
Turning tawny he fell into the abyss.[57] 化黃而淵

[39] Then all could sow the black millet and sticky millet, 咸播秬黍
Where they had planted only reeds and cresses. 莆雚是營

His son rightly sowed the early-blooming and late-blooming crops, 子宜播植穉
Upon the hillocks, upon the rivers: 於丘於川
There the bulrushes, there the cattails, 維莞維蒲
There the water-bamboo, there the reeds.[58] 維菰維蘆
And he raked the soil according to plan; 丕徹以圖
The people then rejoiced and praised him.[59] 民以謹以都

How could they plant all the crops? 何由并投
For Gun's fault only greatened and expanded. 而鯀疾脩盈

Yao was harsh to that father [Gun], 堯酷厥父
But the son Yu was thereby provoked to his achievement. 厥子激以功
He was able to magnify the ancestral offerings, 克碩厥祀
As later generations established suburban sacrifices.[60] 後世是郊

[40] The white nimbus winding around and spreading out, 白蜺嬰茀
Why did it come upon this hall? 胡為此堂
How did [Cui Wenzi] obtain that fine elixir, 安得夫良藥
Which turned out to be incapable of good? 不能固臧

[41] Heaven is configured horizontal and vertical: 天式從橫
When Yang energy disperses then you die. 陽離爰死

57. This response seems moderate, but simply by affirming that Gun died, Liu is effectively rejecting the entire myth.

58. This passage employs the kind of repetition found mainly in *Shijing*, an AXAY structure in each of three lines in succession, and the affirmative particle *wei* 維 repeated four times.

59. For this archaic use of *du* 都, see, e.g., the first stanza of "You nü tong che" 有女同車 (*Odes* 83); Legge, *She King*, 137.

60. As mentioned in *Zuozhuan*, Duke Zhao, year 7. According to Zichan 子產 from the state of Zheng, Gun received the suburban sacrifices in recognition of his achievement, even though he ultimately failed. See Durrant et al., *Zuo Tradition*, 1423.

> Why did the great bird cry out, 大鳥何鳴
> And how did the man's body disappear? 夫焉喪厥體
>
> The Prince [Qiao] was startled and shocked 王子怪駭
> At the nimbus-like form that enfolded his robes.[61] 蜺形蜌裳
> Cui Wenzi stole the garb and wielded the halberd, 文襫操戈
> So he failed to notice the elixir's excellence. 猶憯夫藥良
> The bird cried out as it wandered, 終鳥號以游
> And rose out of the bamboo cases square and round. 奮厥筐筐
> From the tenebrous gloom he could hardly glean 窅漠莫謀
> Where the form was present and where absent.[62] 形胡在胡亡
>
> [42] When Ping cries out to summon the rain, 萍號起雨
> How does he get it to start? 何以興之
>
> The Yang energy stealthily boils up, 陽潛而釁
> While the steam of the Yin then rains down. 陰蒸而雨
> "Ping" (duckweed) arises accordingly, 萍憑以興
> And so the spirit's name was coined.[63] 厥號爰所
>
> Having created those bodies possessing two torsos, 撰體協脅
> How could deer assume them? 鹿何膺之
>
> That energy bizarre and yet divine, 氣怪以神
> Thence created a strange body, 爰有奇軀
> With torsos intertwined and limbs doubled — 脅屬支偶
> Tribute from the sovereign's borderland.[64] 尸帝之隅

61. Here Liu Zongyuan follows the Han commentary's glosses of *ying fu* 嬰茀 to form his own response.

62. This passage only makes sense in light of Wang Yi's convoluted interpretation of the source: "Cui Wenzi studied to be an immortal with Prince Qiao. Ziqiao transformed into a white nimbus spreading out and winding around, and brought the elixir to Wenzi. Cui Wenzi was startled and baffled, and drew his halberd to strike at the nimbus. When he hit it, the elixir fell to the ground. He looked down at it and saw the body of Prince Qiao. That is why it says that the elixir is not good." Liu in turn then reinterprets the story as a kind of optical illusion.

63. This is a clever etymological analysis of the rain god's name Ping 萍 as a variant of *ping* 苹 "duckweed," which is graphically similar.

64. Zuo Si's 左思 (250–305) "Shu Capital Rhapsody" ("Shudu fu" 蜀都賦) refers to a rare type of deer that can consume poison; see *Wenxuan*, 4.193; Knechtges, *Selections of*

[43] *When the mighty mountain-bearing turtles clap,* 鼇戴山抃
  How do they hold them steady in place? 何以安之

  Residing in the hills of the numinous ones, 宅靈之丘
  Though shaken they are not imperiled: 掉焉不危
  The giant turtles stand at their heads, 鼇厥首
  So they are ever tranquil and steady. 而恆以恬夷

  Letting go of the ships to go by land instead, 釋舟陵行
  How are they kept moving through space? 何以遷之

  Should they be released upon the land, 要釋而陵
  They are likely to be banished thence. 殆或謫之
  The giant of the Dragon Earls bore back the bones, 龍伯負骨
  And yet the Lord still shrank his domain.[65] 帝尚窄之

[44] *When Ao arrived at the doorstep,* 惟澆在戶
  What was he seeking from his brother's wife? 何求于嫂
  Why did Shaokang, while on the chase with hounds, 何少康逐犬
  End up decapitating his head? 而顛隕厥首

  Ao's lechery was equal to his strength; 澆嫪以力
  He coupled with his own brother's doe.[66] 兄麛聚之

Refined Literature, 1:365. The commentary by Liu Kui 劉逵 further describes it as a magical deer with two heads, citing Wei Wan's 魏完 gazetteer *Nanzhong zhi* 南中志. Liu seems to be expanding on this rumor with the idea of the strange creature being offered as tribute from the provinces.

65. Although the story of the turtles corresponds to an episode in the *Liezi*, Liu Zongyuan refers to the broader context of the story, in particular the succeeding passage where the giant from the kingdom of the Dragon Earl (Longbo 龍伯), after fishing out the six turtles, roasted their bones and was punished by the Lord of Heaven. See Graham, *Book of Lieh-tzŭ,* 97–98: "But there was a giant from the kingdom of the Dragon Earl, who came to the place of the five mountains in no more than a few strides. In one throw he hooked six of the turtles in a bunch, hurried back to his country carrying them together on his back, and scorched their bones to tell fortunes by the cracks. Thereupon two of the mountains, Daiyu 岱輿 and Yuanjiao 員嶠, drifted to the far North and sank in the great sea; the immortals who were carried away numbered many millions. God was very angry, and reduced by degrees the size of the Dragon Earl's kingdom and the height of his subjects." For Chinese text see Yang Bojun, ed., *Liezi jishi,* 5.161–62.

66. The "doe" is a startlingly bestial metaphor.

Shaokang borrowed the moment of hunting	康假於田
To retake possession of the home.	肆克宇之

[45] When Lady Tangent was sewing an undershirt, 女歧縫裳
They shared lodgings in the same house. 而館同爰止
Why did Shaokang behead the wrong one, 何顛易厥首
So that the lady met with harm instead? 而親以逢殆

Because of the undershirt, because of the lodging, 既裳既舍
It would have been right to remove both their heads at once. 宜咸墜厥首

[46] When Tang plotted to transform the people, 湯謀易旅
How did he treat them generously? 何以厚之

Tang took control of the vassals of Kui [Jie] 湯奮癸旅
By means of endearing gestures. 爰以區拊
He then demonstrated his power in Ge, 載厥德於葛
Punishing those who had made enemies of the provisioners.[67] 以詰仇餉

When [Shaokang] capsized the vessels of Zhenxun, 覆舟斟尋
By what route did he conquer them? 何道取之

Once Shaokang had restored the old ones [the Xia dynasty], 康復舊物
How could Zhenxun preserve itself? 尋焉保之
The capsized vessels are a metaphor for ease; 覆舟喻易
But perhaps they make the task sound still too hard! 尚或艱之

[47] When Jie assaulted Mount Meng, 桀伐蒙山
Whom did he obtain there? 何所得焉
Why was Lady Moxi taken advantage of [by Jie], 妹嬉何肆
And why did Tang destroy him for it? 湯何殛焉

Jie verily was fond of beauty, 惟桀嗜色
And captured Lady Mo of Meng by force. 戎得蒙妹

---

67. Liu Zongyuan is referring to the campaign of Tang against Ge 葛, perhaps to complement the example of his more generous policies in the original poem. See *Shangshu zhengyi*, 8.235; Legge, *Shoo King*, 180–81.

Living lasciviously in dissipation,
His own behavior incurred that man's assault.[68]

淫處暴娛
以大啓厥伐

[48] While Shun was anxious about the household,
Why did his father keep him a bachelor?
Why did sagely Yao not inform the groom's own clan Yaw
When marrying off to Shun his two daughters?

舜閔在家
父何以鱞
堯不姚告
二女何親

[49] When the sprouting of events is at its start,
How can one even speculate upon it?

厥萌在初
何所億焉

The blind father treated Shun as an enemy,
Keeping him a bachelor without mate.
Yao gave him possession of his daughters,
So as to aid him in his own reign.
How filial, obedient, reverent, and gracious!—
At a crook in the river Gui.[69]

瞽父仇舜
鯀以不儷
堯專以女
茲俾允厥世
惟蒸蒸翼翼
於嬀之汭

The agate-studded tower had ten stories;
Who was it who completed it?

璜臺十成
誰所極焉

Zhow's terrace was made of agate,
It was Sir Ji who recognized its foreboding.[70]

紂臺於璜
箕克兆之

[50] When [Fuxi] ascended to the throne as Lord,
By what path was he elevated to it?

登立為帝
孰道尚之

Because of his virtue, he rose to rule as High Lord,
And the people all placed him at the head.

惟德登帝
師以首之

As for the body possessed by Nü Wa,
Who crafted and constructed it?

女媧有體
孰制匠之

Wa's body has been called a serpent,
A diviner must have seen the resemblance.

媧軀虺號
占以類之

68. In this case Liu Zongyuan simply imposes a moralizing gloss on the events.

69. Where Shun was able to marry the two daughters of Yao, according to the *Book of Documents*. See *Shangshu zhengyi*, 2.53; Legge, *Shoo King*, 27.

70. As noted in the Han commentary to these lines, Zhow's extravagance and dissipation were indicated by various of his actions, including the building of the tower, but also the use of ivory chopsticks and other enormities.

> But why say she transformed seventy times in a day? 胡曰日化七十
> Only craftiness could produce such a prodigy. 工獲詭之

[51] Shun served his younger brother, 舜服厥弟
But ultimately met with harm. 終然為害
When Xiang acted wantonly in his cur-like body, 何肆犬體
Why was Shun's person not endangered or ruined? 而厥身不危敗

Shun's younger brother regarded him as an enemy, 舜弟眡厥仇
And ultimately sought to murder him by water and fire. 畢屠水火
How could someone roam freely as a sage, 夫固優游以聖
And yet still perish in these trials? 而孰殆厥禍
The canine are lacking in all virtue, 犬斷於德
And so could not triumph by mere biting. 終不克以噬
The elder still treated him with utmost benevolence, 昆庸致愛
Enfeoffing him with Bi, rich in revenues.[71] 邑鼻以賦富

[52] When the state of Wu was obtained by Gu, 吳獲迄古
Then [his son Taibo] stopped only at the Southern Marchmount. 南嶽是止
Who was it they encountered, after departing [Zhou], 孰期去斯
Who then obtained these two young noblemen? 得兩男子

Ah, humane indeed was Taibo, 嗟伯之仁
And abdicated to Jili so as to travel to the Marchmount.[72] 遜季旅嶽
Zhongyong shared similar capacity in dutifulness, 雍同度厥義
Which brought merit to the Kingdom of Wu. 以嘉吳國

[53] With crane-flavored broth and jade-ornamented tripods, 緣鵠飾玉
Yi Yin made offering to his Sovereign Lord [Tang]. 后帝是饗

---

71. The *Diwang ji* 帝王紀 (perhaps the same as *Diwang shiji*?) is quoted in *Shiji*, 1.53n, as identifying the place of Xiang's enfeoffment as Bi.

72. Liu Zongyuan follows the Han commentary to these lines, as translated above. Taibo, Zhongyong, and Jili 季歷 were the sons of Zhou ancestor Taiwang 太王 (a.k.a. Lord Gu 古公, Danfu 亶父). Since Jili was designated heir, his two older brothers Taibo and Zhongyong traveled south to establish the kingdom of Wu, a model of virtuous deference. See *Shiji*, 31.1747.

Why was he tasked with the plot against Jie of Xia, 何承謀夏桀
Which ultimately resulted in death and destruction? 終以滅喪

Sky Mulberry [Yi Yin] served the tripods to [Tang of] Shang,[73] 空桑鼎殷
Cajoling him with broth of his cranes; 諸饎厥鵠
Only Mencius understood language rightly, 惟軻知言
And perceived that this was not the case.[74] 睭焉以為不
The humane ones replaced, the foolish are endangered; 仁易愚危
But what foresight, what strategy is this? 夫曷揆曷謀
Then all took refuge in the thickets and pools, 咸逃叢淵
Because they had been oppressed by the tyrant.[75] 虐后以劉

[54] The supreme lord [Tang] descended to observe, 帝乃降觀
And below among the people encountered Yi Zhi. 下逢伊摯
Why was it that when [Jie] was punished by exile to Tiao, 何條放致罰
The people did rejoice greatly? 而黎服大說

He descended so as to observe below, 降厥觀於下
If it were not Zhi then who could receive him? 匪摯孰承
At Tiao assaulted, to Nanchao banished, 條伐巢放
The people therefore had that wart expunged for them. 民用潰厥疣
Their skin having been scraped smooth, 以夷於膚
Why not belt out songs of joy? 夫曷不謠

73. For the interpretation of Kongsang 空桑 as the Sky Mulberry at the center of the cosmos, see Chūbachi Masakazu, *Chūgoku no saishi to bungaku*, 34.

74. Liu draws from Mencius throughout this miniature poem in response to quatrain 53. In this case, Mencius had rejected the legend that Yi Yin won over Tang with gifts, rather than by the power of his virtue. See *Mencius*, 5A.7; *Mengzi zhushu*, 9B.307; Legge, *Works of Mencius*, 360–64; Lau, *Mencius*, 146.

75. The argument is that the wicked rulers themselves drive people away, and cause them to take refuge with the sagely ruler, rather than being drawn along intentionally by the sage. Liu adapts the analogies from Mencius: "The one that drives the fish into the deep pool is the otter; the one that drives the sparrows into the thicket is the falcon. Those who drove the people ahead of them, on behalf of Tang and Wu, were Jie and Zhow." 故為淵毆魚者獺也，為叢毆爵者鸇也。為湯、武毆民者，桀與紂也. *Mencius*, 4A.9; *Mengzi zhushu*, 7B.234; Legge, *Works of Mencius*, 300; Lau, *Mencius*, 122.

[55] While Jian Di was at the altar why did High 　簡狄在臺嚳何宜
　　　Lord Ku find it proper?
　　At the gift proffered by the dark bird why was 　玄鳥致貽女何嘉
　　　she so gratified?

　　Highlord Ku and Jian Di prayed for fertility, 　嚳狄禱祺
　　And so Xie formed as a fetus. 　契形於胞
　　Why should feeding like a swallow's fledgling[76] 　胡乙鷇之食
　　Be marveled at and cause for gratification? 　而怪焉以嘉

[56] Embracing and maintaining the virtue of his legacy, 　該秉季德
　　　[Gai] showed the same excellence as his father. 　厥父是臧

　　Gai had virtue inherited from his ancestors, 　該德胤考
　　Such that he could be Reaper of Rushes in the West.[77] 　蓐收於西
　　Claws like a tiger's, at hand battleaxes, 　爪虎手鉞
　　Charged with punishments, he corrects misdeeds. 　尸刑以司愿

　　Why was [Ao] finally murdered by the Youhu Clan 　胡終弊于有扈
　　While tending the cattle and sheep? 　牧夫牛羊

　　The Pastor Proper was stern and rigid,[78] 　牧正矜矜
　　Thereby Ao among the Youhu was destroyed.[79] 　澆扈爰踣

[57] Seeking to pacify with timely tasks, 　干協時舞
　　How did [Shaokang] cause [the people] to obey him? 　何以懷之

---

76. The Fudan commentary reads 乙 as a loan for 鳦, "swallow"; see *Tianwen tiandui zhu*, 54.

77. See discussion in chapter 2 above, showing that Liu's identification of Gai is partly right (though mostly wrong).

78. My "Pastor Proper" (Muzheng 牧正) refers to Xia Shaokang, who served in this post.

79. The Han commentary provides the reference for this: "The Youhu was the name of the kingdom ruled by Ao. When Ao defeated Xiahou Xiang, Xiang's unborn son named Shaokang later became the Chief Herdsman of the Youreng, charged with managing all the cattle and sheep. Then he attacked and killed Ao, defeated the Youhu, and restored the past traces of Yu, making offerings to Xia and matching the blessings of Heaven." 有扈, 澆國名也。澆滅夏后相，相之遺腹子曰少康，後為有仍牧正，典主牛羊，遂攻殺澆，滅有扈，復禹舊跡，祀夏配天也。

On the stairs he sought to entertain them, 階干以娛
And the Youmiao were transformed and came 苗革而格
  to submit.[80]
Since they were no longer threatened with death, 不迫以死
Then why should they be stubborn in their villainy? 夫胡狟厥賊

His full figure and lustrous skin: 平脅曼膚
How did he fatten himself up so? 何以肥之

Lord Xin [Zhow] was reckless and wild, 辛后駮狂
Made plump by lack of any anxiety.[81] 無憂以肥
Abandoning any restraint for his body, 肆蕩弛厥體
He sated his flesh with fat. 而充膏於肌
Chary of jewels to adorn his person, 嗇寶被躬
He was incinerated wearing them as his emblems.[82] 焚以旗之

[58] The lowly oxherds among the Youhu Clan: 有扈牧豎
How was it that they obtained favor? 云何而逢
When they were ambushed upon the couch, 擊床先出
How was it that the mandate had gone? 其命何從

Youhu abandoned his husbandry, 扈釋於牧
And made himself monarch by might. 力使后之
The enmity of the people was lodged therein, 民仇焉寓
And Qi slew him on his couch. 啟牀以斷

[59] Ever upholding the virtue of his legacy, 恆秉季德
How did [Tang] obtain that large ox? 焉得夫朴牛
How is it that [Tang] distributed his takings as bounty, 何往營班祿
Not only [racing all over] in vain? 不但還來

The martial founder of Yin walked in virtue, 殷武踵德
And so he obtained that large ox. 爰獲牛之朴

80. The *Shujing* reports that Shun 舜 and Yu 禹 succeeded in pacifying the Youmiao: "The emperor [Shun] also set about diffusing his accomplishments and virtue more widely. They danced with shields and feathers between the two staircases of the court. In seventy days the prince of Miao came to make his submission." See Legge, *Shoo King*, 66; *Shangshu zhengyi*, 4.119.

81. The virtuous ruler ought to feel anxiety on behalf of his subjects.

82. For Zhow's death see *Shiji*, 3.139.

Only uncouth men would lie about this event,	夫唯陋民是冒
And regard it wrongly as a fair omen.	而丕號以瑞
In the end he distributed what he had obtained,	卒營而班
Thereby buying the people's affection.	民心是市
[60] Men followed the paths through the darkness and obscurity,	昏微遵跡
So that the Youdi were not content.	有狄不寧
Why, like the owls flocking together in the brambles,	何繁鳥萃棘
Did [Xie Jufu] betray his son with untrammelled passions?	負子肆情
Xie Jufu was wild and lascivious;	解父狄淫
Encountering sincerity, he was ashamed.[83]	遭愍以赧
He did not observe what was in the midst of things,	彼中之不目
But perceived only what suited his lust.	而徒以色視
[61] The confused younger brother [Xiang], joining in adultery,	眩弟並淫
Endangered and injured his brother [Shun].	危害厥兄
When [Xiang] transformed his shape to dissimulate and deceive,	何變化以作詐
Why did [Shun's] progeny enjoy rapid increase?	後嗣而逢長
Xiang did not treat his brother with reverence,	象不兄龔
But instead plotted against him while he dug a well.[84]	而奮以謀蓋

83. Liu follows the Han commentary's story, apparently belonging to the Lu school of *Shijing* interpretation for "Gate to the Tombs" ("Mu men" 墓門; *Odes* 141): "This says that when Xie Jufu went to marry in Wu, he passed the gate of a cemetery in Chen, and saw a lady carrying her child. He wanted to engage in licentious deeds with her and give way to his own sensual desires. But the lady quoted the Songs to criticize him, saying: 'There are brambles growing by the gates of the cemetery, / And there are owls that gather there.' Thus the text tells of 'Many owls flocking together in the brambles.' This means that since there are brambles on the gates of the cemetery, even though there may be no people [who would observe us], in the brambles there will be owls, so how can you not be ashamed?" 言解居父聘吳，過陳之墓門，見婦人負其子，欲與之淫泆，肆其情欲。婦人則引《詩》刺之曰：墓門有棘，有鴞萃止。故曰繁鳥萃棘也。言墓門有棘，雖無人，棘上猶有鴞，汝獨不愧也。

84. There is a detailed account of Xiang's plot against his older brother Shun in Mencius. See *Mengzi zhushu*, 9A.290–95; Lau, *Mencius*, 139–41. In particular, "Shun's

Yet the sage was scarcely enraged at that wickedness; 聖孰凶怒
Instead inheritance he used to make lasting his love.[85] 嗣用紹厥愛

[62] *Cheng Tang journeyed east* 成湯東巡
Until he reached the Youshen. 有莘爰極
Why did he request of lesser official [Yi Yin], 何乞彼小臣
And so obtain a propitious consort? 而吉妃是得

There was a jade maiden of the Youxin Clan, 莘有玉女
And Tang journeyed far to obtain her.[86] 湯巡爰獲
Then within his household there could be harmony, 既內克厥合
And he could safeguard his virtue without. 而外弼於德
His recognizing Yi Yin was not his recognizing of 伊知非妃伊之知
   his consort and Yi Yin together;
How could a vassal fail to be recognized?[87] 臣曷以不識

[63] *It was by a tree at the water's margin* 水濱之木
That the little child [Yi Yin] was found, 得彼小子
So why did [the Youshen], detesting him, 夫何惡之
Send him off escorting a bride of their own clan? 媵有莘之婦

Why say the tree transformed into a mother? 胡木化於母
This is poison spoken against Yi Yin's sageliness. 以蝎厥聖
These beaks chattering of nothing good 喙鳴不良
Use slander to pervert the right. 譖以詭正

---

parents sent him to repair the barn. Then they removed the ladder and the Blind Man set fire to the barn. They sent Shun to dredge the well, set out after him and blocked up the well over him." 「父母使舜完廩, 捐階, 瞽瞍焚廩. 使浚井, 出, 從而揜之。」 Lau, *Mencius*, 139; *Mengzi zhushu*, 9A.290.

85. Referring again to Mencius' verdict on the situation: "He, Xiang, came as a loving brother, and so Shun honestly believed him and was pleased. What need was there for pretence?" 彼以愛兄之道來, 故誠信而喜之, 奚偽焉? Lau, *Mencius*, 140; *Mengzi zhushu*, 9A.292.

86. See *Shiji*, 3.122–23.

87. Fudan commentators punctuate in three tetrasyllabic lines, but my eccentric construal of the lines produces a plausible sense, and gives a consistent entering-tone rhyme for this passage. Essentially, Liu seems to be criticizing the original poem for conflating the two different episodes, meeting a consort and meeting a minister, and argues that these were two unrelated events.

If the whole village [of Yi Yin's mother] was submerged,	盡邑以墊
Who could have transmitted her dream?[88]	孰譯彼夢

[64] When Tang emerged from Double Springs,　湯出重泉
Of what crime had he been found guilty?　夫何辠尤
When he could no longer check the will to assault the Sovereign,　不勝心伐帝
Who was it that spurred him on?　夫誰使挑之

Because what Tang had done was not conventional,　湯行不類
He was imprisoned at Double Springs.　重泉是囚
The statutes established, wrongful and tyrannical,　違虐立辟
For that reason harmed the virtuous.　實罪德之由
The people were greatly angered by that exploitation,　師憑怒以割
It was Kui [Jie] himself who provoked enmity.　癸挑而讎

[65] When they met at dawn to make the war compact,　會晁爭盟
Who was it that accomplished their common oath?　何踐吾期
When the gray-black birds assembled in flight,　蒼鳥群飛
Who was it that caused them to flock together?　孰使萃之

[66] Arriving, they struck fiercely at the body of Zhow,　到擊紂躬
But Uncle Dan [Duke of Zhou] did not approve the act.　叔旦不嘉
Why did [the Duke of Zhou] survey and initiate [the return],　何親揆發足
While [the people] sighed in admiration at the mandate bestowed upon Zhou?　周之命以咨嗟

[67] When all under Heaven had been allotted to the Yin,　授殷天下
By what authority did they rule?　其位安施
When in turn success met with destruction,　反成乃亡
What was the fault that caused it?　其罪伊何

[68] Contending to dispatch the weapons of aggression,　爭遣伐器
How did he accomplish it?　何以行之

---

88. Liu's response refers to the fascinating story preserved in the Han commentary (see above), similar to an anecdote in the *Lüshi chunqiu* (Knoblock and Riegel, *Annals of Lü Buwei*, 307 [14/2.2]). Yi Yin's mother has a dream warning of her in a flood but then is drowned by the flood when it comes. As Liu Zongyuan rightly points out, the story does not seem to be logically consistent.

Advancing in stride, striking on both flanks,	並驅擊翼
How did he take command of all this?	何以將之

Jiao Ge was close to destruction,	膠鬲比縶
So he took action in the rain to meet with the deadline.[89]	雨行踐期
Just like hurling forth a pot of water to prevent a burn,	捧盎救灼
When humaneness advances then all follow in its wake.	仁興以畢隨
The goshawks all shared the same intent,	鷹之咸同
And so were caused to flock together there.	得使萃之
Slicing Zhow's neck with a gold battleaxe:	頸紂黃鉞
Why would Dan [Duke of Zhou] delight in that?	旦孰喜之
The father of the people had received his blessing,	民父有瞽
So they sighed in admiration of him.	嗟以美之
Authority is meant to protect the people,	位庸庇民
Only the humane can assume it.	仁克蒞之
Zhow was dissipated and destructive,	紂淫以害
So the people murdered and overthrew him.	師殛圮之
They all chased after his death,	咸諠厥死
Striving to seize weapons of their own.	爭徂器之
As both flanks were incited to overcome and resist,	翼鼓顛禦
With delighted dances they overswept him.	謹舞靡之

[69] *When Lord Zhao completed his excursion*	昭后成遊
Reaching as far as the southern lands,	南土爰底
What was the benefit for him in the end	厥利惟何
From coming upon the white pheasant?	逢彼白雉

On the water's margin they teased Zhao,	水濱翫昭
And the men of Jing then captured and murdered him.	荊陷弒之
What a canard, that he should be welcomed by the Yueshang:	繆迓越裳
For why would they have offered pheasant as tribute?	疇肯雉之

[70] *Why did King Mu, so clever and covetous,*	穆王巧楳
Choose to pursue his world-spanning journey?	夫何為周流

---

89. Liu comments on the legend, in the Han commentary, that King Wu attacked at the appointed time so as to save the life of Zhow's advisor Jiao Ge.

Putting in order all under Heaven,	環理天下
What was it that he was searching for?	夫何索求
King Mu was baffled by the "Prayer and Summons,"[90]	穆憒祈招
And instead set forth roaming in idle abandon.	猖洋以遊
Traveling in a circuit around the nine lands,	輪行九野
Ever seeking after strange sights.	惟怪之謀
Why feign that he entertained a beast in lady's headdress,	胡紿娛戴勝之獸
And toasted her at Chalcedony Pool while exchanging songs?[91]	觴瑤池以迭謠
[71] When the uncanny couple were selling goods,	妖夫曳街
What did they call out in the marketplace?	何號于市
Who was it that King You of the Zhou would execute,	周幽誰誅
So that he obtained his concubine Bao Si?	焉得夫褒姒
The children set out to harm the couple by speech:	孺賊厥說
"Made of mulberry was the bow."[92]	爰㡣其弧
The disaster and muddle of King You was from his wastefulness,	幽禍挐以夸
Fearing that Bao would lure him out.	憚褒以漁
Being extravagantly fond of homicide,	淫嗜藨殺

90. A lost poem composed by Moufu 謀父, intended to rebuke and restrain King Mu. See *Zuozhuan*, Duke Zhao, year 12; Durrant et al., *Zuo Tradition*, 1484 n. 585.

91. King Mu is said to have visited Xiwangmu (The Spirit-Mother of the West) in his travels. According to the *Shanhaijing*, she had "disarrayed hair and ornate headdress" 蓬髮戴勝; see Yuan Ke, ed., *Shanhaijing jiaozhu*, 2.45, and for her bestial form see also quatrain 21 above. The *Mu tianzi zhuan* 穆天子傳 describes their meeting in more detail: "The Son of Heaven toasted the Spirit-Mother of the West upon the Chalcedony Pool. The Spirit-Mother of the West then performed a song for the Song of Heaven..." 天子觴西王母于瑤池之上。西王母為天子謠. This passage is quoted in *Taiping yulan*, 85.3a; see also Wang Yiliang and Chen Jianmin, eds., *Mu tianzi zhuan huijiao jishi*, 3.143.

92. This passage elaborates on the story from the Han commentary, having to do with the downfall of King You and his consort, Bao Si 褒姒: "Long ago in the past age of King You of Zhou there was a children's ditty saying: 'Mulberry bow and willow quiver / Will surely mark the end of the Zhou state!' Later on a couple were selling these items, and so people thought they must be demonic. They were caught, and dragged out into the market to be humiliated." 昔周幽王前世有童謠曰：㡣弧箕服，實亡周國。後有夫婦賣是器，以為妖怪，執而曳戮之於市也.

Advisors slaughtered, critics murdered, 諫尸謗屠
How was the scaly dragon's spittle taken as omen? 孰鱗漦以徵
What crime was attributed to the transformed 而化黿是羞
turtle?[93]

[72] *As the Mandate of Heaven revolves and reverses:* 天命反側
How does it punish and how does it aid? 何罰何佑

Heaven is remote and obscure, 天邈以蒙
Man is miniscule and set apart. 人幺以離
How could their two paths intersect 胡克合厥道
To punish someone's errors or transgressions? 而詰彼尤違

Duke Huan of Qi convened the lords nine times, 齊桓九會
But he too was murdered in the end. 卒然身殺

Duke Huan trumpeted his might, 桓號其大
But ruled his subordinates with arrogance. 任屬以傲
By fortune he was able to convene them nine times, 幸良以九合
But still encountered wickedness and came to ruin.[94] 逮孽而壞

[73] *As for that Zhow the King himself:* 彼王紂之躬
Who set him into disturbance and confusion? 孰使亂惑
Why did he loathe his own aides and assistants, 何惡輔弼
And employ instead the men of slanderous gossip? 讒諂是服
[74] *Why did his adviser Bi Gan revolt,* 比干何逆
Though he was then crushed and destroyed? 而抑沈之
Lei Kai was obsequious and obedient, 雷開阿順
And yet received enfeoffment. 而賜封之
[75] *Why does the virtue of the sages, though constant,* 何聖人之一德
Achieve success in different places? 卒其異方
Sire Mei was ground into meat paste, 梅伯受醢
And Master Ji feigned madness. 箕子詳狂

93. Apart from the children's ditty mentioned above, these lines refer to other popular omens about the downfall of the wicked King You. Bo Yang 伯陽 told of two dragons that appeared to the Xia court, and whose spittle was transmitted across the ages up to their own time, when it transformed into large turtle. A young girl who encountered it later became pregnant, and gave birth to a young girl, who was adopted by the people of Bao 褒, and grew up to be Bao Si, who was said to have caused King You's downfall. *Shiji*, 4.186.

94. Duke Huan's murder, miserable in spite of his excellent treatment of his advisors in the past, is described in *Guanzi*; see Rickett, *Guanzi*, 1:430.

No one in particular caused Zhow's confusion, 紂無誰使惑
Nothing but his own ambition to be leader. 惟志為首
Planning things back to front, his perception was 逆圖倒視
    inverted;
So his supporters and sycophants he slaughtered 輔讒以僇寵
    and honored.[95]
Bi Gan for his contrariness incurred death, 干異召死
Lei Kai for his assistance was made a lord. 雷濟克后
The virtue of King Wen advanced, benefiting all, 文德邁以被
Such that Rui first sued, then submitted to the Way.[96] 芮鞫順道
Mincing up Mei, enslaving Ji: 醢梅奴箕
The worthy all perished, wickedness thrived. 忠咸喪以醜厚

[76] Hou Ji was the primary son already, 稷維元子
Why did the Lord of Heaven honor him? 帝何竺之
When he was discarded on the ice, 投之於冰上
Why did the birds keep him warm? 鳥何燠之
[77] Why was he, with mighty bow and bearing arrows, 何馮弓挾矢
Able beyond all others to lead them? 殊能將之
Since [King Wu] had fiercely startled the sovereign 既驚帝切激
    [Zhow],
How then did he arrive at enduring success? 何逢長之

Qi [the Discarded One] was charmed and deserving; 棄靈而功
But how did [the Lord's] favor make itself evident? 篤胡爽焉
Warmed by the birds' wings on the ice, 翼冰以炎

---

95. I follow the curious grammar of Liu's original poem, which only makes sense if one adds an implicit "respectively" at the end of this line.

96. See *Shiji*, 4.152: "The Sire of the West (the Duke of Zhou) privately performed acts of benevolence, and so the feudal lords all came to him to resolve their troubles. Once men of Yu and Rui had a lawsuit that could not be settled, so they went to Zhou. When they entered, the farmers all yielded the fields, as according to popular custom all yielded to the elder. The men of Yu and Rui did not meet the Sire of the West, but were all ashamed. They told one another 'The matter we are contesting would be a source of shame to the people of Zhou. Why bother going there when it will only bring us humiliation?' So they returned home, and yielded to one another's demands. The feudal lords heard of this and said, 'The Sire of the West is indeed the mandated sovereign.'" 西伯陰行善，諸侯皆來決平。於是虞、芮之人有獄不能決，乃如周。入界，耕者皆讓畔，民俗皆讓長。虞、芮之人未見西伯，皆慚，相謂曰：「吾所爭，周人所恥，何往為，祇取辱耳。」遂還，俱讓而去。諸侯聞之，曰「西伯蓋受命之君」。

What kind of honor or elevation was this?	盍崇長焉
Since he was both majestic and intelligent,[97]	既岐既嶷
He was capable of taking charge of them.	宜庸將焉
Zhow's harshness was such a provocation	紂凶以啟
That King Wu was able long to continue his reign.	武紹尚焉

[78] When Prince Chang exclaimed upon the decline, 伯昌號衰
He wielded the whip and served as master. 秉鞭作牧
Why did [King Wu] take over all the Qi altars, 何令徹彼岐社
And the mandate for the dynasty of Yin? 命有殷國

The Prince wielded the whip in the west, 伯鞭於西
Brought rehabilitation to the banks of Yangzi and Han. 化江漢滸
Exchanging for the Qi altars the Grand Altar,[98] 易岐社以太
The mandate of the state was bequeathed to Wu.[99] 國之命以祚武

[79] When he transported his prized possessions towards Mount Qi, 遷藏就岐
Why did people follow along with him? 何能依

Passing over Liang with great sacks and parcels, 踰梁橐囊
The virtuous were drawn as if ants by gamey odors.[100] 羶仁蟻萃

That bewitching lady in Yin: 殷有惑婦
Why was she so vilified? 何所譏

Da Ji ruined the lascivious Shang, 妲滅淫商
So the wretched populace fled fast. 痡民以亟去

[80] When Zhow presented the bloody paste, 受賜茲醢
The Prince of the West [King Wen] protested to Heaven; 西伯上告

97. *Qini* 岐嶷 is an interesting divisible rhyming compound. It occurs in this same form in "The Birth of the People" ("Sheng min" 生民; *Odes* 245) in *Shijing* (Legge, *She King*, 468), describing the young Hou Ji.

98. The Grand Altar is mentioned as the supreme one in *Liji zhengyi*, 46.1520. The Qi altars were the older ones located at Mount Qi, a little west of modern Xi'an.

99. This is a proper answer to the query that seems to remove any doubt or ambiguity.

100. I follow the Fudan commentary's plausible interpretation here, but the syntax is still impossible. Literally "gamey virtue ants gather"; see *Tianwen tiandui zhu*, 74.

> Why did the High Lord [of Heaven] personally　　何親就上帝
> Revoke the mandate of Yin and not preserve it?　　罰殷之命以不救
>
> As for making Sire Mei the meat of a reward,　　肉梅以頒
> Why should King Wen not then have complained　　烏不台訴
>   to *me*?
> Who exceeded Kui's villainy?[101]　　孰盈癸惡
> Thus his body was struck, his altars razed.　　兵躬殄祀

[81] When Master Wang was in the market,　　師望在肆
　　How did Chang [King Wen] recognize him there?　　昌何識
　　Wielding a knife and raising up a cry,　　鼓刀揚聲
　　Why did the sovereign rejoice therein?　　后何喜

> When Ziya [Lü Wang] concealed himself midst　　牙伏牛漁
>   oxen and fishermen,
> What had concentrated within him flourished　　積內以外萌
>   without.
> The talented man of Qi [King Wen] eyed that mind　　歧目厥心
>   of his,
> Keenly perceiving the light that would shine forth.　　瞭眠顯光
> Exerting his energies to run the kingdom like a　　奮力屠國
>   butcher,
> He split the femur and the hipbone from the Shang.[102]　　以髀髖厥商

[82] When Wu set forth to assault Yin,　　武發殺殷
　　What was it that had infuriated him?　　何所悒
　　When he bore his spirit tablet to join in battle,　　載尸集戰
　　What was it that spurred him on?　　何所急

> How could Wu Fa indulge in slaughter?[103]　　發殺曷逞

---

101. Text is unclear since Kui normally refers to Jie 桀, but the topic here ought to be Zhow 紂. The Fudan editors boldly amend to Zhow; see *Tianwen tiandui zhu*, 75.

102. This passage offers a deft metaphorical account of Lü Wang's achievements, borrowing from the memorable quotation given in the Han commentary: "The inferior butcher is a butcher of cattle; the superior butcher is a butcher of kingdoms."

103. The Han commentary had glossed *yi* 悒 "melancholy, anxious" as *yuanyi* 悁悒 ʔyen-ʔyep, but this is an alliterative compound in which the semantic emphasis probably lies with the first character *yuan* 悁, hence my translation as "infuriated." Liu Zongyuan seems to understand the line as asking why the assault on Shang was justified, with an

He sought to cool the boiling torments of the people.	寒民於烹
Using chestnut wood for King Wen's spirit tablet,	惟栗厥文考
The pious son set forth on campaign.	而虔子以徂征

[83] The elder prince hung himself:[104]
What was the reason for it?
Why did it move the Heavens and tremble the Earth,
And who was still afraid of her [Lady Li]?

伯林雉經
維其何故
何感天抑墜
夫誰畏懼

Suffering slander, unrecognized,
That obedient prince hung himself.
How should the abuse of earthworms, the assault of mites,
Suffice to change Heaven and Earth?

中譖不列
恭君以雉
胡螾訟蟯賊
而以變天地

[84] When awesome Heaven located its Mandate,
Why was [the King] so circumspect?
When the rites were offered to all under heaven,
Why did this result in [the King's] overthrow?

皇天集命
惟何戒之
受禮天下
又使至代之

Heaven located its Mandate
So that only those of virtue could receive it.
Idle inheritors are soon discarded;
Should Heaven yet aid them?

天集厥命
惟德受之
允怠以棄
天又祐之

[85] At first the minister of Tang was Zhi [Yi Yin],
But later this one took on the responsibility of counsellor.
Why did he ultimately serve as officer for Tang,
To honor the offerings of the ancestral succession?

初湯臣摯
後茲承輔
何卒官湯
尊食宗緒

With the alliance of Tang and Zhi
The sacrificial meats could long be consumed.
Blind at the start but perceiving clearly by the end,[105]

湯摯之合
祚以久食
昧始以昭末

---

implicit suggestion that it might have been nothing better than King Wu's penchant for violence.

104. The Han commentary offers the almost incomprehensible gloss "'forest' means 'prince'" 林, 君也. Liu seems to follow this gloss too, and hence also the allusion to the story of Prince Shensheng 申生 of Jin and his stepmother Lady Li (Li Ji 驪姬).

105. The remark simply seems to comment that Tang did not at first fully appreciate Yi Yin's talent. Perhaps referring to *Mencius*: "Tang's relation to Yi Yin was such that first he

    They could complete their lasting deeds. 克庸成績

[86] *The meritorious scion Helu was born of Meng,* 勛闔夢生
    But was cast away in his youth. 少離散亡
    Why was [Helu] so mighty and practiced in arms, 何壯武厲
    That he could spread his reputation far and wide? 能流厥嚴

    Guang [Helu] substantiated the lineage of ancestor Meng; 光徵夢祖
    By regret over his abandonment he further fortified himself. 憾離以屬
    While wandering astray he was stirred and incited, 仿偟激覆
    Till courage overflowed and virtue advanced.[106] 而勇益德邁

[87] *When Peng Keng brewed the pheasant broth,* 彭鏗斟雉
    Why did the Lord consume it? 帝何饗
    When he achieved extraordinary longevity, 受壽永多
    How was it that it extended for such a long time? 夫何久長

    Keng offered the broth to the Lord, 鏗羹於帝
    Why should the sage savor the taste of it? 聖孰嗜味
    At death a man finds his own life's twilight; 夫死自暮
    Who can extend longevity by just one repast? 而誰饗以俾壽

[88] *When the central states shared the pasture,* 中央共牧
    Why was the Sovereign angered? 后何怒
    How could the paltry lives of bees and ants 蠡蛾微命
    Possess the strength to endure? 力何固

    The vipers chomped on their own poison; 魄醟已毒

---

learned from him, and later he made him his minister" 湯之於伊尹，學焉而後臣之. See *Mengzi zhushu*, 4A.126.

106. Wu founder Shou Meng 壽夢 is the patriarch referred to here. Helu took power by assassinating the previous king, his uncle Wang Liao 王僚, whom he saw as a usurper; see *Shiji*, 31.1765–67. The account of the story in the "Tianwen" and embellished by Liu Zongyuan presents him as a sort of heroic, triumphant version of Qu Yuan who returns from exile to lead the kingdom to triumph, although this is rather different from the *Shiji* portrayal in which he seems more like an ambitious schemer who happens by good fortune to attain success.

It was not that it had spread to the outside.[107]	不以外肆
A thin-waisted rabble of stingers—	細腰群蟄
What cause for worry should they be?	夫何足病

[89] When a girl was startled while gathering vetch, 驚女采薇
    Why did a deer protect her? 鹿何祐
    North as far as the Winding Waters, 北至回水
    In meeting there, why did they delight nonetheless? 萃何喜

    Arriving at the Winding Waters and happening on fortune, 萃回偶昌
    Why did the deer aid the lady so?[108] 鹿曷祐以女

[90] When the elder brother had a keen-toothed hound, 兄有嗞犬
    Why did the younger seek it?[109] 弟何欲
    Though bartering it for a hundred [chariots],[110] 易之以百兩
    Why was he ultimately without any estate? 卒無祿

    Qian wanted his elder brother's beloved [hound], 鍼欲兄愛
    To satisfy himself with abundant riches. 以快侈富
    Though Qian's chariots grew more numerous, 愈多厥車
    Ultimately he was driven out a refugee. 卒逐以旅

[91] A bolt of lightning in the twilight sky: 薄暮雷電
    What should I fear if I return? 歸何憂
    If we do not respect his authority, 厥嚴不奉
    How can we importune the Lord [of Heaven]? 帝何求
[92] Hiding and skulking in cavernous places, 伏匿穴處
    What more is there to say? 爰何云
    The army of Jing achieved a meritorious deed, 荊師作勳

---

107. This follows the Han commentary's interpretation about bicephalous serpents, probably unrelated to the original meaning of the text (see discussion in "Text Three").

108. Liu asks reasonable questions about the garbled story provided by the Han commentary, in which a lady happens upon a deer who somehow brings her good fortune.

109. According to the Han commentary, the brothers here are the Prince of Qin 秦 and his younger brother Qian 鍼.

110. There is a note here identified as an "original note" 元注 commenting that the "hundred" should actually refer to chariots, rather than gold as proposed by the Han commentary. But since this is clear enough from Liu's response, it seems to be an explanation by a later scholar rather than Liu himself.

214　Text Two

  But how was it to endure? 夫何長
[93] May he see his faults and change his ways— 悟過改更
  What more ought we to advise? 我又何言

  Singing your lament in the wilds: 咨吟於野
  Why is your resentment so fierce? 胡若之很
  Prestige fallen, duty destroyed, you fulfilled your responsibility, 嚴墜誼殄丁厥任
  If appropriate behavior is violated, you must hide yourself where you are; 合行違匪固若所
  Ah, oh, in the poison of your fury, who will you find to join you? 呷嚘忿毒意誰與
  Reviling Qi and turning to Qin, [the King] swallowed the bait: 醜齊徂秦啗厥詐
  Slanderers ascended, schemers employed, all advances set in reverse; 讒登狡庸咈以施
  Taking pleasure and ease in disaster and peril, all were weeded out; 甘恬禍凶巫鋤夷
  That stubbornness cannot be transformed, so let all your deeds be in vain. 慏不可化徒若罷

  Guang [King Helu] of Wu contested the realm, 吳光爭國
  And was long victorious over us. 久余是勝
[94] Why did she pass by all the lanes and cross the altars, 何環閭穿社
  Even so far as the grave mounds? 以及丘陵
  Such wantonness, such wildness, 是淫是蕩
  So that she gave birth to Ziwen.[III] 爰出子文
[95] I would like to warn the master Duao 吾告堵敖
  That he will not long survive. 以不長
  How could the murder and usurpation of the sovereign 何試上自予
  Cause his reputation for loyalty to gain in glamor? 忠名彌彰

  Helu broadened his martial might, 闔綽厥武
  While this king of ours was rash and indulgent. 滋以侈頹

III. I follow the variant text provided in the Han commentary, which seems to fit better with the prosodic scheme of the poem as a whole. It is also presented as a variant text in *Zengguang zhushi yinbian Tang Liu xiansheng ji*, 14.82b. The alternative reading is 何環穿自閭社丘陵，爰出子文. See *Chuci buzhu*, 4.118; Wen Yiduo, "Tianwen shuzheng," 634–35.

If even Wutu [Lingyin Ziwen] was not able to flourish, 於菟不可以作
To these indolent men how could one give allegiance? 怠焉庸歸
I do lament that Duao 欸吾敖之
Was overthrown and died abroad; 閼以旅尸
But if you did not cherish fame above all, 誠若名不尚
Why expire producing speeches?[112] 曷極而辭

112. If taken as a criticism of the solipsism of literature this might seem to apply to Liu Zongyuan as well. On the other hand, Liu did not write anything like "Sublimating Sorrow" ("Lisao"), which was understood as a direct criticism of the current regime. So perhaps this can be understood as an objection to Qu Yuan's disloyalty, following in the tradition of similar criticisms.

CHAPTER THREE

Towards the Modern Interpretation

> There exists thus a natural tension between the historian and the philologist, who wants to understand a text with respect to its beauty and truth. The historian interprets it with regard to something external that is not stated in the text itself, and so does not need to be placed in the intended sense of the text. The historical and philological consciousness come here into fundamental conflict. However, this tension is no longer present, now that historical consciousness has changed even the position of the philologist. Since then, he has abandoned the claim that texts possess normative value for himself. He sees them no longer as models of speech and in regard to their exemplarity of what is said, but sees them in light of something beyond, which they themselves do not mean at all, that is, he perceives them as a historian.
>
> —Gadamer, *Truth and Method*[1]

One of the purposes of this study is to work out in some detail the consequences of viewing the Chinese textual tradition in the light of hermeneutics; to read original texts in dialogue with their later

---

1. Gadamer, *Wahrheit und Methode*, 319–20: "Es besteht insofern eine natürliche Spannung zwischen dem Historiker und dem Philologen, der einen Text um seiner Schönheit und Wahrheit willen verstehen will. Der Historiker interpretiert auf etwas hin, was nicht im Text selbst ausgesagt wird und durchaus nicht in der gemeinten Sinnrichtung des Textes zu liegen braucht. Das historische und das philologische Bewußtsein geraten hier im Grunde in Konflikt. Indessen ist diese Spannung kaum mehr vorhanden, seit das historische Bewußtsein auch die Haltung des Philologen verändert hat. Er hat seitdem den Anspruch aufgegeben, als besäßen seine Texte für ihn eine normative Geltung. Er sieht dieselben nicht mehr als Vorbilder des Sagens und in der Vorbildlichkeit des Gesagten, sondern auch er sieht sie auf etwas hin an, was sie selber gar nicht meinen, d.h. er sieht sie als Historiker an." Cf. translation, *Truth and Method*, 346.

interpretations. There is no way to understand how a particular text was composed at some particular historical moment, without addressing the historiographical and hermeneutical tradition that crystallized after that moment. On the other hand, there are always important historical facts to be ascertained, since it is true that we can correct errors and fill in lacunae. This study has opened with one remarkable case in which the discovery of the oracle bones helped to confirm the correct reading of the "Heavenly Questions." And yet Wang Guowei's methodology only makes sense in light of his mastery of the received textual tradition as well. That is to say, the discoveries of the twentieth and twenty-first centuries, the oracle bones, the bronze inscriptions, the bamboo and silk manuscripts, are all essential; but the Han scholarship is also essential, and it is only by sifting through all the sources available that we are going to achieve a deeper understanding. And in that process we have much to learn from the traditional exegetes.[2]

For the premodern Chinese scholars—and to some extent also for the modern ones—there does not seem to exist quite the same tension between history and philology to which Gadamer refers above. All the traditional readings of "Heavenly Questions"—or at least all the sympathetic ones—seem to be searching for a moral reading; even some of the scholars who reject the poem as a disorganized mélange of historical trivia are disappointed in it precisely because they do not find the same affirmation of a loyal courtier as in the Qu Yuan poems. Yet Gadamer also rejects this tension as a false one, concluding that: "It is fully appropriate for the poetic tradition of a nation, that we admire not only the poetic ability, the fantasy and artistry of expression in it, but before all of these the superior truth that speaks out from it."[3] Philologists may certainly attempt to focus on the linguistic expression, or the historical reality of their texts, but can hardly blind themselves utterly to the facts behind them. Thus, the gradual

---

2. On the rich significance of Chinese commentaries, though with an emphasis more on the Neoconfucian tradition, see Gardner, "Confucian Commentary and Chinese Intellectual History."

3. Gadamer, *Wahrheit und Methode*, 320: "Vollends trifft es für die dichterische Überlieferung der Völker zu, daß wir an ihr nicht nur die dichterische Kraft, die Phantasie und die Kunst des Ausdrucks bewundern, sondern vor allem auch die überlegene Wahrheit, die aus ihr spricht." Cf. trans., *Truth and Method*, 346–47.

progression in understanding of the "Heavenly Questions" was not solely a matter of technical prowess, or phonological rigor, or even of historical accuracy alone, but also demanded a new recognition of the message of the original text.

To put it another way, we read the "Heavenly Questions" as a single, coherent whole, only by understanding the meaning of individual words and lines. But our glosses of individual words must rely on a sense of the meaning of the whole.[4] The view that the poem had to be read in regard to its enduring moral truth has often been more useful than the stance of pseudoscientific objectivity from which it appears to be merely a heap of historical fragments. Ultimately one must look at the poem from both perspectives, both the general and the specific meanings, but any particular study or interpretation may rely more on one aspect than the other. Some scholars have addressed themselves primarily to making sense of the coherent meaning of the entire poem, while others have made greater contributions to individual lines or words. In principle, it is possible for a single scholar to discover the hidden meaning of a particular line without commenting on anything else in the poem, but this is rarely the case. Most reinterpretations of individual lines are presented within commentaries to the entire poem, so they tend to work in parallel with corresponding reinterpretations of other lines. Even the impressive contribution of the Qing scholars was sometimes vitiated by their failure to offer a comprehensive view of the poem's meaning, a framing for their own brilliant reexamination of individual cruxes.

And yet from another point of view, perhaps there was a spiritual kinship between the "Heavenly Questions" and the critical attitude of the evidential research of the Qing. As we have seen from Liu Zongyuan's searching responses to the "Heavenly Questions," there were readers after the Han who understood it far better than one would expect from the Han commentary alone. Doubtless Liu Zongyuan was not the only such reader, but most other readers of the poem did not record their own interpretations in writing. Even the authoritative Song scholars, Hong Xingzu and

---

4. What philologist Friedrich Ast (1778–1841) called "die Idee des Ganzen," and saw as indispensable to interpretation of the details; see Ast, *Grundlinien der Grammatik*, 188. But cf. discussion of some challenges in interpreting this conception of the "whole" in Gadamer, *Wahrheit und Methode*, 178.

Zhu Xi, did not make much progress in the interpretation of the poem. Both their commentaries to the *Chuci* anthology play important roles in the ongoing "Qu Yuan debate," but are not indispensable for dealing with the puzzles of "Heavenly Questions."

Hong Xingzu's voluminous commentary cites various intertexts that may or may not be applicable, and provides useful material for a proper study of the text, but generally refrains from the essential analytic work of distinguishing which events are referred to or not. For instance, if we look at the challenging quatrain 46:

[46] When Tang plotted to transform the people,   湯謀易旅
   How did he treat them generously?   何以厚之
   When [Shaokang] capsized the vessels of Zhenxun,   覆舟斟尋
   By what route did he conquer them?[5]   何道取之

The Han commentary interprets the first half of this quatrain in relation to Shang founder Tang, and the second half in relation to Xia hero Shaokang 少康. As so often, this division into two different subjects and topics makes the quatrain as a whole nearly incomprehensible. Hong Xingzu's commentary is equally puzzling because it follows the lead of the Han commentary, and treats the two halves of the quatrain as unrelated.[6] For the first half, Hong cites a *Book of Documents* passage on Tang's governance; for the second half, he argues that the protagonist should be strongman Ao 澆, rather than Shaokang, who was responsible for slaying Ao, as mentioned in the preceding lines. This reading makes the chronological sequence of events totally incomprehensible. Moreover, Hong cites the passage in *Zuozhuan*, Duke Xiang, year 4, which describes how Ao defeated the Zhenxun people, without explaining how to interpret the question itself. Probably Hong Xingzu's greatest contribution was to preserve the text of the poem, the Han commentary, and numerous variants of both of these, but he was unable to resolve their own internal contradictions.

After all, an essential part of analysis is the sifting through of existing data. Zhu Xi's main addition to the scholarship consisted less in brilliant

---

- 5. You Guoen et al., eds., *Tianwen zuanyi*, 263.
- 6. *Chuci buzhu*, 3.103.

philology or erudition than in applying critical skepticism to some of the previous interpretations. From the beginning, he was by temperament not profoundly drawn to the "Heavenly Questions." His commentary generally emphasizes "the bond of lord and vassal" 君臣之義,[7] a topic which is alluded to relatively sparsely in the "Heavenly Questions." Nonetheless, Zhu's critical temperament and philological acumen allowed him to sift effectively through the previous exegesis and also to analyze the structure of the poem effectively. He appreciated that the poem was largely coherent, even if it had obscure passages: "The topics queried in this poem may sometimes be strange and fantastical, but if one evaluates them according to reason, in most cases the events concerned can still be discerned." 此篇所問, 雖或怪妄, 然其理之可推, 事之可覽者尚多有之.[8]

In particular, Zhu Xi was able to recognize the local coherence of the poem since he paid attention to the rhyme scheme and structure of the poem, generally arranging its lines into quatrains, and pointing out the rhyme scheme according to the "harmonizing rhyme" 叶韻 practice in which words are pronounced slightly differently from their normal reading so as to complete a rhyme. He had drawn on the previous phonological scholarship of Wu Yu 吳棫 (ca. 1100–1154) and Zheng Qiao 鄭樵 (1104–1162), and appreciated that the rhymes of ancient Chinese needed special attention.[9]

In the example of quatrain 46 above, Zhu Xi immediately recognizes that Tang and the Zhenxun should not be mentioned in conjunction, and proposes that Tang 湯 is an error for Kang 康. Though later scholars have not followed this particular suggestion, modern interpretations generally rely on various theories that Tang is a graphic error for some other character. In this and other cases, Zhu's critical commentary rejects many of the earlier interpretations, casually discarding much of the Han commentary and rejecting Hong Xingzu's additions. Often Zhu Xi does not offer any explanation at all, as for quatrain 42, where he writes, "This stanza is bizarre and fantastic and cannot be explained, so I will not discuss it further now." 此章大抵荒誕無說, 今亦不論.[10] His skepticism and caution are salu-

---

7. *Chuci jizhu*, 1.6.
8. *Chuci jizhu*, 3.49.
9. This important fact is mentioned by Ding Fanzi in the preface to his *Chuci yinyun*, 1b.
10. *Chuci jizhu*, 3.61.

tary, and his willingness simply to write "unclear" (*wei xiang* 未詳) was an important innovation beyond the Han commentary.

Both Zhu Xi and Hong Xingzu are more significant in relation to the *Chuci* as a whole, of course, rather than to "Heavenly Questions" in particular. There have been numerous studies of the interpretive traditions of the *Chuci* anthology as a whole, tending to emphasize the peculiarities of Wang Yi and Zhu Xi in particular.[11] But for the "Heavenly Questions," these famous commentaries are less important, relatively speaking, since these prominent scholars were clearly baffled by significant portions of the text. As a result, the works of later scholars have been equally significant in the hermeneutical tradition of this poem, and force us to take a much broader view.

After the Song, Zhu Xi's philosophical preeminence was firmly established, so his commentaries to the classics and to the *Chuci* also exerted the most influence for centuries. For most of the Ming dynasty, Neoconfucian philosophy and Zhu Xi's views were dominant in *Chuci* studies.[12] By the seventeenth century, however, there were dramatic advances in philological methodology and awareness that made possible a far better understanding of the original "Heavenly Questions."[13] Part of this was simply a matter of methodology. In the Qing dynasty, there was a new "evidential research" (*kaozheng* 考證) methodology that required strict attention to relevant sources. As Benjamin Elman sums up:

> By making precise scholarship rather than pure reason the source of acceptable knowledge, Qing classicists ... contended that the legitimate reach of ancient ideals should be reevaluated impartially through comparative delineation of the textual sources from which all such knowledge derived. This turn to empirically based classical inquiry meant that abstract ideas,

---

11. See two essential studies by Michael Schimmelpfennig, "Quest for a Classic," and "Two Ages, One Agenda?"

12. Sun Qiaoyun, *Yuan Ming Qing Chuci xueshi*, 65–73.

13. Qing philologists themselves sometimes blamed the fall of the Ming on the sloppy thinking of Neoconfucian philosophy: see Elman, *From Philosophy to Philology*, 51. Nathan Vedal has recently discussed ways that Ming scholarship anticipated Qing philology in various aspects, albeit not in phonological rigor. See his *The Culture of Language in Ming China*.

meta-physical diagrams, and rational argumentation gave way as the primary objects of elite discussion to concrete facts, verifiable institutions, ancient natural studies, and historical events.[14]

In this spirit, one of the major innovations of Qing scholarship was simply the incorporation of a greater body of source material into their research. This reflected the triumph of printing and widespread dissemination of texts; even though the technology for woodblock printing dated back to the Tang, manuscripts remained popular, it seems, through to the Ming dynasty, when printing truly exploded.[15] Moreover, midway through the Ming dynasty, less popular historical works began to circulate more widely via printing: "Publishers began to bring out new editions of a wide range of early history texts, ones heretofore not widely available in print."[16] This was the period when scholars began to be proactive about reconstructing historical texts that had been lost, and ingeniously applying them as sources of evidence to fill in gaps in understanding.[17] Rather than simply quoting a single source and then speculating about the meaning, Qing scholars were scrupulous about the precise wording, and hence were able to distinguish between isolated thematic parallels and direct historical references. Moreover, as scholarship advanced, they were able to devote rigorous attention to a greater variety of texts. Whereas a key triumph of Tang scholarship had been the standard commentary to the Five Classics,[18] and the most memorable achievement of Song scholarship in the even narrower domain of the Four Books, Qing scholars devoted disciplined efforts to all kinds of texts, notably the *Bamboo Annals*, which would be especially helpful in interpreting the "Heavenly Questions."

But there was also a specific linguistic knowledge that was useful,

14. Elman, "Early Modern or Late Imperial," 226.
15. See McDermott, "Ascendance of the Imprint."
16. McDermott, "Ascendance of the Imprint," 89. McDermott cites several histories that do not bear directly on the "Heavenly Questions" but would certainly have helped fill in gaps of historical understanding about the topics it engages, notably the *Wu Yue chunqiu* 吳越春秋.
17. See Elman, *From Philosophy to Philology*, 69, for telling examples.
18. For a recent appreciation of its intellectual significance, see Bender, "Corrected Interpretations of the Five Classics."

namely improved understanding of phonology and the new awareness of graphic variants that this enabled. With better recognition of the sound changes that had transformed pronunciations of the Chinese characters, Qing philologists reconstructed the rhyme groups of the *Book of Odes*, and were able to recognize characters that had sounded similar in the Zhou dynasty even if their pronunciations had later diverged. Perhaps the key figure in this development was Gu Yanwu 顧炎武 (1613–1682).[19] Gu was the first to identify systematically ten distinct rhyme groups for the *Book of Odes*.[20] It is not so much his concrete accomplishment that is significant for our purposes, though, as his general approach. He viewed all the classics as history, in a more rigorous way than his predecessors, and fostered the disciplined study of texts.[21]

Gu's key innovation, anticipating modern linguistics, was to examine the sound of the Chinese character, rather than interpreting it based on its written form. A phonological approach allowed for the recognition of loan graphs, in which a different graph was borrowed to write a (spoken) word, even though the two differed in meaning. This technique of reading relied on the phonological advances of Gu Yanwu and others, but as applied to the exegesis of ancient texts. The principle itself had already been established in the Yuan dynasty by Dai Tong 戴侗, who advocated "following the sound to seek the meaning" 因聲以求義 in his text *Liushu gu* 六書故 (Proper meaning of the six modes of writing).[22] But the principle could only be exploited effectively in tandem with explicit awareness and detailed study of the sound changes that had taken place between antiquity and the late imperial era. Since the primary evidence for this was the rhymes of the *Book of Odes*, it would be the work of Qing phonologists establishing these rhyme categories that made possible a more rigorous analysis of loan graphs and other variants and errors in ancient texts.

All in all, there was considerable progress in philological scholarship. There is a tension, though, between the notion of progress and that of historical understanding as a dialogic process. If interpretation were a

19. Gu Yanwu saw himself as correcting the pernicious influences of Wang Yangming's thought and returning to Confucian origins; see Vergnaud, *La Pensée de Gu Yanwu*, 58–62.
20. Baxter, *Handbook of Old Chinese Phonology*, 155.
21. Xu Sumin, *Gu Yanwu pingzhuan*, 264–74.
22. See useful discussion in Deng Wenbin, *Zhongguo gudai yuyanxue shi*, 292–94.

purely subjective phenomenon, there could not be significant technological progress in this field. If it were purely objective, progress in linguistic technique would outstrip any other factors, so that our twenty-first-century readings of ancient texts would be as superior to those of the Qing dynasty as an electric car is to a palanquin. In reality, of course, neither of these is true. Better technologies of printing and data organization and linguistic analysis allow our responses to be better targeted and more precise, so real progress is possible. But technology can only play an ancillary role. Our interpretations are active communications, our own messages-in-bottles that we cast out into the sea in response to the texts we are reading. We may make them more precise, but they remain our own subjective responses conditioned by our own historical moments. If we understand classical texts better—which is not always the case—it can only be because we understand not just those particular texts better, but also because we understand ourselves, in relation to language and the world, better than before. And this composite task of understanding both self and other does not necessarily grow easier with time. To the contrary, the distractions of the Internet doubtless make it more difficult, even as immediate access to rare manuscripts across the oceans is of course is an incalculable advantage.

In the best of Qing dynasty scholarship, then, we see improved technical knowledge permitting a better understanding of the "Heavenly Questions" as a whole, but only because the scholars who have mastered these philological techniques are themselves wise enough to comprehend the depth of the poem they are seeking to interpret. However, their interpretive achievements, as substantive as they were, ultimately came up against the limits of technical scholarship. By comparison, there was even greater progress in the twentieth century, along both hermeneutical and factual trajectories. The mass dissemination of texts and photographic reproduction even of rare texts together have allowed serious scholarship on these issues to take place anywhere in the world. But the proliferation of data may only make more necessary than ever the comprehensive interpretation that enables mastery of scattered detail.

A Sense of the Whole

My own understanding of the hermeneutical tradition regarding the "Heavenly Questions" has been shaped above all by You Guoen's 游國恩 (1899–1978) anthology of premodern commentaries, the *Tianwen zuanyi* 天問纂義. This is not the be-all or end-all of "Heavenly Questions" interpretation, since numerous modern scholars have brought additional insights beyond its scope. But You's anthology remains a superb guide to the traditional interpretations, particularly as he offers brief critical comments that help to sort through the commonalities and differences among the interpreters. The discussion below owes much to You's magnum opus, even if ultimately I may reach different conclusions on specific points.

In the first section of the *Tianwen zuanyi*, You quotes the general comments about "Heavenly Questions" as a whole from numerous scholars of the past, arrayed in chronological order. Many of these are negative, complaining about the disorder of the original poem. Even Hong Xingzu, while defending the "Heavenly Questions," seems also to say that there is no way to address the nature of Heaven and Earth in any coherent sequence. But in the late Ming period, scholars often identified a kind of coherence in the poem, even if they could perceive it only by intuition, as in Lu Shiyong's 陸時雍 (d. 1640) remark:

> These are all things one cannot discuss logically, nor attain by one's feelings, but instead one must trace back the sense, to find it in the surface of the enormous void, within the silence of infinite space.[23]
>
> 此皆不可以理論，不可以情求，逆其意者當得之，遼闊之表，窈冥之中耳。

The suggestive quality of this remark reflects the trend in Ming criticism towards a new kind of commentarial reflection on ancient texts, the "evaluation and punctuation" (*pingdian* 評點). This was an important innovation precisely because of its casual and partial nature. Rather than glossing every word or paraphrasing the meaning of every line, the *pingdian* commentary placed greater weight on impressionistic responses to

---

23. *Qishier jia*, 3.3a. There is a hint here of Pascal's "le silence éternel de ces espaces infinis m'effraie."

passages, even though it might also offer the scholarly glosses or citations familiar from earlier commentaries. Jin Shengtan's 金聖歎 (1608–1661) commentary to the *Shuihu zhuan* 水滸傳 (The water margin) is a famous example of how Ming readers employed this new mode of commentary in their response to works of fiction.[24] But the *pingdian* method was also used to respond to classical texts including the *Chuci*, and flourished in the Ming dynasty, particular in the late Ming.[25] While the *pingdian* commentaries rarely solved philological cruxes, they occasionally offered insightful judgments and reactions on poems or critical passages.

The impressionistic and evaluative mode of the *pingdian* commentaries is also visible in traditional commentaries produced in the same period. Perhaps the first scholar to offer a full-throated defense of the integrity of "Heavenly Questions" was the idiosyncratic polymath Wang Fuzhi 王夫之 (1619–1692). While his writings were proscribed under the Qing, so that he cannot have been directly influential on many of the scholars who followed, nonetheless he appears to be the prophet of a new age of interpretation when he writes:

> In my view, though miscellaneous matters are discussed in the piece, they begin from Heaven and Earth, and mountains and rivers, and continue to human events, recalling what happened in the past, and concluding with the Chu ancestors. It is never the case that no order remains to the contents. Thus it must have been sewn together into a piece by Qu Yuan. Wang Yi is inaccurate in saying that it was inscribed on a wall. He also says, "It does not say 'ask Heaven' but rather 'Heaven asks' because Heaven is lofty and cannot be questioned." This too is wrong. Yuan considers that the transformations of the Creator of Changes, and the successes or failures within human events, are without exception the manifestations of the order of Heaven. Thus he cites examples of Heaven's mystery and ineffability, so as to question those foolish lords and redundant ministers, who "in their wretchedness neglect to regard its brilliance with reverence."[26] That is why it is called "Heavenly Questions," and not "Asking Heaven."

---

24. For a survey of the topic, see Rolston, *Traditional Chinese Fiction and Fiction Commentary*.
25. See Luo Jianbo, *Mingdai* Chuci *pingdian lunkao*.
26. A quotation from the first stanza of "The People Are Burdened" ("Min lao" 民勞; *Odes* 253).

Though the content of the poem reaches far and wide, the central idea is that those who act with the Way will flourish, and those without the Way will perish. To brandish arms needlessly, reject proper counsel, indulge in pleasure, be immoderate and wanton, to doubt the worthy and trust the wicked: all these are the origin of decline and perishing. Yuan's spirit of counselling and criticizing the King of Chu reaches its full extent here. He wants to cause him to inquire about the past so as to question himself, to tread in the beautiful footsteps of the Three Kings and Five Lords, while avoiding the inverted tracks of Jie, Zhow, and Kings You and Li, and to trace back to the crucial starting point for nurturing and maturing the people. Yuan investigates the crucial starting point for nurturing and maturing the people,[27] so as to fulfil the true function of ordering principles for human affairs. Doing his utmost to offer corrections to the jade pendants of the ruler's ears,[28] his words are comprehensive, and not merely intended to express his frustration and worry.[29]

按篇內事雖雜舉，而自天地山川，次及人事，追述往古，終之以楚先，未嘗無次序存焉，固原自所合綴以成章者。逸謂書壁而問，非其實矣。逸又云：「不言問天而言天問，天高不可問」。說亦未是。原以造化變遷，人事得失，莫非天理之昭著，故舉天之不測不爽者，以問憎不畏明之庸主具臣。是為天問，而非問天。

篇內言雖旁薄，而要歸之旨，則以有道而興，無道則喪，黷武忌諫，耽樂淫色，疑賢信姦，為廢興存亡之本。原諷諫楚王之心，於此而至，欲使其問古以自問，而躡三王、五伯之美武，違桀、紂、幽、厲之覆轍，原本權輿亭毒之樞機，以盡人事綱維之實用。規瑱之盡，辭於斯備矣，抑非徒渫憤舒愁已也。

Wang is able to view the poem as a whole in large part because he identifies a unified theme as indicated by the title, which he seems to understand as "Questions on *behalf* of Heaven." I am not sure Wang's gloss on the title of poem is exactly correct, but it poses an intriguing possibility well worth considering. It is of course guided by his assumption of Qu Yuan's authorship, but even leaving that aside, his argument that the poem is concerned above all with the problems of rulership cannot be denied. So Wang's view

---

27. Wang uses the compound *tingdu* 亭毒 deriving from *Laozi* 51, and understood as the variant text of the same line, *chengzhi shuzhi* 成之熟之.
28. This is an allusion to *Guoyu*; see Xu Yuangao, ed., *Guoyu jijie*, 17.505.
29. *Chuci tongshi*, 3.273; also quoted in You Guoen et al., eds., *Tianwen zuanyi*, 2–3.

should be noted as one possible gloss on "Heavenly Questions," which is suggestive as to the meaning of the poem in its entirety.

More importantly, Wang covers the content of the poem in a single grand vision of the rise and decline of regimes as they follow inevitably from the justice or injustice of the ruler's actions. Within this framework—which one derives from a close reading of the text, and not directly from the unreliable paratextual material in the *Chuci zhangju*—the poem turns out to be a coherent work arrayed in a plausible sequence. Though to some extent his insight into the broader meaning of the poem probably derives from his unique genius for a comprehensive view of things, it also signals a broader historical shift towards more accurate appraisals of the poem both in entirety and in detail.[30]

Though Wang's commentary to individual lines mostly does not break new ground, he does occasionally employ the method that would become central and fundamental to reinterpretation of the poem, namely, the recognition of loan graphs. He appears to have been the first scholar to point out that *sui* 遂 in the first line of the poem, *suigu zhi chu* 遂古之初, is simply a loan graph for *sui* 邃, "remote."[31] The two graphs are similar in form and are pronounced the same way, so it is a natural substitution, and one that earlier readers may simply have taken for granted. But the precise analysis of the substitution nonetheless removes a doubt that had long persisted, and the cumulative effect of this kind of annotation, identifying the meaning of individual words with steadily increasing precision, would ultimately be dramatic.

Nor was Wang Fuzhi the only seventeenth-century scholar to appraise the "Heavenly Questions" as a single, coherent narrative on the rise and fall of heroes, the wages of virtue and vice. Huang Wenhuan 黃文煥 (1595–ca. 1667), for instance, presented a similar view of the poem in his influential *Chuci tingzhi* 楚辭聽直 (Assessing uprightness in the *Elegies of Chu*), whose title indicates a moralizing perspective on the anthology. Huang was a successful scholar who served as an editorial aide in the imperial academy (Hanlin yuan bianxiu 翰林院編修), but got caught up in court intrigue

---

30. For other examples of Wang's balanced approach to the anthology as a whole, see Sun Qiaoyun, *Yuan Ming Qing chuci xueshi*, 143–44.

31. *Chuci tongshi*, 3.274. The *Wang Li gu Hanyu zidian* notes that of *sui* 遂 that it can *tong* "*sui*" 通「邃」(p. 1444).

and spent several years in prison. The *Siku quanshu zongmu tiyao* proposes that he actually wrote the commentary while he was in prison.[32] Huang's commentary has been popular in part because of his passionate empathy for Qu Yuan's plight. With regard to the "Heavenly Questions" itself, he remarked bitterly: "If a ruinous lord and venal officials cause men regret, then a sagely lord and honest officials cannot easily satisfy men either." 亡主奸臣，既使人恨，聖主賢臣，亦未易滿人意。[33] Like Wang Fuzhi, Huang was one of relatively few scholars before modern times who argued that "Heavenly Questions" was a coherent composition.[34]

Zhou Gongchen 周拱辰 (1589?–1658?) is a less famous scholar who lived probably a bit earlier than Wang Fuzhi, and was also insightful about the interpretation of the "Heavenly Questions." His dates are uncertain, but it is known that he was designated a Tribute Student (*gongsheng* 貢生) in 1646. Zhou was a native of Tongxiang 桐鄉 in modern Shaoxing city, Zhejiang, and said to be a descendant of the Song thinker Zhou Dunyi 周敦頤 (1017–1073). That he was particularly interested in the "Heavenly Questions" is shown by the existence of a "Tianwen biezhu" 天問別注, but the summation of his *Chuci* scholarship is the *Lisao caomu shi* 離騷草木史 (History of plants and trees in "Sublimating Sorrow"), which in spite of its title is a commentary to the whole anthology and not just "Sublimating Sorrow."[35]

Zhou was a close friend of *Chuci* scholar Lu Shiyong 陸時雍, also of Tongxiang, who compiled the *Chuci shu* 楚辭疏 commentary towards the end of the Ming dynasty. That the two collaborated closely is shown, among other things, by the fact that Zhou's "Tianwen biezhu" was appended to the *Chuci shu*. Zhou uses the mode of commentary to express more open and passionate critique of poor governance, which might reflect his own

32. Pointed out in Sun Qiaoyun, *Yuan Ming Qing chuci xueshi*, 117.
33. *Chuci tingzhi*, 3.63; quoted in Sun Qiaoyun, *Yuan Ming Qing chuci xueshi*, 120.
34. See his "Ting 'Tianwen'" 聽天問 afterword, *Chuci tingzhi*, 245. Notably, he compared the poem to the *Li wen* 禮問 of Zengzi 曾子. See also Sun Qiaoyun, *Yuan Ming Qing chuci xueshi*, 139, and footnote.
35. My information here derives from Peng Lingjing, "Zhou Gongchen shige yanjiu." See also Li and Gao, "Yi zhujie Qu Yuan shuxie junguo qinghuai." Zhou's literary collection is the *Shengyuzhai ji* 聖雨齋集.

historical situation writing after the Qing conquest.[36] For whatever reason, though, Zhou Gongchen's commentary is distinguished by a consistently innovative approach to the "Heavenly Questions."[37] Rather than following the Han or Song commentaries, or complaining about a lack of order in the text, Zhou is frequently willing to present an innovative hypothesis of a line or a whole passage of the poem, reinterpreting it as part of his larger vision of the whole poem.

Zhou writes in his preface to the poem: "Qu Yuan is borrowing Heaven so as to magnify his questions; and also borrowing questions so as to magnify his Heaven." 屈原蓋借天以大其問，亦借問而大其天也與。[38] He sees the poem as corresponding to the "Summons" poems elsewhere in the *Elegies of Chu*, but choosing as the object of summons not Qu Yuan or any individual, but a whole series of heroes and rulers of the past. And indeed, Zhou seems to have thought more carefully and deeply about the interrogative aspect of the text than earlier scholars, and in his commentary is willing to delve deeper into the historical background rather than interpreting the questions at the surface level. If we consider quatrain 47:

When Jie assaulted Mount Meng,	桀伐蒙山
Whom did he obtain there?	何所得焉
Why was Moxi so wanton,	妹嬉何肆
And why did Tang destroy her for it?	湯何殛焉

The Han commentary provides this straightforward explanation of these lines about the wicked ruler Jie who brought the Xia dynasty to its end:

Jie of Xia went to attack the country of Mengshan, where he obtained Moxi. When Jie obtained Moxi and indulged his passions with her, Tang banished him to Nanchao.

言夏桀征伐蒙山之國，而得妹嬉也。言桀得妹嬉，肆其情意，故湯放之南巢也。

---

36. Li Jinshan 李金善 and Gao Chenxi 高晨曦 demonstrate this in their comparison with Lu Shiyong, "Yi zhujie Qu Yuan shuxie junguo qinghuai," 36.
37. Huang Linggeng also points this out in his preface to *Lisao caomu shi*, 14.
38. *Lisao caomu shi*, 3.68.

But Zhou Gongchen writes:

What did he obtain at Mount Meng? He obtained Moxi. According to the *Diwang shiji* (Annals of gods and kings), "Jie was drinking wine night and day with Moxi and her palace ladies, and placed Moxi on his knees. She liked to hear the sound of silk being ripped apart, so he brought out ten thousand pieces of silk and had them ripped apart just to satisfy here."[39] Thus it is said that Jie's fall was on account of Moxi. But I for myself do not fully agree. According to the *Bamboo Annals*, "Jie commanded Bian to attack the Shanrong, where he obtained two ladies named Wan and Yan. He loved them but had no sons, so he inscribed their names on a precious piece of trumpet-vine-blossom jade. The trumpet-vine was for Wan, the blossoms for Yan. But he abandoned his original concubine at Luo, who was named Moxi, and who then had relations with Yi Yin and thence the Xia was destroyed."[40] Or again, according to the *Accounts of the States* (*Guoyu*): "Moxi was the mate of Yi Yin. So it was because Moxi was discarded that the realm was lost, not because she was made the favorite that the realm was lost."[41] When the text says, "whom did he obtain there," does it mean that he first obtained Moxi, and then later Wan and Yan? When it says, "why was Moxi so wanton," it is because after losing her position of favor, she openly had relations with Yi Yin and betrayed her own kingdom, which was extremely wanton behavior. Why is it that Tang captured Jie but did not let him die, and yet executed Moxi and did not pardon her? Is it that the responsibility for the crime lay with Moxi, and so that is why the blame does not attach to Jie, who was allowed to live?

蒙山何得？得妹嬉也。《帝王世紀》：桀日夜與妹嬉及宮女飲酒，置妹嬉膝上。好聞裂繒之聲，發萬繒裂之，以適其意，故曰桀之亡也以妹嬉。愚謂不盡然也。按《竹書紀年》，桀命扁伐山戎，得女子二人，曰琬，曰琰。愛之而無子，斲其名於苕華之玉。苕是琬，華是琰。而棄其元妃于洛，曰妹嬉氏，以與伊尹交，遂以亡夏。又《國語》：妹嬉比伊尹。是妹嬉以棄而亡國，非以嬖而亡國也。曰何所得，前得妹嬉，後得琬與琰乎？曰妹嬉何肆，已失寵而公然與伊尹交

---

39. *Diwang shiji*, 3.26.

40. In the Ancient Text version of the *Zhushu jinian*; see Fang and Wang, eds., *Guben Zhushu jinian jizheng*, 18; also, in the Modern-Text version, see "Jinben Zhushu jinian shuzheng," in *Guben Zhushu jinian jizheng*, A.222.

41. Xu Yuangao, ed., *Guoyu jijie*, 7.250. Not an exact quotation.

以賣國，則肆甚矣。湯所以禽桀，待以不死，而巫誅妺嬉不舍也，歸其罪于妺嬉，所以寬其辜，以存桀也與？[42]

This is not the only way to explain the quatrain. Xu Wenjing 徐文靖 (1667–after 1756), whom we will discuss further below, suggests that the first half of the quatrain refers not to Moxi at all but rather to Wan and Yan, Jie's earlier concubines. This makes the logic of the quatrain even more satisfying, particularly since the first question is not answered directly.[43] Nonetheless, Zhou Gongchen has already come very close to explaining the quatrain in full, by providing the full range of historical sources necessary to comprehend its background.

What is perhaps even more significant than the wide ranges of sources Zhou is using, though, is his hermeneutical method. Zhou is newly attentive to the distinction between questions and answers, and makes a careful attempt to identify both the full historical context, and also the nature of the questions themselves. He is not satisfied to explain what Jie obtained, or why he (or Moxi, depending on our interpretation) was punished, but also wants to explain what the question is, what Heavenly law is being interrogated here. Thus, here he speculates that the true implication of the quatrain has to do with why Moxi was punished more harshly even than Jie. This may not quite be the correct interpretation of the quatrain, then, but it is a wonderful model for how to read a complex, self-questioning work of literature. The point of interpreting an interrogative poem like "Heavenly Questions" is not just to identify the subjects and objects, or even to cite all the appropriate intertexts, but rather to ascertain the purpose of the questioning in relation to the proper historical contexts (including both the contexts of the author and of the events being interrogated).

Of course, it would be hard to attain insights into the meaning of the text without having reflected on these issues in themselves. Like Wang Fuzhi or Liu Zongyuan, Zhou Gongchen had expressed his own reactions to the morality of ancient historical events in other venues as well. In the second of a series of poems on "Reflecting on History" ("Langu shi" 覽古詩), for instance, he had written:[44]

---

42. *Lisao caomu shi*, 3.109. Also quoted in You Guoen et al., eds., *Tianwen zuanyi*, 270–71.
43. I follow this interpretation in my note to the quatrain (*Elegies of Chu*, 198).
44. *Shengyuzhai shiji*, 1.6b. My thanks to Tim Chan for many useful suggestions on the interpretation of this difficult poem.

Ordinary men rescue those who have drowned,	庸人救已溺
But the best take precautions against what has not yet happened.	至人防未然
How can there be a disaster that goes unperceived,	豈有災不省
Until too late to ponder one's mistakes?	垂晚思其愆
[Yu] cleared up Zhi and dried out Yangyu,[45]	剪彘暴陽盱
Then Gun was punished and sent to the Plume Abyss.	殛鯀至羽淵
Why should self-accusation once decreed	胡爲罪已詔
Then have been delayed seven years?	遲之至七年
The aura of disaster must have its cause;	災祲必有以
To punish oneself must be truly difficult.	責躬良獨艱
Yao and Tang were not sages;[46]	堯湯非聖人
When the disease was desperate they prescribed only words.	病劇申藥言
I laugh before Lord Xin of the Shang [Zhow],	吾笑商辛帝
Who ascribed his chastisement to Heaven.[47]	歸獄於其天

In this poem, Zhou Gongchen refers to various famous sages and dynastic founders, especially Yu of Xia, Yao, and Tang, and points out they failed to avert disaster in advance. His ultimate stance seems to be similar to that of Liu Zongyuan, emphasizing the personal responsibility of individuals, and mocking Zhow for blaming his fall on the punishment of Heaven. It is not a coincidence that a sophisticated reader of the "Heavenly Questions" had

45. According to Zheng Xuan's 鄭玄 (127–200) commentary to the *Zhouli*, Mount Huo 霍山 was located at Zhi 彘, which was also the site of Yangyu 陽盱, so here Zhi seems to be a place name identical with Yangyu (see *Zhouli zhushu*, 33.1028), in the area of modern Huozhou 霍州 City, Shanxi. Yu 禹 was said to have stopped the flood waters with his body at Yangyu 陽盱. According to *Huainanzi*: "Thus when Yu managed the waters, he made a ritual offering of his own body at the river on Yangmian" 是故禹之為水, 以身解於陽盱之河 (Liu Wendian, ed., *Huainan honglie jijie*, 19.770). The meaning of *jie* 解 here is glossed by Gao You 高誘 as *jiedao* 解禱, "ritual of expurgation." Even though the place name looks different here, it seems to be the same, as suggested by the entry in *Shanhaijing* on "The mountain of Yangyu" 陽汙之山 (Yuan Ke, ed., *Shanhaijing jiaozhu*, 12.276). Hao Yixing cites a variant text of *Huainanzi*: "Long ago when Yu controlled the great flood, he offered prayers at Yangyu" 昔禹治洪水, 具禱陽紆. This appears to be the same place.

46. Su Shi had famously declared that King Wu of Zhou was not a sage either; see *Dongpo zhilin*, 5.69–70.

47. In the *Shiji* account, Zhow claims just before his fall still to possess the mandate of Heaven; see *Shiji*, 3.138.

also reflected deeply on these issues. Perhaps underlying some of the innovation in classical exegesis was a new adherence to Liu's vision of human agency independent of a correlative cosmos. In general, the creative thinkers of the seventeenth century, such as Wang Fuzhi and Zhou Gongchen, seem newly attuned to the central theme of the "Heavenly Questions" as a whole, the problem of uranodicy, and the moral urgency of these questions in their time pressed them on to a sophisticated recognition of the poem's coherence.

Relating the "Heavenly Questions" to the Riddles of the Bamboo Annals

Though the "Heavenly Questions" touches on ancient historical events that appear in numerous classics and ancient sources, before the Qing dynasty, many of the important extant sources had not been systematically incorporated in research on the text. Thus one of the major innovations in Qing philology was simply in citation practices, as Elman has remarked: "Citation and criticism of sources also were integral aspects of evidential scholarship."[48] In other words, some of the signal achievements of Qing scholarship did not require any great ingenuity or new ideology, but simply the application of knowledge from neglected sources. Rather than reading the *Elegies of Chu* in isolation or in relation to the principal Confucian classics, scholars were bolder about looking for new sources of authority, by which means they could reevaluate the content of the poems.[49]

Consider, for instance, the first couplet of quatrain 50:

> When [somebody] ascended to the throne as Lord,　　登立為帝
> By what path was [that person] elevated to it?　　孰道尚之

The Han commentary identifies the subject of these lines as Fuxi 伏羲, ancient culture hero and inventor of the trigrams. But a different proposal was offered by Mao Qiling 毛奇齡 (1623–1716), prolific scholar and poet.[50]

48. Elman, *From Philosophy to Philology*, 185.
49. See also Ori Sela's discussion (in *China's Philological Turn*, 118ff.) of how Qian Daxin 錢大昕 (1728–1804) incorporated the histories into his study of the Classics.
50. His literary collection is the *Xihe wenji* 西河文集. He was a person of singular

Mao suggested that the first word here, *deng* 登, is not a verb but instead a proper noun, part of the personal name of Nü Deng 女登 (Lady Deng), said to be the mother of god-emperor Yandi 炎帝.[51] What is striking is his sources for the information, which include the *Diwang shiji* 帝王世紀 and the weft text *Chunqiu yuanming bao* 春秋元命苞.[52] The *Diwang shiji* is a historical chronicle attributed to Huangfu Mi 皇甫謐 (215–282), which has been reconstructed in modern times. It turns out to contain much valuable information relevant to the "Heavenly Questions," especially lurid stories about early monarchs that were not preserved in the *Shiji* or other orthodox records.

This is just one of many original proposals in Mao's *Tianwen buzhu* 天問補註 (Supplementary commentary to "Heavenly Questions"). In this particular case, Mao's suggestion probably does not stand up; it was not Lady Deng herself but her son who became the ruler; and moreover, the second half of the quatrain refers explicitly to Nü Wa, and there is no direct connection between Nü Wa and Nü Deng. Yet the methodology is nonetheless admirable; as we have seen, the great innovation in the reading of quatrain 56 just a few lines below this passage relied on a syntactic reinterpretation of *gai* as a proper noun. So this insight could potentially have been a breakthrough.

For quatrain 56, the employment of new materials would also be essential; not just the oracle bones, but other texts that had in fact already been available in the Qing and long before. These include obscure weft texts from the Han dynasty, and the third-century *Diwang shiji*, as cited by Mao Qiling in response to quatrain 50.[53] But one of the most important, and

---

temperament who at first responded to the Qing conquest by retiring to his home region of Zhejiang (he was a native of Xiaoshan), for a considerable time was an itinerant scholar, but late in life succeeded in passing the *boxue hongci* examination in 1679. According to the biography of Tu Lien-chê (Hummel, *Eminent Chinese*, 564): "A man of outstanding ability, but tenacious and dogmatic in his opinions, he was often subjected to severe criticism when he engaged in controversy with the scholars of his time." On Mao's scholarship, see Ch'ien Mu, *Zhongguo jin sanbainian xueshu shi*, 220–58.

51. See You Guoen et al., eds., *Tianwen zuanyi*, 281.

52. The *Chunqiu yuanming bao* is a weft text from the Han dynasty, associated with the *Chunqiu* classic as its name indicates. For this reference, see Yasui and Nakamura, *Jūshū isho shūsei*, 4A.26.

53. The weft texts (*wei shu* 緯書, also "apocrypha") themselves do not seem to have

one which illustrates the new approach of Qing philologists best, is the *Bamboo Annals* (*Zhushu jinian* 竹書紀年), which deserves some special attention here.

The *Bamboo Annals* belonged to a vast trove of texts that were discovered in a tomb in Ji 汲 Commandery (modern Ji county, Henan) around 279 CE, during the Western Jin dynasty.[54] The tomb has been identified as belonging to various figures, including King Xiang'ai 襄哀 of Wei 魏, who reigned from 319 to 296 BCE.[55] Because of the gap of nearly six centuries during which the texts had been buried, they would have been authentic Warring States-era documents that were not necessarily preserved or available to Han scholars. There is an account of the discovery and the documents in the *Jinshu* 晉書, so they have a well-attested pedigree. The *Bamboo Annals*, in particular, is a detailed chronicle (a history in which events are generally ordered chronologically by year within reign periods) that provides much additional information and alternative accounts of ancient history, particularly in the remote eras of Xia and Shang.

The *Bamboo Annals* in its transmitted form (Modern Text, *jinben* 今本) has been accused of being a Ming forgery, and scholars have attempted to reassemble a more authentic version from quotations in various sources, notably the *Shuijing zhu* 水經注 and *Shiji suoyin* 史記索引. Ultimately, though, it is difficult to distinguish two such lineages. Instead, it seems apparent that all the surviving materials from the *Bamboo Annals* have been scattered and confused in various ways. For instance, Edward Shaughnessy suggests that some other texts from the Ji tomb may have been conflated with the *Bamboo Annals* in at least one version.[56] Perhaps the best solution

---

resolved many of the problems in "Heavenly Questions," but they may be considered emblematic of the general problem; numerous historical sources were not preserved in full, because they might be found to offer support for alternative political regimes. On the complex political debates intertwined with the question of the weft texts in the Han, see van Ess, "The Apocryphal Texts of the Han Dynasty and the Old Text/New Text Controversy."

54. My account here relies on the detailed treatment in Shaughnessy, *Rewriting Early Chinese Texts*, chapter 3, "The Discovery and Editing of the Ji *Zhong* Texts," 131–84, and chapter 4, "The Editing and Editions of the *Bamboo Annals*," 185–256.

55. Shaughnnessy provides good reason for skepticism about this and other royal attributions, however (*Rewriting Early Chinese Texts*, 136–37).

56. Shaughnessy, *Rewriting Early Chinese Texts*, 224.

is simply to collect them all and sift through them on an individual basis, as modern scholars have done.[57] For our purposes, the edition of Fang Shiming and Wang Xiuling is more than adequate, since it contains both a new reconstruction of the ancient text version and also Wang Guowei's collation of the Modern-Text version of the *Bamboo Annals*, quoting all the relevant passages.[58]

Even if it is an ancient text, of course, the content of the *Bamboo Annals* is not necessarily accurate with regard to events further back in the past than the date of its own composition. But one reason that Qing philologists were particularly interested in this text was because of its detailed chronology of ancient history, which related to their contemporary inspiration from Western astronomy and mathematics.[59] Though scholars have often been skeptical of its accuracy, some modern researchers like David Nivison have continued to treat it seriously.[60] For our purposes it does not matter exactly how accurate it is, and indeed many of the events discussed by both the *Bamboo Annals* and the "Heavenly Questions" are at least semi-mythical. The more important thing for our purposes here is that the *Bamboo Annals* provides a set of accounts of ancient history that may represent a more accurate picture of the kind of historical records to which the "Heavenly Questions" was composed in response. In particular, the "Heavenly Questions" seems in some cases to be asking skeptical questions about legends of the Shang ancestors, which had not been considered appropriate for inclusion in the *Book of Documents*, or even about the founding of the Zhou. These kinds of revisionist narratives were not deemed legitimate for inclusion in the *Shiji*.

One of the remarkable developments in Qing scholarship on the "Heavenly Questions," reflecting the new orientation of Qing learning in general, was special attention to the poem by classical scholars. In contrast to the Song learning, Qing evidentiary scholars were willing to devote greater attention to unorthodox works like the *Bamboo Annals*, the *Diwang shiji*, and the *Classic of Mountains and Seas*, treating all of

57. Shaughnessy demonstrates one possible methodology in *Rewriting Early Chinese Texts*, 242–56.
58. Fang and Wang, eds., *Guben Zhushu jinian jizheng*.
59. Elman, *From Philosophy to Philology*, 81–82, citing Sivin, "Copernicus in China."
60. See in particular Nivison, *The Riddle of the Bamboo Annals*.

these as valuable sources of information on the remote past. Thus it is no coincidence that some of the most insightful comments on the "Heavenly Questions" from the Qing dynasty came from a scholar who had also specialized in the *Bamboo Annals*. This is Xu Wenjing 徐文靖 (1667–after 1756), who was a native of Dangtu 當塗 (modern Anhui). He only achieved a limited success as a scholar, quite late in life.[61] Attaining *juren* 舉人 in 1723, he attempted the *boxue hongci* 博學宏辭 exam in 1736 but failed it. However, he was recommended to the Qianlong Emperor by the poet Zhang Pengchong 張鵬翀 (1688–1745) in 1744, and similarly again in 1750. In 1751, Xu was awarded a rank of "corrector" in the Hanlin Academy, but spent the end of his life lecturing at the Tsuiluo 翠螺 Academy in Dangtu. Most of his writings have been lost, except for a collection containing the following six works:[62]

1. *Tianxia shanhe liangjie kao* 天下山河兩戒考 (14 *juan*; maps 1 *juan*)
2. *Zhushu jinian tongjian* 竹書紀年統箋 (12 *juan*; miscellaneous records 1 *juan*; previous compilation 1 *juan*)
3. *Yugong huijian* 禹貢會箋 (14 *juan*; maps 1 *juan*)
4. *Guancheng shuoji* 管城碩記 (30 *juan*)
5. *Jingyan shiyi* 經言拾遺 (14 *juan*)
6. *Zhiningtang quangao* 志甯堂全稿 (No *juan* divisions)

The first and third of these books both deal extensively with geography, the first being focused on the traditional *fenye* 分野 system of "astrogeography" which attempts to correlate geographical boundaries with astrological ones. The fifth, in spite of its title, is dedicated mainly to the *Yijing* (Book of changes), and the preface to this work was composed when Xu was already ninety years old.

The second, though, is Xu's remarkable edition of the *Bamboo Annals*, which actually goes beyond the conventional requirements of a scholarly edition, since it cites much supplementary material to corroborate the original text. It is one fine example of the Qing scholarship that finally reha-

---

61. Little information is available on Xu in modern sources, so the capsule biography in Hummel, *Eminent Chinese*, 326, by Rufus O. Suter is extremely helpful.
62. *Xu Weishan liuzhong* 徐位山六種. On the loss of most of his writings, see Suter's biography, apparently deriving his information from the local gazetteer *Dangtu xian xiangtuzhi* 當塗縣鄉土志.

bilitated the historical value of this text. Xu's sixth surviving work, *Jingyan shiyi* 經言拾遺, also suggests elements of Xu's critical methodology that distinguish his interpretation of the "Heavenly Questions."[63] For instance, Xu interprets two lines of the "After Completion" (Jiji 既濟) hexagram (no. 63) in terms of events from ancient history:[64]

> Six in the fourth place:
> The finest clothes turn to rags. Be careful all day long.
>
> 六四：繻有衣袽終日戒。

Here Xu cites a story which he attributes to the *Bamboo Annals* entry for the nineteenth and final year of the reign of King Zhao 昭 of Zhou.[65] The Modern-Text *Bamboo Annals* merely says that the king "lost the six armies at the Han river, and expired" 喪六師于漢, 王陟.[66] But Xu's own edition of the *Bamboo Annals* also cites a story according to which, during King Zhao's campaign towards Chu, he attempted to cross the Han River. The boats he used had been pasted together and the paste dissolved midcourse, leading to his death by drowning.[67] The recovery of this narrative would turn out to be relevant to the interpretation of the "Heavenly Questions" as well.[68]

It is the fourth of the books in Xu's surviving collection, the *Guancheng shuoji*, which contains extensive and illuminating notes on the *Elegies of Chu* and other classics. This is a collection of scholarly notes on minute philological points, whose title might perhaps have been one source of

---

63. Not directly relevant to my argument here, but a memorable example of Xu's analytic powers, is his comment on the introductory statement "On your own day you are believed" 己日乃孚, for the Ge 革 hexagram (no. 49). Xu argues that this does not refer to a single, specific day, since revolutions are by definition cyclical and recurring. *Jingyan shiyi*, 2.10b–11b. The text may also be read as 巳日. See *Zhouyi zhengyi*, 5.236; translation quoted from Wilhelm, *I Ching*, 189.

64. *Zhouyi zhengyi*, 6.295.

65. *Jingyan shiyi*, 2.21a/b.

66. Fang and Wang, eds., *Guben Zhushu jinian jizheng*, 46.

67. *Zhushu jinian tongjian*, 8.6a. The story is not cited in the modern edition *Guben Zhushu jinian jizheng*. Its *locus classicus* seems to be a citation in the subcommentary of *Chunqiu Guliang zhuan zhushu*, 7.134.

68. See quatrain 69 in "Text Three" below.

inspiration for Qian Zhongshu's 錢鍾書 (1910–1998) masterwork, *Guanzhui bian* 管錐編 (Limited views). Qian's title is an allusion to *Zhuangzi*,[69] but Xu's title *Guancheng shuoji* has a more intricate pedigree, as explained in the charming preface to the volume:

> Having clung stubbornly to a single Classic, I have not been able to collect all the books of the world, and glean the treasures of past and present. All that my ears and eyes have traversed does not exceed a few thousand fascicles. And with my features and talents being clumsy and stupid, I have also been unable to remember widely and recall precisely what I accumulated over time. Even something I have perused for a full year I will forget as soon as I close the book. Recalling my life I find that my belly remains empty just as always. So I have no choice but to entrust it to the Master of Shaft Citadel, and borrow that name to title my own studio. Regarding classics and commentaries, the philosophers and histories, the elegies and rhapsodies, and miscellaneous collections, wherever I have had some mixture of doubt and confidence, where the order seems to be contradictory, then I have rapidly wetted my brushtip and wielded the shaft, so by the steady accumulation of each inch and peck, these have gathered into one collection, thirty fascicles in all.[70]

> 余株守一經，不能盡蓄天下之書，羅古今之富，凡耳目所經涉者，不過數千卷書耳。而姿稟愚鈍，又不能博聞強記，積貯逾時。縱窮年繙閱，掩卷輒忘。廻憶平生，枵腹如故。不得已而托之管城子，假以記室，凡經傳、子史、騷賦、雜集，過有疑信相參，先後互異者，則速為濡豪摛翰，寸積銖累，裒為一集，凡三十卷。

The term "Shaft Citadel" or Guancheng 管城 refers to the final resting place of Mao Ying 毛穎, i.e. the writing brush, in Han Yu's 韓愈 (768–824) mock biography.[71] Thus the title in entirety might be rendered as

---

69. *Zhuangzi jishi*, 17.601: "Thus you confusedly and confoundedly seek it out with investigation, and inquire by means of analysis. This is no more than to use a pipe to peer up at Heaven, or to use an awl to point to the earth: how petty indeed!" 子乃規規然而求之以察，索之以辯，是直用管闚天，用錐指地也，不亦小乎.

70. *Guancheng shuoji*, 1–2. For this work I cite the modern typeset edition.

71. I am not satisfied with "Shaft Citadel," nor by the alternatives of Elling Eide in "Another Go at Mao Ying Chuan": "Ferule City"; or both Hightower in "Han Yü as Humorist," 13, and Nienhauser in "An Allegorical Reading of Han Yü's 'Mao Ying Chuan,'" 162: "Tube City." Eide's "ferule" is apparently an error for "ferrule," the ring at the end of the

Reliable Notes from the Shaft Citadel. In spite of this unprepossessing and indeed somewhat self-satiric title, the volume contains important insights on countless points of classical philology.

Within the section of this book on *Elegies of Chu*, Xu Wenjing devotes considerable attention to "Heavenly Questions," and in his analysis of interpretive problems, often alludes effectively to the *Bamboo Annals* or other early texts. With regard to quatrain 47, discussed above as an example of Zhou Gongchen's interpretation, we saw that Xu goes further than Zhou in tying the quatrain to the historical episode. And he is full of insights that help to maintain the coherence of the poem, as when he proposes that quatrain 83, which the Han commentary identifies with Prince Shensheng 申生 (seventh century BCE), might instead relate to Guanshu Xian 管叔鮮 (ca. eleventh century BCE), younger brother of King Wu, who rebelled against King Cheng 成 of Zhou and had to commit suicide.[72] Since the quatrain follows immediately on discussions of the Zhou founding, this fits far better with the chronological sequence than an incongruous reference to the Spring and Autumn period.

But what is most impressive of all is Xu's comment on the great crux of quatrain 56:[73]

> According to the "Table of Personages Past and Present" in the *History of the Former Han dynasty*, Di Ku's 帝嚳 consort Jian Di 簡邐 gave birth to Xie. Xie's fifth-generation descendant was named Ming 冥, and Ming's son was Gai 垓. Yan Shigu 顏師古 (581–645) said: Gai is pronounced like Gai 該.[74] So this is the same Gai. According to the *Bamboo Annals* for year 13 of Lord Zhu, "Marquis of Shang, Ming, died in the Yellow River." According to the *Rites*: "Ming was diligent in his office but died in the water."[75] This refers to the same event. These lines in "Heavenly Questions" follow [the following lines from quatrain 55]: "While his concubine Jian Di was at the altar, /

---

brush handle that holds the brushtip in place. Even though the handle is made of a bamboo "tube," this word also seems to lack the appropriate connotations here. The implication is not the same as in the title of Qian Zhongshu's *Guanzhui bian*, where it is a matter of looking through a hollow tube, not writing with one.

72. *Guancheng shuoji*, 16.291; *Shiji*, 35.1888.
73. *Guancheng shuoji*, 16.285. Quoted in You Guoen et al., eds., *Tianwen zuanyi*, 308.
74. *Hanshu*, 20.882.
75. *Liji zhengyi*, 46.1524.

Why did High Lord Ku find it proper?" As for Gai being able to uphold the virtuous legacy of Xie and Shang, and carry on his father Ming's excellence and goodness, that is what is referred to in the line "he showed the same excellence as his father." What does this have to do with Qi [as claimed in the Han commentary]?

按漢書古今人表, 帝嚳妃簡遏生高, 高五世孫冥, 冥子垓。師古曰, 垓音該, 是即該也。竹書帝杼十三年, 商侯冥死于河。禮曰冥勤其官而水死, 是也。此承上簡遏在臺, 玄鳥致貽, 至于該而能秉高商之季德, 以承父冥之臧善, 所謂厥父是臧也。與啓何與?

Xu's reading of quatrain 56 is grounded in his own long and disciplined study of the *Bamboo Annals*, including his own commentary to that text, where he cites this same line for Lord Zhu (Di Zhu 帝杼), year 13: "The Marquis of Shang, Ming, died in the Yellow River" 商侯冥死於河.[76] Furthermore, in relation to quatrain 59, he quotes the *Shanhaijing* passage about Wang Hai and the Youyi people, as well as the corresponding *Bamboo Annals* passage: "The son of the lord of Yin, Hai, was a guest of the Youyi, but they killed and discarded him" 殷侯子亥賓于有易, 殺而放之.[77] This episode occurs in different forms in both the Ancient-Text and Modern-Text versions of the *Bamboo Annals*, and is a good illustration of Shaughnessy's thesis that both versions actually do reflect an authentic original text, albeit one edited and transmitted in different ways.[78]

Xu Wenjing's bold insights into the "Heavenly Questions" were based on three key methodological advances. First, he took seriously a wide range of textual evidence, and never limited himself to the orthodox classics or literary collections. Second, he was interested in the whole narratives underlying cryptic references in the *Changes* or "Heavenly Questions"; his insights there anticipate some of the twentieth-century reconstructions of ancient myth and early history. Finally, he appreciated that the "Heavenly Questions" was asking serious questions about antiquity, and by following through on the premise that it was a coherent work about authentic histor-

---

76. *Zhushu jinian tongjian*, 3.16a. This story comes from the Modern-Text version of the *Zhushu jinian*. See Wang Guowei's edition, in Fang and Wang, eds., *Guben Zhushu jinian jizheng*, 217.

77. Xu Wenjing's comments are also quoted in You Guoen's *Tianwen zuanyi*, 329. *Zhushu jinian tongjian*, 4.1a.

78. Fang and Wang, eds., *Guben Zhushu jinian jizheng*, 12 and 219.

ical issues, he was able to resolve the ancient crux of the word *gai* 該 centuries before Wang Guowei. Even though his interpretation of the poem as a whole is not explicit in *Guancheng shuoji*, his confidence in its historical reality underlies his concrete insights, which were later to be verified by the discovery of the oracle bones, affirming the validity of his interpretive vision in a way almost unprecedented for philological scholarship.

Xu Wenjing's poetic oeuvre, insofar as it survives, seems to confirm the stereotype of Qing scholarship as being pedantic and hobbled in imaginative scope. His literary collection *Zhiningtang quangao* 志甯堂全稿, compiled by his student in 1735, contains just a few dozen poems, which are dominated by a series of "Seven Particle Verses" ("Yuzhu qizi shi" 語助七字詩), which obey the remarkable formal restriction of using each of the seven fundamental particles *zhi zai hu yi zhe ye yan* 之哉乎矣者也焉 each at the beginning of a line.[79] Nonetheless, Xu was a brilliant scholar whose highest achievement took the form of the isolated notes to particular cruxes in classical texts. The narrowness suggested by his verse and even the title of *Guancheng shuoji* did not negate the reverberating influence of his discoveries.

A New Precision in Late Qing Philology

The period from the reign of the Qianlong Emperor (r. 1735–1799) to the end of the Qing dynasty showed considerable achievement in the area of classical philology, and not just in the synthesis of old ideas but often in innovative ways as well. The aforementioned survey by Benjamin Elman, *From Philosophy to Philology*, discusses the broader social environment of this scholarship. Hamaguchi Fujio's study demonstrates how profoundly the philological methods of these scholars were inspired by and grounded in a quest for the ethical foundations of the Confucian sages.[80] At the same time, it is important to be aware of the limitations of the school as well.

---

79. See *Zhiningtang gao*, 184–90. I use the modern pagination since the original chapter/fascicle divisions are opaque.

80. Hamaguchi Fujio, *Shindai kōkyōgaku no shisōshiteki kenkyū*, passim. The thesis of the book is implied by its title, which is that the philology of the Qing needs to be understood as the realization of trends in intellectual history.

Ch'ien Mu has objected that the *kaozheng* scholars of this period failed to appreciate the Song Neoconfucian scholars they loved to vilify, but never succeeded fully in appreciating the Han scholars they claimed to idolize.[81] More recently, Kinoshita Tetsuya has argued that these Qing scholars should not be regarded as proto-scientific, and proposed instead that the new philological trends might better be described as a kind of individualization of scholarship, interpreting the classics in idiosyncratic ways.[82]

There would be no way to resolve or even to contribute to these debates by means of the present study. The writings of late-Qing scholars generally were not centered on the *Elegies of Chu*, let alone "Heavenly Questions," but rather on the Confucian classics, so the commentaries to the "Heavenly Questions" can only afford us an oblique view of larger trends. From the limited perspective of this study, however, it is reasonably clear that the more detailed and phonologically grounded scholarship of the late Qing scholars, in particular their attention to phonetic variants, was able to solve quite a few cruxes in the "Heavenly Questions," but at the same time had its own limitations. While their interpretations of particular lines are often superior to any earlier interpretations, it is not clear that they offered better readings of the poem as a whole.

Dai Zhen 戴震 (1724–1777), for instance, was a prolific scholar and philologist of the Qing, and his *Qu Yuan fu zhu* 屈原賦注 is a detailed study, even if not especially groundbreaking with regard to the "Heavenly Questions."[83] Dai Zhen was one of the philologists who elevated to prominence the principle of *yin sheng qiu yi* 因聲求義, "seeking the meaning by means of the sound."[84] This has been a central principle of Chinese historical linguistics in modern times, since twentieth-century linguistics has taken as an axiom the view that writing is a transcription of spoken

---

81. Ch'ien Mu, "'Qingdai Hanxue' henglun."

82. See in particular Kinoshita, "*Shinchō kōshōgaku*" to sono jidai, 23; critiquing the work of Hamaguchi.

83. Both a "first draft" 初稿 and the final version of the commentary can be found in his complete works, *Dai Zhen quanshu*, 3:531–604 and 3:605–811, respectively. Liao Tung-liang has a useful discussion of Dai Zhen's *Chuci* scholarship, focusing on his analysis of the "Lisao." See Liao, *Lingjun yuying*, 167–226.

84. For the identification of Dai Zhen as a key figure in establishing this principle for later philologists, see Hamaguchi, *Shindai kōkyogaku no shisōshiteki kenkyū*, 469ff.

language.⁸⁵ This was a critical transformation in the analysis of ancient texts, because it allowed for quite bold reinterpretations of familiar words and lines. One character sometimes had to be read as a graphic variant (a different way of writing) for an entirely different written character; but this was logically consistent and indeed necessary, once one recognized that different characters could be used to inscribe the same (spoken) word.

For instance, with regard to line 71 in "Sublimating Sorrow," "I raise up osmanthus braided with sweet clover" 矯菌桂以紉蕙兮, Dai glosses *jiao* 矯 as *ju* 舉, and helpfully comments that this is "a transposition of the spoken word" 語之轉.⁸⁶ That is, *jiao* 矯 (OCM *kao?) makes sense as a loan for *ju* 舉 (OCM *kla?) because they are so close phonologically. As in many such cases, they remain similar in modern Mandarin pronunciation (the same initial consonant and tone), but knowledge of historical phonology allows one to confirm their proximity in ancient times as well. Modern linguists have continued to expand on this method and have made more systematic analyses of ancient word families, considering both etymology and phonology in tandem.⁸⁷ But the essential principles were already established by Dai Zhen and his peers.

In spite of the reputation of Qing scholarship for focusing on minutiae, Dai was more attuned to philosophical questions. As Hamaguchi Fujio has shown, Dai's philological analysis was inspired by his conviction that knowledge of ancient language was a key to the way of the sages.⁸⁸ Thus his commentary is not especially detailed but notable more for its attempts to clarify the structures of poems on the basis of proper identification of semantics. In the case of "Heavenly Questions," Dai analyzes the rhymes of the poem and in general analyzes the text according to its structure in quatrains. He seems to have been baffled, though, by quatrain 56 and the succeeding lines, providing no commentary at all to quatrains 58–64.⁸⁹ He

---

85. In other words, both Qing philologists and modern linguistics rejected the "ideographic myth" that Chinese characters represent ideas directly. For a comprehensive comparative study of this issue, see O'Neill, *Ideography and Chinese Language Theory*.

86. *Qu Yuan fu zhu*, 1.3.

87. This relationship is confirmed and placed in context of a broader range of vocabulary in, for instance, Wang Li's *Tongyuan zidian*, 207–8.

88. Hamaguchi Fujio, *Shindai kōkyogaku no shisōshiteki kenkyū*, 193–205.

89. *Qu Yuan fu zhu*, 3.31–32.

also states explicitly that his method is to explain only the "near and proper" (*jinzheng* 近正) terms and ignore the other, more exotic ones (recalling Zhu Xi's reluctance to speculate on difficult passages in the poem).[90]

Wang Niansun 王念孫 (1744–1832), who studied with Dai Zhen, employed similar philological methods but on a larger scale and more systematically. Wang did not attempt to interpret the "Heavenly Questions" itself, but his philological approach was determinative for later readers, and his discoveries on the meanings of words are frequently cited and reapplied to the "Heavenly Questions" by other scholars.[91] Perhaps more than any other Qing scholar, Wang's work established a new and comprehensive model of classical philology, that explored the meanings of words throughout the ancient canon, rather than glossing individual texts in isolation. One of the masterworks of this sophisticated approach was Wang Niansun's *Guangya shuzheng* 廣雅疏證. The original *Guangya* is a synonymicon, an extended collection of words with related meanings, categorized loosely by topic. It was compiled by Zhang Yi 張揖 around 227 CE and was based on the earlier *Erya* 爾雅, which eventually was established as one of the Thirteen Classics. Wang Niansun's *Guangya shuzheng* is an elaborate commentary to the original *Guangya* with extensive citations used to verify or elaborate on the meanings of words, delicately distinguishing how they are related and demonstrating their usage within ancient texts. Wang cites widely from other philological resources, especially the *Fangyan* 方言 of Yang Xiong 揚雄, but also from the usage of the words in different classics and historical texts. Throughout the work, Wang's fundamental principle is to investigate the sounds of language rather than just to examine the meanings of characters, allowing him to recognize phonetic loans and word families.[92]

In the *Guangya shuzheng*, Wang employs evidence from the *Elegies of Chu* widely, and hence the commentary can help to understand the glosses of words in the *Elegies*, even while it also uses them as a source for the

---

90. *Qu Yuan fu zhu*, 3.23; cited in Sun Qiaoyun, *Yuan Ming Qing chuci xueshi*, 177.

91. His notes on the *Chuci*, which only touch directly on "Heavenly Questions" once, may be found in the "Dushu zazhi yubian" 讀書雜志餘編, included in *Dushu zazhi*. There is a comprehensive study of his philological methods by Liu Jingsheng, *Wang Niansun zhi xunguxue yanjiu*.

92. Liu Jingsheng, *Wang Niansun zhi xunguxue yanjiu*, 36–38.

ancient language in general (the hermeneutic circle). For instance, the second quatrain of "Heavenly Questions" includes the tricky lines:

> In that chaotic congeries of semblances, 馮翼惟像
> How could anything be differentiated? 何以識之

The most challenging word here is *pingyi* 馮翼, which seems to be related to a similar expression in the Huainanzi.[93] *Pingyi* is identified in a cryptic entry of the *Guangya*, but Wang Niansun's further citations to the term help to substantiate this reading and explain why the *Guangya* entry lists this term along with a number of reduplicative compound descriptive of "primal energy" (*yuanqi* 元氣).[94]

Wang's research was part of the work necessary to achieving a macroscopic view of ancient language and usage, work that remains indispensable even with the aid of electronic databases, since philologists like Wang made scrupulous efforts to distinguish different usages of the same character, while also recognizing the phenomenon of phonetic variants, when one character can be used in place of another one with similar pronunciation (at the time, meaning Old Chinese). For instance, he has a useful suggestion for understanding quatrain 16:[95]

> When he divided the earth into nine levels, 地方九則
> How could he build it into embankments? 何以墳之

Wang cites evidence supporting Wang Yi's own gloss of *fen* 墳 here as a homonym, *fen* 分. In my own translation I have chosen not to follow this gloss, because it seems to me that the sense of division is already implicit in the previous line with the phrase "nine levels," and that interpreting *fen* as an active verb, "to build the embankments," fits the traditional gloss of the character and the context better. The *Shuowen jiezi* also glosses it as *mu* 墓, "tomb" or "tumulus," referring to the earth mound over a tomb. Nonetheless, Wang Niansun's point that it may also be interpreted as a phonetic variant for *fen*, "to divide," cannot be ignored. Perhaps this can be understood as a form of graphophonemic word play: the most natural

---

93. This term was also discussed in chapter 1, from a different perspective.
94. *Guangya shuzheng*, 6A.25a.
95. *Guangya shuzheng*, 1A.33b.

understanding of the word, based on its pronunciation, is as the verb "to divide," and it is only the specific graphic form that adds an additional layer of meaning.⁹⁶

The *Chuci* anthology did form one of the main subjects of one of Wang Niansun's works, namely, *Maoshi qunjing Chuci gu yunpu* 毛詩群經楚辭古韻譜 (Rhyme table for the Mao Odes, various classics, and Elegies of Chu), a comprehensive study of pre-Qin rhyming.⁹⁷ This great work followed in a long tradition of phonological scholarship on the anthology dating back to the Sui dynasty.⁹⁸ But Wang and Jiang Yougao 江有誥 (d. 1851) achieved the highest sophistication of any Qing scholars in their analysis of ancient rhymes, and established the foundation of modern analysis.⁹⁹ With 22 rhyme groups (21 in Jiang's case), they were able to analyze the *Chuci* in a relatively satisfying way. In fact their results are quite similar to those of the great modern linguist Wang Li 王力, who pays homage to Jiang in the title of his work, *Chuci yundu* 楚辭韻讀.

Wang Niansun's contribution to the interpretation of the "Heavenly Questions" was primarily linguistic, relying on a more rigorous analysis of Chinese script and phonology. But a more traditional kind of scholarship, the eclectic commentary more like reading notes than an analytical treatise, also continued in the Qing. Another major philologist of the late Qing, Ding Yan 丁晏 (1794–1875), was a native of Shanyang, Jiangsu, and spent most of his life there, leading efforts to defend the city against the British in

---

96. It may also have been Wang Niansun who decisively showed that *gu zang* 固臧 in quatrain 40 should be interpreted as "keep secure" with 臧 merely a graphic variant for *cang* 藏, "keep, hide." See Wang Niansun, "Dushu zazhi yubian," 3b–4a, and also commentary to "Text Three" below.

97. The title is also given as simply *Gu yunpu*.

98. See discussion in Sun Qiaoyun, *Yuan Ming Qing chuci xueshi*, 178. The only surviving phonological study from the Song is Wu Yu 吳棫 (ca. 1100–1154), *Chuci shiyin* 楚辭釋音. But the earliest phonological work of which we know is Zhixian's 智騫 (Sui) *Chuci yin* 楚辭音. This is not extant in its entirety, but is quoted by Hong Xingzu, and survives in part in a Dunhuang manuscript, p. 2494. See study by Jiang Liangfu, "Dunhuang xieben Sui Shi Zhixian *Chu ci yin* ba" 敦煌寫本隋釋智騫楚辭音跋, in *Chuci xue lunwen ji*, 367–85. I follow Jiang's correction of the author's name to Zhixian 智騫 (the latter character with the bird radical) rather than Daoqian 道騫. As Jiang himself shows, however, the names were conflated and confused from an early date, so the evidence is insufficient.

99. Baxter, *Handbook of Old Chinese Phonology*, 169.

1842 and again against the Nian 捻 rebels in 1860.¹⁰⁰ He was a prolific classical scholar, and twenty-three of his numerous works are included in the collectanea *Yizhizhai congshu* 頤志齋叢書. Ding authored one of the rare works in premodern times devoted explicitly to the "Heavenly Questions," the *Chuci Tianwen jian* 楚辭天問箋. As noted above, Ding offered the excellent suggestion that quatrain 40 is about the moon goddess Chang'e 嫦娥 rather than Prince Qiao.¹⁰¹ As with Xu Wenjing, Ding's contribution lies mainly in quoting from apposite sources that had previously been neglected, such as *The Classic of Mountains and Seas*.

Though he lived slightly later than these other prominent scholars of the Qing, completing much of his work even after the Taiping Rebellion as the Qing faced its demise, Yu Yue 俞樾 (1821–1907) deserves special attention because he proposed several truly original corrections to the text of "Tianwen." Yu was an extraordinary scholar and prolific writer.¹⁰² He was a precocious student who had already become a *xiucai* in 1836, and spent most of his life in Suzhou and Hangzhou. He was also a diligent teacher, among whose many prominent students was Zhang Taiyan 章太炎 (1869–1936).

Yu Yue clearly stated the three key principles of his philological research: "The way of editing the classics has just three essential elements: correcting punctuation, examining the meanings of characters, and the phonetic loans (*jiajie*) of ancient writing." 余嘗謂治經之道，其要有三曰：正句讀，審字義通，古文假借。¹⁰³ The third principle, in particular, shows that

---

100. Biography in Hummel, *Eminent Chinese*, 727–28, authored by Eduard Erkes.
101. *Chuci Tianwen jie*, 33a/b.
102. See *Eminent Chinese*, 944–45. Probably the best source for Yu's biography is his own autobiographical poem, "Quyuan zishu shi" 曲園自述詩, accompanied by Yu's prose commentary; see Zhang Yanying, ed., *Yu Yue shiwen ji*, 2:861–96. Yu's poetry is distinguished by his devotion to his family; see his "Baiai pian" 百哀篇, lamenting the death of his wife (*Yu Yue shiwen ji*, 3:1000–1009), in particular, but also occasional pieces like the regulated verse matching the rhymes of a poem from his granddaughter (2:436). Many of his poems also remark on the incidental pleasures of daily life, notably the joy of eating tofu (2:788). For a splendid appreciation of writings by Yu Yue and his family, in particular his grandson Yu Pingbo 俞平伯 (1900–1990), see Huntington, *Ink and Tears*.
103. "Zuo Zhiwen Zhuzi bujiao xu" 左祉文諸子補校序, in Yu Yue, *Chunzaitang zawen*, 5.7.2b. See also the discussion in Luo Xiangfei, *Yu Yue de jingxue sixiang yu jingxue yanjiu fengge*, 62.

the legacy of Wang Niansun and Dai Zhen's scholarship was still strong. In one striking example of his method, Yu reinterpreted a line in the second stanza of *Odes* 89, "On the Levelled Earth by the East Gate" ("Dongmen zhi shan" 東門之墠): "The chestnuts by the East Gate" 東門之栗, based on a parallel in the *Zuozhuan*, Duke Xiang, year 9, "to cut down the tree markers along the road" 斬行栗.¹⁰⁴ Yu understands *li* "chestnut" to be a loan for *lie* 列 "row."¹⁰⁵

Yu's notes to the *Chuci* occupy just sixty (traditional woodblock-print) pages in a large compilation of his brief scholarly writings, the *Yulou zazuan* 俞樓雜纂. For the "Heavenly Questions," he offers remarks on only five quatrains out of the whole poem (14, 31, 43, 76, and 77), and he disregards the quatrain structure to discuss only individual couplets. In spite of the limitations of scale, though, his notes are essential reading. With regard to quatrain 76, for instance:

76 Hou Ji was the primary son,   稷維元子
   So why did the High Lord **revile** him?   帝何竺之
   When he was discarded on the ice,   投之於冰上
   Why did the birds keep him warm?   鳥何燠之

Yu argues convincingly that *du* 竺 (*tûk, usually read as equivalent to *du* 篤) is a loan graph for *du* 毒 (*dûk), which I accordingly render as "revile." Though one has to be cautious about this kind of phonological substitution, in this case the logic of the text makes it seem overwhelmingly plausible. The question is only legible if the High Lord is treating Hou Ji in a way contrary to expectation, which is that the primary or eldest son ought to be revered, not reviled. The meaning of this character had long been debated, but it seems to me that Yu basically settled the controversy with his suggestion, solidly grounded in historical phonology. In spite of Yu's accomplishments, one does regret that the notes are so few and so isolated, without a hint of a broader interpretation.

The legacy of Qing philology continued into the twentieth century without a sharp break; though modern scholars have had new insights,

---

104. See Luo Xiongfei, *Yu Yue de jingxue sixiang yu jingxue yanjiu fengge*, 63; *Qunjing pingyi*, 8.29a/b; compare Durrant et al., *Zuo Tradition*, 957, translating *li* as "chestnuts."

105. The two words are quite close in Baxter's reconstruction, *C-rjit and *C-rjat, though they do not actually rhyme since they have different main vowels.

in most cases they have built upon the achievements of premodern ones. The continuity of philological progress here is most visibly represented in You Guoen's remarkable work, *Tianwen zuanyi*, the summation of the achievements of traditional Chinese philology in interpreting the poem. Published posthumously in 1982, this book is a synthesis that quotes dozens of commentators, ranging from the earliest surviving commentary of the *Chuci zhangju* up through the beginning of the twentieth century. In other words, rather than simply resolving problems according to his own theories, You sketches the ongoing debates and gradual evolution of understanding on each particular issue. The commentary becomes an *omnium gatherum* of earlier interpretations, and the final interpretation is the synthesis of everything that has gone before. This conception of scholarly tradition in commentary is not unprecedented in the Chinese tradition. With regard to the "Heavenly Questions" itself, one of You Guoen's major sources and doubtless an inspiration for his own work is the *Qishier jia piping Chuci jizhu* 七十二家批評楚辭集注 (Collected commentaries to *Chuci*, evaluated by 72 experts), compiled by Jiang Zhiqiao 蔣之翹. This is technically just a new edition of Zhu Xi's classic anthology, but with additional marginal commentary by some seventy-two past scholars (many of whom, it should be noted, are cited only once or twice).[106] But it is You Guoen's great achievement that he does not merely quote and accumulate information, but rather sifts carefully through it so as to draw his own conclusions, which become all the more powerful because they are reached in response, in self-differentiation, and even in outright opposition to the views of earlier scholars.

You Guoen was of course not the only master of the *Chuci* in the twentieth century. Among many other Chinese readers of the anthology, it may be particularly worth comparing him with his contemporary Jiang Liangfu 姜亮夫 (1902–1995).[107] Both men studied with Wang Guowei at Peking University in the 1920s, just before his suicide in 1927, and imbibed both the deep erudition, and the cosmopolitan outlook, of the great scholars of that era. Jiang's edition of the *Elegies*, the *Qu Yuan fu jiaozhu* 屈原賦校注, focuses, as its name indicates, on the works that Jiang considers attributable to Qu Yuan himself, including the "Heavenly Questions." This

---

106. See discussion in Luo Jianbo, *Mingdai* Chuci *pingdian lunkao*, 219–25.
107. See Liu and Jiang, "Jiang Liangfu xiansheng ji qi *Chuci* yanjiu."

was completed in 1931 but only published in 1957 by Renmin chubanshe, and then published in a revised version in 1987. It contains countless valuable insights into the content and style of the poems, as well as editorial emendations and explication of cruxes, and I have cited it frequently in my commentary to my translation of "Heavenly Questions" below. Moreover, Jiang was also the author of the astonishing encyclopedia, *Chuci tonggu* 楚辞通故, which contains thousands of entries on nearly every word or name that is mentioned in the anthology as a whole.

Though Jiang Liangfu was in some ways more original than You Guoen, and probably advanced the understanding of the *Elegies of Chu* further, it nonetheless seems to me that his work on the "Heavenly Questions" itself is not quite as important as You's.[108] The reason is simple. The study of the "Heavenly Questions" is not a field where originality and idiosyncratic insight can resolve every problem. To the contrary, in regard to many of the puzzling issues that arise in reading the poem, all one can do is compile the best guesses of previous scholars. Once this has been accomplished, of course, there is still room for revisionist interpretations; as I have emphasized throughout this study, there are many cases where the Han commentary was incorrect and set future scholarship on the wrong track. On the whole, though, there is no way to gain a comprehensive view of the poem without a close study of the commentarial tradition itself, and this is what You's edition provides in exemplary fashion.

In the present century, other Chinese scholars have continued to build on You's achievement. To return to quatrain 46:

46 When Shaokang prepared the army for ambush,   汤谋易旅
    How did he strengthen it?   何以厚之
    When Ao capsized the vessels of Zhenxun,   覆舟斟寻
    By what route had he conquered them?   何道取之

As we have seen, Zhu Xi perceptively noted the difficulty of understanding the subject as Tang, even though Tang 汤 is the first character here. He rightly analyzed the logic of the poem quatrain by quatrain and so could be confident there was a textual difficulty here. You Guoen then

---

108. For an insightful comparison of the two scholars' work in general, see Cao Jianguo, "You Guoen yu Jiang Liangfu *Chuci* yanjiu bijiao." My comments here are limited to their work on "Heavenly Questions."

cites additional evidence to support an emendation of *tang* to *kang* 康. In my own interpretation, I follow a similar approach, but supplement it with an insight from the great twenty-first-century scholar, Huang Linggeng 黃靈庚. Huang's achievement, like that of You Guoen and other major interpreters of Chinese of the past, is summative; two highlights of his prolific output are a five-volume collation and subcommentary to the *Chuci zhangju*, the *Chuci zhangju shuzheng* 楚辭章句疏證; and an eighty-volume compilation of significant scholarship, the *Chuci wenxian congkan* 楚辭文獻叢刊. And yet Huang is also capable of the philological aperçu more distinctive of the Wang Niansun tradition. In this case, he argues cogently for an emendation of *tang* 湯 to *yang* 陽 in its sense of "pretend," so that the line would refer to a strategy used by Shaokang, just mentioned as the subject of the previous quatrain, involving some kind of ambush.[109]

Though I have adopted Huang's solution in my own translation, the other point that should not be overlooked is that many of the traditional readings on which Huang builds his own interpretations, just like the traditional exegeses cited by You Guoen, are themselves potentially valid, even if we may prefer alternatives today. "Heavenly Questions" is not a legal document with a sole intended meaning and many erroneous interpretations; it is a poem that has often been interpreted erroneously, but has always offered many potential implications, some of them more pointed and explicit than others. Reading the history of its interpretation is not just an exercise in metascholarship, but is indispensable to understanding the poem itself.

Towards a Comparative Reading

In retrospect we can see that Qing scholarly trends were leading towards the new insights of the twentieth century.

Even though he made numerous breakthroughs in scholarship and occasionally boasted of his own originality, Wang Guowei would have been the last to assert that any of these were paradigm shifts.[110] To the contrary, in his preface to the *Guoxue congkan* 國學叢刊, which he cofounded with

---

109. Huang Linggeng, ed., *Chuci zhangju shuzheng*, 4.1120.
110. See Hu Qiuhua's recent study, *Konfuzianisches Ethos und westliche Wissenschaft*.

Luo Zhenyu in 1911, Wang wrote this sensitive consideration of the relation between cultural understanding and verifiable fact:

> Thus I have declared that learning cannot be said to be new or old, Chinese or Western, practical or impractical. I may be more precise here. Why do I say that learning is not new or old? For all things under Heaven can be examined either scientifically or historically, and in each case one will make different kinds of observations. Examined scientifically, one must exhaust their reality, and the principle is to seek out how they are. Whenever there is something my intelligence cannot penetrate or where my mind cannot be at rest, then even if it is affirmed by the sages I will not believe it, and even if it was practiced by the sages I will have some dissatisfaction. Why is this? The sages are used to distinguish truth and falsity, truth and falsity do not derive from the sages. They are used to distinguish right and wrong, right and wrong are not established by the sages. From the historical perspective, it is not only the truth and actuality of things that furnishes the materials of research. That which today we see as untrue accounts, and the institutions and customs we reject, must have had their own reasons for being established, and causes that they were useful to their own times. Their causes existed in antiquity, and their results have passed on to the future, so all these materials are worthy of investigation and reference, and even the most trivial we dare not discard. Thus in the history of physical sciences, half the assertions are false. In the history of philosophy, half of it is fantasy. Of the whole history of institutions and customs, half is to be discarded with the youth's black cap and the child's parted bangs.[III] But the historical scholars do not reject them. This is the difference between the two kinds of scholarship, and yet those who practice the scientific kind of scholarship must rely on the materials of the historians; and those who practice scholarship also cannot do with scientific knowledge. Yet the fine people today either disparage antiquity or revere antiquity. Those who disparage antiquity are inspired by the scientific perspective but do not know there is historical scholarship too. Those who revere antiquity are guided by the historical perspective, but do not know there is scientific scholarship too. But there are those who try to mediate between the two, and yet do not understand how to choose from one or the other, and this is why there arise the theories of ancient and modern or new and old.

III. "Jet-black cap or the first clippings of an infant's hair" (*bianmao* 弁髦) is an expression deriving from *Zuozhuan*, Duke Zhao, year 9, for outmoded things; see Durrant, et al., *Zuo Tradition*, 1447.

故吾所謂學無新舊,無中西,無有用、無用之說,可得而詳焉。何以言學無新舊也?夫天下之事物,自科學上觀之與自史學上觀之,其立論各不同。自科學上觀之,則事物必盡其真,而道理必求其是。凡吾智之不能通而吾心之所不能安者,雖聖賢言之有所不信焉。雖聖賢行之有所不慊焉。何則圣賢所以別真偽也,真偽非由聖賢出也。所以明是非也,是非非由聖賢立也。自史學上觀之,則不獨事理之真與是者,足資研究而已,即今日所視為不真之學說,不是之制度風俗,必有所以成立之由,與其所以适于一時之故。其因存于遼古,而其果及于方來,故材料之足資參考者,雖至纖悉不敢棄焉。故物理學之歷史,謬說居其半焉。哲學之歷史,空想居其半焉。制度、風俗之歷史,弁髦居其半焉。而史學家弗棄也。此二學之異也。然治科學者,必有待於是史學上之材料。而治史學者,亦不可無科學上之知識。今之君子,非一切蔑古,即一切尚古。蔑古者,出于科學上之見地,而不知有史學。尚古者,出于史學上之見地,而不知有科學。即為調停之說者,亦未能知取舍之所以然,此所以有古今新舊之說也。[112]

In 1911, with the Qing dynasty on the verge of collapse, all these issues were not theoretical. The civil service examinations had finally been abandoned in 1905, and intellectuals were actively rethinking China's education system. The relative value that should be accorded to different kinds of learning and study was actively under debate. Wang's answer is that history and science are intertwined, and neither can be extricated from the other. This is clear enough when one looks at a field like what is called "political science" today. If you are going to examine how monarchy and democracy have functioned, you cannot run experiments in a laboratory, but must resort to historical information. By the same token, in studying ancient Chinese poetry, you will be more successful the more information you have about the world: about the astronomical phenomena referred to at the beginning of the "Heavenly Questions," about the internal contradictions of autocracy, about the nature and regularity of linguistic change; the humanities cannot be separated from physical sciences, but incorporate their discoveries into their own picture of the human condition.

When Wang Guowei drew on the oracle bone inscriptions to examine the institutions and regimes of antiquity, he could not discard transmitted

---

112. German translation and text in Hu Qiuhua, *Konfuzianisches Ethos und westliche Wissenschaft*, 345–52; Chinese text in *Wang Guowei yishu*, 3:4.6b–9b (202–8).

Fig. 3: Kong Kai Ming 江啟明, *Wang Guowei* 王國維, drawing: pencil, pen and ink, and watercolor, 51 x 38 cm, in *Hong Kong Baptist University Library Art Collections*, accessed February 5, 2024, https://bcc.lib.hkbu.edu.hk/artcollection/kc-26-wangguowei. Courtesy of Hong Kong Baptist University Library.

texts, but rather integrated this new objective data from Anyang into his historical study. And it is this same integrative process of objective knowledge and subjective interpretation that we have seen throughout this book. In this chapter, it was first the highly original and intuitive thinkers of the seventeenth century who offered bold new readings of "Heavenly Questions" as a whole. Then it was the patient historical scholarship of Xu Wenjing that provided documentary corroboration from the *Bamboo Annals* and other sources to demonstrate that the poem had a substantive coherence and correspondence to historical fact. Later it was the linguistic acumen of Wang Niansun and others that clarified readings of individual characters; and in the late nineteenth century it would be a combination of lucid phonological analysis and sheer erudition on the part of Ding Yan and Yu Yue that would clarify several ancient cruxes.

Throughout this history of interpretation, then, it has been some combination of analytical insight and cumulative integration of knowledge that has allowed us to penetrate the mysteries of the "Heavenly Questions." Of all the scholarly works published in China or abroad, You Guoen's *Tianwen zuanyi* must be the book that demonstrates this point as fully and substantively as any. Though he also compiled a similar book on "Subli-mating Sorrow," it is not as compelling as the *Tianwen zuanyi* because the diversity of opinion regarding "Sublimating Sorrow" has more to do with the inherent richness and multiplicity of meanings in the original poem. The case of "Heavenly Questions" is different, because we have the polysemy of a great literary work combined with so many substantive mysteries of history, mythology, language, and script.

But we should conclude this chapter by considering more recent innovations in scholarship on the "Heavenly Questions," which have integrated both new archaeological discoveries and also comparative data from outside China. Perhaps the one study that best combines comparative analysis with scholarly rigor is the 1976 essay "'Tianwen' wenti de yuanliu: 'fawen' wenxue zhi tantao" 〈天問〉文體的源流——「發問」文學之探討 ("The sources of the genre of 'Heavenly Questions': an investigation of 'interrogative' literature") by the Hong Kong scholar Jao Tsung-i 饒宗頤 (1917–2018). In this major study, Jao compares the "Heavenly Questions" not just to other interrogative writings from the Chinese tradition, but also to a wide range of Indic and foreign texts. While Jao is enthusiastic about a wide-ranging comparative investigation of these interrogative texts, what he calls "literary anthropology" after Northrop Frye, he is cautious about making any specific claims of foreign influence on the text.[113] Instead, he employs a huge range of citations to demonstrate how common "interrogative literature" per se is throughout world literature and religion. The weight of his evidence suggests to me that one should not look for any direct line of influence, but rather recognize that the impulse to ask questions about human origins is common through many cultures.

The interrogative mood is common in poetry even just within the Chinese tradition, and one of Jao's contributions here is to point out a number of lesser-known Chinese texts. This turns out to be useful primarily for distinguishing the "Heavenly Questions" from other early Chinese texts that at first appear similar. For instance, the Mawangdui medical text "Shi wen" 十問 (Ten questions), cited by Jao, contains ten dialogues.[114] Note that in the dialogues, though, it is the sovereign, whether Yu, the Yellow Emperor, or another king, who is asking questions of various

---

113. Jao, "Tianwen wenti de yuanliu: Fawen wenxue zhi tantao," 53.
114. Jao, "Tianwen wenti de yuanliu: Fawen wenxue zhi tantao," 50.

experts, and that the questions are concise compared to the expansive explanations of the medical experts.[115] As with similar examples in the various Warring States philosophical texts, the answers are much longer than the questions; in spite of interrogative framing, the emphasis is on providing information and explanation, not on inquiry itself.

A number of transmitted texts also contain extensive passages framed as questions, such as *Guanzi* 管子 and *Zhuangzi*.[116] The opening of the fourteenth chapter of *Zhuangzi*, "Heavenly Revolutions" ("Tianyun" 天運), reads:

> "Does heaven revolve?
> Does earth stand still?
> Do the sun and moon jockey for position?
> Who controls all of this?
> Who unfolds all of this?
> Who ties it all together?
> Who dwells in inactivity,
> Yet impels things on their course?
>
> May it be that there are levers and threads
> That drive them inexorably?
> Or may it be that they just keep turning
> And are unable to stop by themselves?
> Do the clouds make the rain?
>
> Or does the rain make the clouds?
> Who bestows them so generously?
> Who dwells in inactivity,
> Yet urges things on to all this lusty joy?
> The winds arise in the north
>
> And, first to the east, then to the west,
> They drift back and forth above us.
> Who breathes them?

---

115. For a full translation, see Harper, *Early Chinese Medical Literature*, 385–411.

116. For instance, *Guanzi* contains a chapter entitled "Queries" 問. See *Guanzi jiaozhu*, 24.534–58. Ricketts discusses its prominent differences from "Heavenly Questions" (*Guanzi*, 1:366). Field also discusses the relevance of *Guanzi* with appropriate skepticism at "Cosmos, Cosmograph, and the Inquiring Poet," 85, n.8.

> Who dwells in inactivity,
> Yet does this fanning?
> I venture to ask the reasons for all this."
>
> "Come, and I shall tell you," said the Magus Xian.[117]

天其運乎？地其處乎？日月其爭於所乎？孰主張是？孰維綱是？孰居無事推而行是？意者其有機緘而不得已邪？意者其運轉而不能自止邪？雲者為雨乎？雨者為雲乎？孰隆施是？孰居無事淫樂而勸是？風起北方，一西一東，有上彷徨，孰噓吸是？孰居無事而披拂是？敢問何故？巫咸袑曰：「來！吾語女。」

There is an intriguing parallel here, but also a fundamental difference. *Zhuangzi*, exceptional as it is in many particulars of style and thought, nonetheless resembles the other philosophical works of the Warring States in attempting to present explanations of phenomena. Even in this case, Magus Xian goes on to answer the questions in some detail.

By contrast, the "Heavenly Questions" itself does not attempt to resolve any of its questions. Instead its whole method is simply to peer back into the past and to expose the mysteries, not to resolve them. This is, after all, why readers needed the corroboration of oracle bones to understand some of the questions posed by the poem about Shang ancestors, all of which the author(s) took for granted. Rather than reading the poem in dialogue with Warring States thinkers, it may make sense to look further back in time. For instance, there is an old theory that the state of Chu inherited the legacy of Shang dynasty culture. We could selectively quote from "Heavenly Questions" to substantiate this connection:

55	While his concubine Jian Di was at the altar,	簡狄在臺
	Why did High Lord Ku find it proper?	譽何宜
	At the gift proffered by the dark bird	玄鳥致貽
	Why was she so gratified?	女何嘉

Jian Di is said in the *Shiji* to be the younger concubine of High Lord Ku, mythic Shang ruler. She swallowed the egg of the Dark Bird, and then gave

---

117. Mair, *Wandering on the Way*, 130–31; *Zhuangzi jishi*, 14.499. Demiéville has an insightful discussion of this parallel in his essay, "Enigmes taoistes." He explicitly distinguishes the Daoist, mystical implications of the *Zhuangzi* from the skepticism of the "Heavenly Questions."

birth to Xie 契, ancestor of the Shang people. As "Dark Bird" ("Xuan niao" 玄鳥; *Odes* 303) describes it: "Heaven bade the dark bird / To come down and bear the Shang, / Who dwelt in the lands of Yin so wide. / Of old God bade the warlike Tang / To partition the frontier lands" 天命玄鳥、降而生商、宅殷土芒芒。古帝命武湯、正域彼四方。[118] Nor should one ignore the detailed knowledge of the Shang ancestors that is interrogated in quatrains 56 and following, as we have seen in chapter one; these are events whose memory is recorded in the oracle bone inscriptions, but was largely lost to later historians.

But this parallel could only serve as one example of many that can also be cited as part of other hypotheses for the historical origins of "Heavenly Questions." The poem also contains extensive discussion of pre-Shang and of Zhou mythology. David Hawkes argues convincingly that we should also be cautious of expecting a single cultural lineage to survive over centuries; instead, the people of Chu, as in other states, were able to pick and choose among mythological traditions as necessary to negotiate their relations with other powers.[119] In other words, it may be more profitable to look at how myth is used within particular texts and contexts rather than looking for an ur-myth. Allan's work is very useful for this purpose because of her emphasis on structuralist motifs and contrasts, as in her first book, *The Heir and the Sage*. The "Heavenly Questions" also offers a number of mythic archetypes, including the great flood, heir-sage dichotomy (such as Yu's 禹 abdication to Yi 益 rather than son Qi 啟), mystic birds, the strongman hero betrayed by an unfaithful wife, man-animal metamorphoses, etc.

It is with these materials in mind that previous scholars have attempted a comparative approach. August Conrady (1864–1925) had already published perhaps the earliest attempt to relate the "Heavenly Questions" to foreign texts, citing *Rigveda* 10.136.[120] Hellmut Wilhelm (1905–1990) instead proposed to compare *Rigveda* 10.129, the "Hymn of Creation."[121]

---

118. Waley, trans., *Book of Songs*, 320. For more on this background, see Sarah Allan's great work, *Shape of the Turtle*, as well as Chen Zhi's "Study of the Bird Cult."

119. Hawkes, "Heirs of Gaoyang." Hawkes sums up, "Theology was the handmaiden of political expediency" (p. 21).

120. Conrady, "Indische Einflüsse in China im 4. Jh. v. Chr."

121. Wilhelm, "Bemerkungen zur T'ien-wen Frage." He further points out *Rigveda* 1.164 and 10.90; and *Atharvageda* 10.7, 8.

But Wilhelm is more cautious about drawing any conclusions from this evidence, and also makes the critical point that these kinds of questioning pseudo-liturgies are not limited to Indic tradition, citing also the Old Norse Edda. Su Hsüeh-lin (cited above) also proposed Indo-European parallels, and expanded the breadth of the comparison to take in the Avesta and numerous other foreign parallels. There has been further interest in this comparison, including by Victor H. Mair, who ends up calling the poem "pan-Eurasian."[122]

Jao Tsung-i, in the study mentioned above, treats the comparative problem with relative sobriety, and pointedly objects to Su's thesis of direct transmission. In reality, few of the other texts that include questions and answers on cosmic topics attain anything like the historical vision of "Heavenly Questions"; most even go on to answer explicitly the questions posed, just as, as we have seen, the Magus Xian does in *Zhuangzi*. As Paul Demiéville also pointed out, even the cosmological questions in the *Zhuangzi* are fundamentally different from those in "Heavenly Questions," since the former belong to a broader philosophical argument leading towards one unifying, mystical Dao.[123] To take, for instance, the Old Norse "Lay of Vafthrudnir," it presents a number of remarkable riddles but goes on to answer them immediately:

> Whence shall come the Sun to the smooth heaven
> After Fenris has eaten her up?
>
> Elf-Candle shall have a daughter
> Before she is seized by Fenris:
> The maid shall ride her mother's highway
> When all the High Ones are dead.[124]

Probably most writers throughout history have been more interested in answering questions than posing them. After all, the posing of an unanswerable question is a hard and unrewarding task.

Though the "Heavenly Questions" treat a disparate set of topics and the

---

122. See Mair's comments in his prefatory note to his excellent translation of the poem, "Heavenly Questions," 373.
123. In his essay "Énigmes taoïstes."
124. See Taylor and Auden, trans., *The Elder Edda*, 77–78.

narrative thread sometimes seems to be lacking, all the different materials ultimately converge on a central question about the relationship between Heaven and Man. The poem repeatedly asks whether Heaven punishes the wicked and aids the virtuous, or not; and if not, is there some other logic or justification behind the course of events? Thus, while some scholars have suggested that the questions in the poem are merely rhetorical or originally accompanied by fixed answers, it seems more likely that they are open-ended. If there is any implied answer that unifies the poem, it must be the sustained scepticism and doubt of the interrogative mode itself. In this sense it is closest to the spirit of the "Book of Job" in the *Old Testament*:[125]

> And the Lord answered Job from the whirlwind and He said:
> Who is this who darkens counsel
> in words without knowledge?
> Gird your loins like a man,
> that I may ask you, and you can inform Me.
> Where were you when I founded earth?
> Tell, if you know understanding.
> Who fixed its measures, do you know,
> or who stretched a line upon it?
> In what were its sockets sunk,
> or who laid its cornerstone,
> when the morning stars sang together,
> and all the sons of God shouted for joy?
> Who hedged the sea with double doors,
> when it gushed forth from the womb,
> when I made cloud its clothing,
> and thick mist its swaddling bands?

The essential difference between "Heavenly Questions" and "Job," on one side, and the other examples that have been cited, is that these two masterpieces of "interrogative literature" delve much farther into the unknowable aspects of the universe. In "Heavenly Questions" the emphasis is on history and politics, while for "Job" it is on ethics and theology, but the interrogative element is shared by both works. They do not simply cite a few curiosities about the scope of the cosmos so as to praise the Creator,

---

125. In Robert Alter's new translation, *The Wisdom Books*, 158–59.

but instead use it as material to set forth on a deeper journey of inquiry. In "Job," the questions are partly resolved, but leave a considerable remainder of skepticism.[126] The "Heavenly Questions" are not answered explicitly, and the poignant effect of the poem can only be a lingering query, an assay of doubt, a recognition of how hard it ought to be to make sense of the political history leading up to the contemporary Chu regime.

Thus the grand tradition of Chinese scholarship illuminating this difficult text, a tradition that had originated in the efforts of Han scholars fiddling with bamboo strips, reached its culmination in the Qing dynasty and twentieth century as scholars in China and abroad were able to restore and explicate the entire poem. On this more accurate reading of its lines and quatrains, we are able to appreciate how well it deserves to stand alongside the *Book of Job* and other classics from around the world as a literary inquiry to human action and cosmic justice. Nonetheless, the "Heavenly Questions" ultimately remains distinct from all these texts, with its unparalleled queries into the obscurities and contradictions of Shang and Zhou founders. Though comparative literature has much to add, the messages and questions of the poem remain intrinsically the province of Sinological investigation, since they demand such careful scholarship of both transmitted and recently excavated Chinese texts. It has taken an extraordinary amount of Sinological erudition to determine how unanswerable the "Heavenly Questions" must remain.

---

126. See Dell, *The Book of Job*.

APPENDIX TO CHAPTER THREE

Text Three: "Heavenly Questions" as We Can Read It Today

The translation below is divided into seven sections and an epilogue. These divisions are somewhat arbitrary and are intended solely to guide the reader and to clarify the chronological and thematic progression of the poem. However, the divisions into quatrains are not arbitrary but rather follow the rhyme scheme.

This volume focuses on the Chinese scholarly tradition because it is these scholars who have made the greatest contributions by far, but it is worth noting previous translations which I have consulted:

Hawkes, David. *The Songs of the South. An Anthology of Ancient Chinese Poems by Qu Yuan and Other Poets.* Harmondsworth: Penguin Books, 1985.

Field, Stephen. *Tian wen: A Chinese Book of Origins.* New York: New Directions, 1986.

Mair, Victor H., trans. "Heavenly Questions." In *The Columbia Anthology of Traditional Chinese Literature*, 371–87. New York: Columbia University Press, 1994.

Mathieu, Rémi. *Elégies de Chu.* Paris: Gallimard, 2004.

Sukhu, Gopal. *Songs of Chu.* New York: Columbia University Press, 2017.

This translation is based on my own version previously published in:

Williams, Nicholas Morrow. *Elegies of Chu: An Anthology of Early Chinese Poetry.* Oxford: Oxford University Press, 2022.

The notes after each quatrain are not intended to be comprehensive—that would require an additional volume—but more to point out some key considerations that have shaped my own translation.

I. Formation of the Universe

It was said:	曰
1 Regarding the beginnings of the primordial age,	遂古之初
Who recorded the events and told us of them?	誰傳道之
Before all above and below had taken shape,	上下未形
What way was there to investigate it?	何由考之

The opening with the term *yue* 曰 marking reported discourse is a formal usage also found in the *Book of Documents* and other ancient texts, and one of the linguistic features suggesting an early date of the poem. Wang Fuzhi's remark that *sui* 遂 should be read *sui* 邃, "remote," is helpful here (*Chuci tongshi*, 3.274).

This stanza is relatively straightforward to translate, but its implications for the poem as a whole are immense. In particular, it immediately contradicts any facile assumption that the questions are intended to have straightforward answers, or that the poem is some kind of crib for shamanistic examinations, or an instruction manual for princes, etc.: the whole point of this quatrain is that some matters are unknowable.

2 When light and dark were still hazy and indistinct,	冥昭瞢闇
Who could fully comprehend them?	誰能極之
In that chaotic congeries of semblances,	馮翼惟像
How could anything be differentiated?	何以識之

Like the first quatrain, this one again emphasizes the difficulty of describing or understanding what is excessively remote, thereby setting the tone for the entire poem. The second half of this quatrain has to be read in light of the opening of the third chapter of *Huainanzi* describing the nature of the cosmos "Before Heaven and Earth were formed" and employing the descriptive term *pingping yiyi* 馮馮翼翼, here simply *pingyi* (see Liu Wendian, ed., *Huainan honglie jijie*, 3.79). This is not a rhyming or alliterative compound according to the normal phonological categories, but the Baxter-Sagart reconstruction *[b]rəŋ-gwrək suggests the velar euphony that may have made it an effective onomatopoeic descriptive in early times.

3 Light in its brilliance and dark in its obscurity,	明明闇闇
How were they formed separately and created?	惟時何為

> Of Yin, Yang, and [with Heaven] the Three Conjoined: 陰陽三合
> Which is original and which is altered? 何本何化

The Han commentary interprets light and dark here as representing Yin and Yang, which is reasonable. In view of my own interpretation of the poem as a whole, however, I would like to suggest that the issue of clarity and obscurity of interpretation is also implicit here. One is tempted to translate *shi* 時 here literally as "time" as does Sukhu (*Songs of Chu*, 76), so that the second line of the quatrain would read, "How was time created?" But we should instead submit to the consensus of the commentators that *shi* should be read (as frequently in the *Odes* and *Documents*) as a demonstrative, *shi* 是.

According to one view, Yin, Yang, and Heaven cannot produce life independently, but all three must work in conjunction (see *Guliang zhuan*, Duke Zhuang, year 3; *Chunqiu Guliang zhuan zhushu*, 5.78). Alternatively, some scholars emend *san* 三 to *can* 參, meaning simply that Yin and Yang forces mix together and combine. But the received text is more interesting as it distinguishes the complementarity of Yin and Yang from their threefold union.

> 4 The Heavenly Sphere divided ninefold,   圜則九重
>   Who can traverse round and measure it?   孰營度之
>   What craft was responsible for it?   惟茲何功
>   Who could have created it in the beginning?   孰初作之

According to *Huainanzi*, "Heaven has nine layers, just as man has nine orifices" 天有九重，人亦有九竅 (Major et al., *Huainanzi*, 143; Liu Wendian, ed., *Huainan honglie jijie*, 3.150–51). But "Heavenly Questions" may be inquiring about a different configuration specific to Chu cosmology. The conception is of nine components of Heaven arrayed horizontally, corresponding to the nine continents of earth, and including the four cardinal directions, four intercardinal directions, and the center.[1] Qu Yuan swears by the Ninefold Heavens in "Sublimating Sorrow," l. 43, and Jao Tsung-i has identified this as a belief specific to Chu culture ("Jing-Chu wenhua," 874).

---

1. Jiang Liangfu gives a thorough account in *Chuci tonggu*, 1:40–41, although to some extent he is reliant on the Han commentary.

You Guoen's argument here that *ying* 營 means "circumference" or "circumnavigate" seems convincing (*Tianwen zuanyi*, 32).

5   Where are the axle and mainstays attached?   斡維焉繫
      Where is the fulcrum of Heaven placed?   天極焉加
      How do the Eight Pillars support [the Earth]?   八柱何當
      Why is the Southeast truncated?   東南何虧

The word *wo/guan* 斡 is related to *guan* 筦, "tube." According to Shirakawa it originally indicated a flagpole, and by extension the Northern Dipper, axle of the universe (*Jitsū*, 10). By the Han dynasty the reading of this graph was disputed, leading to its two unrelated pronunciations.

The Eight Pillars are apparently those placed below the earth (not supporting heaven). The Southeast is said in the *Huainanzi* to be have been truncated by the mighty Gonggong, who warred with Qu Yuan's ancestor Zhuanxu (Major et al., *Huainanzi*, 58; Liu Wendian, ed., *Huainan honglie jijie*, 1.58). But see also quatrain 18 below.

6   Regarding the margins of the Nine Heavens: 九天之際
      Where are they placed and where do they connect?   安放安屬
      Though corners and interstices are many,   隅隈多有
      Who can know their number in full?   誰知其數

Heaven was said to be divided into nine parts, as we saw above in quatrain 4.

7   With what is Heaven imbricated?   天何所沓
      How are the Twelve Stations divided?   十二焉分
      To what entity are subjoined the sun and moon?   日月安屬
      And where are the serried stars disposed?   列星安陳

The Twelve Stations are the twelve regions of the sky through which the sun passes on its course, the elliptic, and which in turn correspond to the twelve months. The stars are arrayed into the twenty-eight mansions.

8   Rising out of Sunny Vale   出自湯谷
      To lodge at Murky Strand,   次于蒙汜
      From dawning all the way to dusk,   自明及晦
      How many miles does the sun travel?   所行幾里

Tanggu 湯谷 (Sunny Vale) can also be written Yanggu 暘谷, which helps to make clear its sense as the home of the sun. It is mentioned in numerous early texts as the starting point of the sun's journey. In Old Chinese the name was an alliterative compound: *lang-lok.

9	What power has the nocturnal radiance,	夜光何德
	That it may die and then grow back again?	死則又育
	What sort of singularity does it possess,	厥利維何
	That a rabbyt is perceived within its belly?	而顧菟在腹

The "nocturnal radiance" of the moon was associated with the growth and decline of the human soul (in particular the *po*, the earthsoul). The "rabbyt perceived" *gutu* 顧菟 has been interpreted in various ways, and might refer to a toad (tadpole, *kedou* 蝌蚪) instead of a rabbit, but there is no definitive evidence for this early period (see Lin Geng, "Tian wen lunjian," 186–87). I translate "rabbyt," seeing 菟 as an obscure graphic variant of the conventional *tu* 兔.

10	Lady Tangent had no mate,	女歧無合
	So how could she obtain Nine Sons?	夫焉取九子
	Where does the Sire of Might reside?	伯強何處
	Where do the gentle airs abide?	惠氣安在

Lady Tangent (Lady Qi 歧, whose personal name I translate somewhat freely) seems to be a celestial or astrological deity here. But her name is shared with that of Ao's wife in quatrain 54 below and I translate them identically (it is not an unusual phenomenon for mythical figures to recur in different stories and historical periods). But the myth referenced here is uncertain. Jiang Liangfu proposes that Lady Tangent might refer to the moon goddess Chang Yi 常儀 or Chang'e 嫦娥, following the previous quatrain (*Qu Yuan fu jiaozhu*, 274–76). The Nine Sons were eventually identified with the Tail constellation, representing the tail of the Dark Dragon in the eastern quadrant of the sky (*Shiji*, 27.1298). So Lady Tangent seems to be another name for this same constellation of which the Nine Sons form a part. There are further legends involving her but it is unclear what is intended.

There are various interpretations of "Sire of Might" (Boqiang 伯強) but the *Chuci zhangju* explanation is plausible: he is a god for those who have died by violence, just like the recipient of "Martyrs of the Realm" in the "Nine Songs." Corresponding to the Tail constellation of Lady Tangent, he represents the neighboring Winnow constellation. Thus this quatrain sets in opposition two mythic representatives of feminine fertility and masculine violence.

11   What is it that closes when darkness falls?   何闔而晦
       What is it whose opening brings light?   何開而明
       When the Horn Portal has not yet dawned,   角宿未旦
       Where does the radiant spirit conceal itself?   曜靈安藏

The Horn Portal is the answer to the first two questions above: it is the Gate of Heaven. It is the first of seven constellations composing the Dark Dragon, the eastern quadrant of the sky. Henri Maspero argued that this poses quite a subtle problem of astronomy ("Review of Conrady and Erkes," 64).

The "radiant spirit" is the sun, just as it is properly identified in the Han commentary. With this conundrum of concealment and unveiling, the poem concludes its astronomical section and turns to human or humanlike figures from myth and history.

II. Heroes from the Age of Floods

12   Were Gun not appointed to control the floods,   不任汩鴻
       Why would the masses have elevated him?   師何以尚之
       The officials said: "Why be anxious?   僉曰何憂
       Why not test him with the challenge?"   何不課而行之

This quatrain corresponds loosely to the account in both the *Shiji* and *Shujing*, in which Yao is at first skeptical about appointing Gun to control the flood, but then convinced by the Four Marchmounts (Siyue 四岳). See *Shiji*, 2.64; *Shangshu zhengyi*, 2.47. The following quatrains, however, seem to refer to a more detailed account of Gun's labors than is available in other received texts.

13   As for the mighty turtles drawing and dragging,   鴟龜曳銜
       How did Gun follow their example?   鯀何聽焉
       When he had fulfilled our desires and completed the task,   順欲成功
       Why did the Lord then punish him?   帝何刑焉

This episode is not mentioned in other sources. Commentators hypothesize either that Gun was aided by these animals in the dike's construction, or that the dike was somehow modelled on these animals. A later source tells us that: "Yu exhausted his strength in cutting dikes and ditches and in conducting the courses of rivers and levelling mounds. The yellow dragon dragged its tail in front of him, while the dark turtle carried green mud on its back behind him."[2] Thus the Qing scholar Xu Huanlong argued that *chigui* should be instead the name of a type of turtle.[3] Accordingly, I interpret *yexian* 曳銜 as referring to the activities of the turtles as they aided Yu.

14 When imprisoned at Plume Mountain till his death,   永遏在羽山
    Why was the corpse not displayed for three years?   夫何三年不施
    When Prince Yu was born from Gun's belly,   伯禹愎鯀
    How were these metamorphoses contrived?   夫何以變化

Gun's death at Plume Mountain is mentioned in "Sublimating Sorrow," lines 131–32, as well. Lady Xu mentions in her cautionary speech that, "Gun lost his life for his honesty and frankness – / ultimately he perished in the wilds of Mount Plume" 鯀婞直以亡身兮, 終然殀乎羽之野; see Williams, *Elegies*, 7, and Huang Linggeng, ed., *Chuci zhangju shuzheng*, 1.252–57. The *locus classicus* for this quatrain as a whole is in *Zuozhuan*, Duke Zhao, year 7: "Long ago when Yao executed Gun at Plume Mountain, his spirit was transformed into a tawny terrapin, and plunged into the Plume Abyss" 昔堯殛鯀于羽山, 其神化為黃熊, 以入于羽淵 (cf. different translation in Durrant et al., *Zuo Tradition*, 1423). The text originally refers to a "yellow bear," but this is more likely the *nai* 能, a mythical sea turtle that recurs in ancient myth, hereafter rendered as "terrapin."[4]

The divination manual *Guicang* 歸藏 reports that even after three years Gun's body did not decay, and that when cut with a Wu sword, he transformed into a yellow dragon.[5] This source includes the text "did not putrefy for three years" 三歲不腐. Some scholars read *shi* 施 as a loan for *chi* 弛,

2. See Birrell, *Chinese Mythology*, 242, citing *Shi yi ji* 拾遺記, in *Han Wei congshu*, 2.2b.
3. *Qu ci xisui*, 3.2b. Cf. the term *chizhu* 鴟豬 "big as a hog," in *Yiqie jing yinyi*, 793a.
4. See Jiang Liangfu's helpful remarks after quatrain 25 in *Qu Yuan fu jiaozhu*, 3.291.
5. The story is quoted in Guo Pu's commentary to *Shanhaijing*; see Yuan Ke, ed., *Shanhaijing jiaozhu*, 18.396, n.4.

but it is more simply understood to mean "display the corpse," as in *Guoyu* (Episode 9/3, *Guoyu jijie*, 306). The word *bi* 憊 is best explained by the same line in *Shanhaijing*, which reads simply "Gun then (by means of belly) gave birth to Yu" 鯀復生禹: *fu* 復 "then" may be a loan graph for *fu* 腹 "belly." There were also other myths regarding the birth of Yu prevalent in early China (see Allan, *Buried Ideas*, 153–55).

15 Continuing the legacy of his predecessors, 纂就前緒
    Yu ultimately accomplished the task of his father. 遂成考功
    Why, to resume the start and advance the work, 何續初繼業
    Did he use such different stratagems? 而厥謀不同

In contrast to the lexical or historical puzzles of many other lines in the poem, this quatrain is relatively straightforward, and even You Guoen dispenses with it succinctly. Yu is a model for the scholar-writer, putting into order the inchoate efforts of his predecessors.

16 The abyss of the floodwaters was most deep, 洪泉極深
    So how could he block the flow? 何以窴之
    When he divided the earth into nine levels, 地方九則
    How could he build it into embankments? 何以墳之

Yu is described in various sources as playing a pivotal role not just in stemming the flood but also in establishing the geographical divisions of China. The *locus classicus* for these stories is the "Tribute of Yu" ("Yu gong" 禹貢) chapter in the *Shujing*.

17 How did the Responsive Dragon measure them? 應龍何畫
    Why did the rivers and oceans pour out? 河海何歷
    [A couplet seems to have been lost here.] □□□□
    □□□□

I translate the variant text cited by Zhu Xi and Hong Xingzu, but the received text is instead 河海應龍, 何盡何歷. The *Chuci zhangju* offers an alternative commentary that seems to follow the variant text, so either alternative is equally plausible. Note that this text creates a rhyme in *-ek* (though the text still seems to be corrupted, since it is only a couplet rather than a quatrain). Tang Bingzheng suggests instead that *ying* 應 is a loan for 鷹, "goshawk," implying that the dragon is winged, which fits with the Han commentary (*Chuci leigao*, 290). Yu is supposed to have had help from a dragon in measuring out the land and rivers.

The Responding Dragon also appears in *The Classic of Mountains and Seas*: "Responding Dragon lives at the South Pole. He killed the gods Jest Much and Boast Father. But then Responding Dragon could not go back up to the sky. That is why down on earth there are so many droughts. When there is a drought, people make an image of Responding Dragon, and then they receive a heavy rainfall" 應龍處南極,殺蚩尤與夸父,不得復上。故下數旱,旱而為應龍之狀,乃得大雨 (Yuan Ke, ed., *Shanhaijing jiaozhu*, 14.306; Birrell, trans., *Classic of Mountains and Seas*, 162). The motif of the hidden dragon in the first hexagram of the *Changes* may also be pertinent.

18	What did Gun himself construct?	鯀何所營
	What did Yu himself achieve?	禹何所成
	In the crack and the clash of furious flashing,	康回馮怒
	Why did the earth buckle down to the southeast?	墬何故以東南傾

This event is referred to already in quatrain 5 above. There is a myth that the earth collapsed because of the violent contest of Gonggong and Zhuanxu, but Lin Geng points out that it does not appear in pre-Qin texts, but only in *Huainanzi* ("Tianwen lunjian," 193). "Kang Hui" is thus probably not an alternative name for Gonggong, as the Han commentary suggests, but instead an alliterative compound (Tang Bingzheng, *Chuci leigao*, 291).[6] Lin Geng's proposal is that this line is instead descriptive of lightning.

In context, the whole quatrain may then imply that it was Gun's fault the topography of the earth was transformed. Often the organization of the poem is questioned by scholars who even attempt to rearrange it. But here there is a subtle and very effective transition from the efforts to Gun and Yu to control the flood, to the organization of geography afterwards.

III. On the Geography of the World

19	How are the Nine Continents arranged?	九州安錯
	How were the rivers and valleys carved out?	川谷何洿

---

6. Perhaps something like *khâŋ-kwəi. The 2014 Baxter-Sagart reconstruction gives *[kʰ]ˤaŋ-[ɢ]ʷˤəj.

Flowing to the east they do not overflow:	東流不溢
Who knows the reason behind all this?	孰知其故

These Nine Continents appear to be continents of the entire world, belonging to a legendary geography of the cosmos, and do not refer to the provinces of the central plain of China, as in the *Documents*.[7] Thus, this quatrain and the succeeding ones are mapping out a comprehensive geography of the world.

20	East and west, south and north:	東西南北
	Which direction extends the farthest?	其脩孰多
	If south and north follow an oval course,	南北順橢
	How far do they protrude there?	其衍幾何

The *Huainanzi* provides potential answers to these questions: "The expanse within the four seas measures 28,000 li from east to west and 26,000 li from south to north."[8] The same passage provides information relevant to the succeeding quatrains 21 and 22 as well. Since the *Huainanzi* was compiled in the Han dynasty under the auspices of Prince Liu An 劉安 (179–122 BCE) of Huainan, it is unclear if there is any direct textual linkage. Perhaps both this poem and the *Huainanzi* were inspired by some earlier work of world geography.

21	The Hanging Garden of Kunlun's Peaks:	崑崙縣圃
	In what locale may they be found?[9]	其居安在
	The nine walls of the Tiered Palisade:	增城九重
	How many miles high do they stand?	其高幾里

The "Tiered Palisade" and "Hanging Gardens" are both mythical sites within the Kunlun Mountains at the center of the world. The same passage of *Huainanzi* mentioned above answers these questions: the Tiered Palisade

---

7. Following Jiang Liangfu, ed., *Qu Yuan fu jiaozhu*, 6.236–37, and also Chūbachi, *Chūgoku no saishi to bungaku*, 45–46.

8. See Major et al., *Huainanzi*, 155–58; Liu Wendian, ed., *Huainan honglie jijie*, 4.159–63, for the whole passage.

9. It might be preferable to adopt the emendation to *jiu* 尻 "bottom" for *ju* 居, suggested by Dai Zhen, which would produce a rendering of "Where does it have a bottom?" See Huang Linggeng, ed., *Chuci zhangju shuzheng*, 4.1050.

stands 11,000 li tall, and the Hanging Garden is located within the Changhe 閶闔 Gate of Kunlun.¹⁰

22	Who is it who passes through	四方之門
	The Gates of the Four Directions?	其誰從焉
	When the Northwest opens up wide,	西北辟啓
	What kind of air blows through it?	何氣通焉

The *Huainanzi* identifies gates for the eight directions, and in the northwestern direction lies the Broken Mountain.¹¹ But its account does not really answer the question posed here directly.

23	Why does the sun not reach its mark	日安不到
	Till Xihe lifts the reins of the sun carriage?	羲和之未揚
	What does the Torch Dragon illumine?	燭龍何照
	What gleams on the blossoms of the Dimming Wood?	若華何光

I invert the order of the second and third lines of this quatrain to create an ABAB rhyme in keeping with the remainder of the poem. The Torch Dragon is a deity providing constant illumination. For Xihe, the charioteer of the sun, compare "Nine Songs: Lord of the East" (Williams, *Elegies of Chu*, 31). For "Dimming Wood," see also "Sublimating Sorrow," line 195: "I pluck a branch of Dimming Wood to block the sun —" 折若木以拂日兮 (Williams, *Elegies of Chu*, 9; Huang Linggeng, ed., *Chuci zhangju shuzheng*, 1.347). The Dimming Wood or Ruo 若 tree is variously identified in early sources, though often located in the far west as the place where the sun sets; see Yuan Ke's note to *Shanhaijing jiaozhu*, 17.368.

24	What place is warm in the wintertime?	何所冬暖
	What place will freeze in the summer?	何所夏寒
	Where is there a forest of stone?	焉有石林
	What beast is capable of speech?	何獸能言

The stone forest, as well as the nine-headed serpent in quatrain 26, are

---

10. See Major et al., *Huainanzi*, 156; Liu Wendian, ed., *Huainan honglie jijie*, 4.159 and 162.
11. See Major et al., *Huainanzi*, 158; Liu Wendian, ed., *Huainan honglie jijie* 4.166.

alluded to in conjunction in Zuo Si's 左思 "Wu Capital Rhapsody" ("Wudu fu" 吳都賦). Zuo Si's use of the images suggests that they seemed fantastical to him: "Though there be a stone forest rugged and steep, / Each warrior would willingly bare his arm and reduce it to rubble. / Though there be a great nine-headed serpent, / All would gladly lift their feet and stomp it to the ground" (*Wenxuan* 5.228; Knechtges, *Selections of Refined Literature*, 1:411–13). For the beast that can speak, recall that the Han commentary quotes the *Book of Rites* on the orangutan: "The orangutan can speak, but is not distinct from the birds and beasts" 猩猩能言, 不離禽獸也. See *Liji zhengyi*, 1.17.

25 Where is the coiled dragon 焉有虯龍
    Diving with a terrapin on its back? 負熊以遊
    [A couplet seems to have been lost here.] □□□□
      □□□□

The word *xiong* 熊, "bear," in ancient mythology is often interchangeable with the graphic variant *nai* 能 or *huangnai* 黃能, a mythical animal, or perhaps a three-legged turtle as in the *Erya* (*Erya zhushu*, 16.332). Though this question remains obscure, it seems to refer an episode involving water deities. It might refer to the story of Yu handling the flood—see note to quatrain 13 above.

26 The fierce hamadryad of nine heads, 雄虺九首
    Where does it go in its rampages? 儵忽焉在
    What place is there without death? 何所不死
    Where do the giants abide? 長人何守

The monstrous *hui* 虺 is glossed as a kind of snake, so it seems appropriate to use the term "hamadryad," a synonym for the king cobra; cf. "Summons to the Soul," line 41. Note that in early China the question "what place is without death" is not a fanciful one, since a substantial subset of the population was actively pursuing immortality as *xian* "transcendents." The land of the transcendents is thus a proper subject of geographical speculation, as in *The Classic of Mountains and Seas*, for example: "The Neverdie folk are to its east. Its people are black and they live to a great age. They never die.

One author says they are east of the borechest country" 不死民, 在其東, 其爲人黑色, 壽, 不死。一曰在穿匈國東。[12]

The rhyme scheme here is unusual. Gu Yanwu identified an ABBA rhyme scheme, comparing it to *Odes* 179/5 (*Shi benyin*, 5.17a). The final words in each line are as follows:

Final words	OCM reconstruction
shou 首	lhuʔ
zai 在	dzə̂ʔ
si 死	siʔ
shou 守	śuʔ

However, although *shou* 首 and *shou* 守 do rhyme in Old Chinese just as they do in modern Mandarin (though in Mandarin they constitute a perfect rhyme, which would again be irregular), I would prefer to identify a lax version of the regular XAXA rhyme scheme. All four words end in glottal stop, and the rhyme between *zai* and *shou* can be considered a lax rhyme or half rhyme. Even the *Odes* example proposed by Gu Yanwu, moreover, relies on an unusual rhyme between *tong* 同 (*dôŋ) and *tiao* 調 (*liû). Probably both cases are better understood as examples of lax rhyming that follow the typical scheme within their context (XAXA here, AAXA in the *Odes* case).

27 Waterlily blossoms branching ninefold　　　　靡萍九衢
　　And soma flowers: where are they to be found?　　枲華安居
　　When a snake swallowed an elephant,　　　　一蛇吞象
　　How gigantic must it have been?　　　　　　　厥大何如

As seen in "Text Two," Liu Zongyuan called the *Chuci zhangju* commentary here a fraud, because it read *qu* 衢 as a literal road. *The Classic of Mountains and Seas* mentions an exotic plant with a five-pointed formation: "On the summit of this mountain there is a tree; its name is the gods-rest tree. Its leaves are like the poplar, and its branches are in a fiveways crossroads formation" 其上有木焉, 其名曰帝休, 葉狀如楊 (*Shanhai-*

---

12. Yuan Ke, ed., *Shanhaijing jiaozhu*, 6.182; Birrell, trans., *Classic of Mountains and Seas*, 110.

jing jiaozhu, 5.135; Birrell, trans., *Classic of Mountains and Seas*, 82). "Soma flowers" (*xihua* 枲華) could simply refer to a variety of ordinary hemp, but then the question would be trivial, so it seems preferable to relate this term to the *shuma* 疏麻 in "Nine Songs: Greater Controller of Destinies" (*xi* in Old Chinese is *sə?, quite close to *shu* *sra?).[13] For details on the legendary snake see again *The Classic of Mountains and Seas*: "The Snake of the Ba region eats elephants and after three years it disgorges their bones. Gentlemen take a dose of this snake so they will never have heart disease or illnesses of the belly" 巴蛇食象，三歲而出其骨，君子服之無心腹之疾。[14]

28   Blackwater and Mystic Base　　　　　　　黑水玄趾
　　And Mount Triperil: where are they found?　三危安在
　　Though years without dying may be prolonged,　延年不死
　　When must longevity come to an end?　　　壽何所止

Blackwater and Triperil are place names attested in *The Classic of Mountains and Seas*. "The River Black rises there and flows south to empty into the sea. It contains numerous sturgeon which look like perch but have the bristles of a hog" 黑水出焉，而南流注于海。其中有鱄魚，其狀如鮒而彘毛。[15] Again, on Mount Triperil (Sanwei 三危): "Three green birds live on it. This mountain has a girth of a hundred leagues all round" 三青鳥居之。是山也，廣員百里。[16] They figure in the "Tribute of Yu" chapter of the *Book of Documents* as well, where the Blackwater is identified as the western boundary of the realm, and said to flow past Mount Triperil (see Legge, *Shoo King*, 123, 125). The Han commentary says that *xuanzhi* is another mountain, which I have loosely translated as "Mystic Base."

---

13. For more detailed argument, see my "Shamans, Souls, and Soma."
14. Yuan Ke., ed., *Shanhaijing jiaozhu*, 10.247; translation modified from Birrell, 10.136. An interesting variant has 靈 for 一, which would make the third line: "When the numinous snake swallowed an elephant." See Huang Linggeng, ed., *Chuci jijiao*, 555.
15. Yuan Ke, ed., *Shanhaijing jiaozhu*, 1.16; Birrell, trans., *Classic of Mountains and Seas*, 9.
16. Yuan Ke, ed., *Shanhaijing jiaozhu*, 2.48; Birrell, trans., *Classic of Mountains and Seas*, 25.

IV. Heroes of the Xia Dynasty

29   Where is the home of the mermen?   鯪魚何所
     Where do the griffins abide?   鬿堆焉處
     How did Archer Yih shoot down the suns?   羿焉彃日
     How were the suncrows then deplumed?   烏焉解羽

These mermen are identified in *The Classic of Mountains and Seas*: "there the people have a human face, hands, and feet, but a fish's body" 陵魚人面, 手足, 魚身.[17] Another proposal is that the term refers to the fish-like pangolin. My "griffins" (*qidui* 鬿堆) are also described therein: "There is a bird here which looks like a chicken, but it has a white head and rat's feet with tiger claws.... It also eats humans" 有鳥焉, 其狀如雞而白首, 鼠足而虎爪……亦食人 (*Shanhaijing jiaozhu*, 4.63).

Yih shot down nine of the ten suns, and the corresponding nine suncrows all died. However, the story is presented in various ways in the earliest sources. Perhaps a representative example is this *Huainanzi* passage, omitting the crows entirely: "Yao therefore commanded Yih [the Archer] to slaughter Chisel Tusk in the water meadows of Chouhua, to kill Nine Gullet on the banks of the Xiong River, to shoot down Typhoon in the wilds of Greenhill, upward to shoot the ten suns and downward to kill Chayu, to chop Long Snake in two at Dongting Lake, and to capture Mound Pig in Mulberry Forest. The multitudes of people all were happy and established Yao as Son of Heaven." 堯乃使羿誅鑿齒於疇華之野, 殺九嬰於凶水之上, 繳大風於青邱之澤, 上射十日而下殺猰貐斷修蛇於洞庭, 擒封豨於桑林。萬民皆喜, 置堯以為天子。(Liu Wendian, ed., *Huainan honglie jijie*, 8.305). This is a central origin story elaborated on in the mythology of the Shang (see Allan, *The Shape of the Turtle*, 36ff). I write the name of the Archer as Yih rather than Yi to distinguish from the ruler Yi mentioned below.

30   Yu exerted himself to complete the task,   禹之力獻功
     He descended to watch over all four parts of the earth.   降省下土四方
     How did he find that lady of Mount Soil,   焉得彼嵞山女
     And mate with her at the Platform of Mulberries?   而通之於台桑

---

17. Yuan Ke, ed., *Shanhaijing jiaozhu*, 12.280; Birrell, trans., *Classic of Mountains and Seas*, 147.

For the verb "to descend" (*jiang* 降), cf. "Sublimating Sorrow," line 4: "on the twenty-seventh day I descended from Heaven" 惟庚寅吾以降 (Williams, *Elegies*, 1; Huang Linggeng, ed., *Chuci zhangju shuzheng*, 1.31). In *Chuci*, gods and superior men both arrive upon the earth by descending from heaven, as Huang Linggeng observes, and we will see again below in quatrains 35 and 54. This episode is also described in more positive terms in the *Book of Documents*, "Yi and Ji" chapter. Yu says, "When I married in Tushan, I remained with my wife only the days *xin, ren, gui,* and *jia*. When my son Qi was wailing and weeping, I did not regard him, but kept planning with all my might my labour on the land" 予創若時，娶于塗山，辛壬癸甲。啓呱呱而泣，予弗子，惟荒度土功。[18]

There are various identifications of Tushan or "Mount Soil" and of the lady from this place. Rather than investigate its geographical location, I take it as a symbolic place name. *Tu* 塗 can have a neutral sense of "route" but more commonly means "to corrupt, defile."[19] To preserve something of the ambiguity I use the comparable "soil."[20]

31	Caring for that maiden he made a match with her,	閔妃匹合
	In order to perpetuate himself;	厥身是繼
	Why did he, relishing such unlike flavors,	胡維嗜不同味
	Yet hasten for dawn's consummation?	而快鼂飽

According to *The Annals of Lü Buwei*, Yu left his bride to stop the flood only four days after consummating the marriage. This is recorded in a fragment not part of the received text (see Knoblock and Riegel, *Annals of Lü Buwei*, 674).

The rhyme here seems to be irregular. Guo Moruo made the suggestion of substituting *ji* 飢 "hungry" for *bao* 飽 "satiated," but an even simpler solution is to posit a reversal of the third and fourth lines.

---

18. Legge, *Shoo King*, 84–85; *Shangshu zhengyi*, 5.147.

19. For a vivid example of the pejorative usage, see *Zhuangzi*, where Bo Yi and Shu Qi assert "Rather than ally with the Zhou and thereby besmirch (*tu*) our persons, it would be better to shun them and thereby preserve the purity of our conduct." 其並乎周以塗吾身也，不如避之以潔吾行。*Zhuangzi jishi*, 28.990; Mair, *Wandering on the Way*, 28.296.

20. Whereas with Mount Soil this sense is not necessarily obvious, the "mulberry" in the following line is a sex symbol; see Diény, *Pastourelles et magnanarelles*.

280   Text Three

32 When Qi replaced the minister Yi as heir—　　　　　啟代益作后
　　All of a sudden meeting with disaster—　　　　　　卒然離蠥
　　Why was it that Qi was still beset by anxiety,　　　何啟惟憂
　　And succeeded in imprisoning him?　　　　　　　　而能拘是達

Qi was the product of Yu's aforementioned union. He is said to have murdered Yi, Yu's wise minister to whom Yu entrusted the succession, in order to take the throne. Though early sources do not present a detailed account, these events are mentioned in the *Bamboo Annals* and elsewhere.[21] The questions here seem to refer to a version of the story that has not been preserved in other texts, so both the text itself and all the commentarial interpretations seem garbled. I take *wei* 惟 as a graphic variant of *li* 罹, "meet with."

33 Since all obeyed and bowed to him,　　　　　　　　皆歸射鞠
　　And none did harm to that man's body,　　　　　　而無害厥躬
　　Why did Qi overthrow the Lord Yi,　　　　　　　　何后益作革
　　Though Yu had rendered blessings to him?　　　　　而禹播降

For the difficult compound *sheju* 射鞠,[22] I follow Jiang Liangfu's suggested emendation to *gongju* 躬鞠, as in *Analects* 10/5, meaning "to bow the body" (*Qu Yuan fu jiaozhu*, 6.250).[23] But no reading of this exceptionally difficult quatrain is satisfactory.

34 Qi had sped to make audience with the High Lord,　　啟棘賓商
　　Chanting the "Nine Phases" and the "Nine Songs,"　　九辯九歌
　　Why did his diligent son rupture his mother,　　　　何勤子屠母
　　And, dying, make new division in the earth?　　　　而死分竟地

The first line here is extraordinarily difficult and has been the subject of several dedicated studies (such as Yuan Ke, "*Chuci yu shenhua* duhou"). The word *ji* 棘 here originally represents the "jujube," but also has a paronomas-

---

21. See Fang and Wang, eds., *Guben Zhushu jinian jizheng*, 2. This is one of the archetypal conflicts between "the heir and the sage" discussed by Sarah Allan in her seminal study by that name.

22. Variants include 䠶 and 鞠. See Huang Linggeng, ed., *Chuci jijiao*, 564.

23. See also D. C. Lau's translation of this line (*Analects: Bilingual Edition*, 89): "When he held the jade tablet, he drew himself in as though its weight was too much for him" 執圭, 鞠躬如也, 如不勝.

tic usage in the sense of *ji* "urgent," which is well-documented (Liu Zhao, "Shi jiaguwen zhong de 'bingji'"). Moreover, the term *shang* 商 may be a graphic error for *di* 帝.[24] I read the first line here in accordance with both these substitutions.[25]

The violent birth of Qi is not well-attested, but can be found in at least one early source, a fragment of the Mohist text *Sui Chaozi* 隨巢子. According to the fragment (quoted in *Yishi*, 12.13b), "Yu married the lady of Mount Soil, and stopped the flood waters. He opened up Mount Xuanyuan, and was transformed into a bear. When the lady of Mount Soil saw this, she regretted it and departed. When she reached the base of high Mount Song, she was transformed into a stone. Yu said, 'Return my child.' The stone cracked open on the north side and gave birth to Qi" 禹娶塗山, 治鴻水, 通轘轅山, 化為熊。塗山氏見之, 慚而去, 至嵩高山, 化為石。禹曰：「歸我子。」石破北方而生啓。

35 The High Lord sent down Archer Yih for the   帝降夷羿
    Yee tribes,
    And he purged the evil from the people of Xia.   革孽夏民
    But why did he shoot at the Sire of the Yellow River,   胡射夫河伯
    And take the nymph of the Luo River as his wife?   而妻彼雒嬪

Yih the Archer was the ruler of the Youqiong people, here referred to as the Yee (written Yee to differentiate from Yi). Archer Yih defeated the Xia people when they were ruled by the imprudent ruler Taikang, thus inspiring the composition of the "Song of the Five Brothers" 五子之歌 in the pseudo-Ancient Text *Book of Documents* (see Legge, *Shoo King*, 153–56). There may also be some confusion of mythology here. The god Sire of the Yellow River (Hebo) seems in the earliest sources to be the name of a tribe competing with the Shang people. Here it is placed in tandem with the goddess of the Luo River, also known as Fu Fei.

24. Zhu Junsheng, *Shuowen tongxun dingsheng*, 18.34b. There are also parallel expressions in the oracle bone inscriptions; see Huang Linggeng, *Chuci zhangju shuzheng*, 4.1087.

25. On the other hand, Xu Wenjing quotes the *Zhushu jinian*, Shun year 29, as mentioning that Shun's son Yijun 義鈞 was enfeoffed at Shang, and thereby argues that the line makes sense on its face; Shang was the vassal state of Shun. See *Zhushu jinian tongjian*, 2.136.

36 When with his mighty bow of nacre and keen gauntlet　馮珧利決
    The giant boar he shot dead,　　　　　　　　　　　　封狶是射
    Why, upon presenting the rich offering of meat,　　　何獻蒸肉之膏
    Did his sovereign Lord not approve?[26]　　　　　　　而后帝不若

Zhong Xing 鍾惺 (1574–1625), one of the 72 scholars quoted in Jiang Zhiqiao's 蔣之翹 Ming-dynasty compendium, comments that this quatrain "accords with" (*dou ci* 逗此) "Sublimating Sorrow," lines 149–50 (*Qishier jia*, 1.11a):

> Archer Yih was a dissolute man who　　　　　羿淫遊以佚畋兮
>   overindulged in hunting –
> But succeeded in shooting the great boar.　　又好射夫封狐

In both cases the appraisal of Archer Yih seems to be ambivalent: a great hero but possessing notable moral weaknesses. I use the en-dash to represent the rhythmic particle *xi* 兮, which is one of the distinctive features of *Chuci* poetry, even though it is absent from "Heavenly Questions".

37 When Han Zhuo seduced Pure Fox,　　　　　　浞娶純狐
    That beguiling consort conspiring with him,　　眩妻爰謀
    Why was it that the hide-piercing Archer Yih　　何羿之射革
    Suffered that they plot to devour him?　　　　而交吞揆之

Pure Fox seems to be the name of one of the wives of Archer Yih whom Han Zhuo took for himself after he had overthrown Archer Yih by wiles and deceit.

Perhaps the fullest account of Han Zhuo is in *Zuozhuan*, Duke Xiang, year 4. I quote the translation of Stephen Durrant, Wai-yee Lee, and David Schaberg (with Archer Yi's name modified to Yih for clarity):

> Han Zhuo was the deviant, slanderous son of the Boming lineage. Boming Lord Han had cast him off, and Archer Yih took him in, trusted him, and gave him assignments, making him his own assistant. Han Zhuo flattered and seduced those inside the palace, offered bounties to those outside it,

---

26. This quatrain continues to discuss Archer Yih. On *feng* 馮 see Tang Bingzheng, *Chuci leigao*, 297. Tang reads it as *peng* 弸, glossed as 'appearance of a strong bow' in the *Shuowen*.

fooled and cajoled the people, and misled Archer Yih, making him engrossed with hunting. Having planted in him deceit and iniquities, he took Archer Yih's domain and patrimony from him, and those inside and outside all submitted to him. Even then Archer Yih did not repent. When he was about to return to the court from the fields, his own men killed him, boiled him, and fed his flesh to his sons. His sons could not bear to eat it and died at the Gate of Qiong. Mi fled to the Youge lineage. Han Zhuo took over Archer Yih's wives and concubines and fathered Ao and Yi. Relying on his slanderous wickedness and deceitful treachery, he showed no virtue toward the people and sent Ao to employ troops to eliminate the Zhenguan and Zhenxun lineages. He placed Ao in Guo and Yi in Ge. Mi, coming from the Youge lineage, collected the last embers—the remnant forces of Zhenguan and Zhenxun—to extinguish Han Zhuo and established Shaokang as ruler. Shaokang killed Ao at Guo, and his son Lord Zhu killed Yi at Ge. That the Youqiong lineage thus perished was because it had failed in the proper use of men.[27]

38	When blocked at Desperation Rock while traveling westward,	阻窮西征
	How was it that he managed to cross those cliffs?	嚴何越焉
	When Gun was transformed into a tawny terrapin,	化為黃熊
	How did the shaman bring him back to life?	巫何活焉

Xu Wenjing points to *Zuozhuan*, Duke Xiang, year 4 with the line "Archer Yih moved from Chu to Qiongshi [Desperation Rock] and, with the support of the Xia people, took over Xia rule" 后羿自鉏遷于窮石, 因夏民以代夏政.[28] Thus *zu* 阻 could be a loan for Chu 鉏. Similarly, Yuan Ke suggests that Qiong is short for Mount Qiong 窮山 in *The Classic of Mountains and Seas* (*Shanhaijing jiaozhu*, 7.202). The broader meaning is overdetermined, but the surface syntax is problematic.

The episode in the latter couplet is also mentioned in *Zuozhuan*, Duke Zhao, year 7 (Durrant et al., *Zuo Tradition*, 1423). But note that this and other sources do not mention the Shaman's involvement (cf. quatrain 14 above). *Huangxiong* 黃熊 could also mean "brown bear," but Gun and Yu were originally associated with sea dragons, and so I have followed the

---

27. Durrant, et al., *Zuo Tradition*, 917.
28. *Guancheng shuoji*, 16.280; Durrant et al., *Zuo Tradition*, 917. See also *Diwang shiji*, 3.24.

alternate reading *huangnai* 黃能, where 能 is read *nai* and glossed as "three-legged turtle," just as in quatrain 25 above.

39 Though all were sowing black millet and sticky millet,　　咸播秬黍
    There they planted only reeds and cresses;　　　　　　　　莆蘿是營
    Why is that after they had fled and taken refuge,　　　　　何由并投
    When Gun was ill, only Xiu Ji nursed him?　　　　　　　　而鮌疾脩盈

The first line describes the land crops, the second the water plants. Xu Wenjing provides a novel and clear interpretation of this quatrain: Gun could plant only wetland crops after he had been removed to Plume Abyss. His wife was named Xiu Ji 脩己, and she helped him in his hardship. See *Guancheng shuoji*, 16.281.

40 With necklace and tiara glittering in a white nimbus,　　白蜺嬰茀
    Why did Chang'e display such magnificence?　　　　　　　胡為此堂
    Where did she obtain that superb elixir,　　　　　　　　　安得夫良藥
    That she was unable to conceal safely?　　　　　　　　　　不能固臧

For this stanza and the next one we may ignore the fanciful interpretation of the Han commentary regarding certain transcendents. That the subject is instead Chang'e, the moon goddess, was proposed by Ding Yan, as discussed above in chapter 3. Yih had received an elixir of immortality from Xiwangmu, but Chang'e stole it and fled to the moon (Liu Wendian, ed., *Huainan honglie jijie*, 6.260).

Wang Niansun had several insightful suggestions for this quatrain. In his annotations to the *Guangya* 廣雅 synonymicon, he showed that *tang* 堂 can represent the reduplicative compound *tangtang* meaning "bright, glorious" (*Guangya shuzheng*, 4A.9a). Wang also made a compelling argument that *zang* 臧 needs to be read as *cang* 藏, not just for semantic reasons but because the collocation with *gu* 固 only makes sense in that reading.[29]

41 Heaven is configured horizontal and vertical:　　　　　天式從橫
    When Yang energy disperses then you die;　　　　　　陽離爰死
    Why did the mighty bird cry out,　　　　　　　　　　大鳥何鳴
    And how was it deprived of mortal frame?　　　　　　夫焉喪厥體

---

29. See "Dushu zazhi yubian" 讀書雜志餘編, in *Dushu zazhi*, 3b–4a; and discussion in You Guoen et al., eds., *Tianwen zuanyi*, 242.

The Han commentary identifies this with a story about Prince Qiao, who after death was transformed into a great bird that cried out and then flew away. But it is better to take it at its surface meaning, following the hint in the excavated bamboo-slip text "Fan wu liu xing" 凡物流形 ("All Things Change Their Forms"): "Flowing forms complete the body; what makes them never die? / Having been completed, having been born, what makes them cry and wail?" 流形成體, 奚得而不死? 既成既生, 奚呱而鳴.[30] See my more detailed discussion of this comparison in the "Epilogue" below.

42	When Pingyi summons the rain into being;	蓱號起雨
	How does he cause it to be created?	何以興之
	As for that body possessing two torsos,	撰體協脅
	How could a deer assume it?	鹿何膺之

Pingyi 蓱翳 the rain god is also known as Pinghao 蓱號, as Hong Xingzu already showed (*Chuci buzhu*, 3.101). Meanwhile the Thunder God, Feilian 飛廉, is described by Guo Pu 郭璞 as a "dragon bird with bird body and deer head" 飛廉, 龍雀也, 鳥身鹿頭.[31] On the other hand, Zuo Si's "Shu Capital Rhapsody" refers to a rare type of deer that can consume poison.[32] The commentary by Liu Kui 劉逵 further mentions that this was known as a magical deer with two heads, citing Wei Wan's 魏完 gazetteer *Nanzhong zhi* 南中志.

43	When the mighty mountain-bearing turtles start to dance,	鼇戴山抃
	How does one hold them steady in place?	何以安之
	Setting loose the ships to go by land instead,	釋舟陵行
	How are they kept moving through space?	何以遷之

Bian 抃 originally means "to clap," by extension "to dance in time with the rhythm." For the sea turtles who carry continents on their backs, see

---

30. Quoted in Huang Linggeng, ed., *Chuji jijiao*, 4.579; for a transcription and study, see Cao Feng, "Shangbo Chu jian 'Fan wu liu xing' de wenben jiegou yu sixiang tezheng"; see also Sukhu, *Songs of Chu*, 62. For a detailed study and translation, see Huang, *A Walk in the Night with Zhuangzi*.

31. Note to *Shiji*, 117.3034. According to some sources this is simply a monster, not a deity. See Knechtges, *Selections of Refined Literature*, 1:136, note to line 330 of the "Western Capital Rhapsody."

32. *Wenxuan*, 4.193; Knechtges, *Selections of Refined Literature*, 1:365.

the "Questions of Tang" chapter in the *Liezi*: "God was afraid that they would drift to the far West and he would lose the home of his sages. So he commanded Yuqiang 禺彊 to make fifteen giant turtles carry the five mountains on their lifted heads, taking turns in three watches, each sixty thousand years long; and for the first time the mountains stood firm and did not move." 帝恐流於西極，失羣仙聖之居，乃命禺彊使巨鼇十五舉首而戴之。迭為三番，六萬歲一交焉。五山始峙而不動. See Yang Bojun, ed., *Liezi jishi*, 5.160–61; Graham, *Book of Lieh-tzŭ*, 97. As we saw above, Liu Zongyuan's response to this same quatrain borrows further material from the same passage.

Yu Yue argues that the source of the latter couplet is *Analects* 14/6 (trans. Legge, *Confucian Analects*, 277, modified): "Yih was skillful at archery, and Ao could move a boat along upon the land, but neither of them died a natural death. Yu and Ji personally wrought at the toils of husbandry, and they became possessors of the kingdom." 羿善射，奡盪舟，俱不得其死然；禹稷躬稼，而有天下. This is already a close textual parallel, and then the succeeding quatrain turns to the strongman Ao. Considering the immediate context, though, these lines ought also to be relevant to the turtles. Perhaps this is an example of two different modes of progression within the poem: one by topic and historical era, but another by conceptual association. Within this quatrain, both couplets are inspired by the *Liezi* vision of turtles carrying continents around on their backs, with the latter lines preparing the way for the succeeding quatrain through the conjunction of boats and land, as Yu Yue suggests in "Du Chuci," 8a.

Rather than treating this quatrain as a riddle and looking to decipher it, though, we can also enjoy the whimsical questions on their own terms. Note the neat rhyme and antithesis between rhyming lines, mirrored in my translation.

44	When Ao arrived at the doorstep,	惟澆在戶
	What was he seeking from his brother's wife?	何求于嫂
	Why did Shaokang, while on the chase with hounds,	何少康逐犬
	End up decapitating only the other one?	而顛隕厥首

Beginning with this quatrain, we enter a sequence of questions all about a related series of events from Xia history/myth. This quatrain refers to the story of the strong man Ao 澆 committing adultery with Lady Tangent. Shaokang is then said to have killed Ao while hunting.

45 When Lady Tangent was sewing an undershirt,　　女歧縫裳
　　Why did they share lodgings in the same house?　而館同爰止
　　Why did Shaokang behead the wrong one,　　　何顛易厥首
　　So that the lady met with harm instead?　　　　而親以逢殆

This Lady Tangent, Ao's sister-in-law, is said by most commentators to be different from the goddess mentioned in quatrain 10, but I wonder if it was not originally the same mythical figure, later attached to different historical chronologies. The story referred to here seems to be that Shaokang first attacked Ao at night and accidentally killed Lady Tangent; only later did he succeed in killing Ao, as referred to in the previous quatrain.

46 When Shaokang prepared the army for ambush,　湯謀易旅
　　How did he strengthen it?　　　　　　　　　　何以厚之
　　When Ao capsized the vessels of Zhenxun,　　　覆舟斟尋
　　By what route had he conquered them?　　　　　何道取之

I follow Huang Linggeng's emendation of Tang 湯 to yang 陽 (*Chuci zhangju shuzheng*, 4.1120). It is easy to understand how related words could misread as Tang given the focus on ancient rulership here, and the reading of *yang* makes this quatrain far more coherent, because it allows us to retain the subject Shaokang from the previous quatrain.

Zhenxun was a kingdom whose rulers were of the same clan as the Xia royal house. The Xia ruler Xiang took refuge there, so Ao attacked them and killed him (*Zuozhuan*, Duke Ai, year 1; Durrant et al., *Zuo Tradition*, 1835). The capsized vessels are apparently a metaphor like "ship of state."

47 When Jie assaulted Mount Meng,　　　　　　　桀伐蒙山
　　Whom did he obtain there?　　　　　　　　　何所得焉
　　Why was Moxi abandoned by him,　　　　　　妹嬉何肆
　　And why did Tang destroy Jie for it?　　　　　湯何殛焉

Tang Bingzheng points out that "Mount Meng" here is probably the same as Mount Min 岷. According to the *Bamboo Annals*, "Jie captured Mount Min, and there obtained two women, named Wan and Yan." 桀伐珉山, 得女二人, 曰琬, 曰琰.[33] There is thematic repetition of the "two brides," as

---

33. Tang Bingzheng, *Chuci leigao*, 298–300; Fang and Wang, eds., *Guben Zhushu jinian jizheng*, 17.

in the princesses of the Xiang River. Moreover, since the next event in the story is that Jie abandons his original consort Moxi for these new brides, *si* 肆 should be glossed simply as "discard" rather than "wanton."

48 While Shun dealt with discontent within the household,	舜閔在家
Why did his father keep him a bachelor?	父何以鰥
Why did sagely Yao not inform the groom's own clan Yaw	堯不姚告
When marrying off to Shun his two daughters?	二女何親

Shun was born at Yaw 姚 and so obtained his clan name from that place. Both Shun's family plotting against him, and the propriety of not informing Shun's parents, are discussed in *Mencius*.[34] Mencius explains that this was the only way that Shun could have been married, and also explains Shun's attitude to his brother Xiang. In a more rudimentary way, this quatrain addresses the same complex moral dilemmas as the more extensive treatment in *Mencius*. However, Huang Linggeng also points out that there is little evidence for this story outside of *Mencius*, and these questions may refer to a different version of the legend (Huang, *Chuci yu jianbo wenxian*, 255).

49 When the sprouting of events is at its start,	厥萌在初
How can one perceive their significance?[35]	何所億焉
The agate-studded tower had ten stories;	璜臺十成
By whom was it completed?	誰所極焉

The Han commentary explains this quatrain by reference to a story about the profligate king of Shang, Zhow 紂. As before, I romanize his name this way to distinguish from the Zhou 周 people who overthrew him and established the succeeding dynasty. Zhow's advisor Jizi 箕子 criticized him for using ivory chopsticks, and warned that this was the beginning of a slippery slope to disaster: "If he makes ivory chopsticks, then this will inevitably lead to using goblets of jade; after making the goblets, then he will long for exotic beasts from far-off lands to ride. The ruin of the impe-

---

34. *Mengzi zhushu*, 9A.290–91; trans. D. C. Lau, *Mencius*, 100.

35. I translate according to the variant *yi* 意 for *yi* 億 (already one sense of the latter graph as well). See *Chuci buzhu*, 3.103.

rial carriage and palaces begins from this, and they cannot be revived." 彼為象箸，必為玉梪；為梪，則必思遠方珍怪之物而御之矣。輿馬宮室之漸自此始，不可振也 (*Shiji*, 38.1933–34). In the event, Jizi's prophecy proved accurate, and Zhow would later build a ten-story tower decorated with precious stones. Yet it is also possible to understand this as an abstract question about a general issue: how drastic transformations can occur through gradual accumulation over time rather than a unique event.

50	When she ascended to the throne as Lord,	登立為帝
	By what path was she elevated to it?	孰道尚之
	As for the body possessed by Nü Wa,	女媧有體
	Who crafted and constructed it?	孰制匠之

This quatrain resembles no. 42 above, also concerned with the body of a deity. The Han commentary identifies the subject of the first couplet as Fu Xi, but Zhou Gongchen points out that there are several quatrains, such as 52 below, where the main subject is only identified in the latter couplet.[36] So the former couplet should also be referring to Nü Wa, whose body is frequently described and depicted as being that of a snake.

The insertion of Nü Wa here seems like a digression within the poem; but the next quatrain does continue along the theme of the bestiality of human character and bodies.

51	Shun was subservient to his younger brother,	舜服厥弟
	But ultimately met with harm;	終然為害
	Why in spite of that wanton, cur-like body of his brother Xiang,	何肆犬體
	Was his own person not endangered or ruined?	而厥身不危敗

Shun's younger half-brother Xiang "The Elephant" and their father Gusou 瞽瞍 "The Blind Old Man" together attempted to murder Shun, as apparently referred to more obliquely in quatrain 48 above. There is an interesting variant *quanshi* 犬豕 for the original text *quanti* 犬體. Xiang's violation of fraternal duty makes him equivalent to a dog or pig. I prefer the received text with "body" because of the associative link with the previous quatrain.

---

36. You Guoen cites this extremely perceptive remark at *Tianwen zuanyi*, 280, but I have not been able to find it in the text of the *Lisao caomu shi*.

52 Shun of Yu had obtained, from ancient times, 吳獲迄古
    Territory reaching to the Southern Marchmount; 南嶽是止
    Who would have predicted that at this place 孰期去斯
    He would encounter the two young noblemen? 得兩男子

This quatrain is typically read as referring to the founders of the state of Wu. A more coherent interpretation, though, proposed by Qing scholar Liu Mengpeng 劉夢鵬 (b. 1728), follows from reading the first character, Wu 吳, as a variant of Yu 虞 (in which it is phonetic), the clan name of Shun. Then the quatrain is asking about Shun and his two sons, which keeps it within the timeline of the surrounding text. According to Liu, the two sons' names were Yigou 義鈞 and Jili 季釐.[37] Huang Linggeng elaborates on this new interpretation, suggesting that the two men are Shun's son Shangjun 商均 (also known as Shujun 叔均) and Danzhu 丹朱, Yao's son who did not inherit the throne (*Chuci zhangju shuzheng*, 4.1136–39). *The Classic of Mountains and Seas* mentions in different entries that Shun was buried at Mount Cangwu 蒼梧 along with Danzhu, and also with his son Shujun.[38]

Thus, a series of questions relating to Shun's ascendancy and rule conclude with this quatrain interrogating the limits of his rule and the succession. The more common reading of this quatrain in relation to the Wu founding is also possible, of course. The word *wu* 吳 / *yu* 虞 here (phonetically interchangeable, since *wu* is the phonetic component of *yu*) might even be intended to convey a double meaning, with both historical episodes illustrating a single message about the contingency of fate.

V. The Shang and Its Ancestors

53 When with crane-shaped tripods and ornamented jade 緣鵠飾玉
    [Yi Zhi] made offering to his Sovereign Lord, 后帝是饗
    Why was he tasked with the plot against Jie of Xia, 何承謀夏桀
    Which resulted in [Jie's] death and destruction? 終以滅喪

---

37. *Quzi zhangju*, 4.17b–18a; see also the discussion in You Guoen et al., eds., *Tianwen zuanyi*, 290–92, noting that You himself rejects this reading.

38. Yuan Ke, ed., *Shanhaijing jiaozhu*, 10.242 and 15.310, respectively.

According to the *Chuci zhangju*, the quatrain as a whole is about Tang's minister Yi Yin 伊尹, counsellor to Shang founder Tang 湯 and later Shang kings, who is not explicitly mentioned till the next quatrain, there under the name of Yi Zhi. Some commentators understand Houdi 后帝 here as the Lord of Heaven rather than Tang, but since Di is mentioned again in the following quatrain, it is much more straightforward to understand the word as referring to Tang in both cases (although of course the ruler of All Under Heaven would ordinarily be understood as ruling with Heavenly mandate, so this may be a distinction without a difference).

The bamboo-strip manuscript "When Red Pigeons Gathered on Tang's House" ("Chi jiu zhi ji Tang zhi wu" 赤鳩集湯之屋), from the Tsinghua University collection, opens with Tang shooting down red pigeons and then commanding his minister to make them into a soup. This quatrain and its Han commentary have been used to help interpret that text, although it is unclear whether it conversely helps to illuminate this quatrain (Allan, "When Red Pigeons Gathered on Tang's House," 454). The minister there is identified only as Xiaochen 小臣, but that is how Yi Yin is identified in quatrain 62 below.

54	After the High Lord descended to observe,	帝乃降觀
	And down below had rendezvous with Yi Zhi,	下逢伊摯
	Why was it that when Jie was punished by exile to Tiao,	何條放致罰
	The people did rejoice greatly?	而黎服大說

This quatrain continues with the narrative of the Shang founder Tang (identified only by the general term *di* 帝, which I render as "High Lord" to preserve something of its open-endedness), first returning to his encounter with Yi Yin and then asking why the people were glad to be rid of Jie. Tiao is short for Mingtiao 鳴條 (north of modern Anyi 安邑 in Shanxi province), where Jie, wicked final king of Xia, was exiled by Tang.[39]

55	While his concubine Jian Di was at the altar,	簡狄在臺
	Why did High Lord Ku find it proper?	嚳何宜
	At the gift proffered by the dark bird	玄鳥致貽
	Why was she so gratified?[40]	女何嘉

39. See *Shiji*, 2.88; Nienhauser, *Grand Scribe's Records*, 1:38.

40. I follow the graphic variant *jia* 嘉 for *xi* 喜, which improves the OC rhyme (*-aj), as Wen Yiduo points out in "*Chuci jiaobu*," 165–66.

This quatrain goes back in time to the ancestors of the Shang kings. Though that is an inversion of chronological order, it is a natural digression in terms of the historical issues at play. Jian Di is said in the *Shiji* to be the younger concubine of High Lord Ku (Di Ku 帝嚳), mythic Shang ruler. She swallowed the egg of the Dark Bird, and then gave birth to Xie 契, ancestor of the Shang people.[41] Jian Di belonged to the Yousong 有娀 Clan, as in "Sublimating Sorrow," line 238.

56 When Wang Hai upheld the virtue of Ming,　　該秉季德
    He showed the same excellence as his father.　　厥父是臧
    Why was he ultimately murdered by the Youyi Clan　　胡終弊于有扈
    While tending the cattle and sheep?　　牧夫牛羊

Gai 該 refers to Shang ancestor Wang Hai 王亥. The identification of *gai* as a proper name is already suggested by Liu Zongyuan, was developed by later scholars, and confirmed by Wang Guowei through an analysis of names mentioned in the Shang oracle bones (see "Yin buci zhong suo jian xiangong xianwang kao"). I also accept Wang Guowei's emendation of Ji 季 to Ming 冥, the name of Wang Hai's father. The Youyi Clan were an ancient people located in modern Hu 戶 county, Shaanxi. This story is also mentioned in the *Bamboo Annals*: "Prince Hai of the Yin was a guest with the Yi Clan when he committed adultery. Mianchen, the King of the Youyi Clan, murdered him and let go his oxen. Thus the ruler of Yin, Jia Wei, borrowed an army from the Hebo to attack the Youyi Clan, destroyed them, and killed their ruler Mianchen" 殷王子亥賓于有易而淫焉, 有易之君綿臣殺而放之。是故殷上甲微假師于河伯以伐有易, 滅之, 遂殺其君綿臣也。[42] Based on this text I amend "Youhu" to "Youyi," again following Wang Guowei. It seems that the following series of quatrains up to 60 and possibly 61 all refer to this story, including a number of plot details that have not survived in other texts.

---

41. See "Dark Bird" ("Xuanniao" 玄鳥; *Odes* 303): "Heaven bade the dark bird / To come down and bear the Shang, / Who dwelt in the lands of Yin so wide. / Of old God bade the warlike Tang / To partition the frontier lands" (trans. Waley, *Book of Songs*, 320); cf. Allan, *Shape of the Turtle*, 38–41, and Chen Zhi, "Study of the Bird Cult."

42. The "Ancient Text" version as quoted in the commentary in Yuan Ke, ed., *Shanhaijing jiaozhu*, 14.351.

57 How by timely showing of the shield dance　　干協時舞
    Did he draw his rivals into friendship?　　　　何以懷之
    With their plump torsos and delicate complexions　平脅曼膚
    How did they then fatten him up so?　　　　　　何以肥之

Some premodern scholars identified these lines as referring to Shun's pacification of the Miao Clan in the "Da Yu mo" chapter of the *Book of Documents* (Legge, *Shoo King*, 62), but this is one of the pseudo-Ancient Text chapters. Huang Linggeng emends 干協時舞 to 干舞協時, based on the order of the *Chuci zhangju* glosses (*Chuci zhangju shuzheng*, 4.1155). It seems plausible that a benighted copyist put *wu* 舞 at the end of the line to create a supererogatory rhyme with *hu* 膚 below.

The commentaries do not offer convincing explanations of these lines, which seem to refer to another, unknown story about Wang Hai.

58 The lowly oxherds among the Youyi Clan:　　有扈牧豎
    How did he come upon them?　　　　　　　　云何而逢
    When they ambushed him upon the couch,　　擊床先出
    How was it that his life was spared?　　　　　其命何從

According to the *Bamboo Annals*, Wang Hai's son Shangjia Wei attacked the Youyi in revenge (see note to quatrain 56 above). I take it that this quatrain is referring loosely to these events, though the syntax is obscure.

59 Wang Heng too upheld the virtue of his father Ming,　恆秉季德
    But where did he obtain the tame oxen?　　　　　　焉得夫朴牛
    When he went to manage ranks and rewards,　　　　何往營班祿
    Why did he not return in vain?　　　　　　　　　　不但還來

Heng was Wang Hai's younger brother. The story behind this quatrain is obscure and interpretations vary widely even today.

60 As Twilight Wei followed the old paths,　　　　　　昏微遵跡
    So that the Youdi were not content,　　　　　　　　有狄不寧
    Why, like the myriad birds flocking in the brambles,　何繁鳥萃棘
    Did he betray his son with untrammelled passions?　　負子肆情

The first couplet refers to Wang Hai's son Shangjia Wei 上甲微. Liu Pansui suggested reading Hun 昏 "Twilight" (alternatively, "benighted") as a name for Shangjia Wei (*Tianwen jiaojian*, 278). It seems not necessarily pejorative, since he is introduced in reference to a martial victory: Wang Guowei and others have identified Youdi with Youyi, since the *Bamboo Annals* records Shangjia Wei's defeat of the Youyi. It would be odd, although not unprecedented, for the text to refer to the same people by two different, but similar, terms twice in succession. As with this whole sequence of quatrains, it is clear there is even more historical background that has been lost and makes it nearly impossible to recover the full implications of the poem. Shangjia Wei is also praised in a recently excavated text, the *Bao xun* 保訓 (Allan, *Buried Ideas*, 285–88).

61	The confused younger brother, joining in adultery,	眩弟並淫
	Endangered and injured his brother.	危害厥兄
	Though he transformed his shape to dissimulate and deceive,	何變化以作詐
	Why did his progeny enjoy rapid increase?	後嗣而逢長

This quatrain is taken by some commentators as referring back to the story of Shun and Xiang. While this is possible, it would be a needless repetition. I take it perhaps to be referring both to Wang Hai's family *and* to Shun's. In other words, it links together these disparate threads by posing a general question about the apparently inevitable conflict between brothers.

62	When Cheng Tang journeyed east	成湯東巡
	Until he arrived at the Youshen Clan,	有莘爰極
	Why did he make a request of that lesser official	何乞彼小臣
	And so obtain a propitious consort?	而吉妃是得

With this quatrain we turn from the remote ancestors of the Shang dynasty to its founder Tang. Note that the progression also follows the parallel that Tang, like Wang Hai, is encountering an alien clan. The ancient kingdom of the Youshen Clan was in the region of modern Kaifeng, Henan province, and this episode is described in the *Lü shi chunqiu* (Knoblock and Riegel, *Annals of Lü Buwei*, 307). For "propitious consort," Huang Linggeng suggests we read *ji* 吉 as the surname Ji 姞 (*Chuci yu jianbo wenxian*, 267–68).

63	It was by a tree at the water's margin	水濱之木
	That that little child was found.	得彼小子
	So why did the Youshen then, detesting him,	夫何惡之
	Send him off escorting a bride of their own clan?	媵有莘之婦

This passage refers to the Moses-like origin story of Yi Yin, also recounted in the same passage of *Lü shi chunqiu* (see previous note). He was discovered by a girl of the Shen Clan while she was harvesting silkworms from a mulberry tree.[43]

64   When Tang emerged from the double springs,   湯出重泉
        Of what crime had he been found guilty?   夫何辠尤
        When he could not muster courage to assault the Sovereign,   不勝心伐帝
        Who was it that spurred him on?   夫誰使挑之

According to the *Shiji*, Tang was imprisoned at the Terrace of Xia by Jie (*Shiji*, 2.88). Whether "double springs" is the same place is unclear. Presumable the answer to the latter question is Yi Yin, Tang's great counsellor. Mori Yasutarō suggested that Tang was originally a sun deity (*Kōtei densetsu*, 13–29). This supposition is helpful in understanding how some of the more mysterious legends arose, and were then by the time of the *Shiji* assimilated to more straightforward histories of regime change.

VI. Founding of the Zhou Dynasty

65   When they met at dawn to make the war compact,   會晁爭盟
        Who was it that accomplished their common oath?   何踐吾期
        When the gray-black birds assembled in flight,   蒼鳥群飛
        What is it that caused them to flock together?   孰使萃之

This quatrain seems to refer to King Wu's founding of the Zhou and conquest of Shang at the battle of Muye. It relates to the depiction of the same events in the eighth stanza of "Great Illumination" ("Daming" 大明; *Odes* 236), which concludes: "The captain was Shang-fu [Taigong Wang]; / Like a goshawk he uprose. / Ah, that King Wu / Swiftly fell upon Great Shang, / Who before daybreak begged for a truce." 維師尚父, 時維鷹揚, 涼彼武王, 肆伐大商, 會朝清明 (trans. Waley, *Book of Songs*, 230, modified). The goshawk there might provide the inspiration for the ques-

---

43. On the consort of Tang, see also Kinney, *Exemplary Women of Early China*, 6.

tion about birds here, but alternatively, You Guoen cites Liu Mengpeng's explanation that one of the good omens for King Wu's conquest of Shang was a fire that fell from Heaven and transformed into a crow.[44] We have no external evidence beyond the Han commentary that the bird here is the *ying* 鷹, so the crow episode might be more pertinent.

66 When they struck fiercely at the body of Zhow,   到擊紂躬
    Lord Dan did not approve the act.   叔旦不嘉
    Why did he nonetheless survey the starting point himself,   何親揆發足
    And sigh in admiration at the mandate bestowed upon Zhou?   周之命以咨嗟

Lord Dan, literally "Uncle Dan," was the younger brother of King Wu and is more commonly known as the Duke of Zhou. I follow the *Chuci buzhu* variant of *lie* 列 for *dao* 到, and understand it as a graphic variant of *lie* 烈 "fierce" (Yu Xingwu, *Zeluoju Chuci xinzheng*, 276–77). Hong Xingzu also cites the *Liutao* 六韜, attributed to Taigong 太公, in which the Duke of Zhou counsels against the attack on Shang because of various ill omens (*Taiping yulan*, 328.7a). This quatrain may also refer to the story that King Wu personally decapitated Zhow's body and hung the head up on a flagpole (*Yi Zhou shu huijiao jizhu*, 36.346).

67 When all under Heaven had been allotted to the Yin,   授殷天下
    By what authority did they rule?[45]   其位安施
    When in turn success met with destruction,   反成乃亡
    By what crime was the fall incurred?   其罪伊何

This quatrain may be the clearest statement of the theme of the poem. Heavenly favor is granted to some, whether deservedly or not; when it is revoked, inevitably, what is the cause? Though various answers are suggested in the poem none is or can be final. There are various alternative interpretations, though, including the view that *cheng* 成 "success" is actually a proper noun, referring to King Cheng of Zhou (Jiang Liangfu, ed.,

---

44. You Guoen et al., eds., *Tianwen zuanyi*, 360. The bird might also be a hawk, as in the Modern-Text version of the *Shujing*, quoted in *Shiji*, 4.121n.

45. The *Chuci buzhu* quotes a variant of 德 for 位, which Wen Yiduo prefers. See "Tianwen shuzheng," 609.

Qu Yuan fu jiaozhu, 3.362–63). The subject here would then be the Duke of Zhou, and the question why he came into conflict with King Cheng, as recounted in the *Shujing* (Legge, *Shoo King*, 357–60).

68	Contending to dispatch the weapons of war,	爭遣伐器
	How did [King Wu] accomplish it?	何以行之
	Advancing in stride, striking on both flanks,	並驅擊翼
	How did he take command of all this?	何以將之

Regarding the difficult term *jiyi* 擊翼 "striking on both flanks," Huang Linggeng demonstrates the frequency of this term in contemporary military discourse (*Chuci yu jianbo wenxian*, 270).

69	When Lord Zhao completed his excursion	昭后成遊
	Reaching as far as the southern lands,	南土爰底
	What was the benefit for him in the end	厥利惟何
	From coming upon the white pheasant?	逢彼白雉

According to the *Bamboo Annals*, King Zhao in the sixteenth year of his reign campaigned against Chu, where he came upon a rhinoceros, and in the nineteenth year journeyed further south and startled the pheasants and hares there.[46] According to another early source, he drowned in Chu after the lacquer boat he had received from the local people dissolved in the river.[47]

70	Why did King Mu, so clever and covetous,	穆王巧梅
	Choose to pursue his world-spanning journey?	夫何為周流
	Putting in order all under Heaven,	環理天下
	What was it that he was searching for?	夫何索求

King Mu of Zhou, historically the fifth king of Zhou, was famous for his journeys to distant lands, and even so far as to see the Spirit Mother of the West, as recorded in the mythic narrative *Mu tianzi zhuan* (Biography of

---

46. Fang and Wang, eds., *Guben Zhushu jinian jizheng*, 45–46; Legge, "Annals of the Bamboo Books," 149.

47. See *Diwang shiji*, 5.44, as quoted in *Shiji*, 4.134n; also *Zhushu jinian tongjian*, 8.6a. The story is not cited in the Modern-Text *Zhushu jinian* or in the Ancient-Text version as edited by Fang Shiming and Wang Xiuling, and its *locus classicus* seems to be a citation in the subcommentary of *Chunqiu Guliang zhuan zhushu*, 7.134.

King Mu). *Mei* 梅 "prunus" is a difficult crux, and Wang Fuzhi emends to the homophone *mei* 枚 "rein" (*Chuci tongshi*, 3.290.). I follow instead the lexical variant of *mu* 梅 meaning "to seek" (*Chuci buzhu*, 3.110.).

For this quatrain cf. "Sublimating Sorrow," l. 192: "I will seek throughout the world above and below" 吾將上下而求索 (Williams, *Elegies*, 9; Huang Linggeng, ed., *Chuci zhangju shuzheng*, 1.341).

71	When the uncanny couple were selling goods,	妖夫曳衒
	What did they call out in the marketplace?	何號于市
	Who was it that King You of the Zhou would execute,	周幽誰誅
	So that he obtained his concubine Bao Si?	焉得夫褒姒

King You 幽 (r. 781–770), "the benighted," was the final ruler of the Western Zhou. His unrestrained passion for femme fatale Bao Si led to his downfall. She was the adopted daughter of a man sentenced to execution, who offered her up to the king in exchange for a pardon.[48]

According to the *Guoyu*, King You's fall was anticipated by a children's ditty popular under the previous reign: "With mulberry bow and willow quiver, / That will surely mark the end of the Zhou state!" 檿弧箕服，實亡周國 (*Guoyu jijie*, 16.473). A married couple were seen selling precisely these items, and they were captured and dragged through the streets. The wood of this bow is identified in the second stanza of "How Great!" ("Huang yi" 皇矣; *Odes* 241) as mulberry; the wood of the quiver is identified only as *ji* 箕, not normally a plant name but resonant as the name of Master Ji 箕子, mentioned below, and perhaps a loan for the nearly homophonous *qi* 杞 "purple willow."

72	As the Mandate of Heaven revolves and reverses:	天命反側
	Wherefore chastening, wherefore succor?	何罰何佑
	Duke Huan of Qi convened the lords nine times,	齊桓九會
	But he too was murdered in the end.	卒然身殺

Duke Huan of Qi was famous for convening alliances with the other states (not necessarily nine times, but frequently). The biography of Guan Zhong 管仲 in the *Shiji* mentions that he had helped Duke Huan to "convene the feudal lords nine times" 九合諸侯, a kind of formula also used to describe

---

48. On Bao Si, see Kinney, *Exemplary Women of Early China*, 138–39.

the achievements of other leaders during the Warring States era (*Shiji*, 62.2131). Yet his virtuous efforts at leadership and diplomacy ended in failure; Duke Huan's miserable death is described in *Guanzi*, and occurred after four wicked retainers revolted, following his wise adviser Guan Zhong's death (see Rickett, *Guanzi*, 1:430).

It is possible that the order of "chastisement" and "succor" has been reversed by editors unaware of the rhyme scheme, since the final of "chastisement" 罰 (OCM *bat) fits better to rhyme with "murder" 殺 (OCM *srât).

Conrady points out the relevance of *Laozi* 79, which ends with a tetrasyllabic quatrain that would indeed fit rather well here:

Those with power (virtue) wield the tallies,	有德司契
Those without power wield the carriage-ruts.	無德司徹
The Way of Heaven is without partiality,	天道無親
And generally aids those who are good.[49]	常與善人

However, contrary to expectation, the *Laozi* seems to present a more Confucian vision of virtue rewarded, whereas "Heavenly Questions" quatrain 72 more harshly depicts Heaven as treating human beings as "straw dogs."

73	As for that Zhow the King himself:	彼王紂之躬
	Who set him into disturbance and confusion?	孰使亂惑
	Why did he loathe his own aides and helpers,	何惡輔弼
	And surrender to slanderous gossip?	讒諂是服

This quatrain refers to the episodes of Bi Gan and Sire Mei, Zhow's loyal counselors whom he executed, and who are mentioned by name in the two succeeding quatrains 74 and 75, respectively. But *wu* 惡 "loathe" may also be a proper noun, referring to Wulai 惡來, one of Zhow's ministers: "Why, even though Wu[lai] aided and supported him, / Did he surrender to slanderous gossip?"

74	Why did his adviser Bi Gan revolt,	比干何逆
	Though he was then crushed and destroyed?	而抑沈之
	Lei Kai was obsequious and obedient,	雷開阿順
	And yet received enfeoffment.	而賜封之

---

49. Conrady and Erkes, *Das älteste Dokument*, 32. *Laozi daodejing zhu jiaoshi*, 188–90.

This quatrain presents us with two opposing models of behavior: Bi Gan protested Zhow's corruption and was executed in a particularly grisly fashion, while Lei Kai was one of the flattering ministers of Zhow. Lei Kai is not mentioned in the *Shiji*, but the Qing scholar Jiang Ji cites the *Huangwang daji* 皇王大紀, which does mention him as a flatterer, but in no more detail than is implicit here (*Shandaige zhu Chuci*, 10.34b). The opposition of the two figures is dramatic and is formally articulated by the syntactic parallelism between the two couplets.

75 Why does the virtue of the sages, though constant,　　何聖人之一德
    Yet conclude in such contrary ways?　　卒其異方
    Sire Mei was ground into meat paste,　　梅伯受醢
    And Master Ji affected madness.　　箕子詳狂

Sire Mei and Master Ji were two ministers of Zhow, both of whom protested at Zhow's wickedness. But Sire Mei did so directly, and was executed in this gruesome way, while Master Ji feigned madness and survived to serve the Zhou. This quatrain provides a devastating conclusion to the whole section on the founding of the Zhou dynasty.

VII. Manifestations of Virtue through the Ages

76 Hou Ji was the primary son,　　稷維元子
    So why did the High Lord revile him?　　帝何竺之
    When he was discarded on the ice,　　投之於冰上
    Why did the birds keep him warm?　　鳥何燠之

This quatrain refers to the story of the mythic ancestor Hou Ji, "Lord Millet," and seems to correspond to "Birth of the People" ("Sheng min" 生民; *Odes* 245), which describes his virgin birth:

    She who in the beginning gave birth to the people　　時維姜嫄
    This was Jiang Yuan.　　厥初生民
    How did she give birth to the people?　　生民如何
    Well she sacrificed and prayed　　克禋克祀
    That she might no longer be childless.　　以弗無子
    She trod on the big toe of God's footprint,　　履帝武敏歆

Was accepted and got what she desired.	載震載夙
Then in reverence, then in awe,	載介載止
She gave birth, she nurtured;	載生載育
And this was Hou Ji.	時維后稷

In the third stanza, though, the same poem describes how he was abandoned: "Indeed, they put him on the cold ice; / But the birds covered him with their wings. / The birds at last went away, / And Hou Ji began to wail." 誕寘之寒冰、鳥覆翼之。鳥乃去矣、后稷呱矣。[50] But I would note that neither the *Book of Odes* passage, nor any other ancient text I know, provides the answers to these questions.

My interpretation follows Yu Yue, who argues that *zhu* 竺 actually means *du* 毒, 'to revile," with which it is interchangeable ("Du Chuci," 8a/b). He also identifies the High Lord as Di Ku 帝嚳, though it may also be the supreme Lord of Heaven.

77	Why was he, with mighty bow and bearing arrows,	何馮弓挾矢
	Able beyond all to lead them?	殊能將之
	Since he startled his lord, grievously and scathingly,	既驚帝切激
	How then did he arrive at enduring success?	何逢長之

The Han commentary explains this quatrain with respect to King Wu's conquest of Shang. But Yu Yue relates these lines to the birth of Hou Ji as described in "Birth of the People." Legge, Waley, and Karlgren all elide the dramatic conflict between the newborn Hou Ji and his father in these lines, which might literally be translated: "When he [Hou Ji] thus made manifest his numinous power, / The God on High was *not* at ease." 以赫厥靈, 上帝不寧. Legge and Karlgren read the negative as a rhetorical question, while Waley seems to translate it as a loan for *pi* 丕.[51] But the plain sense of the text is more effective and fits well with this quatrain of "Heavenly Questions."

Tang Bingzheng reads *ping* 馮 as a variant of the homophonous *peng* 弸, glossed as "appearance of a strong bow" in the *Shuowen*, as in quatrain 36 above (*Chuci leigao*, 297). *Ping* is usually understood as a Chu dialect word, but that hypothesis is unnecessary.

---

50. Waley, *Book of Songs*, 244–45, slightly modified. See also Legge, *She King*, 465–67, for Chinese text and alternative translation.

51. Cf. Legge, *She King*, 467; Waley, *Book of Songs*, 245; Karlgren, *Book of Odes*, 200.

78 When Prince Chang exclaimed upon the decline, 伯昌號衰
    He wielded the whip and served as master. 秉鞭作牧
    Why did he command the Qi altars be re-established, 何令徹彼岐社
    And the mandate for the dynasty of Yin? 命有殷國

This seems to refer to King Wen of Zhou and the conquest of Shang, since King Wen's personal name was Chang 昌. Mount Qi [sometimes written 岐 for 歧, literally 'forking path' or my 'Tangent' in the name of Lady Tangent above] was a sacred site in the founding myth of the Zhou, as the place where Gugong Danfu and Jiang Yuan come to settle in "Spreading" ("Mian" 緜; *Odes* 237).

79 When he transported his prized possessions towards Mount Qi, 遷藏就岐
    Why did people follow along with him? 何能依
    As for the bewitching lady of Yin-Shang: 殷有惑婦
    Why was she so reviled by them? 何所譏

According to the Han commentary, the first couplet refers to when Zhou ancestor King Tai 太王, Gugong Danfu 古公亶父, settled at Mount Qi, and the second to Zhow's concubine Da Ji 妲己, killed during the Zhou conquest. This admittedly looks like a place where the quatrain does not cohere around a single topic, an exception to the rule I have set forth for interpreting the poem in general.

80 When Zhow presented him the bloody paste, 受賜茲醢
    The Prince of the West protested to Heaven; 西伯上告
    Was it because he personally addressed the Lord on High, 何親就上帝
    That the mandate of Yin was reproached and not saved? 罰殷之命以不救

The Han commentary misconstrues this quatrain by taking *shou* 受 as a common verb, when it is actually the style name of Zhow. The Prince of the West is King Wen of Zhou. The likely source for this story is the *Diwang shiji*: Zhow murdered and then fed King Wen's own son, Bo Yikao 伯邑考, to him, to show he was no sage. King Wen then protested to God on high. See *Diwang shiji*, 5.40.

81 When Master Wang was in the market, 師望在肆
    How did Chang [King Wen] recognize him there? 昌何識

Wielding a sword and raising up a cry—	鼓刀揚聲
Why did the sovereign rejoice therein?	后何喜

This quatrain refers to the well-known origin story of Lü Wang, hired to serve as chief adviser to King Wen when he was working as a butcher. This episode, inspiring to many unappreciated scholars with unsavory jobs, is referred to also in "Sublimating Sorrow," ll. 293–94.

82	When Wu set forth to assault Yin,	武發殺殷
	What was it that had infuriated him?	何所悒
	When he bore his spirit tablet to join in battle,	載尸集戰
	What was it that spurred him on?	何所急

This quite straightforward quatrain inquires about King Wu's motivation for going into battle against the Shang. Quatrain 80 above has just provided one indication of an answer.

According to the *Shiji*, King Wu brought the spirit tablet (*muzhu* 木主) of his father along with him and proclaimed that he was fighting on behalf of his father (*Shiji*, 4.156).

83	For what reason could it have been	伯林雉經
	His brother was hanged in the Northern Forest?	維其何故
	Why did it stir the Heavens and strike the Earth,	何感天抑墬
	And who was still in awe and fear of him?	夫誰畏懼

This quatrain is more than usually obscure. The premodern commentaries following the Han commentary generally relate it to Prince Shensheng 申生 of Jin, but no name is mentioned in the text. I follow instead Xu Wenjing's interpretation relating these lines to the story of Guanshu Xian 管叔鮮, King Wu's younger brother, which keeps us in the same approximate period as the preceding and following lines (*Guancheng shuoji*, 16.291). Guanshu Xian rebelled against King Cheng and was defeated and slain by the Duke of Zhou. This interpretation understands the difficult words *bolin* 柏林 as a phonetic loan for Beilin 北林, the "Northern Forest," identified as a place name in modern Xingyang 滎陽, Zhengzhou City, in the ancient state of Zheng.

84	When mighty Heaven located its Mandate,	皇天集命
	What was worth reprimanding him?	惟何戒之

| When Zhow had already offered the rites to all under heaven, | 受禮天下 |
| Why did this result in his own overthrow? | 又使至代之 |

As in quatrain 80, Shou 受 should be understood as the style name of Zhow rather than as a verb. This is another example of the paronomastic manner of the poem.

85	At first the minister of Tang was Zhi,	初湯臣摯
	But later this one took on the responsibility of counsellor.	後茲承輔
	Why did he ultimately serve as officer for Tang,	何卒官湯
	To honor the offerings of the ancestral succession?	尊食宗緒

The minister of Tang was Yi Yin, personal name Zhi, who figured prominently in section V of the poem. The quatrain seems to ask why he was elevated to such a prominent role. Though on the whole the chronology of the poem is consistent, this quatrain appears to be another exception.

86	The meritorious scion Helu was born of Meng,	勳闔夢生
	But was cast away in his youth.	少離散亡
	Why was he so mighty and practiced in arms,	何壯武厲
	That he could spread his reputation far and wide?	能流厥嚴

These lines refer to Shou Meng 壽夢 (?–561 BCE), grandfather of the famous King of Wu, Helu 闔廬, originally Sir Guang 光. The succession was contested among Shou Meng's grandsons, and Helu ultimately won the throne by murdering his cousin in cold blood, using a dagger concealed inside a fish (*Shiji*, 31.1767). Being "cast away" refers to the fact that Sir Guang was the son of Shou Meng's eldest son, and so felt himself to be the rightful heir to the throne, but instead the throne was occupied by his cousin, King Liao 僚, who was the son of Shou Meng's third son.

87	When Peng Keng brewed the pheasant soup,	彭鏗斟雉
	Why did the High Lord consume it?	帝何饗
	When he achieved extraordinary longevity,	受壽永多
	Why was he still so long distressed?	夫何久長

Peng Keng is also known as Peng Zu 彭祖. According to the Han commentary, he cooked pheasant soup for Yao, bringing him longevity, but there is no external confirmation of this, and Wen Yiduo suggests instead that it was an offering to the Lord of Heaven ("Tianwen shuzheng," 627).

Peng Zu is a prominent figure in ancient lore, but also a man of mystery who is hard to pin down to a specific historical setting. He may also be the same person as Shaman Peng of "Peng and Xian" 彭咸 in "Sublimating Sorrow." The *Shenxian zhuan* 神仙傳 identifies Peng Zu as a descendant of the Yellow Emperor who lived 767 years, his lifespan intersecting with the Xia, Shang, and Zhou (as quoted in Hong Xingzu's commentary to *Chuci buzhu*, 3.116). Peng Zu is identified in the *Liexian zhuan*, however, as a nobleman of the Shang who lived over eight hundred years (Wang Shumen, ed., *Liexian zhuan jiaojian*, A.38). Huang Linggeng suggests that Peng Zu was originally the name of a clan that persisted for generations, which was later misinterpreted as the name of an individual (*Chuci zhangju shuzheng*, 4.1235). In any case, here Peng Keng is a man of extreme longevity who still feels regret that he could not live even longer. I read *chang* 長 "long-lasting" as an error for *chang* 悵 "distressed," again following Wen Yiduo.

The use of *shou* 受 "receive" (translated as "achieved") in the first position of the third line mirrors quatrain 84 just above, where it was a proper name (the personal name of wicked King Zhow), but here it has to be read as a verb. This might be an example of intentional wordplay on the part of the author.

88 When the central states were governed by Earl Gong,   中央共牧
    Why was the sovereign angered?   后何怒
    How could the paltry lives of bees and ants   蠭蛾微命
    Possess the strength to endure?   力何固

There is a variant noted by Hong Xingzu of *shou* 收 for *mu* 牧 (*Chuci buzhu*, 3.116). According to the Han commentary, the bees and ants represent the surrounding peoples, the Man 蠻 and Yi 夷, joining together to drive out the wicked King Li 厲 of Zhou (r. ?–ca. 841 BCE). The Han commentary then adds the amusing theory that "central" stands for a place known for its many-headed vipers who contest the crops. It seems to have been Ma Qichang who did the best to resolve the crux by pointing out that *gong* 共 is not an adverb "together" but rather a proper name, Earl Gong 共伯, personal name He 和 (*Qu fu wei*, A.37a). According to the *Bamboo Annals*, it was Earl Gong who governed in place of the incompetent King Li (Fang Shiming and Wang Xiuling, eds., *Guben Zhushu jinian jizheng*, 58; Legge, *Shoo King*, 154). On the other hand, *pace* Jiang Liangfu, who criticizes later commentators for interpreting this quatrain in general terms rather than only in relation to a specific historical event (*Qu Yuan fu jiaozhu*, 3.384), there is also a case for taking this quatrain to refer to a general type of situation rather than a single event: why should the king be upset if the lesser lords choose to collaborate rather than to undermine one another? And yet on the other hand, if it comes to a contest, can the lesser states (paltry as bees or ants) survive even if they ally with one another?

89 When they startled a woman while gathering vetch,　　驚女采薇
    Why did a deer protect them?　　鹿何祐
    North as far as the winding currents,　　北至回水
    In meeting there why did they delight nonetheless?　　萃何喜

Li Shan's *Wenxuan* commentary quotes a source called the *Gu shi kao* 古史考 to provide the legend of Bo Yi and Shu Qi, the mythic Shang loyalists who starved themselves on Mount Shouyang (located south of modern Yongji city, Shanxi) rather than submit to Zhou. According to the legend, they only starved after a woman came to them and told them that even the vetch they were harvesting belonged to Zhou, and so they could no longer consume even that (note to *Wenxuan*, 54.2394). Another source mentions that Heaven first sent a white deer to nourish them when they had been starving for seven days (*Diaoyu ji*, 12.29). For both these points, see Wen Yiduo, "Chuci jiaobu," 172–73.

The "winding currents" may refer to the rough waters of the Yellow River. Mount Shouyang, where Bo Yi and Shu Qi took refuge, is located near the sharp eastward bend in the Yellow River later known as "Yellow River's Crook" 河曲 (*Tianwen buzhu*, 18b).

It is worth noting the coincidence that "Gathering Vetch" is also the title of a poem in the *Odes* (167) about soldiers separated from their families while on an expedition.

90 When the elder brother had a keen-toothed hound,　　兄有嗜犬
    Why did the younger seek it?　　弟何欲
    Though bartering for a hundred chariots,　　易之以百兩
    Why was he ultimately without any estate?　　卒無祿

The Han commentary offers an explanation of this quatrain based on a story about the Duke of Qin and his younger brother Qian 鍼. It has no other extant source, but corresponds in part to the account in *Zuozhuan*, Duke Zhao, year 1. Qian was the younger brother of the Duke and was forced to flee to Jin because otherwise he might be perceived as a threat to the ruler: "Qian of Qin had been a favourite son of Lord Huan [r. 604–577] and was like a second ruler under Lord Jing [r. 576–537]. Their mother said to Qian, 'If you do not depart, I fear that you will be sent away. In the fifth month, on the *guimao* day (25), when Qian went to Jin, his chariots numbered one thousand." (Durrant et al., *Zuo Tradition*, 1319).

None of this fully explains the dog, but Huang Linggeng cites a proverb quoted in *Zuozhuan*, Duke Ai, year 12: "When a tall tree dies, there is nothing it will not fall upon; when the best dog in the domain goes rabid, there is no one it will not bite" 長木之斃無不摽也, 國狗之瘈無不噬也 (*Chuci zhangju shuzheng*, 4.1247; Durrant et al., *Zuo Tradition*, 1909). The proverb would apply to situations like this one, because the older brother, like a rabid dog, was a threat even to his innocent brother Qian. But it is still difficult to construe the first question in this quatrain accordingly.

VIII. Epilogue

91 A bolt of lightning in the twilight sky: 薄暮雷電
    What worry for those returning? 歸何憂
    If his authority they did not respect, 厥嚴不奉
    What still to request from the Lord? 帝何求

There are various proposals for identifying the subject matter here. The Han commentary and Jiang Liangfu both see this section as returning to contemporary circumstances, or at least recent Chu history (*Chuci buzhu*, 3.117; *Qu Yuan fu jiaozhu*, 318–19). The latter interpretation seems to comport well with the literary effect of the bolt of lightning, which has not been identified as a historical allusion. In other words, the quatrain shifts the focus of the poem from heroes of the more remote past, especially the founders of Zhou, and towards the confrontations of Chu political history.

The topic of returning home, in particular as applied to soldiers on campaign, is a common one in the *Book of Odes*, as in "Four Steeds" ("Simu" 四牡; *Odes* 162), first stanza: "My four steeds are weary / The high road is very far. / Indeed, I long to come home; / But the king's business never ends. / My heart is sick and sad." 四牡騑騑, 周道倭遲。豈不懷歸, 王事靡盬, 我心傷悲 (trans. Waley, *Book of Songs*, 134). See also Michael Hunter's study of this theme in the *Odes* and *Chuci*: "To Leave or Not to Leave."

92	Hiding and skulking in cavernous places,	伏匿穴處
	What more is there to say?	爰何云
	May he see his faults and change his ways—	悟過改更
	What more ought we to advise?	我又何言

This quatrain might be inspired by an episode in *Zhuangzi* about a prince who took refuge underground. After three successive kings of the southern state of Yue were killed by their own subjects, it is said that: "Prince Sou fled to the Cinnabar Caves, leaving the state of Yue without a ruler. The people searched for Prince Sou but could not find him, till finally they tracked him to the Cinnabar Caves. Prince Sou was unwilling to come out, but they smoked him out with mugwort and made him ride in the royal chariot. As Prince Sou held on to the straps to mount the chariot, he looked up to heaven and cried out, 'A ruler! Oh, to be a ruler! Couldn't I alone have been spared from this?'" 越人三世弒其君, 王子搜患之, 逃乎丹穴。而越國無君, 求王子搜不得, 從之丹穴。王子搜不肯出, 越人薰之以艾。乘以王輿。王子搜援綏登車, 仰天而呼曰:「君乎君乎! 獨不可以舍我乎!」 (*Zhuangzi jishi*, 28.968; trans. Mair, *Wandering on the Way*, 286).

I have reversed the positions of the latter couplet of quatrain 92 and the former couplet of quatrain 93 to correct the rhyme, and also incidentally to improve the sense (the received text has 伏匿穴處, 爰何云。荊師作勳, 夫何長。悟過改更, 我又何言。吳光爭國, 久余是勝).

93	The army of Jing achieved a meritorious deed,	荊師作勳
	But how was it to endure?—	夫何長
	As Guang of Wu contested the realm,	吳光爭國
	And was long victorious over us.	久余是勝

Guang is the personal name of Helu 闔廬 (r. 514–496), famous king of Wu who won the throne by murdering his uncle King Liao 僚, and later led the state to its destruction by rival Yue. Before that, however, Wu established supremacy over Chu, invading its capital Ying in 506 BCE.

94	Why did they encircle the shrines and trample the altars,	何環閭穿社
	Even offending the very tomb mounds?—	以及丘陵
	It was that wantonness, that wildness,	是淫是蕩
	Which led to the appearance of Sir Wen.	爰出子文

Dou Bobi 鬬伯比 (the son of Chu leader Ruoao 若敖) had an adulterous liaison with a lady of Yun 鄖, which produced the son Ziwen, who became Lingyin, chief minister of Chu, from 664 to 637. But: "Lady Yun had him abandoned at Meng Marsh. A tigress suckled him. When the Master of Yun went hunting, he saw this and returned in fear. His wife told him what had happened, and he thus had the child brought back" (*Zuozhuan*, Duke Xuan, year 4; Durrant et al., *Zuo Tradition*, 613). Ziwen's full name is Dou Gouwutu 穀於菟, said to mean "suckled by a tigress" in Chu dialect. The whole story is related at this point in the *Zuozhuan* to provide the context for the episode of a ruinous rebellion by Ziwen's nephew Dou Jiao 椒.

For this quatrain I follow the variant text cited by Hong Xingzu and Zhu Xi (*Chuci buzhu*, 3.118; *Chuci jizhu*, 3.70). According to Xu Wenjing, the "tomb mounds" refer to Wu Zixu's desecration of the tomb of King Ping of Chu during Wu's conquest of Chu (*Guancheng shuoji*, 16.294).

95	I would like to warn the ruler Duao	吾告堵敖
	That he will not long survive;	以不長
	But how could an admonition from me	何試上自予
	Burnish a loyal reputation any further?	忠名彌彰

My translation of *shi* 試 is suggested by the variant of *jie* 誡 for *shi* 試, noted in the *Chuci buzhu*, 3.118. Duao is Xiong Jian 熊艱, an early ruler of Chu also known as Zhuang'ao. His son killed him and usurped the throne to reign as King Mu 穆 (626–614). The mother of Duao is mentioned in *Zuozhuan*, Duke Zhuang, year 14 (680 BCE; Durrant et al., *Zuo Tradition*, 175). There are numerous contradictions and alternative names in the sources, but I follow the account in Blakeley, "King, Clan, and Courtier in Ancient Ch'u," 6–10, based on the *Zuozhuan*.

As discussed in chapter 1 above, this conclusion would seem at first to place the poem neatly in the voice of Qu Yuan speaking about recent events, and yet the events referred to in fact seem to have happened centuries before Qu Yuan's own time. Alternatively, the implied speaker might be considerably more ancient than Qu Yuan, and the poem as a whole gazing even further down into the well of history.

EPILOGUE

No Literature without Lacunae

> Normative concepts like the sense of the author or the understanding of the original readers represent in reality only a blank space, which is filled at each occasion by a new understanding.
>
> —Gadamer, *Truth and Method*[1]

One of the principal assumptions of the hermeneutical conception of literary tradition is that ancient texts have something to say to us as well. Meaning is not entirely unstable, imposed on the text by the interpreter, but is constructed by means of a dialogical process. And from this point of view the "Heavenly Questions," like other poems in the *Chuci*, ought to have its own message of use to us. This does not mean that an academic study should devote itself to, say, searching for political lessons in the poem that we might apply to contemporary regimes, although we may certainly hope that philological studies clarifying the interpretation of ancient texts may ultimately assist these texts in providing guidance or inspiration to future readers. Nonetheless, in keeping with the goals of this study, it may be worth suggesting, at the very least, one concrete lesson that the reading of the "Heavenly Questions" has to teach the literary scholar.

The "Heavenly Questions" and the history of its interpretation over two millennia can show, based on the various elements highlighted in this study, to what extent literary study cannot be a quantitative or mechanical process. So many aspects of twenty-first century life are controlled by digital processes that there is an easy temptation to apply these processes to literary texts, or even to find resemblances between literary compositions and mechanical processes. All this ignores the role that silence and

---

1. Gadamer, *Wahrheit und Methode*, 373: "Normbegriffe wie die Meinung des Verfassers oder das Verständnis das ursprünglichen Lesers repräsentieren in Wahrheit nur eine leere Stelle, die sich von Gelegenheit zu Gelegenheit des Verstehens ausfüllt."

emptiness play in literary composition and interpretation, and this is one thing that "Heavenly Questions" tells us, not once but over and over again in every line. The interpretation of literature has to leave room for lacunae, for the spaces left empty and silent in the midst of linguistic motion and noise.

To illustrate this lesson in a different way, we might consider, from a different literary tradition, a remarkable moment in Gadamer's short book, *Who Am I and Who Are You*, on Romanian-born German-language poet Paul Celan (1920–1970). In a revised edition of the text, Gadamer confesses that he has had to alter his interpretation of one poem because he had previously missed its references to geology.[2] The poem in Celan's collection *Atemwende* (Breath-turn) is brief and can be quoted in full, as translated by Richard Heinemann and Bruce Krajewski:[3]

ARMORED RIDGES,	HARNISCHSTRIEMEN,
fold-axes,	Faltenachsen,
Breakthrust-	Durchstich-
points:	punkte:
your terrain.	dein Gelände.
At both poles	An beiden Polen
of the cleft-rose, legible:	der Kluftrose, lesbar:
your banished word.	dein geächtetes Wort.
North-true. South-bright.	Nordwahr. Südhell.

In the revised version of his essay, Gadamer admits that the terms "Farnischstriemen," "Faltenachsen," "Durchstichpunkte," and "Kluftrose" from Celan's poem had led him astray ("haben mich in die Irre geführt"). He had mistakenly thought the imagery was drawn from that of violent combat, weaponry and armor. In fact, as he later realized, these are all technical terms of geology. "Harnischstriemen," which should probably be

---

2. The poem and discussion can be found in "Wer bin Ich und wer bist Du," in *Gesammelte Werke*, 9:419. This long essay, about sixty pages in his collected works, was originally published as an independent volume of 134 pages by Bibliothek Suhrkamp Frankfurt in 1973, but then revised and reprinted in 1986, before being incorporated into Gadamer's collected works. It has also been published as an independent English volume, with introduction by Gerald L. Bruns and including two other short essays on Celan, as *Gadamer on Celan*.

3. I quote both text and translation from *Gadamer on Celan*, 115.

translated "slickensides" or "slickenslide striation," refers to the striations on a fissure in the earth, produced by friction between the two surfaces. "Faltenachsen" refers to "fold axes" (where "axes" is the plural of a mathematical "axis," not "axe"), which is "a line which, when moved parallel to itself, traces out a folded surface." "Durchstichpunkte" are "piercing points," "A point of intersection of a geologically defined line with a fault surface that can be used to determine the net slip along the fault."[4] Finally, "Kluftrose" refers to a particular type of contour diagram used to represent geological data, and is probably best rendered as "cleft girdle."[5]

With all this in mind, it becomes clear that the translation provided above represents Gadamer's initial, mistaken impression of the poem as one about a violent interaction between two forces parallel to the "you" and the "I." Following the geological terminology more closely one would correct to:

SLICKENSLIDE STRIATIONS,
    folded surfaces,
Puncture
points:
    your terrain.

At both poles
of the cleft girdle, legible:
your banished word.
North-true. South-bright.

The corrected translation then accentuates the theme of the "legibility" of earth, environment, self, and other. The "striations" are the inscription of history upon the earth's crust, measured by human perception in surfaces and points, "your terrain." The cleft girdle too is a mathematical representation of geological contours with its own poles, making legible the uncomprehensible stuff of experience only by "banishing" words that would distract from it.

It is to Gadamer's credit that he recognized his own error and makes

---

4. Neuendorf, Mehl, and Jackson, *Glossary of Geology (Fifth Edition)*, s.v. "puncture point."

5. Neuendorf, Mehl, and Jackson, *Glossary of Geology (Fifth Edition)*, s.v. "cleft girdle": "On a fabric diagram, an annular maximum occupying a small circle of the net."

clear in the revised discussion that this geologically-informed reading of the poem is indisputably correct: "this language is also concerned with describing the stratification and classification of the earth's crust on the basis of the visible formations that orientate the geologist in her task of fathoming the secret of the earth's interior."[6] But what Gadamer reiterates, even in light of better information, is that the poem is not a technical statement of geological science, but is merely borrowing this imagery so as to describe "the terrain of language."[7] Moreover, the poem's center of gravity remains not the technical terminology but in fact its opposite, "your banished word" (dein geächtetes Wort), the word that is banished and despised, one that Gadamer rightly interprets as many-layered, suggesting "the word of the true God, the word of the true poet, and the true word itself."[8]

Identifying correctly the references contained within the poem thus draws us closer to its intended meaning, but does not immediately allow us to identify any explicit message. The authentic meaning of the poem is surely not to advertise to us that geology is a worthy field of scientific inquiry. Rather it is to explore, within a geological realm of linguistic imagery, the limits of our verbal orientation towards reality, and above all of our recognition of both self and other. A more refined perception of geological contours is to be strived for but leaves much unanswered.

In reading ancient literature, as well, one constantly makes this sort of discovery. A poem that looks like a placid scene of nature turns out to contain oblique references to a political upheaval; terms that at first had seemed vaguely decorative turn out to refer to a particular site or historical figure. Literary scholarship is rife with objective facts of no small importance. And yet it is equally important, when reading ancient literature, to identify zones of ignorance and uncertainty; to understand the questions being asked, not just to recover the answers that have been forgotten. The "Heavenly Questions" is a historical document but it is also a poem which shares some literary features, not just with the poetry of Liu Zongyuan or Du Fu, but also with the cryptic work of Celan.

There are powerful moments in the "Heavenly Questions" in which

---

6. Gadamer, *Gadamer on Celan*, 116.
7. Gadamer, *Gadamer on Celan*, 119.
8. Gadamer, *Gadamer on Celan*, 118.

nothing is expressed; not only are questions left unanswered, but the motivations for questions never indicated. A poem may belong to a corpus of texts but it may also be used to define spaces where no corpus remains to be found. For instance, quatrain 41 of "Heavenly Questions" reads:

> Heaven is configured horizontal and vertical: 天式從橫
> When Yang energy disperses then you die; 陽離爰死
> Why did the mighty bird cry out, 大鳥何鳴
> And how was it deprived of mortal frame? 夫焉喪厥體

The Han commentary identifies this with a story about transcendent Prince Qiao, who after death was transformed into a great bird that cried out and then flew away. This explanation runs into some chronological difficulties since that story probably belongs to the Han dynasty itself. But even leaving that aside, there is nothing in this quatrain that identifies it with Prince Qiao specifically. This is all the more true when we look at it as a coherent quatrain rather than two couplets, as early and medieval readers generally did. Seen as an integral quatrain, the topic is the great matrix of Yin and Yang, between Heaven and Earth, in which life comes into being and then perishes.

There is another excavated text that fits well into this perspective, the "Fan wu liu xing" 凡物流行 ("All Things Change Their Forms") from the Shanghai Museum collection.[9] The text is a piece of (mainly) tetrasyllabic verse in the interrogative mode, just like "Heavenly Questions," and it uses the same verb for the bird's cry (*ming* 鳴, subject unclear) right in the sixth line:

> All things flow into form; what brings them to completion?
> Flowing forms complete the body; what makes them never die?
> Having been completed, having been born, what makes them cry and wail?
> Having budded, having taken root, what do they follow, and what do they precede?

9. Quoted in Huang Linggeng, *Chuji jijiao*, 4.579; for a transcription and study, see Cao Feng, "Shangbo Chu jian 'Fan wu liu xing' de wenben jiegou yu sixiang tezheng"; see also Sukhu, *Songs of Chu*, 62. For a detailed English translation and study, see Huang, *A Walk in the Night*. See also Ma, ed., *Shanghai bowuguan cang Zhanguo Chu zhujian (qi)*, 223–300; Asano Yūichi, "Shanhaku Sōkan 'Banbutsu ryūkei' no zentai kōsei."

The respective abodes of Yin and Yang, what keeps them stable?

凡物流形，奚得而成？流形成體，奚得而不死？既成既生，奚呱¹⁰而鳴？既拔既根，奚後之奚先？陰陽之處，奚得而固？¹¹

This might be seen as simply another interrogative poem on creation like those discussed above, such as the "Heavenly Revolutions" chapter of Zhuangzi.¹² It does not turn to the historical or mythical subject matter of the "Heavenly Questions," so it does not really deserve to be compared with it as a similar type of composition in entirety, but it seems parallel to, and instructive for, our reading of quatrain 41.

In particular, the "Fan wu liu xing" suggests that the cry of the dying bird is a rather fitting and conventional metaphor for the passage of life and death.¹³ The first couplet describes the universal motion of *qi* energy within the cosmos, forming life and then expiring; the second couplet asks why the living shapes that form, such as the bodies of animals or a bird, cry out before they die. It is possible a better explanation will be provided at some point, and indeed it would be foolhardy to assert that any interpretation here is final, but the original explanation of the Han commentary really does not make much sense here. Instead, Huang Linggeng's proposal to relate the quatrain to these enigmatic questions about creation and metamorphosis makes far better sense.

It is also striking that, even though Liu Zongyuan's response to this passage follows the Prince Qiao episode cited by the Han commentary, his conclusion somehow ends up elaborating on the general issue of uncertainty, of mysterious metamorphosis, rather than on the specific episode of immortals:

> He was unable to glean from the tenebrous gloom　　簡漢莫謀
> Where the form was present and where absent.　　　形胡在胡亡

---

10. This is the reading proposed by Cao Jinyan in "Shanghai bowuguan cang Zhanguo zhushu *Chuci*." Other scholars such as Cao Feng have suggested *gua* 寡.
11. Translation slightly modified from Huang, *A Walk in the Night*, 3.
12. Asano Yūichi interprets the first half of the text as an independent series of questions which he titles the "Wen wu" 問物. He then compares this to a "Song of the Creation of the World" of the Miao people.
13. "Fan wu liu xing" can also be seen as an early statement of the relation between Man and Heaven. See Lin Chi-ping, "Zhongguo gudai tianren sixiang yu 'Fan wu liu xing.'"

I wonder if this does not suggest that Liu himself recognized that the key point was the hiddenness, the mystery, not the narrative which the Han commentary has unnecessarily tied to these lines.

But what does it mean? The quatrain tells us nothing directly; it is a poem, not a newspaper. What does it ask? It asks about why living things speak out; why people write poems, for instance. And what does it suggest about the answers to that question? The answer, I would suggest, is *nothing*. In a cosmos filled with change and death, all is uncertain and some aspects of experience remain simply unknowable. This is a rebuke not just to certain philosophers and priests, but also to many interpreters of this very text, notably the Han scholars who attempted to fill in the lacuna here with the story of Prince Qiao. The story of Prince Qiao is not totally irrelevant. Even magicians who transform into birds will die, but they may cry out first in such a way that they are long remembered. But to limit the meaning of this quatrain to that story of Prince Qiao is a misunderstanding. The primary sense of the quatrain is that we are mortal, and speak out before we die, but who knows why? It is a message that can only be appreciated if we have some tolerance and even some relish for the unanswered question, the undefined generality, and the lacunae of all our interpretations.

Bibliography

Allan, Sarah. *The Heir and the Sage: Dynastic Legend in Early China.* San Francisco: Chinese Materials Center, 1981.

———. *The Shape of the Turtle: Myth, Art, and Cosmos in Early China.* Albany: State University of New York Press, 1991.

———. "'When Red Pigeons Gathered on Tang's House': A Warring States Period Tale of Shamanic Possession and Building Construction Set at the Turn of the Xia and Shang Dynasties." *Journal of the Royal Asiatic Society* 25, no. 3 (2015): 419–38.

Alter, Robert. *The Wisdom Books: Job, Proverbs, and Ecclesiastes.* New York: Norton, 2010.

Asano Yūichi 浅野裕一. "Byōzoku sōseika to Shanhaku Sokan *Banbutsu ryūkei* 'Tonbutsu'—*Soji* 'Tenmon' no engen" 苗族創世歌と上博楚簡『凡物流形』《問物》—『楚辞』天問の淵縁. In *Chikukan ga kataru kodai Chūgoku shisō (san): Shanhaku Sokan kenkyū* 竹簡が語る古代中国思想（三）：上博楚簡研究, 95–124. Tokyo: Kyūko shoin, 2010.

———. "Shanhaku Sokan 'Banbutsu ryūkei' no zentai kōsei" 上博楚簡『凡物流形』の全体構成. In *Chikukan ga kataru kodai Chūgoku shisō (san)*, 37–94.

Ast, Friedrich (1778–1841). *Grundlinien der Grammatik, Hermeneutik und Kritik.* Landshut: Thomann, 1808.

Baxter, William. *A Handbook of Old Chinese Phonology.* Berlin: Mouton de Gruyter, 1992.

Bender, Lucas Rambo. "The Corrected Interpretations of the Five Classics (*Wujing zhengyi*) and the Tang Legacy of Obscure Learning (*Xuanxue*)." *T'oung Pao* 105 (2019): 76–127.

Bielenstein, Hans. *The Bureaucracy of Han Times.* Cambridge: Cambridge University Press, 1980.

Birrell, Anne. *Chinese Mythology: An Introduction.* Baltimore: Johns Hopkins University Press, 1993.

———, trans. *The Classic of Mountains and Seas.* London: Penguin Books, 1999.

Blakely, Barry B. "King, Clan, and Courtier in Ancient Chu." *Asia Major*, third series, 5.2 (1992): 1–39.

Bokenkamp, Stephen R. *Early Daoist Scriptures.* Berkeley: University of California Press, 1997.

Bol, Peter. *"This Culture of Ours": Intellectual Transitions in T'ang and Sung.* Stanford: Stanford University Press, 1994.

Burkert, Walter. *Structure and History in Greek Mythology and Ritual*. Berkeley: University of California Press, 1982.

Cao Fangxiang 曹方向. "Shangbo jian suo jian Chuguo gushi lei wenxian jiaoshi yu yanjiu" 上博簡所見楚國故事類文獻校釋與研究. PhD diss., Wuhan University, 2013.

Cao Feng 曹峰. "Shangbo Chu jian 'Fan wu liu xing' de wenben jiegou yu sixiang tezheng" 上博楚簡《凡物流形》的文本結構與思想特徵. *Qinghua daxue xuebao (zhexue shehui kexue ban)* 25 (2010): 73–82.

Cao Jianguo 曹建國. "Chuci zhangju yuntizhu kaolun"《楚辭章句》韻體注考論. *Wenxue pinglun* 2010.5: 118–25.

———. "You Guoen yu Jiang Liangfu *Chuci* yanjiu bijiao" 游國恩與姜亮夫楚辭研究比較. *Guji yanjiu* 2003.4: 126–30.

Cao Jinyan 曹錦炎. "Shanghai bowuguan cang Zhanguo zhushu *Chuci*" 上海博物館藏戰國竹書楚辭. *Wenwu* 2010.2: 59–62.

Chan, Chok Meng (Travis). "Writing for the Empire: A Study of Ban Gu's (32–92 CE) 'Dian yin' (Elicitation of the Canon)." MA thesis, University of Hong Kong, 2019.

Chan Hung To 陳鴻圖. "Lun *Chuci zhangju* yunwen zhu de xingzhi yu shidai" 論《楚辭章句》韻文注的性質與時代. *Tamkang Journal of Chinese Literature* 39 (2018): 1–31.

———. *Wang Yi Chuci zhangju xinlun* 王逸楚辭章句新論. Shanghai: Shanghai guji chubanshe, 2021.

Chan, Timothy W. K. *Considering the End: Mortality in Early Medieval Chinese Poetic Representation*. Leiden: Brill, 2012.

———. "The *Jing/Zhuan* Structure of the *Chuci* Anthology: A New Approach to the Authorship of Some of the Poems." *T'oung Pao* 84 (1998): 293–327.

———. "A New Reading of an Early Medieval Riddle: 'Utterly Wonderful, Lovely Words?'" *T'oung Pao* 99 (2013): 53–87.

———. "Wang Yi on Integrity and Loyalty." In *Considering the End: Mortality in Early Medieval Chinese Poetic Representation*, 7–40. Leiden: Brill, 2012.

Chang, I-jen, William G. Boltz, and Michael Loewe. "Kuo yü." In *Early Chinese Texts: A Bibliographical Guide*, ed. Michael Loewe, 263–68. Berkeley: Society for the Study of Early China, 1993.

Chen Hong 陳洪 and Zhao Jibin 趙紀彬. "Liu Zongyuan shige Foxue yuanyuan tanxi" 柳宗元詩歌佛學淵源探析. *Beifang luncong* 2011.2: 14–17.

Chen, Jo-shui. *Liu Tsung-yüan and Intellectual China in T'ang China*. Cambridge: Cambridge University Press, 2006.

Chen Weisong 陳維松. "Wang Yi zhujie *Chuci* de wenxue shijiao: *Chuci zhangju* zhi 'bazi zhu' tanxi" 王逸注解《楚辭》的文學視角———《楚辭章句》之"八字注"探析. *Zhongguo wenxue yanjiu* 2003.1: 77–82.

Chen, Zhi. "A Study of the Bird Cult of the Shang People." *Monumenta Serica* 47 (1999): 127–47.

Ch'ien Mu 錢穆. "'Qingdai Hanxue' henglun" 「清代漢學」衡論. In *Liang Han sixiangshi* 兩漢思想史, 3:567–629. Taiwan: Xuesheng shuju, 1979.

———. *Zhongguo jin sanbainian xueshu shi* 中國近三百年學術史. Taipei: Taiwan shangwu yinshuguan, 1966.

Chūbachi Masakazu 中鉢雅量. *Chūgoku no saishi to bungaku* 中国の祭祀と文学. Tokyo: Sōbunsha, 1989.

Chuci buzhu 楚辭補注. Compiled by Wang Yi. Further edited by Hong Xingzu 洪興祖 (1090–1155). Based on the Jiguge 汲古閣 edition, collated with the *Sibu congkan* edition and *Wenxuan*. Punctuated by Bai Huawen 白化文 et al. Beijing: Zhonghua shuju, 1983.

Chuci jizhu 楚辭集注. By Zhu Xi 朱熹 (1130–1200). Punctuated by Jiang Lifu 蔣立甫. Shanghai: Shanghai guji chubanshe, 2001.

Chuci Tianwen jian 楚辭天問箋. By Ding Yan 丁晏 (1794–1875). *Chuci wenxian congkan*, vol. 64. Guangxu era print.

Chuci tingzhi 楚辭聽直. By Huang Wenhuan 黃文煥 (1595–ca. 1667). Punctuated by Huang Linggeng 黃靈庚 and Li Fengli 李鳳立. Shanghai: Shanghai guji chubanshe, 2019.

Chuci tongshi 楚辭通釋. By Wang Fuzhi 王夫之 (1619–1692). In *Chuanshan quanshu* 船山全書, 14:205–480. Changsha: Yuelu shushe, 1988.

Chuci tuzhu 楚辭圖注. Illustrated by Xiao Yuncong 蕭雲從 (1596–1673). 1645. Electronic reproduction. Cambridge, MA: Harvard Library Preservation, 2014. (Harvard-Yenching Library Chinese Rare Books Digitization Project-Collected Works). Copy digitized: Harvard-Yenching Library: T 5240 4212.

Chuci wenxian congkan 楚辭文獻叢刊. Edited by Huang Linggeng 黃靈庚. Shanghai: Shanghai guji chubanshe, 2017.

Chuci yinyun 楚辭音韻. By Ding Fanzi 丁繁滋. *Chuci wenxian congkan*, vol. 64. 1800 print.

Chuci yundu 楚辭韻讀. By Jiang Yougao 江有誥 (1773–1851). *Chuci wenxian congkan*, vol. 64. 1819 print.

Chuci yunjie 楚辭韻解. By Qiu Yangwen 邱仰文 (1733 *jinshi*). 8 *juan*. *Chuci wenxian congkan*, vols. 57–58. 1772 edition.

Chunqiu Guliang zhuan zhushu 春秋穀梁傳注疏. In *Shisanjing zhushu* 十三經注疏. Edited by Li Xueqin 李學勤 et al. Beijing: Beijing daxue chubanshe, 2000.

Chunqiu jizhuan zuanli 春秋集傳纂例. Compiled by Lu Chun 陸淳. *Siku quanshu* 四庫全書. Vol. 146. Taipei: Taiwan shangwu yinshuguan, 1983–1986.

Chunqiu Zuozhuan zhengyi 春秋左傳正義. In *Shisanjing zhushu* 十三經注疏. Edited by Li Xueqin 李學勤 et al. Beijing: Beijing daxue chubanshe, 2000.

Conrady, August. "Indische Einflüsse in China im 4. Jh. v. Chr." *Zeitschrift der Deutschen Morgenländischen Gesellschaft* 60 (1906): 335–51.

Conrady, August, and Eduard Erkes. *Das älteste Dokument zur chinesischen Kunstgeschichte, T'ien-wen* 天問: *Die "Himmelsfragen" des K'üh Yüan*. Leipzig: Verlag Asia Major, 1931.

Dai Zhen quanshu 戴震全書. Edited by Yang Yingqin 楊應芹 and Zhu Weiqi 諸偉奇. 7 vols. Hefei: Huangshan shushe, 2010.

DeBlasi, Anthony. *Reform in the Balance: The Defense of Literary Culture in Mid-Tang China*. Albany: State University of New York Press, 2002.

Declercq, Dominik. *Writing against the State: Political Rhetorics in Third and Fourth Century China*. Leiden: Brill, 1998.

Dell, Katherine J. *The Book of Job as Sceptical Literature*. Berlin: Walter de Gruyter, 1991.

de Man, Paul. "Introduction." In *Toward an Aesthetic of Reception*, by Hans Robert Jauss, translated from the German by Timothy Bahti. Minneapolis: University of Minnesota Press, 1982.

Demiéville, Paul (1894–1979). "Enigmes taoistes." In *Silver Jubilee Volume of the Zinbun-Kagaku Kenkyushyo*, 54–60. Kyōto: Kyōto University, 1954.

Deng Shengguo 鄧聲國. *Wang Yi "Chuci zhangju" kaolun* 王逸"楚辭章句"考論. Beijing: Guojia tushuguan chubanshe, 2011.

Deng Wenbin 鄧文彬. *Zhongguo gudai yuyanxue shi* 中國古代語言學史. Chengdu: Ba Shu shushe, 2002.

Diaoyu ji 琱玉集. Tang dynasty. *Xuxiu siku quanshu* 續修四庫全書. Vol. 1212. Shanghai: Shanghai guji chubanshe, 2013.

Diény, Jean-Pierre. *Pastourelles et magnanarelles: essai sur un thème littéraire chinois*. Paris: Droz, 1977.

Ding Fulin 丁福林, ed. *Jiang Wentong ji jiaozhu* 江文通集校注. 4 vols. Shanghai: Shanghai guji chubanshe, 2017.

Diwang shiji 帝王世紀. Compiled by Huangfu Mi 皇甫謐 (215–282). In *Diwang shiji; Shiben; Yi Zhou shu; Guben zhushu jinian* 帝王世紀・世本・逸周書・古本竹書紀年. Punctuated by Lu Ji 陸吉. Jinan: Qi Lu shushe, 2010.

Dongpo zhilin 東坡志林. By Su Shi 蘇軾. In *Congshu jicheng* 叢書集成. Shanghai: Shangwu yinshuguan, 1939.

Du, Heng. "The Author's Two Bodies: The Death of Qu Yuan and the Birth of *Chuci zhangju* 楚辭章句." *T'oung Pao* 105 (2019): 259–314.

Durrant, Stephen, Wai-yee Li, and David Schaberg. *Zuo Tradition – Zuozhuan* 左傳: *Commentary on the "Spring and Autumn Annals."* Seattle: University of Washington Press, 2016.

Dushu zazhi 讀書雜志. By Wang Niansun 王念孫 (1744–1832). Shanghai: Saoye shanfang, 1924.

Elman, Benjamin. "Early Modern or Late Imperial? The Crisis of Classical Philology in Eighteenth-Century China." In *World Philology*, ed. Sheldon

Pollock, Benjamin Elman, and Ku-ming Kevin Chang, 225–44. Cambridge, MA: Harvard University Press, 2015.
———. *From Philosophy to Philology: Intellectual and Social Aspects of Change in Late Imperial China*. Cambridge, MA: Harvard University Asia Center, 1984.
Erkes, Eduard. "A Reply to Mr. Achilles Fang." *Monumenta Serica* 12 (1947): 229.
———. "Zu Chü Yüan's T'ien-wen 天問: Ergänzungen und Berichtigungen zu Conrady-Erkes, *Das älteste Dokument zur chinesischen Kunstgeschichte*." *Monumenta Serica* 6 (1941): 273–339.

Fang, Achilles. "On the T'ien-wen 'Reconstruction' by Professor Erkes." *Monumenta Serica* 7 (1942): 285–87.
Fang Shiming 方詩銘 and Wang Xiuling 王修齡, eds. *Guben Zhushu jinian jizheng* 古本竹書紀年輯證. Shanghai: Shanghai guji chubanshe, 2005.
Field, Stephen. "Cosmos, Cosmograph, and the Inquiring Poet: New Answers to the 'Heaven Questions.'" *Early China* 17 (1992): 83–110.
———. *Tian wen: A Chinese Book of Origins*. New York: New Directions, 1986.
Fogel, Joshua. *Politics and Sinology: The Case of Naitō Konan*. Cambridge, MA: Harvard University Press, 1984.
Franke, Herbert. "On Chinese Traditions Concerning the Dates of the Buddha." In *The Dating of the Historical Buddha / Die Datierung des historischen Buddha*, part 1, ed. Hanz Bechert, 441–48. Göttingen: Vandenhoek & Ruprecht, 1991.
Fu Gang 傅剛. *Wenxuan banben yanjiu* 文選版本研究. Beijing: Beijing daxue chubanshe, 2000.
Fu Xiren 傅錫任. "Jiang Yougao *Chu ci yundu* bianzheng" 江有誥楚辭韻讀辨證. *Danjiang xuebao* 6 (1967): 93–113.

Gadamer, Hans-Georg. *Gadamer on Celan: "Who Am I and Who are You?" and Other Essays*. Translated and edited by Richard Heinemann and Bruce Krajewski, with an Introduction by Gerald L. Bruns. Albany: State University of New York Press, 1997.
———. *Gesammelte Werke*. Tübingen: J. C. B. Mohr, 1993.
———. *Truth and Method*. Translation revised by Joel Weinsheimer and Donald G. Marshall. London: Bloomsbury, 1989.
———. *Wahrheit und Methode*. 2nd ed. Tübingen: J. C. B. Mohr, 1965.
———. "Wer bin Ich und wer bist Du?" In *Gesammelte Werke*, 9:383–451.
Gardner, Daniel K. "Confucian Commentary and Chinese Intellectual History." *Journal of Asian Studies* 57 (1998): 397–422.
Goldin, Paul R. "On the Meaning of the Name *Xi wangmu*, Spirit-Mother of the West." *Journal of the American Oriental Society* 122.1 (2002): 83–85.
Graham, A. C. *The Book of Lieh-tzŭ*. London: John Murray, 1960.
Gu, Ming Dong. *Chinese Theories of Reading and Writing: A Route to Hermeneutics and Open Poetics*. Albany: State University of New York Press, 2005.

Guancheng shuoji 管城碩記. By Xu Wenjing 徐文靖 (1667–1756?). Punctuated by Fan Xiangyong 范祥雍. Beijing: Zhonghua shuju, 1992.
Guangya shuzheng 廣雅疏證. By Wang Niansun 王念孫. Nanjing: Fenghuang chubanshe, 2000.
Guanzi jiaozhu 管子校注. Compiled by Li Xiangfeng 黎翔鳳 (*jinshi* 1847). 3 vols. Edited by Liang Yunhua 梁運華. Beijing: Zhonghua shuju, 2018.
Gu yunpu 古韻譜. By Wang Niansun 王念孫. Shanghai: Shanghai guji chubanshe, 1995.

Hamaguchi Fujio 濱口富士雄. *Shindai kōkyogaku no shisōshiteki kenkyū* 清代考拠学の思想史的研究. Tokyo: Kokusho kankōkai, 1994.
Han shi waizhuan 韓詩外傳. *Siku quanshu* 四庫全書. Vol. 89. Taipei: Taiwan shangwu yinshuguan, 1983–1986.
Hanshu 漢書. Compiled by Ban Gu 班固 (32–92). 12 vols. Beijing: Zhonghua shuju, 2013.
Harper, Donald. *Early Chinese Medical Literature*. London: Kegan Paul International, 1998.
Hawkes, David. "The Heirs of Gao-yang." *T'oung Pao* 49 (1983): 1–21.
———. *The Songs of the South. An Anthology of Ancient Chinese Poems by Qu Yuan and Other Poets*. Harmondsworth: Penguin Books, 1985.
Hessler, Peter. *Oracle Bones: A Journey through Time in China*. New York: Harper Perennial, 2007.
Hightower, James R. *Han Shih Wai Chuan: Han Ying's Illustrations of the Didactic Application of the Classic of Songs*. Cambridge, MA: Harvard University Press, 1952.
Hollander, John. *Melodious Guile: Fictive Pattern in Poetic Language*. New Haven: Yale University Press, 1988.
Hou Hanshu 後漢書. Compiled by Fan Ye 范曄 (398–446). 12 vols. Beijing: Zhonghua shuju, 1965.
Hu, Qiuhua. *Konfuzianisches Ethos und westliche Wissenschaft: Wang Guowei (1877-1927) und das Ringen um das moderne China*. Abingdon, Oxon: Routledge, 2016.
Huang, Kuan-yun. *A Walk in the Night with Zhuangzi*. Albany: State University of New York Press, 2023.
Huang Linggeng 黃靈庚, ed. *Chuci jijiao* 楚辭集校. 3 vols. Shanghai: Shanghai guji chubanshe, 2009.
———. *Chuci yu jianbo wenxian* 楚辭與簡帛文獻. Beijing: Renmin chubanshe, 2011.
———, ed. *Chuci zhangju shuzheng* 楚辭章句疏證. Ordering based on the anonymous *Chuci shiwen* 楚辭釋文. 5 vols. Beijing: Zhonghua shuju, 2007.

Hummel, Arthur W. *Eminent Chinese of the Ch'ing Period (1644–1912)*. Washington, DC: United States Government Printing Office, 1943.
Hunter, Michael. "To Leave or Not to Leave: The *Chu ci* 楚辭 (Verses of Chu) as Response to the *Shi jing* 詩經 (Classic of Odes)." *Early China* 42 (2019): 111–46.
Huntington, Rania. *Ink and Tears: Memory, Mourning, and Writing in the Yu Family*. Honolulu: University of Hawai'i Press, 2018.

Ishikawa Misao 石川三佐男. "Kodai So ōkoku kokusaku to kōko shutsudo shiryō kara mita Soji bungaku no hassei to tenkai" 古代楚王国国策と考古出土資料から見た楚辞文学の発生と展開. In *Soji to So bunka no sōgōteki kenkyū* 『楚辞』と楚文化の総合的研究, ed. Ōno Keisuke 大野圭介, 83–146. Tokyo: Kyūko shoin, 2014.
———. *Soji shinkenkyū* 楚辭新研究. Tokyo: Kyūko shoin, 2002.
———. "So Shō ō no jinbutsu jiseki kō: Soji Tenmon hen seiritsu no seijiteki kikkake o tsukutta So ō 'shikkaku' no ō" 楚昭王の人物事跡考——楚辞天問篇成立の政治的きっかけを作った楚王「失格」の王. *Shutsudo bunken to Shin-So bunka* 6 (2012): 50–68.

Jao Tsung-i 饒宗頤. "Jing-Chu wenhua" 荊楚文化. Repr. in *Rao Zongyi ershiwu shijixueshu wenji* 饒宗頤二十五世紀學術文集, 9:845–913. Taipei: Xinwenfeng, 2003.
———. "Tianwen wenti de yuanliu: Fawen wenxue zhi tantao" 〈天問〉文體的源流———「發問」文學之探討. Repr. in *Rao Zongyi ershiwu shijixueshu wenji* 饒宗頤二十五世紀學術文集, 16:35–56.
———. *Yindai zhenbu renwu* 殷代貞卜人物. Repr. in *Rao Zongyi ershiwu shijixueshu wenji* 饒宗頤二十五世紀學術文集, 2:1–1362.
Jiaguwen heji 甲骨文合集. Edited by Guo Moruo 郭沫若 et al. 13 vols. Beijing: Zhonghua shuju, 1978–1983.
Jiang Liangfu 姜亮夫. *Chuci tonggu* 楚辭通故. 4 vols. Jinan: Qi Lu shushe, 1985.
———. "Dunhuang xieben Sui Shi Zhixian *Chu ci yin ba*" 敦煌寫本隋釋智騫楚辭音跋. In *Chuci xue lunwen ji* 楚辭學論文集, 367–85. Shanghai: Shanghai guji chubanshe, 1984.
———, ed. *Qu Yuan fu jiaozhu* 屈原賦校注. Rev. ed. Tianjin: Tianjin guji chubanshe, 1987.
———. "*Shiji* Qu Yuan liezhuan shuzheng" 史記屈原列傳疏證. In *Chuci xue lunwen ji*, 1–28.
Jiang Sheng 姜生. *Han diguo de yichan: Han gui kao* 漢帝國的遺產：漢鬼考. Beijing: Kexue chubanshe, 2016.
Jingyan shiyi 經言拾遺. Included in *Xu Weishan liuzhong*.

Karlgren, Bernhard. *The Book of Odes: Chinese Text, Transcription, and Translation*. Stockholm: Museum of Far Eastern Antiquities, 1950.

Keightley, David N. *Sources of Shang History: The Oracle-Bone Inscriptions of Bronze Age China*. Berkeley: University of California Press, 1978.

———. *These Bones Shall Rise Again: Selected Writings on Early China*. Albany: State University of New York Press, 2014.

Kennedy, George A. "Metrical 'Irregularity' in the *Shih-ching*." *Harvard Journal of Asiatic Studies* 4 (1939): 284–96.

Kern, Martin. "Cultural Memory and the Epic in Early Chinese Literature: The Case of Qu Yuan 屈原 and the *Lisao* 離騷." *Journal of Chinese Literature and Culture* 9 (2022): 131–69.

———. "The Poetry of Han Historiography." *Early Medieval China* 10–11 (2004): 23–65.

———. "'Xi shuai' 蟋蟀 (Cricket) and Its Consequences: Issues in Early Chinese Poetry and Textual Studies." *Early China* 42 (2019): 39–74.

Kinney, Anne Behnke. *Exemplary Women of Early China: The Lienü zhuan of Liu Xiang*. New York: Columbia University Press, 2014.

Kinoshita Tetsuya 木下鉄矢. "*Shinchō kōshōgaku*" *to sono jidai: Shindai no shisō*「清朝考証学」とその時代：清代の思想. Tokyo: Sōbunsha, 1996.

Knechtges, David R. *The* Han shu *Biography of Yang Xiong (53 B.C.–A.D. 18)*. Occasional Paper No. 14. Tempe, AZ: Center for Asian Studies, Arizona State University, 1982.

———. "A Journey to Morality: Chang Heng's *The Rhapsody on Pondering the Mystery*." In *Essays in Commemoration of the Golden Jubilee of the Fung Ping Shan Library (1932–1982)*, 2 vols., 162–82. Hong Kong: Hong Kong University Press, 1982.

———, trans. *Wen xuan, or Selections of Refined Literature*, vol. 1: *Rhapsodies on Metropolises and Capitals*. Princeton: Princeton University Press, 1982.

Knechtges, David R.; and Taiping Chang, eds., *Ancient and Early Medieval Chinese Literature: A Reference Guide*. 4 vols. Leiden: Brill, 2010–2013.

Knoblock, John, and Jeffrey Riegel. *The Annals of Lü Buwei: A Complete Translation and Study*. Stanford: Stanford University Press, 2000.

Kominami Ichirō 小南一郎. "Ō Itsu *Soji shōku* to *Soji* bungei no denshō" 王逸「楚辭章句」と楚辞文藝の伝承. In *Soji to sono chūshakushatachi* 楚辞とその注釈者達, 299–369. Kyōto: Hōyū shoten, 2003.

———. "Tenmon hen no seiri" 天問篇の整理. In *Soji to sono chūshakushatachi*, 173–247.

Kroll, Paul W. "Huilin on Black and White, Jiang Yan on *Wuwei*: Two Buddhist Dialogues from the Liu-Song Dynasty." *Early Medieval China* 18 (2012): 1–24.

Kroll, Paul W., et al. *A Student's Dictionary of Classical and Medieval Chinese*. 3rd ed. Boston: Brill, 2022.

Lai, Whalen. "Looking for Mr. Ho Po: Unmasking the River God of Ancient China." *History of Religions* 29 (1990): 335–50.

Lamont, H. G. "An Early Ninth Century Debate on Heaven: Liu Tsung-yüan's *T'ien Shuo* and Liu Yü-hsi's *T'ien lun*: An Annotated Translation and Introduction." *Asia Major* new series 18.2 (1973): 181–208, and 19.1 (1974): 37–85.

Laozi daodejing zhu jiaoshi 老子道德經注校釋. Commentary by Wang Bi 王弼. Edited by Lou Yulie 樓宇烈. Beijing: Zhonghua shuju, 2018.

Lau, D. C., trans. *The Analects*. Bilingual Edition. Hong Kong: Chinese University Press, 2000.

———, trans. *Mencius*. Harmondsworth: Penguin, 19.

Legge, James. "The Annals of the Bamboo Books." In *The Shoo King or the Book of Historical Documents*, 105–76.

———. *The Chinese Classics, with a Translation, Critical and Exegetical Notes, Prolegomena, and Copious Indexes*. 5 vols. Repr. Taipei: SMC Publishing, 2000.

———. *The Confucian Analects*. In *The Chinese Classics*, vol. 2.

———. *The Lî Kî*. 2 vols. In *The Sacred Books of China: The Texts of Confucianism*, parts III–IV. Oxford: Clarendon Press, 1885.

———. *The She King, or the Book of Poetry*. In *The Chinese Classics*, vol. 4.

———. *The Shoo King or the Book of Historical Documents*. In *The Chinese Classics*, vol. 3.

———. *The Works of Mencius*. In *The Chinese Classics*, vol. 2.

Li Daming 李大明. *Han Chuci xue shi* 漢楚辭學史. Beijing: Shehui kexue chubanshe, 2004.

Li Daoping 李道平 and Pan Yuting 潘雨廷, eds. *Zhouyi jijie zuanshu* 周易集解纂疏. 10 vols. Beijing: Zhonghua shuju, 1994, 2004.

Li Jinshan 李金善 and Gao Chenxi 高晨曦. "Yi zhujie Qu Yuan shuxie junguo qinghuai: Lu Shiyong *Chuci shu* yu Zhou Gongchen *Lisao caomu shi* zhushi zhi bijiao" 以注解屈原抒寫君國情懷———陸時雍《楚辭疏》與周拱辰《離騷草木史》注釋之比較. *Hebei daxue xuebao (zhexue shehui kexue ban)* 47.2 (2022): 33–39.

Li Xueqin 李學勤. *Zhouyi suyuan* 周易溯源. Chengdu: Ba Shu shushe, 2006.

Liao Tung-liang 廖棟樑. "Chuwei zhi shi: Wang Yi *Chuci zhangju* de yunti shiwen" 出位之詩———王逸《楚辭章句》的韻體釋文. In *Lunli, lishi, yishu: Gudai Chuci xue de jiangou* 倫理・歷史・藝術：古代楚辭學的建構, 365–415. Taipei: Liren, 2008.

———. *Lingjun yuying: Gudai Chuci xue lunji* 靈均餘影：古代楚辭學論集. Taipei: Liren, 2008.

Liji zhengyi 禮記正義. Commentary by Zheng Xuan 鄭玄 (127–200). Subcommentary by Kong Yingda 孔穎達 (574–648). In *Shisanjing zhushu* 十三經注疏. Edited by Li Xueqin 李學勤 et al. Beijing: Beijing daxue chubanshe, 2000.

Lin Chi-ping 林啟屏. "Zhongguo gudai tianren sisiang yu 'Fan wu liu xing'" 中國古代天人思想與《凡物流形》. In *Chuanhe Kangsan jiaoshou rongxiu jinian wenji* 川合康三教授榮休紀念文集, ed. Lin Tsung-cheng 林宗正 and Jiang Yin 蔣寅, 1–19. Nanjing: Fenghuang chubanshe, 2017.

Lin Geng 林庚. "Tianwen lunjian" 天問論箋. In *Lin Geng Chuci yanjiu liangzhong* 林庚楚辭研究兩種. Beijing: Qinghua daxue chubanshe, 2006.

Lin Lianshan 林蓮山. *Chuci yinyun* 楚辭音韻. Hong Kong: Zhaoming chubanshe, 1979.

Lin Weichun 林維純. "Liu Xiang bianji *Chuci* chutan" 劉向編集《楚辭》初探. *Jinan xuebao* 25 (1984): 86–92.

———. "Shilun *Chuci zhangju* 'xuwen' de zuozhe wenti" 試論《楚辭章句》「序文」的作者問題. *Jinan xuebao* 27 (1986): 47–56, 62.

Lisao caomu shi 離騷草木史. By Zhou Gongchen 周拱辰. Edited by Huang Linggeng 黃靈庚. Shanghai: Shanghai guji chubanshe, 2019.

Lisao fu buzhu 離騷賦補注. By Zhu Junsheng 朱駿聲 (1788–1858). 1882. Repr. in *Chuci wenxian congkan*, vol. 65.

Liu Hedong ji 柳河東集. Original commentary by Han Chun 韓醇 (Song dynasty). Included in the *Siku quanshu*. Punctuated ed. Shanghai: Shanghai guji chubanshe, 2008.

Liu Jingsheng 劉精盛. *Wang Niansun zhi xunguxue yanjiu* 王念孫之訓詁學研究. Changchun: Jilin daxue chubanshe, 2011.

Liu Wendian 劉文典, ed. *Huainan honglie jijie* 淮南鴻烈集解. Punctuated by Feng Yi 馮逸 and Qiao Hua 喬華. 2 vols. Beijing: Zhonghua shuju, 2013.

Liu Yuejin 劉躍進 and Jiang Linchang 江林昌. "Jiang Liangfu xiansheng ji qi *Chuci* yanjiu" 姜亮夫先生及其楚辭研究. *Wenxue yichan* 1998.3: 99–109.

Liu Zongyuan ji 柳宗元集. 4 vols. Beijing: Zhonghua shuju, 1979.

Loewe, Michael. *A Biographical Dictionary of the Qin, Former Han, and Xin Periods (221 BC–AD 24)*. Leiden: Brill, 2000.

Lu Jui-ching 魯瑞菁. *Fengjian shuqing yu shenhua yishi: Chuci wenxin lun* 諷諫抒情與神話儀式：楚辭文心論. Taipei: Liren, 2002.

Lunyu zhushu 論語注疏. In *Shisanjing zhushu* 十三經注疏. Edited by Li Xueqin 李學勤 et al. Beijing: Beijing daxue chubanshe, 2000.

Luo Changpei 羅常培 and Zhou Zumo 周祖謨. *Han Wei Jin Nanbeichao yunbu yanbian yanjiu* 漢魏晉南北朝韻部演變研究. Beijing: Kexue chubanshe, 1958.

Luo Jianbo 羅劍波. *Mingdai Chuci pingdian lunkao* 明代《楚辭》評點論考. Taipei: Weiwei chubanshe, 2018.

Luo Xiongfei 羅雄飛. *Yu Yue de jingxue sixiang yu jingxue yanjiu fengge* 俞樾的經學思想與經學研究風格. Beijing: Dianzi keji daxue chubanshe, 2014.

Ma Chengyuan 馬承源, ed., *Shanghai bowuguan cang Zhanguo Chu zhujian (qi)* 上海博物館藏戰國楚竹書(七). Shanghai: Shanghai guji chubanshe, 2008.

Mair, Victor H., trans. "Heavenly Questions." In *The Columbia Anthology of Traditional Chinese Literature*, 371–87. New York: Columbia University Press, 1996.

———. *Wandering on the Way: Early Taoist Tales and Parables of Chuang Tzu*. Honolulu: University of Hawai'i Press, 1988.

Major, John S., Sarah A. Queen, Andrew Seth Meyer, and Harold D. Roth, eds. and trans. *The Huainanzi: A Guide to the Theory and Practice of Government in Early Han China*. New York: Columbia University Press, 2010.

Maoshi zhengyi 毛詩正義. In *Shisanjing zhushu* 十三經注疏. Edited by Li Xueqin 李學勤 et al. Beijing: Beijing daxue chubanshe, 2000.

Maspero, Henri. Review of *Das älteste Dokument zur chinesischen Kunstgeschichte, T'ien-wen . . . die 'Himmelsfragen' des K'üh Yüan*. By August Conrady and Eduard Erkes. *Journal Asiatique* 222 (1933): 59–74.

Mathieu, Rémi. *Elégies de Chu*. Paris: Gallimard, 2004.

Matsumoto Hajime 松本肇. *Ryū Sōgen kenkyū* 柳宗元研究. Tokyo: Sōbunsha, 2000.

McDermott, Joseph. "The Ascendance of the Imprint in China." In *Printing and Book Culture in Late Imperial China*, ed. Cynthia J. Brokaw and Kai-wing Chow, 55–104. Berkeley: University of California Press, 2004.

McMullen, David. *State and Scholars in T'ang China*. Cambridge: Cambridge University Press, 1988.

McNeal, Robin. "Constructing Myth in Modern China." *Journal of Asian Studies* 71 (2012): 679–704.

Mengzi zhushu 孟子注疏. In *Shisanjing zhushu* 十三經注疏. Edited by Li Xueqin 李學勤 et al. Beijing: Beijing daxue chubanshe, 2000.

Mori Yasutarō 森安太郎. *Kōtei densetsu: Kodai Chūgoku shinwa no kenkyū* 古代中国神話の研究. Kyōto: Kyōto joshi daigaku jinbun gakukai kan, 1970.

Naitō Konan zenshū 內藤湖南全集. 14 vols. Tokyo: Chikuma shobō, 1969–1976.

Needham, Joseph. *Science and Civilisation in China, Volume 3: Mathematics and the Sciences of Heaven and Earth*. Cambridge: Cambridge University Press, 1959.

Neuendorf, Klaus K. E., James P. Mehl, and Julia A. Jackson. *Glossary of Geology (Fifth Edition)*. Alexandria, VA: American Geosciences Institute (AGI), 2011. Retrieved from https://app.knovel.com/hotlink/toc/id:kpGGE00002/glossary-geology-5th/glossary-geology-5th.

Nienhauser, William H., Jr., ed. *The Grand Scribe's Records*, vol. 1: *The Basic Annals of Pre-Han China*. Bloomington: Indiana University Press, 1994.

Nivison, David S. *The Riddle of the Bamboo Annals*. Taipei: Airiti, 2009.

Nugent, Christopher M. B. *Manifest on Words, Written on Paper: Producing and Circulating Poetry in Tang China*. Cambridge, MA: Harvard University Asia Center, 2010.

O'Neill, Timothy. *Ideography and Chinese Language Theory: A History*. Berlin: De Gruyter, 2016.

Owen, Stephen. Review of *Liu Tsung-yüan*, edited by William H. Nienhauser. *Journal of the American Oriental Society* 95 (1973): 519–20.

Peng Lingjing 彭靈靜. "Zhou Gongchen shige yanjiu" 周拱辰詩歌研究. MA thesis, Nanjing Normal University, 2014.

Pulleyblank, Edwin G. *Lexicon of Reconstructed Pronunciation in Early Middle Chinese, Late Middle Chinese, and Early Mandarin*. Vancouver: University of British Columbia Press, 1991.

———. "Neo-Confucianism and Neo-Legalism in T'ang Intellectual Life, 755–805." In *The Confucian Persuasion*, ed. Arthur F. Wright, 77–114. Stanford: Stanford University Press, 1960.

———. *Outline of Classical Chinese Grammar*. Vancouver: University of British Columbia Press, 1995.

Qishier jia piping Chuci jizhu 七十二家批評楚辭集注. Original title *Chuci jizhu* 楚辭集注. Originally compiled by Zhu Xi 朱熹 (1130–1200). Additional commentary compiled by Jiang Zhiqiao 蔣之翹 (Ming dynasty). Preface 1610. Zhongyatang 忠雅堂, 1626. At Kyōto University Library.

Qu Tuiyuan 瞿蛻園, ed. *Liu Yuxi ji jianzheng* 劉禹錫集箋證. Shanghai: Shanghai guji chubanshe, 1989.

Quan Tang shi 全唐詩. Compiled by Peng Dingqiu 彭定求 et al. 25 vols. Beijing: Zhonghua shuju, 1960, 1979.

Quan Tang wen 全唐文. Compiled by Dong Gao 董誥 (1740–1818) et al. 11 vols. Beijing: Zhonghua shuju, 1983.

Qu ci xisui 屈辭洗髓. Compiled by Xu Huanlong 徐煥龍 (Qing dynasty). 1698 edition. Repr. in *Chuci wenxian congkan*, vol. 48.

Qu fu wei 屈賦微. Compiled by Ma Qichang 馬其昶 (1855–1930). Taipei: Guangwen shuju, 1963.

Qunjing pingyi 群經平議. By Yu Yue 俞樾 (1821–1907). Guangxu printing. In *Chunzaitang quanshu* 春在堂全書. Zhongguo jiben gujiku 中國基本古籍庫. http://er07.com/home/pro_3.html.

Qu Yuan fu zhu 屈原賦注. By Dai Zhen 戴震 (1724–1777). In *Guoxue jiben congshu* 國學基本叢書. Shanghai: The Commercial Press, 1930.

Quzi zhangju 屈子章句. By Liu Mengpeng 劉夢鵬 (b. 1728). *Siku quanshu cunmu congshu* 四庫全書存目叢書. "Jibu" 集部, vol. 2. Jinan: Qi Lu shushe, 1997.

Rao Zongyi ershi shiji xueshu wenji 饒宗頤二十世紀學術文集. 20 vols. Taipei: Xinwenfeng, 2003.

Richter, Matthias. *The Embodied Text: Establishing Textual Identity in Early Chinese Manuscripts.* Leiden: Brill, 2013.
Rickett, W. Allyn. *Guanzi* 管子: *Political, Economic, and Philosophical Essays from Early China.* 2 vols. Princeton: Princeton University Press, 1985 and 1998.
Rolston, David L. *Traditional Chinese Fiction and Fiction Commentary: Reading Between the Lines.* Stanford: Stanford University Press, 1997.

Schafer, Edward H. "The Idea of Created Nature in T'ang Literature." *Philosophy East and West* 15.2 (1965): 153–60.
Schimmelpfennig, Michael. "The Quest for a Classic: Wang Yi and the Exegetical Prehistory of his Commentary to the *Lisao*." *Early China* 29 (2004): 109–60.
———. "Qu Yuans Weg von 'wahren Menschen' zum wirklichen Dichter: Der Han-zeitliche Kommentar von Wang Yi zum 'Lisao' und den Liedern von Chu." PhD diss. University of Heidelberg, 1999.
———. "Two Ages, One Agenda? Zhu Xi's Rules of Interpretation versus Wang Yi's Exegesis of the Songs of Chu." In *Interpretation and Intellectual Change: Chinese Hermeneutics in Historical Perspective,* ed. Ching-I Tu, 149–62. New Brunswick: Transaction Publishers, 2005.
Schlegel, Gustave. *Uranographie chinoise.* 2 vols. Leiden: Brill, 1875.
Schuessler, Axel. *ABC Etymological Dictionary of Old Chinese.* Honolulu: University of Hawai'i Press, 2007.
Sela, Ori. *China's Philological Turn: Scholars, Textualism, and the Dao in the Eighteenth Century.* New York: Columbia University Press, 2018.
Shandaige zhu Chuci 山帶閣注楚辭. By Jiang Ji 蔣驥. Shanghai: Shanghai guji chubanshe, 1984.
Shangshu zhengyi 尚書正義. In *Shisanjing zhushu* 十三經注疏. Edited by Li Xueqin 李學勤 et al. Beijing: Beijing daxue chubanshe, 2000.
Shaughnessy, Edward L. *Rewriting Early Chinese Texts.* Albany: State University of New York Press, 2006.
———. "Unearthed Documents and the Question of the Oral vs. Written Nature of the 'Classic of Poetry.'" *Harvard Journal of Asiatic Studies* 75 (2015): 331–75.
———. *Unearthing the Changes: Recently Discovered Manuscripts of the Yijing (I Ching) and Related Texts.* Columbia: Columbia University Press, 2014.
Shengyuzhai shiji 聖雨齋詩集. By Zhou Gongchen 周拱辰. Early Qing woodblock print, courtesy of Zhongguo jiben gujiku. Beijing Airusheng shuzihua jishu yanjiu zhongxin 北京愛如生數字化技術研究中心.
Shiben 世本. Punctuated and collated by Zhou Weiqing 周渭卿. In *Diwang shiji, Shiben, Yizhoushu, Guben zhushu jinian* 帝王世紀‧世本‧逸周書‧古本竹書紀年. Jinan: Qi Lu shushe, 2010.
Shi benyin 詩本音. By Gu Yanwu 顧炎武 (1613–1682). *Siku quanshu* 四庫全書. Vol. 241. Taipei: Taiwan shangwu yinshuguan, 1983–1986.

Shiji 史記. By Sima Qian (ca. 145–ca. 86 BCE). Repunctuated edition. 10 vols. Beijing: Zhonghua shuju, 2014.

Shimosada Masahiro 下定雅弘. *Ryū Sōgen: Gyakkyō o ikinuita utsukushiki tamashii* 柳宗元：逆境を生き抜いた美しき魂. Tokyo: Bensei, 2009.

Shirakawa Shizuka 白川静. *Jitō: fukyūban* 字統：普及版. Tokyo: Heibonsha, 1994.

———. *Jitsū* 字通. Tokyo: Heibonsha, 1996.

Shi sanjia yi jishu 詩三家義集疏. Edited by Wang Xianqian 王先謙 (1842–1917). Beijing: Zhonghua shuju, 1987.

Shi yi ji 拾遺記. In *Han Wei congshu* 漢魏叢書. Compiled by Cheng Rong 程榮. Repr. Changchun: Jilin daxue chubanshe, 1992.

Sivin, Nathan. "Copernicus in China." *Colloquia Copernica II: Études sur l'audience de la théorie héliocentrique*. Warsaw: Union Internationale d'Historie et de Philosophie des Sciences, 1973.

Smith, Jonathan Z. *Imagining Religion: From Babylon to Jonestown*. Chicago: University of Chicago Press, 1982.

Strassberg, Richard A. *A Chinese Bestiary: Strange Creatures from the Guideways through Mountains and Seas*. Berkeley: University of California Press, 2018.

Su Hsüeh-lin 蘇雪林 (1897–1999). *Tianwen zhengjian* 天問正簡. 1974. Repr. Taipei: Wenjin chubanshe, 1992.

Sukhu, Gopal. *The Shaman and the Heresiarch: A New Interpretation of the* Li sao. Albany: State University of New York Press, 2012.

———. *Songs of Chu: An Anthology of Ancient Chinese Poetry by Qu Yuan and Others*. New York: Columbia University Press, 2017.

Sun Changwu 孫昌武. *Liu Zongyuan pingzhuan* 柳宗元評傳 (1998). In *Sun Changwu wenji* 孫昌武文集, vol. 5. Beijing: Zhonghua shuju, 2019.

———. *Liu Zongyuan zhuanlun* 柳宗元傳論 (1982). In *Sun Changwu wenji* 孫昌武文集, vol. 1. Beijing: Zhonghua shuju, 2019.

Sun Qiaoyun 孫巧雲. *Yuan Ming Qing Chuci xueshi* 元明清楚辭學史. Hangzhou: Zhejiang gongshang daxue chubanshe, 2013.

Sun Zuoyun 孫作雲. *Tianwen yanjiu* 天問研究. Beijing: Zhonghua shuju, 1989.

T = *Taishō shinshū daizōkyō* 大正新脩大藏經. Edited by Takakusu Junjirō 高楠順次郎 et al. Tokyo: Taishō issaikyō kankōkai, 1924–1935.

Taiping yulan 太平御覽. Compiled by Li Fang 李昉 (925–996). 4 vols. Beijing: Zhonghua shuju, 1960.

Takeji Sadao 竹治貞夫. *Soji kenkyū* 楚辞研究. Tokyo: Kazama shobō, 1978.

Tang Bingzheng 湯炳正. "Chuci chengshu zhi tansuo" 《楚辭》成書之探索. In *Qu fu xintan* 屈賦新探, 85–109. Jinan: Qi Lu shushe, 1984.

———. *Chuci leigao* 楚辭類稿. Chengdu: Ba Shu shushe, 1988.

―― et al., eds. *Chuci xinzhu* 楚辭新注. 2nd ed. Shanghai: Shanghai guji chubanshe, 2012.
Tangchao Wenxuan jizhu huicun 唐鈔文選集注彙存. Shanghai: Shanghai guji chubanshe, 2000.
Taylor, Paul B., and W. H. Auden, trans. *The Elder Edda*. London: Faber and Faber, 1969.
Tianwen buzhu 天問補註. Compiled by Mao Qiling 毛奇齡. Qing woodblock print. Repr. in *Chuci wenxian congkan*, vol. 46.
Tianwen Tiandui jie 天問天對解. By Yang Wanli 楊萬里. Originally published in 1917. Repr. in *Chuci wenxian congkan*, vol. 30.
Tianwen Tiandui yizhu 天問天對譯注. Edited by Jilin shifan daxue lishi xi 吉林師範大學歷史系. Beijing: Renmin chubanshe, 1976.
Tianwen Tiandui zhu 天問天對註. Edited by Fudan daxue zhongwen xi gudian wenxue jiaoyanzu 復旦大學中文系古典文學教研組. Shanghai: Shanghai renmin chubanshe, 1973.
Tozaki Tetsuhiko 戸崎哲彦. "*Ryū Sōgen shū* chū ni mirareru 'jichū' ni kansuru shohonkan no idō ni tsuite" 『柳宗元集』中に見られる"自注"に関する諸本間の異同について. *Shiga daigaku keizai gakubu kenkyū nenpō* 1 (1994): 43–68.
――. "Tōdai chūki ni okeru jukyō shingaku e no teikō: Tenmei, shōzui no shisō o meguru Kan Yu, Ryū Sōgen no tairitsu to sono seijiteki haikei" 唐代中期における儒教神学への抵抗―天命・祥瑞の思想をめぐる韓愈・柳宗元の対立とその政治的背景. *Shiga daigaku keizai gakubu kenkyū nenpō* 3 (1996): 81–122.
Tu, Ching-I, ed. *Interpretation and Intellectual Change: Chinese Hermeneutics in Historical Perspective*. New Brunswick, NJ: Transaction Publishers, 2005.

Van Ess, Hans. "The Apocryphal Texts of the Han Dynasty and the Old Text/New Text Controversy." *T'oung Pao* 85 (1999): 29–64.
Vedal, Nathan. *The Culture of Language in Ming China: Sound, Script, and the Redefinition of Boundaries of Learning*. New York: Columbia University Press, 2022.
Vergnaud, Jean-François. *La Pensée de Gu Yanwu (1613–1682): Essai de synthèse*. Paris: École française d'extrême-orient, 1990.

Waley, Arthur, trans. *The Book of Songs: The Ancient Chinese Classic of Poetry*. Edited with additional translations by Joseph R. Allen. New York: Grove Press, 1996.
Walker, Galal. "Towards a Formal History of the *Chuci*." PhD diss., Cornell University, 1982.

Wang Guoan 王國安, ed. *Liu Zongyuan shi jianshi* 柳宗元詩箋釋. Shanghai: Shanghai guji chubanshe, 2020.

Wang Guowei 王國維. "Yin buci zhong suo jian xiangong xianwang kao" 殷卜辭中所見先公先王考. In *Guantang jilin* 觀堂集林, 9.409–37. Beijing: Zhonghua shuju, 1973.

Wang Guowei yi shu 王國維遺書. 10 vols. Shanghai: Shanghai shudian chubanshe, 2011.

Wang Li 王力. *Chuci yundu* 楚辭韻讀. Shanghai: Shanghai guji chubanshe, 1980.

———. *Tongyuan zidian* 同源字典. Beijing: Zhonghua shuju, 2014.

——— et al., eds. *Wang Li gu Hanyu zidian* 王力古漢語字典. Beijing: Zhonghua shuju, 2000.

Wang Shaoying 汪紹楹, ed. *Soushen ji* 搜神記. By Gan Bao 干寶 (d. 336 CE). Beijing: Zhonghua shuju, 1979.

Wang Shumin 王叔岷 (1914–2008), ed. *Liexian zhuan jiaojian* 列仙傳校箋. Beijing: Zhonghua shuju, 2007.

Wang Xianshen 王先慎, ed. *Han Feizi jijie* 韓非子集解. Beijing: Zhonghua shuju, 1998.

Wang Yiliang 王貽樑 and Chen Jianmin 陳建敏, eds. *Mu tianzi zhuan huijiao jishi* 穆天子傳匯校集釋. Beijing: Zhonghua shuju, 2019.

Wen Yiduo 聞一多. "*Chuci* jiaobu" 楚辭校補. In *Wen Yiduo quanji* 聞一多全集, 5:111–248. Changsha: Hubei renmin chubanshe, 1993.

———. "Tianwen shuzheng" 天問疏證. In *Wen Yiduo quanji*, 5:523–636.

Wenxuan 文選. Compiled by Xiao Tong 蕭統 (501–531). 6 vols. Shanghai: Shanghai guji chubanshe, 2019.

Wilhelm, Hellmut. "Bemerkungen zur T'ien-wen Frage." *Monumenta Serica* 10 (1945): 427–32.

Wilhelm, Richard. *The I Ching or Book of Changes*. Rendered into English by Cary F. Baynes. Princeton: Princeton University Press, 1967.

Wilkinson, Endymion. *Chinese History: A New Manual*. 5th ed. Cambridge, MA: Harvard University Asia Center, 2018.

Williams, Nicholas Morrow. *Chinese Poetry as Soul Summoning: Shamanistic Religious Influences on Chinese Literary Tradition*. Amherst, NY: Cambria Press, 2022.

———. *Elegies of Chu: An Anthology of Early Chinese Poetry*. Oxford: Oxford University Press, 2022.

———. "The Half-Life of Half-Rhyme." *Early Medieval China* 17 (2011): 22–50.

———. *Imitations of the Self: Jiang Yan and Chinese Poetics*. Leiden: Brill, 2015.

———. "The Pity of Spring: A Southern Topos Reimagined by Wang Bo and Li Bai." In *Southern Identity and Southern Estrangement in Medieval Chinese Poetry*, ed. Wang Ping and Nicholas Morrow Williams, 137–63. Hong Kong: Hong Kong University Press, 2015.

———. "Shamans, Souls, and Soma: Comparative Religion and Early China." *Journal of Chinese Religions* 48.2 (2020): 148–73.

———. "Tropes of Entanglement and Strange Loops in the 'Nine Avowals' of the *Chuci*." *Bulletin of the School of Oriental and African Studies* 81.2 (2018): 277–300.

Wu, Hung. *The Wu Liang Shrine: The Ideology of Early Chinese Pictorial Art*. Stanford: Stanford University Press, 1989.

Wubaijia zhu Liu xiansheng ji 五百家註柳先生集. Compiled by Wei Zhongju 魏仲舉. Originally printed 1200. *Siku quanshu zhenben chuji* 四庫全書珍本初集. Vols. 244 and 245. Taipei: Shangwu yinshuguan, 1970.

Xiang Xi 向熹. *Shijing yuyan yanjiu* 詩經語言研究. Chengdu: Sichuan renmin chubanshe, 1987.

Xiang Zonglu 向宗魯, ed. *Shuoyuan jiaozheng* 說苑校證. Beijing: Zhonghua shuju, 1987.

Xiao Ai 蕭艾, ed. *Wang Guowei shici jianjiao* 王國維詩詞箋校. Changsha: Hunan renmin chubanshe, 1984.

Xiao Bing 蕭兵. *Chuci xintan* 楚辭新探. Tianjin: Tianjin guji chubanshe, 1988.

Xie Jun 謝君. *Zhu Xi Chuci xue yanjiu* 朱熹楚辭學研究. Hong Kong: Zhongguo guwenxian chubanshe, 2014.

Xihe jingyi cunchun 西河經義存醇. By Mao Qiling 毛奇齡. Compiled by Ma Junliang 馬俊良. In *Longwei mishu*, collection #8. Kyōto University Library.

Xu Sumin 徐蘇民. *Gu Yanwu pingzhuan* 顧炎武評傳. Nanjing: Nanjing daxue chubanshe, 2007.

Xu Weishan liuzhong 徐位山六種. 1876 printing. Kyōto University, Jinbunken.

Xu Weiyu 許維遹, ed. *Lüshi chunqiu jishi* 呂氏春秋集釋. 2 vols. Beijing: Zhonghua shuju, 2009.

Xu Yuangao 徐元誥, ed. *Guoyu jijie* 國語集解. Rev. ed. Beijing: Zhonghua shuju, 2002.

Yang Bo 楊博. *Zhanguo Chu zhushu shixue jiazhi tanyan* 戰國楚竹書史學價值探研. Shanghai: Shanghai guji chubanshe, 2019.

Yang Bojun 楊伯峻, ed. *Liezi jishi* 列子集釋. Beijing: Zhonghua shuju, 2018.

Yasui Kōzan 安居香山. *Isho no seiritsu to sono tenkai* 緯書の成立とその展開. Tokyo: Kokusho kankō-kai, 1979.

Yasui Kōzan 安居香山 and Nakamura Shōhachi 中村璋八. *Jūshū isho shūsei* 重修緯書集成. Tokyo: Meitoku shuppansha, 1980.

Yiqie jing yinyi 一切經音義. T 2128: 54.793a.

Yishi 繹史. Compiled by Ma Su 馬驌 (1621–1673). *Siku quanshu* 四庫全書. Vols. 365–68. Taipei: Taiwan shangwu yinshuguan, 1983–1986.

Yiwen leiju 藝文類聚. Shanghai: Shanghai guji chubanshe, 1982.

Yi Zhou shu huijiao jizhu 逸周書彙校集注. Edited by Huang Huaixin 黃懷信, Zhang Maorong 張懋鎔, and 田旭東. Shanghai: Shanghai guji chubanshe, 2007.

You Guoen 游國恩 et al., eds. *Tianwen zuanyi* 天問纂義. Beijing: Zhonghua shuju, 1982.

Yu, Pauline. *The Reading of Imagery in the Chinese Poetic Tradition*. Princeton: Princeton University Press, 1987.

Yu Xingwu 于省吾. *Zeluoju Chuci xinzheng* 澤螺居楚辭新證. In *Yu Xingwu zhuzuo ji* 于省吾著作集, vol. 10. Beijing: Zhonghua shuju, 2009.

Yu Yue 俞樾 (1821–1907). "*Chuci* renming kao" 楚辭人名考. In *Yu lou zazuan* 俞樓襍纂, 30.569–88. In *Yu Yue quanji*. Nanjing: Fenghuang chubanshe, 2021.

———. *Chunzaitang zawen* 春在堂襍文. 43 *juan*. 1899 edition. Zhongguo jiben gujiku.

———. "Du *Chuci*" 讀楚辭. In *Yu lou zazuan* 俞樓襍纂, 24.423–40. Nanjing: Fenghuang chubanshe, 2021.

———. *Yu Yue quanji* 俞樾全集, 32 vols. Nanjing: Fenghuang chubanshe, 2020–2021.

Yuan Ke 袁珂. "*Chuci yu shenhua* duhou: Jianlun 'Tianwen' 'Qi ji bin shang' siyu de zhenggu" 《楚辭與神話》讀後———兼論「天問」「啓棘賓商」四語的正詁. *Sixiang zhanxian* 1988.6: 53–56.

———, ed. *Shanhaijing jiaozhu* 山海經校注. Beijing: Beijing lianhe, 2014.

Zengguang zhushi yinbian Tang Liu xiansheng ji 增廣註釋音辯唐柳先生集. Edited by Tong Zongshuo 童宗說 et al. *Sibu congkan* 四部叢刊. Shanghai: Shangwu yinshuguan, 1929.

Zha Pingqiu 查屏球. *Tangxue yu Tangshi: Zhong wan Tang shifeng de yizhong wenhua kaocha* 唐學與唐詩：中晚唐詩風的一種文化考察. Beijing: Shangwu yinshuguan, 2000.

———. "Wenxue de chanshi yu chanshi de wenxue: Guanyu Wang Yi *Chuci zhangju* yunti zhuwen de kaolun" 文學的闡釋與闡釋的文學———關於王逸《楚辭章句》韻體注文的考論. *Wenxue pinglun* 2008.2: 133–38.

Zhang Guodong 張國棟. "Cong 'Tianwen' 'Tiandui' kan Qu Yuan yu Liu Zongyuan de bianzhe xintai" 從〈天問〉〈天對〉看屈原與柳宗元的貶謫心態. *Gansu guangbo dianshi daxue xuebao* 17.3 (2007): 3–5.

Zhang Lianke 張連科. *Wang Guowei yu Luo Zhenyu* 王國維與羅振玉. Tianjin: Tianjin renmin chubanshe, 2002.

Zhang Shuguo 張樹國. "Cong Wu Zixu tuyong lun 'Tianwen' chuangzuo shidi wenti" 從伍子胥圖詠論〈天問〉創作時地問題. *Zhejiang xuekan* 2018.2: 183–95.

———. "Han chu libian *Chuci* yu *Shiji*, 'Qu Yuan Jia sheng liezhuan' de cailiao laiyuan" 漢初隸變楚辭與《史記・屈原賈生列傳》的材料來源. *Zhonghua wenshi luncong* 2018.1: 66–99.

Zhang Yanying 張燕嬰, ed. *Yu Yue shiwen ji* 俞樾詩文集. 7 vols. Beijing: Renmin wenxue chubanshe, 2022.

Zhang Yong 張勇. *Liu Zongyuan Ru Fo Dao sanjiao guan xinlun* 柳宗元儒佛道三教觀新論. Beijing: Zhonghua shuju, 2020.

Zheng Zhenduo 鄭振鐸. *Zhongguo wenxueshi* 中國文學史. Beijing: Beiping pushe, 1932.

Zhiningtang gao 志甯堂稿. By Xu Wenjing 徐文靖. In *Qingdai shiwen ji huibian* 清代詩文集彙編, vol. 220. Shanghai: Shanghai guji chubanshe, 2010.

Zhouyi jijie zuanshu 周易集解纂疏. Compiled by Li Daoping 李道平. Punctuated by Pan Yuting 潘雨廷. Beijing: Zhonghua shuju, 1994, 2004.

Zhouyi zhengyi 周易正義. In *Shisanjing zhushu* 十三經注疏. Edited by Li Xueqin 李學勤. Beijing: Beijing daxue chubanshe, 2000.

Zhu Junsheng 朱駿聲. *Shuowen tongxun dingsheng* 說文通訓定聲. Beijing: Zhonghua shuju, 1984.

Zhuangzi jishi 莊子集釋. Edited by Guo Qingfan 郭慶藩 (1844–1896?). Punctuated by Wang Xiaoyu 王孝魚. Beijing: Zhonghua shuju, 2016.

Zhushu jinian tongjian 竹書紀年統箋. By Xu Wenjing 徐文靖. 1873. Repr. Taipei: Yiwen yinshuguan, 1966.

Index

Figures are indicated by *italicized* page references.

Accounts of the States. See *Guoyu*
"Against the *Accounts of the States*" ("Fei Guoyu") (Liu Zongyuan), 157, 160, 170
Allan, Sarah, 260
"All Things Change Their Forms" ("Fan wu liu xing"), 315–16
älteste Dokument zur chinesischen Kunstgeschichte, Das (Conrady and Erkes), 31
Analects, 96, 96n37; Yu Yue and, 286
Annals of Gods and Kings (*Diwang shiji*), 110n67, 198n71, 231, 235, 302
Annals of Lü Buwei (*Lüshi chunqiu*) (Knoblock and Riegel), 8, 38, 106n58, 107n60, 204n88, 279, 294–95
Ao, 70, 95, 96n37; in *Analects*, 96; Lady Tangent and, 96, 155, 286–87; Shaokang and, 219, 287; Xiahou Xiang and, 200n79; Zhenxun and, 219
Asano Yūichi, 316n12
Ast, Friedrich, 218n4
Atemwende (*Breath-turn*) (Celan), 312–14
Azure Dragon, 180, 180n12

Bamboo Annals (*Zhushu jinian*), 7, 8–9, 8n15, 71; *Book of Documents* and, 237; Earl Gong in, 305–6; "Heavenly Questions" and, 234–43; on King Zhao, 297; Mount Meng in, 287; in Qing dynasty, 13, 222, 234–43; Shang and, 236; Shangjia Wei in, 293–94; Wang Gai and, 294; on Xia dynasty heroes, 280; Xu Wenjing and, 241, 242, 256
Ban Gu, 110n68. See also *Hanshu*
Bao Si, 206n92, 207n93, 298
Baxter, William H., 50, 65–67

Bi Gan, 60, 113, 299; Zhow and, 300
Bin, Mount, 115, 115n76
Biographies of the Transcendents, 95
"Birth of the People, The" ("Sheng min"), 139, 209n97, 300–301
Blackwater, 277
Bokenkamp, Stephen, 188n40
Book of Changes (*Yijing*), 10; Liu Zongyuan and, 176n3; Xu Wenjing and, 238
Book of Documents, 189n44; *Bamboo Annals* and, 237; Blackwater in, 277; on formation of world, 277; "Heavenly Questions" and, 237; Hong Xingzu and, 239; Huang Linggeng and, 279; Liu Zongyuan and, 150; particle *yue* in, 265; Shun in, 293; "Song of the Five Brothers" in, 281; on Tang, 219; "Tribute of Yu" in, 182n22; Wang Fuzhi and, 265; on Xia dynasty heroes, 279
"Book of Job," 262–63
Book of Odes. See *Shijing*
Book of Rites, 275
Boqiang (Sire of Might), 179, 179n11, 268–69
Boxer Rebellion, 6
Bo Yang, 207n93
Bo Yi, 121n85, 306
Bo Yikao, 302
Breath-turn (*Atemwende*) (Celan), 312–14
Broken Mountain, 274
Buddhism: Duke Zhuang and, 131n17; Jiang Yan and, 131–32; Liu Zongyuan and, 168, 172, 172n106
Bujiang, 188, 188n39

340   Index

Cao Jianguo, 44n56
Celan, Paul, 312–14
Chan, Timothy W. K., 28, 36, 41
Chang'e (Chang Yi), 22; Ding Yan on, 249; on formation of universe, 268
Chaos, 31
Chen Jo-shui, 133n19, 135n25
Chen Weisong, 45
Cheng, King. *See* King Cheng
Cheng Hung To, 44
Cheng Tang. *See* Tang (Shang dynasty founder)
"Chen lao" ("Journey's Woes") (Wang Guowei), 14
Ch'ien Mu, 244
"Chi jiu zhi ji tang zhi wu" ("When Red Pigeons Gathered on Tang's House"), 291
Chinese Theories of Reading and Writing (Gu Ming Dong), 16n38
"Chousi" ("Unraveled Yearnings"), 42–43
Chuci (*Elegies of Chu*), 2; authorship of, 40–46; "Chousi" ("Unraveled Yearnings"), 42–43; Du Heng on, 72, 72n119; "Embracing the Sand" ("Huai sha"), 24; on formation of world, 276; "Great Summons" ("Dazhao") of, 59; *Guancheng shuoji* and, 239; *Guangya shuzheng* and, 246–47; in Han dynasty, 26, 40–67, 73; "Heavenly Questions" and, 15, 22, 25–40, 47, 49–50, 55–58, 59, 60, 127, 145, 148, 175, 228; Hong Xingzu and, 221; Huang Linggeng and, 43n53; Jiang Yan and, 129; Liu Xiang and, 26–27; Liu Zongyuan and, 133, 138, 151–52, 276–77; "Nine Longings" ("Jiuhuai"), 44; "Nine Yearnings" ("Jiusi"), 43, 45–46; in Qing dynasty, 244; Qu Yuan and, 27, 47, 55–58, 68–69; rhyme scheme of, 66–67; *Shijing* and, 51; Wang Guowei on, 12n32; Wang Yi and, 25–42, 40n45, 44, 45; Xu Wenjing and, 241; on Yi Yin, 291; You Guoen and, 251; Yu Yue and, 250; Zhou Gongchen and, 230; Zhu Xi and, 221. *See also* "Heavenly Questions"; "Nine Phases"; "Nine Songs"; "Sublimating Sorrow"; "Summons to the Soul"
"Chuci bianzheng" (Zhu Xi), 53n81
Chuci buzhu, 309; *Chuci shiwen* and, 27n14; Hong Xingzu and, 27, 49–50; Liu Xiang and, 26n12
"Chuci in the Mountains" ("Shan zhong Chuci") (Jiang Yan), 129
Chuci jizhu (Zhu Xi), 44n55, 53n81
Chuci shiwen: *Chuci buzhu* and, 27n14; of Tang dynasty, 148n53
Chuci shu (Lu Shiyong), 229
Chuci Tianwen jian (Ding Yan), 249
Chuci tingzhi (Huang Wenhuan), 228–29
Chuci tuzhu (Xiao Yuncong), 143, 153
Chuci wenxian congkan (Huang Linggeng), 253
Chuci zhangju shuzheng (Huang Linggeng), 253
Chunqiu (Spring and autumn annals), 156–57, 156n67, 162
Chunqiu Guliang zhuan zhushu (*Guliang zhuan*), 187n36
Chunqiu yuanming bao, 235, 235n52
Cinnabar Caves, 308
Classic of Mountains and Seas, 7, 8–10, 188n39; on geography of world, 275–76; Gun in, 271; in Qing dynasty, 237–38; Responding Dragon in, 272; on Shang dynasty, 9–10; Wang Hai and, 242
Collingwood, R. G., 18
Confucianism, 41, 55; of Gun, 181n18; Liu Zongyuan and, 135n25, 136, 168, 172, 181n18; philology in, 243; in Qing dynasty, 243, 244; Three Teachings of, 168, 172; The Way of, 60n99, 135n25. *See also* Neoconfucianism
Conrady, August, 31, 59, 260, 299
Cui Wenzi, 52n79, 94, 161–62, 194n62; Prince Qiao and, 51–52
Cultural Revolution, 134–35

Dai Tong, 223
Dai Zhen, 244–46; on "Heavenly Questions," 245–46; Liao Tung-ling and, 244n83; on "Sublimating Sorrow," 245
Da Ji, 113n72, 116, 302
"Daming" ("Great Illumination"), 164, 295
Dan, Lord, 296
Dan Zhu, 156
Daoism, 22; aims of, 188n40; in Han dynasty, 120n83, 161; "Heavenly Questions" and, 261; "Heavenly Responses" and, 168
"Dark Bird" ("Xuan niao"), 260, 292
Dark Dragon, 268–69
"Da Wei Zhongli lun shidao shu" (Liu Zongyuan), 144n45
"Dazhao" ("Great Summons"), 59
Declercq, Dominik, 136n28
Demiéville, Paul, 261
Deng, Empress Dowager, 41
"Determination of the Tallies of Divination" ("Zhenfu") (Liu Zonghuan), 162
Di, 11n30; Tang and, 291; Yi and, 104n65, 111, 120
Dimming Wood, 274
Ding Yan, 53, 248–49, 284
"Disquisition on Abolishing Punishments" ("Duanxing lun") (Liu Zongyuan), 167
"Divination" ("Buju"), 136
Diwang shiji (Annals of gods and kings), 110n67, 198n71, 231, 235, 302
Dou Bobi, 56n90, 309
Dou Gouwutu. See Ziwen
Dowager Deng, Empress, 41
Dragon Earl, 195n65
Du Heng, 41–42; on *Chuci zhangju*, 72, 72n119
"Duanxing lun" ("Disquisition on Abolishing Punishments") (Liu Zongyuan), 167
Duao, 34–35, 34n37, 39
"Dui hezhe" ("Responding to One Who Congratulated Me") (Liu Zongyuan), 136

Duke Huan, 112–13, 207n94; Guan Zhong and, 298–99
Duke of Qin, 122n86, 307
Duke of Zhou ("The Sire of the West"), 73, 108, 108n64, 208n96, 296; King Cheng and, 297, 303; in *Shujing*, 297
Duke Xiang, 219, 282, 283; Yu Yue on, 250
Duke Zhao, 93n33, 122n86, 193n60, 307
Duke Zhuang: Buddhism and, 131n17; in *Zuozhuan*, 34n37
Durrant, Stephen, 282
"Dushu" ("On Reading") (Liu Zongyuan), 146–48

Earl Gong, 305–6
Eight Pillars, 267
Eight Sacred Mountains, 171
Elegies of Chu. See *Chuci*
Elman, Benjamin, 221–22, 234, 243
"Embracing the Sand" ("Huai sha"), 24
Emperor Shunzong, 132–33
Emperor Yao, 120
Empress Dowager Deng, 41
"Encomium to the Tangerine" ("Ju song"), 59n95
Erkes, Eduard, 31, 59
Erya, 246, 275

Fang Shiming, 9n20, 237
Fangyan (Yang Xiong), 246
"Fan wu liu xing" ("All Things Change Their Forms"), 315–16
"Far Roaming," 130, 152n60
"Fei *Guoyu*" ("Against the *Annals of the State*") (Liu Zongyuan), 157, 160, 170
Feng, Mount, 86, 86n19, 187, 187n36
Field, Stephen, 171
"Fisherman" ("Yufu"), 24, 136
Five Classics (*Wujing zhengyi*), 129, 222
Four Books, 222
Four Marchmounts, 269
"Four Steeds" ("Simu"), 308
From Philosophy to Philology (Elman), 243
Fuxi, 98–99, 197, 234, 289

Gadamer, Hans-Georg, 16–18, 16n38, 33, 142, 217; on Celan, 312–14; *Truth and Method* by, 1, 18, 21, 126, 216, 311; *Who Am I and Who Are You* by, 312
"Gate to the Tombs" ("Mu men"), 202n83
"Gathering Vetch," 306–7
Ge, 196, 196n67, 239n63, 283
Geibun zasshi, 8
Gong Bo, 71
Gonggong, 272
Grand Altar, 209, 209n97
"Great Illumination" ("Daming"), 164, 295
"Great Summons" ("Dazhao"), 59
Gu, Lord, 198n72
Gu Ming Dong, 16n38
Gu Yanwu, 223; rhyme scheme of, 276; Wang Yangming and, 223n19
Guan Zhong, 112; Duke Huan and, 298–99; in *Shiji*, 298–99
Guancheng (Shaft Citadel), 240–41
Guancheng shuoji, 238, 239–40; King Wu and, 303; Xu Wenjing and, 243
Guangya (Zhang Yi), 246
Guangya shuzheng (Wang Niansun), 246–47, 284
Guanshu Xian, 241, 303
Guantang jilin (Wang Guowei), 8
Guanzhui bian (Qian Zhongshu), 240, 240n71
Guben Zhushu jinian jizheng (Fang Shiming and Wang Xiuling), 9n20
Gugong Danfu, 116, 302
Guicang, 270–71
Guliang zhuan (*Chunqiu Guliang zhuan zhushu*), 187n36
Gun, 52; Confucianism of, 181n18; great flood by, 2, 55, 80–84, 269–72; in "Heavenly Responses," 159–60, 159n78, 171; as *huangxiong*, 93, 158; Yao and, 92–93
Guo Moruo, 279
Guo Pu, 285
Guoxue congkan, 253–54
Guoyu (*Accounts of the States*), 157–58, 231; on King You, 298

Hai, Prince, 292. *See also* Wang Hai
Hamaguchi Fujio, 243, 243n80
Han Chun, 145
Han Yu, 240
Han Zhuo, 282
Han dynasty: *Bambo Annals* in, 236; *Chuci zhangju* in, 26, 40–67, 73; *Chunqiu yuanming bao* from, 235n52; Daoism in, 120n83, 161; on formation of universe, 266, 267; on geography of world, 273; "Heavenly Questions" in, 2, 4, 7, 8, 13, 18, 21–22, 25–26, 28–29, 31–34, 37, 47–125, 141n41, 218, 230; "Sublimating Sorrow" in, 127; Yin-Yang cosmology in, 29n19, 80, 94
Han Feizi, 120n84, 141n41
"Hanging Gardens," 273–74
Hanshi waizhuan, 37
Hanshu: Liu Xiang in, 26n12; Wang Gai in, 8; Ying Shao and, 52n79
Hao Yixing, 233n45
Hawkes, David, 59, 59n92, 67, 260
"Heavenly Questions": archetypes in, 67–74; *Bamboo Annals* and, 234–43; *Book of Documents* and, 237; Celan and, 312–14; *Chuci* and, 15, 22, 25–40, 47, 49–50, 55–58, 59, 60, 127, 145, 148, 175, 228; Dai Zhen on, 245–46; Daoism and, 261; earliest interpretations of, 21–125; formation of universe in, 265–69; on geography of world, 272–77; Gun in, 181n18; in Han dynasty, 2, 4, 7, 8, 13, 18, 21–22, 25–26, 28–29, 31–34, 37, 47–125, 141n41, 218, 230; heroes from age of floods in, 269–72; *Huainanzi* and, 60; irregularities in, 64–65; Jiang Liangfu and, 251–52; Jiang Yan and, 129–32; linguistic analysis of archaicity in, 59–67; Liu Xiang and, 36, 40, 46; Liu Zongyuan and, 4, 12–13, 19, 126–215; in Ming dynasty, 19, 229–30; modern interpretation of, 216–317; mural thesis in, 31–33, 35, 73; in Qin dynasty, 6, 21, 49; in Qing dynasty, 6, 13, 19, 49, 102n50, 129, 218, 221–24, 226–28, 236–38, 243–63;

Qu Yuan and, 5–6, 11–19, 24, 27, 29–31, 33–40, 51–52, 55–58, 59, 67–74, 72n119, 121–23, 125, 152–56, 217, 219, 227, 229, 230, 310; rhyme scheme of, 65–66; sense of the whole for, 225–34; on Shang dynasty, 2, 6–7, 24, 37–38, 54, 71, 237, 290–95; *Shijing* and, 63–66; in Song dynasty, 19, 148, 218–19, 237; "Sublimating Sorrow" and, 67; in Tang dynasty, 4, 7, 12, 129, 134–35; Text One of, 75–125; Text Three of, 264–310; Text Two of, 175–215; on virtue through the ages, 300–307; Wang Guowei and, 255–56; Wang Niansun and, 246, 248–49; Wang Yi and, 36–37, 38, 39, 40, 44, 46; in Xia dynasty, 2, 54, 230, 278–90; Xu Wenjing and, 242–43; Yang Xiong and, 36, 40, 46; You Guoen and, 251; on Zhou dynasty, 2, 32, 54, 237
"Heavenly Responses" ("Tiandui") (Liu Zongyuan), 128, 132–44; Cultural Revolution and, 134–35; Daoism and, 168; as dialogue with Heaven, 166–74; Gun in, 159–60, 159n78, 171; Jiang Yan and, 130–32; opening lines of, 137–38; in Song dynasty, 145; on superstition, 156–66; of Tang dynasty, 138n31; on Zhou conquest, 162–64
"Heavenly Revolutions" ("Tianyun"), 258–59, 316
heaven speaks (*tian yu*) (Wang Guowei), 15
Hebo (Sire of the Yellow River), 9, 9n17, 10, 91, 91n31; Shang and, 281
Heinemann, Richard, 312
Heir and the Sage, The (Allan), 260
Helu, King. *See* King Helu
"Hen fu" ("Rhapsody on Bitter Regret") (Jiang Yan), 132
hermeneutics, 1–19, 16n38, 85n15; You Guoen and, 225; Zhou Gongchen and, 232
Hessler, Peter, 6n9
Hetu kuodi xiang, 86n19
"Hollow of Return" ("Guixu"), 183n24
Hong Xingzu, 148, 218–19, 271, 305–6, 309;

Book of Documents and, 239; *Chuci buzhu* and, 27, 49–50; *Chuci zhangju* and, 221
Horn Portal, 269
Hou Hanshu, 40, 40n45
Hou Ji (Lord Millet), 114–15, 114n73, 138, 139, 300–301
Hu Qiuhua, 14n34
Huai, King, 148, 155
Huainanzi, 84n14, 88; on formation of universe, 266, 267; on geography of world, 273–74; "Heavenly Questions" and, 60; Liu Zongyuan and, 184n27; on Xi dynasty heroes, 278; Yu in, 233n45
"Huai sha" ("Embracing the Sand"), 24
Huan, Duke. *See* Duke Huan
Huang Linggeng, 3, 27, 39; *Book of Documents* and, 279; *Chuci wenxian congkan* by, 253; *Chuci zhangju* and, 43n53; *Chuci zhangju shuzheng* by, 253; on Daoism, 120n83; on Shun, 288, 290; "Sublimating Sorrow" and, 43n54; on Tang, 287
Huang Wenhuan, 228–29
Huangfu Mi, 110n67, 198n71, 231, 235
Huangwang daji, 300
huangxiong, 283–84; Gun as, 93, 158
Huo, Mount, 233n45

"Idea of Created Nature, The" (Schafer), 168n100
Interpretation and Intellectual Change (Tu Ching-I), 16n38
Ishikawa Misao, 68
Isle of Fire, 186, 186n31

Jao Tsung-i, 257–58, 261
Jauss, Hans Robert, 25
Jia Yi, 23
Jian Di, 101, 101n47, 200, 241, 259, 291–92
Jiang Ji, 300
Jiang Liangfu, 251–52, 307
Jiang Yan, 129–32; Buddhism and, 131–32
Jiang Yougao, 248
Jiang Yuan, 114, 114n73, 302
Jiang Zhiqiao, 281

"Jiang xue" ("Snow on the River") (Liu Zongyuan), 173
Jiao Ge, 107, 163–64, 163n88; King Wu and, 205n89
Jili, 290
Jin, Marquis of, 158
Jin Shengtan, 226
Jin dynasty, 236
Jingyan shiyi (Xu Wenjing), 238, 239
Jinshu, 236
"Jiubian." See "Nine Phases"
"Jiuhuai" (Nine Longings), 44
"Jiusi" ("Nine Yearnings"), 43, 45–46
"Jiuzhang" ("Nine Avowals"), 24
Jizi, 288
"Journey's Woes" ("Chen Iao") (Wang Guowei), 14
"Ju song" ("Encomium to the Tangerine"), 59n95

Karlgren, Bernhard, 66
Keightley, David N., 11, 11n30
Kennedy, George, 53n80, 63–64
Kern, Martin, 33, 33n35
King Cheng, 110, 241; Duke of Zhou and, 296–97, 303; Guanshu Xian and, 303
King Helu, 56–58, 119–20, 119n81, 123, 124, 212n106; Liu Zongyuan on, 150n56; personal name Guang of, 308
King Huai, 148, 155
King Li, 141n42, 306
King Liao, 119, 123n87, 212n106, 304, 309
King Mu, 34, 110–111, 110n69; Spirit Mother of the West and, 206n91, 297–98
King of Chu, 122–24, 237
King Ping, 309
King Wen, 114, 115, 115n75, 116; Lü Wang and, 303; Mandate of Heaven and, 100; Shang and, 302; Zhow and, 302
King Wu, 107–9, 107n62, 108nn63–64, 109n66, 117, 139, 210n103; Guanshu xian and, 241; *Guancheng shuoji* and, 303; Jiao Ge and, 205n89; King of Chu and, 123–24; Liu Mengpeng on, 296; Liu Zongyuan on, 164–65; Qi and, 115; Shang and, 301, 303; in *Shiji*, 303; Su Shi on, 233n46; Zhou dynasty and, 295
King You, 111–12, 206, 206n92, 207n93; *Guoyu* on, 298
King Zhao, 54, 56, 68, 110, 124, 239; *Bamboo Annals* on, 297
Kinoshita Tetsuya, 244
Knoblock, John, 8, 38, 106n58, 107n60, 204n88, 279, 294–95
Kominami Ichirō, 3, 31n28, 42, 44, 48
Konfuzianisches Ethos und westliche Wissenschaft (Hu Qinhua), 14n34
Krajewski, Bruce, 312
Ku, Lord, 101, 101n47, 200, 241, 259, 291–92
Kuodi xiang, 86n19

Lady Li, 117–18, 117n77, 118n78
Lady Tangent (Lady Qi), 69–70, 155n65, 179n10; Ao and, 96, 155, 286–87; Change Yi and, 268; on formation of universe, 268–69; Shaokang and, 287
Lady Xu, 270
"Lamenting Ying" ("Ai Ying"), 24
Lamont, H. G., 167
"Langu shi" ("Reflecting on History") (Zhou Gongchen), 232–33
Laozi, 299
"Lay of Vafthrudnir," 261
Lei Kai, 60, 113, 300
Li Fang-kuei, 66
Li, King, 141n42, 306
Li Shan, 86n19; on *Wenxuan*, 129, 306
Li Xueqin, 10, 12
Liao, King, 123n87, 304, 309
Liao Tung-liang, 45; Dai Zhen and, 244n83
Liexian zhuan, 52n79, 95; Peng Zu in, 305
Liexian zhuan jiaojian, 52n79, 94n34, 305
Liezi, 183n24, 195n65, 286
Liji zhengyi, 209n98
Lin Geng, 3, 48n70, 50n75, 268, 272
Lingyin, 309
"Lisao." See "Sublimating Sorrow"
Liu An, Prince, 28, 28n18, 273

Liu Chenweng, 22
Liu E, 6
Liu Hedong ji, 145
Liu Kui, 285
Liu Mengpeng, 290; on King Wu, 296
Liu Pansui, 293–94
Liu Tsung-yüan (Chen Jo-shui), 133n19
Liu Xiang: *Chuci buzhu* and, 26n12; *Chuci zhangju* and, 26–27; in *Hanshu*, 26n12; "Heavenly Questions" and, 36, 40, 46
Liu Yuxi, 142n44
Liu Zongyuan, 4, 12–13, 19, 126–215, 218, 232; "Against the *Annals of the State*" by, 157, 160, 170; atheism of, 179n10; *Book of Changes* and, 176n3; *Book of Documents* and, 150; Buddhism and, 168, 172, 172n106; *Chuci zhangju* and, 133, 138, 151–52, 276–77; Confucianism and, 135n25, 136, 168, 172, 181n18; "Da Wei Zhongli lun shidao shu" by, 144n45; "Determination of the Tallies of Divination" by, 162; "Disquisition on Abolishing Punishments" by, 167; *Guoyu* and, 157–58; *Huainanzi* and, 184n27; on King Helu, 150n56; on King Wu, 164–65; Mandate of Heaven and, 165; on Prince Qiao, 316–17; Qu Yuan and, 133, 148, 152–56, 155n64, 212n106; "On Reading" by, 146–48; "Responding to One Who Congratulated Me" by, 136; Shang and, 162–63, 210n103; "Snow on the River" by, 173; "Sublimating Sorrow" and, 155n64, 178n7; on Wang Hai, 292; Wang Yi and, 161, 188n41, 194n62; Yin-Yang cosmology and, 176n3; Zhou Gongchen and, 233; on Zhow, 164–65. *See also* "Heavenly Responses"
Liu Zongyuan zhuanlun (Sun Changwu), 133n19
Lord Dan, 296
Lord Gu, 198n72
Lord Ku, 101, 101n47, 200, 241, 259, 291–92
Lord Millet (Hou Ji), 114–15, 114n73, 138, 139, 300–301
Lord Zhu (Di Zhu), 241, 242; Yi and, 283
Lu Chun, 156, 156n67
Lu Jui-ching, 72n120
Lu Shiyong, 225, 229
Lü Wang, 107, 117, 210, 210n102; King Wen and, 303
"Lu Linguang dian fu" ("Rhapsody on the Hall of Numinous Blessings in Lu") (Wang Yanshou), 31–32
Luo Zhenyu, 7; *Guoxue congkan* and, 253–54
Lüshi chunqiu (*Annals of Lü Buwei*) (Knoblock and Riegel), 8, 38, 106n58, 107n60, 204n88, 279, 294–95

Ma Qichang, 305
Magus Xian, 261
Mair, Victor H., 261
Man, Paul de, 25
Mandate of Heaven, 23, 112–13, 118, 171, 207, 298; King Wen and, 100; Liu Zongyuan and, 165; at Meng Ford, 108; in Shang dynasty, 24, 164
Mao Qiling, 234–35
Mao Ying, 240
Maoshi qunjing Chuci guyunpu (Wang Niansun), 248
Marquis of Jin, 158
Mencius, 190n43, 190n46, 199nn74–75; Shun in, 288
Meng, Mount, 231, 287
Meng Ford, 108, 108n63
"Mian" ("Spreading"), 302
Miao Clan, 293
Millet, Lord (Hou Ji), 114–15, 114n73, 138, 139, 300–301
Ming dynasty: *Bamboo Annals* in, 236; *Chuci shu* in, 229; "Heavenly Questions" in, 19, 229–30; Neoconfucianism in, 221, 221n13; printing in, 222
Minimal Old Chinese (OCM), 50, 50n76
Mogan, Mount, 86n19, 187n36
Mountain of the Mad, 185, 195n29
Mount Bin, 115, 115n76

Mount Feng, 86, 86n19, 187, 187n36
Mount Huo, 233n45
Mount Meng, 231; in *Bamboo Annals*, 287
Mount Mogan, 86n19, 187n36
Mount Qi, 115, 115n76, 302
Mount Shouyang, 306
Mount Song, 281
Mount Triperil, 277
Mount Yu, 86, 86n19, 187, 187n36
Moxi, 231, 232
Mu, King. *See* King Mu
"Mu men" ("Gate to the Tombs"), 202n83
mural thesis, 31–33, 35, 73
Mu tianzi zhuan, 297–98

Naitō Konan, 8
Nanzhong zhi, 285
Neoconfucianism, 217n2; in Ming dynasty, 221, 221n13; philology and, 221n13; of Song dynasty, 244
"Neo-Confucianism and Neo-Legalism in T'ang Intellectual Life" (Pulleyblank), 156n66
Nienhauser, William H., 133n19
"Nine Avowals" ("Jiuzhang"), 24
Nine Continents, 83, 183, 272–73
Nine Heavens, 177, 177n5, 266
"Nine Longings" ("Jiuhuai"), 44
"Nine Phases" ("Jiubian"), 45, 90; Qu Yuan and, 59, 59n92
"Nine Songs," 9n17, 90; on formation of universe, 268–69; Jiang Yan and, 130–31; Wang Yi and, 44
"Nine Yearnings" ("Jiusi"), 43, 45–46
Nivison, David, 237
Nü Deng (Lady Deng), 235
Nü Qi. *See* Lady Tangent
Nü Wa, 235, 289

OCM. *See* Minimal Old Chinese
Old Possum's Book of Practical Cats, 72n119
"On Reading" ("Dushu") (Liu Zongyuan), 146–48
Oracle Bones (Hessler), 6n9
Owen, Stephen, 133n19

Peng Keng, 120, 305
philology, 18; in Confucianism, 243; history and, 217; of Neoconfucianism, 221n13; of Qing dynasty, 221n13, 234, 236, 237, 243–53; on Qu Yuan, 72; Zhu Xi and, 220
Ping, King, 309
pingyi, 247, 285
Plato, 18
Plume Mountain, 270
"Poems in Diverse Forms" ("Zati shi") (Jiang Yan), 129
Prince Hai, 292
Prince Liu An, 28, 28n18, 273
Prince of Qin, 122, 213, 213n109
Prince Qiao, 161, 194n62, 285, 315; Cui Wenzi and, 51–52; Ding Yan on, 249; Liu Zongyuan and, 316–17
Prince Shensheng, 117n77, 118n78, 241
Pulleyblank, Edwin G., 60–61, 140, 154, 156n66
Pure Fox, 282

Qi (son of Yu), 189n44, 190n46; in *Book of Documents*, 279; King Wu and, 115; Shang and, 90; Yi and, 89; Youhu Clan and, 89, 103; Yu and, 90, 280, 281
Qi, Mount, 115, 115n76, 302
Qian, 122, 122n86, 213, 213n109, 307
Qian Zhongshu, 240, 240n71
Qianlong Emperor, 243
Qiao, Prince. *See* Prince Qiao
Qin, Duke of, 122n86, 307
Qin dynasty, 6, 21, 49
Qing dynasty: *Bamboo Annals* in, 13, 222, 234–43; *The Classic of Mountains and Seas* in, 237–38; Confucianism in, 243, 244; "Heavenly Questions" in, 6, 13, 19, 49, 102n50, 129, 218, 221–24, 226–28, 236–38, 243–63; philology of, 221n13, 234, 236, 237, 243–53; *Shijing* in, 223
Qishier jia piping Chuci jizhu, 48n71, 251
Qu Yuan, 2–19, 23; *Chuci* and, 27, 47, 55–58, 68–69; Confucianism and, 41; dialogues about, 136n28; exile of, 39; on formation

of universe, 266; "Heavenly Questions" and, 5–6, 24, 27, 29–31, 33–40, 51–52, 55–58, 59, 67–74, 72n119, 121–23, 125, 152–56, 217, 219, 227, 229, 230, 310; Huang Wenhuan and, 229; Liu Zongyuan and, 133, 148, 152–56, 155n64, 212n106; "Nine Phases" and, 59, 59n92; philology on, 72; *Shiji* and, 110n69; "Sublimating Sorrow" and, 59, 59n92, 72, 127, 133, 266; suicide of, 28, 127; "Summons to the Soul" and, 133; surnames of, 34n36; Wang Yi and, 43–44; Zhou Gongchen and, 230
Qu Yuan fu jiaozhu (Jiang Liangfu), 251
Qu Yuan fu zhu (Dai Zhen), 244
"Questioning the Great Potting Wheel" (Liu Yuxi), 142n44

Reaper of Rushes (Rushou), 152, 152n59, 153
"Reflecting on History" ("Langu shi") (Zhou Gongchen), 232–33
Responding Dragon, 272
"Responding to One Who Congratulated Me" ("Dui hezhe") (Liu Zongyuan), 136
"Rhapsody on Bitter Regret" ("Hen fu") (Jiang Yan), 132
"Rhapsody on the Hall of Numinous Blessings in Lu" ("Lu Linguang dian fu") (Wang Yanshou), 31–32
Rigveda, 260–61
Rushou (Reaper of Rushes), 152, 152n59, 153

Schaberg, David, 282
Schafer, Edward, 168, 168n100
Schimmelpfennig, Michael, 28, 41
Schuessler, Axel, 50, 50n76, 65
"Sedge-stepping Song" ("Ta suo xing") (Wang Guowei), 15
"Seven Particle Verses" ("Yuzhu gizi shi") (Xu Wenjing), 243
Shaft Citadel (Guancheng), 240–41
Shangjia Wei, 10; in *Bamboo Annals*, 293–94

Shang/Shang dynasty: *Bamboo Annals* and, 236; *The Classic of Mountains and Seas* on, 9–10; founding myth of, 101n48; "Heavenly Questions" on, 2, 5–7, 24, 37–38, 54, 71, 117, 237, 290–95; "Heavenly Responses" on, 162–64; Hebo and, 281; King Wen and, 302; King Wu and, 301, 303; Liu Zongyuan and, 162–63, 210n103; Mandate of Heaven and, 24, 164; objects of worship in, 11n30; Qi and, 90; *Shiji* and, 110n69; *Shijing* and, 104n55; Tang and, 219, 291, 294; Wang Guowei and, 292
Shanhaijing. See *Classic of Mountains and Seas*
Shanhaijing jiaozhu, 274
"Shan zhong *Chuci*" ("*Chuci* in the Mountains") (Jiang Yan), 129
Shaokang, 102, 155n65, 253; Ao and, 219, 287; Lady Tangent and, 287; Tang and, 219; Zhenxun and, 97, 196, 219, 287
Shaughnessy, Edward, 236–37, 242
Shen Clan, 295
"Sheng min" ("The Birth of the People"), 139, 209n97, 300–301
Shensheng, Prince, 117n77, 118n78, 241
Shiben, 8
Shiji (Records of the Grand Historian), 8, 23, 23n5, 55; *Diwang shiji* and, 198n71; Guan Zhong in, 298–99; King Wu in, 303; Qu Yuan and, 110n69; Tang in, 295; Yao in, 269; Zhow in, 233n47
Shijing (Book of Odes), 2, 60; "The Birth of the People" ("Sheng min"), 139, 209n97, 300–301; *Chuci zhangju* and, 51; "Dark Bird" ("Xuan niao"), 260, 292; "Four Steeds" ("Simu"), 308; "Gate to the Tombs" ("Mu men"), 202n83; "Gathering Vetch," 306–7; "Great Illumination" ("Daming"), 164, 295; "Heavenly Questions" and, 63–66; irregularities in, 53n80, 63–66; Lin Geng and, 50n75; in Qing dynasty, 223; Shang and, 104n55; "Spreading" ("Mian"), 302
Shiji suoyin, 236
Shirakawa Shizuka, 267

"Shi wen" (Ten questions), 257–58
Shou Meng, 119, 212n106, 304
Shouyang, Mount, 306
"Shu Capital Rhapsody" ("Shudu fu") (Zuo Si), 194n64, 285
Shu Diao, 112–13
"Shudu fu" ("Shu Capital Rhapsody") (Zuo Si), 194n64, 285
Shuihu zhuan (*The Water Margin*), 226
Shujing: Duke of Zhou in, 297; Shun in, 201n80; Yao in, 269; Yu in, 201n80
Shuijing zhu, 236
Shun, 197, 197n69; in *Book of Documents*, 293; Huang Linggeng on, 288, 290; in *Mencius*, 288; Miao Clan and, 293; in *Shujing*, 201n80; Wang Hai and, 294; Xiang and, 289–90; Xu Wenjing and, 281n25; Yaw and, 98n40, 288
Shunzong, Emperor, 132–33
Shuowen jiezi, 247
Shu Qi, 121n85, 306
Sibu congkan, 132, 144; *Zengguang zhushi yinbian Tang Liu xiansheng ji* from, 145, 175
Siku quanshu, 145
Sima Qian, 23, 24, 25–28, 29, 35–36, 54, 67, 72
"Simu" ("Four Steeds"), 308
Sire Mei, 116, 299
Sire of Might (Boqiang), 179, 179n11, 268–69
Sire of the West, The. *See* Duke of Zhou
Sire of the Yellow River. *See* Hebo
Sir Guang, 304
Six Dynasties, 129, 132
Smith, Jonathan Z., 55
"Snow on the River" ("Jiang xue") (Liu Zongyuan), 173
Song, Mount, 281
Song Yu, 43, 127
Song dynasty: Five Classics of, 222; "Heavenly Questions" in, 19, 148, 218–19, 237; "Heavenly Responses" in, 145; Neoconfucianism of, 244

"Song of the Five Brothers," 281
Spirit Mother of the West (Xiwangmu), 184n26; King Mu and, 206n91, 297–98
"Spreading" ("Mian"), 302
Spring and Autumn Annals (*Chunqiu*), 156–57, 156n67, 162
Su Hsüeh-lin, 48, 261
Su Shi, 233n46
"Sublimating Sorrow" ("Lisao"), 15, 24, 27, 62; Dai Zhen on, 245; on formation of universe, 266; in Han dynasty, 127; "Heavenly Questions" and, 67; Huang Linggeng and, 43n54; Liu Zongyuan and, 155n64, 178n7; Peng Zu in, 305; Plume Mountain in, 270; Qu Yuan and, 59, 59n92, 72, 127, 133, 266; Wang Yi and, 28, 41, 42–43, 44; in Warring States period, 127; on Xia dynasty heroes, 279, 282; Zhou Gongchen and, 229
Sui dynasty, 248
Sukhu, Gopal, 41
"Summons to the Soul" ("Zhaohun"), 27–28, 127–28; Jiang Yan and, 130–31; Qu Yuan and, 133
Sun Changwu, 133n19, 159n78, 172n105
Sun Kuang, 48–49
Sunny Vale (*Tanggu*), 268
Supreme Brightness, 60n99

Tai, King, 116–17, 302
Taibo, 99–100, 198n72
Taiping Rebellion, 249
Tang (Shang dynasty founder): *Book of Documents* on, 219; Di and, 291; Ge and, 196, 196n67; Huang Linggeng on, 287; Shang and, 219, 291, 294; Shaokang and, 219; in *Shiji*, 295; Yi Yin and, 118–19, 199n74, 211n105, 231; You Guoen on, 252–53; Zhou Gongchen on, 233; Zhu Xi and, 252
Tang Bingzheng, 271–72, 287, 301–2
Tang dynasty: *Chuci shiwen* of, 148n53; Five Classics and, 222; "Heavenly Questions" in, 4, 7, 12, 129, 134–35; printing in, 222

Tanggu (*Sunny Vale*), 268
Tao Yuanming, 146
"Ta suo xing" ("Sedge-stepping Song") (Wang Guowei), 15
Ten Questions ("Shi wen"), 257–58
Thirteen Classics, 246
Three Teachings, 168, 172
tian bu yu (Heaven does not speak) (Wang Guowei), 15
"Tiandui." *See* "Heavenly Responses"
Tianwen buzhu (Mao Qiling), 235
"Tianwen lunjian" (Lin Geng), 3, 48n70, 50n75, 268, 272
"Tianwen shuzheng" (Wen Yiduo), 8n9, 305
Tianwen tiandui zhu, 175–215
Tianwen zhengjian (Su Hsüeh-lin), 48
Tianwen zuanyi (You Guoen), 3, 225, 251, 256–57
Tianxia shanhe liangjie kao, 238
tian yu (Heaven speaks) (Wang Guowei), 15
"Tianyun" ("Heavenly Revolutions") (*Zhuangzi*), 258–59, 316
"Tiered Palisade," 273–74
Torch Dragon, 274
Tozaki Tetsuhiko, 145, 152n59
"Tribute of Yu" ("Yu gong"), 182n22, 271
Triperil, Mount, 277
Truth and Method (Gadamer), 1, 18, 21, 126, 216, 311
Tu Ching-I, 16n38
Twelve Stations, 78, 78n6, 267

"Unraveled Yearnings" ("Chousi"), 42–43

Vedal, Nathan, 221n13
"Verses on the Creator of Transformations" ("Zaohua pian") (Jiang Yan), 129
"Verses on the Remote Past" ("Suigu pian") (Jiang Yan), 129, 132

Walker, Galal, 66
Wan, concubine of Jie, 232
Wang Bao, 44

Wang Fuzhi, 110n69, 226–28, 232; *Book of Documents* and, 265; on formation of universe, 265
Wang Guowei, 7–10, 8n15, 9n20, 14, 14n34, 217; *Bamboo Annals* and, 237; on *Chuci* anthology, 12n32; *Guoxue congkan* and, 253–54; "Heavenly Questions" and, 255–56; Shang and, 292
Wang Hai, 7–11, 8n15, 13, 18, 54; Liu Zongyuan and, 292; *Shanhaijing* and, 242; Shun and, 294; son of, 293–94; Xu Wenjing and, 241–43
Wang Heng, 293
Wang Li, 65
Wang Niansun, 246–49, 248n96, 284; "Heavenly Questions" and, 246
Wang Shumin, 52n79
Wang Shuwen, 132–33, 135
Wang Xiuling, 9n20, 237
Wang Yangming, 223n19
Wang Yanshou, 31–32, 31n28
Wang Yi, 5, 6, 7, 19, 73, 152; *Chuci zhangju* and, 25–42, 40n45, 44, 45; "Heavenly Questions" and, 36–40, 44, 46; Liu Zongyuan and, 161, 188n41, 194n62; "Nine Songs" and, 44; "Nine Yearnings" and, 45–46; Qu Yuan and, 43–44; "Sublimating Sorrow" and, 28, 41, 42–43, 44; "Unraveled Yearnings" and, 42–43
Wang Yirong, 6
Warring States period, 23, 62; *Bamboo Annals* and, 236; Duke Huan in, 299; "Heavenly Questions" and, 32, 35, 171; phonology in, 65; "Shi wen" in, 258; "Sublimating Sorrow" in, 127; *Zhuangzi* in, 259
Waste Land, The, 72n119
Water Margin, The (*Shuihu zhuan*), 226
Wei Wan, 285
Wen, King. *See* King Wen
Wenxuan, 86n19; Li Shan commentary on, 129, 306
Wen Yiduo, 8n9, 120n82, 305

"When Red Pigeons Gathered on Tang's House" ("Chi jiu zhi ji tang zhi wu"), 291
White Pheasant, 110, 110n68
Who Am I and Who Are You (Gadamer), 312
Wilhelm, Hellmut, 260–61
Writing against the State (Declercq), 136n28
Wu, King. *See* King Wu
Wu Yu, 53; Zhu Xi and, 220
Wu Zixu, 119, 119n81
Wubaijia zhu Liu xiansheng ji, 144
"Wu Capital Rhapsody" ("Wudu fu") (Zuo Si), 275
Wujing zhengyi (Corrected interpretations to the Five Classics), 129, 222
Wulai, 62
Wu Liang shrine, 32

Xia Shaokang, 200n78
Xiahou Xiang, 102; Ao and, 200n79
Xiang, 289–90
Xiang, Duke. *See* Duke Xiang
Xiang'ai, King, 236
Xiao Yuncong, 142, 143
Xia/Xia dynasty: *Bamboo Annals* in, 236; "Heavenly Questions" in, 2, 54, 230, 278–90; heroes of, 278–90; Shenxun and, 287; Zhou Gongchen on, 233
Xie Jufu, 104
Xihe, 185, 195n29, 274
Xiong Jian, 34
Xiu Ji, 284
Xiwangmu. *See* Spirit Mother of the West
Xu Huanlong, 270
Xu Wenjing, 13, 232, 238–43, 239n63, 309; *Bamboo Annals* and, 241, 242, 256; *Book of Changes* and, 238; *Chuci* and, 241; *Guancheng shuoji* and, 243; "Heavenly Questions" and, 242–43; Shun and, 281n25; Zhou Gongchen and, 241; *Zuozhuan* and, 283. See also *Guancheng shuoji*
"Xuan niao" ("Dark Bird"), 260, 292

Yan, concubine of Jie, 232
Yandi, 235
Yang Xiong, 14, 15; *Fangyan* by, 246; "Heavenly Questions" and, 36, 40, 46
Yao, 197, 197n69; Gun and, 92–93; in *Shiji*, 269; in *Shujing*, 269; Zhou Gongchen on, 233
Yao, Emperor, 120
Yaw Clan, 98n40, 288
"Yellow River's Crook," 306
Yi, 190nn47–48; in *Book of Documents*, 279; Di and, 104n65, 111, 120; Lord Zhu and, 283; Qi and, 89
Yi Yin, 37–38, 100–101, 106n58, 295, 304; *Chuci zhangju* on, 291; Moxi and, 231; Tang and, 118–19, 199n74, 211n105, 231; Youshen Clan and, 106
Yigou, 290
Yih, 88, 90–92, 191, 191n52, 281, 282–83
Yijing. *See Book of Changes*
Yin. *See* Shang dynasty
Ying Shao, 52n79
Yinxu shuqi kaoshi (Luo Zhenyu), 7
Yin-Yang cosmology: on formation of universe, 266; in Han dynasty, 29n19, 80, 94; Liu Zongyuan and, 176n3
Yiwei, 119
Yi Ya, 112–13
You Guoen, 3, 225; on formation of universe, 267; on King Wu, 296; on Tang, 252–53; *Tianwen zuanyi* by, 256–57
You, King. *See* King You
Youdi Clan, 294
Youhu Clan, 103n52, 200n79; Qi and, 89, 103
Youshen Clan, 294; Yi Yin and, 38, 106
Youyi Clan, 292, 294
Yu, 182, 182nn19–20, 189nn42–43; in *Book of Documents*, 277, 279; great flood by, 2; in "Heavenly Responses," 171; in *Huainanzi*, 233n45; Qi and, 90, 280, 281; in *Shujing*, 201n80; Zhou Gongchen on, 233

Yu, Mount, 86, 86n19, 187, 187n36
Yu, Pauline, 38n44
Yu Yue, 249–50, 249n102, 301; *Analects* and, 286
Yuan Ke, 274
Yuan dynasty, 223
"Yufu" ("Fisherman"), 24, 136
"Yu gong" ("Tribute of Yu"), 182n22, 271
Yugong huijian, 238
"Yuzhu gizi shi" ("Seven Particle Verses") (Wu Wenjing), 243

"Zaohua pian" ("Verses on the Creator of Transformations") (Jiang Yan), 129
"Zati shi" ("Poems in Diverse Forms") (Jiang Yan), 129
Zengguang zhushi yinbian Tang Liu xiansheng ji, 145, 175
Zha Pingqiu, 44, 156n66
Zhang Pengchong, 238
Zhang Yi, 246
Zhang Yong, 172n105
Zhao, Duke, 93n33, 122n86, 193n60, 307
Zhao, King. *See* King Zhao
Zhao Kuang, 156
"Zhaohun." *See* "Summons to the Soul"
"Zhenfu" ("Determination of the Tallies of Divination") (Liu Zongyuan), 162
Zheng Qiao, 220
Zheng Xuan, 233n45
Zheng Zhenduo, 48
Zhenxun, 28–29, 220, 283, 287; Ao and, 219; Shaokang and, 97, 196, 219
Zhiningtang quangao (Xu Wenjing), 238, 243
Zhong Xing, 282

Zhongyong, 100, 198n72
Zhou, Duke of. *See* Duke of Zhou
Zhou Dunyi, 229
Zhou Gongchen, 229–30, 232–33, 289; Xu Wenjing and, 241
Zhou dynasty, 115; "Heavenly Questions" on, 2, 32, 54, 237; King Wu and, 295; Lord Millet and, 138
Zhow, 107–9, 108n64, 113, 116, 117, 288–89, 296, 304; Bi Gan and, 300; concubine of, 113n72; extravagance of, 197n70; King Wen and, 302; Liu Zongyuan on, 164–65; in *Shiji*, 233n47; Zhou Gongchen on, 233
Zhu, Lord (Di Zhu), 241, 242, 283
Zhu Xi, 53, 53n81, 148, 219–20, 271, 309; *Chuci jizhu* by, 44n55, 53n81; *Chuci zhangju* and, 221; Tang and, 252; Wu Yu and, 220; Zheng Qiao and, 220
Zhuan Shezhu, 119
Zhuang, Duke. *See* Duke Zhuang
Zhuangzi, 240, 258–59; "Four Steeds" and, 308
Zhuanxu, 272
Zhufan, 119
Zhushu jinian. *See Bamboo Annals*
Zhushu jinian tongjian, 238
Zichan, 158, 193n60
Ziqiao, 94, 194n62. *See also* Prince Qiao
Ziwen, 56–57, 56n90, 124, 309
Zuo Qiuming, 157
Zuo Si, 194n64, 275
Zuozhuan, 56n90, 57n91, 60, 307; Duke Xiang in, 219, 250, 282, 283; Duke Zhang in, 34n37; Duke Zhao in, 93n33, 122n86; *Guoyu* and, 157; Xu Wenjing and, 283

Harvard-Yenching Institute Monographs
(most recent titles)

104. *Li Mengyang, the North-South Divide, and Literati Learning in Ming China*, by Chang Woei Ong
105. *Bannermen Tales (Zidishu): Manchu Storytelling and Cultural Hybridity in the Qing Dynasty*, by Elena Suet-Ying Chiu
106. *Upriver Journeys: Diaspora and Empire in Southern China, 1570–1850*, by Steven B. Miles
107. *Ancestors, Kings, and the Dao*, by Constance A. Cook
108. *The Halberd at Red Cliff: Jian'an and the Three Kingdoms*, by Xiaofei Tian
109. *Speaking of Profit: Bao Shichen and Reform in Nineteenth-Century China*, by William T. Rowe
110. *Building for Oil: Daqing and the Formation of the Chinese Socialist State*, by Hou Li
111. *Reading Philosophy, Writing Poetry: Intertextual Modes of Making Meaning in Early Medieval China*, by Wendy Swartz
112. *Writing for Print: Publishing and the Making of Textual Authority in Late Imperial China*, by Suyoung Son
113. *Shen Gua's Empiricism*, by Ya Zuo
114. *Just a Song: Chinese Lyrics from the Eleventh and Early Twelfth Centuries*, by Stephen Owen
115. *Shrines to Living Men in the Ming Political Cosmos*, by Sarah Schneewind
116. *In the Wake of the Mongols: The Making of a New Social Order in North China, 1200–1600*, by Jinping Wang
117. *Opera, Society, and Politics in Modern China*, by Hsiao-t'i Li
118. *Imperiled Destinies: The Daoist Quest for Deliverance in Medieval China*, by Franciscus Verellen
119. *Ethnic Chrysalis: China's Orochen People and the Legacy of Qing Borderland Administration*, by Loretta E. Kim
120. *The Paradox of Being: Truth, Identity, and Images in Daoism*, by Poul Andersen
121. *Feeling the Past in Seventeenth-Century China*, by Xiaoqiao Ling
122. *The Chinese Dreamscape, 300 BCE–800 CE*, by Robert Ford Campany
123. *Structures of the Earth: Metageographies of Early Medieval China*, by D. Jonathan Felt

124. *Anecdote, Network, Gossip, Performance: Essays on the* Shishuo xinyu, by Jack W. Chen
125. *Testing the Literary: Prose and the Aesthetic in Early Modern China*, by Alexander Des Forges
126. *Du Fu Transforms: Tradition and Ethics amid Societal Collapse*, by Lucas Rambo Bender
127. *Chinese History: A New Manual (Enlarged Sixth Edition)*, Vol. 1, by Endymion Wilkinson
128. *Chinese History: A New Manual (Enlarged Sixth Edition)*, Vol. 2, by Endymion Wilkinson
129. *Wang Anshi and Song Poetic Culture*, by Xiaoshan Yang
130. *Localizing Learning: The Literati Enterprise in Wuzhou, 1100–1600*, by Peter K. Bol
131. *Making the Gods Speak: The Ritual Production of Revelation in Chinese Religious History*, by Vincent Goossaert
132. *Lineages Embedded in Temple Networks: Daoism and Local Society in Ming China*, by Richard G. Wang
133. *Rival Partners: How Taiwanese Entrepreneurs and Guangdong Officials Forged the China Development Model*, by Wu Jieh-min; translated by Stacy Mosher
134. *Saying All That Can Be Said: The Art of Describing Sex in* Jin Ping Mei, by Keith McMahon
135. *Genealogy and Status: Hereditary Office Holding and Kinship in North China under Mongol Rule*, by Tomoyasu Iiyama
136. *The Threshold: The Rhetoric of Historiography in Early Medieval China*, by Zeb Raft
137. *Literary History in and beyond China: Reading Text and World*, edited by Sarah M. Allen, Jack W. Chen, and Xiaofei Tian
138. *Dreaming and Self-Cultivation in China, 300 BCE–800 CE*, by Robert Ford Campany
139. *The Painting Master's Shame: Liang Shicheng and the Xuanhe Catalogue of Paintings*, by Amy McNair
140. *The Cornucopian Stage: Performing Commerce in Early Modern China*, by Ariel Fox
141. *The Collapse of Heaven: The Taiping Civil War and Chinese Literature and Culture, 1850–1880*, by Huan Jin
142. *Elegies for Empire: A Poetics of Memory in the Late Work of Du Fu*, by Gregory M. Patterson
143. *The Manchu Mirrors and the Knowledge of Plants and Animals in High Qing China*, by He Bian and Mårten Söderblom Saarela
144. *A Historical Taxonomy of Talking Birds in Chinese Literature*, by Wilt L. Idema
145. *Health and the Art of Living: Illness Narratives in Early Medieval Chinese Literature*, by Antje Richter
146. *Dialogues in the Dark: Interpreting "Heavenly Questions" across Two Millennia*, by Nicholas Morrow Williams